BOOKS BY FINIS FARR

O'HARA

A BIOGRAPHY

O'HARA

A BIOGRAPHY
BY FINIS FARR

W. H. ALLEN   London & New York
A division of Howard & Wyndham Ltd
1974

Printed in Great Britain by Fletcher & Son Ltd, Norwich
for the publishers W. H. Allen & Co. Ltd.
44 Hill Street, London W1X 8LB
Bound by Richard Clay (The Chaucer Press) Ltd, Bungay, Suffolk

ISBN 0 491 01482 1

ACKNOWLEDGMENTS

I OWE A SPECIAL DEBT to Mrs. John O'Hara for much of the material used in writing this biography, and I am grateful to Wylie O'Hara Holahan for sharing memories of her father. John's sister Mary E. O'Hara has been generous with time and memory, and my debt to Tom O'Hara will be seen throughout the book. I also received valuable help from Martin E. O'Hara, for which I record my best thanks. And I am deeply obligated to Joseph W. Outerbridge for his patience in answering questions. My thanks go also to Arlene Boone, Mrs. Gerald Bramwell, C. D. B. Bryan, Niven Busch, Noel F. Busch, Anita Colby (Mrs. Palen Flagler), John Durant, C. Pardee Foulke, Kathleen O'Hara Fuldner, Mrs. Henry Gardiner, Peter Gates, Elizabeth Hart (Mrs. George Edge), John K. Hutchens, Mr. and Mrs. Roger B. Kirkpatrick, Joel Sayre, Don A. Schanche, Marian V. Sheafer, Robert T. Simonds, Frank Sullivan, Mrs. Louis N. Ulmer, the late Alfred M. Wright, Jr., Dr. Robert Wylie, David Yocum, and Frank Zachary. The view of O'Hara and his work offered here is my own, but I owe more than writers usually owe publishers to Harry Sions, a creative editor.

— F. F.

CONTENTS

ILLUSTRATIONS

ONE

AT THE HOUR
OF OUR DEATH

THE INTERSECTION of Province Line and Pretty Brook Roads, five miles northwest of Princeton, is one of the most attractive locations for a house in the eastern United States. You come off the extension of Elm Road, with its big houses and spacious lawns, and go out along Pretty Brook through a wooded glen that might be in the Berkshires instead of only a little more than an hour from New York and Philadelphia. This is estate country, as the experienced eye will note from the inconspicuous gateways framing narrow private roads that wind back into the evergreen forests. Around here the land is closely held by people with no desire for publicity. The gateposts carry no signs announcing THE WATERBURYS, nor do they show that familiar syntactic solecism, THE THOMPSON's. Perhaps, as John O'Hara would have said, that might be not so much an unsuccessful attempt to form the possessive plural, as a tribute to some notable grandee and family founder, The Thompson. Then he would smile his sudden smile, which started at the mouth and ended around the eyes. It was a singularly pleasing smile, and he himself had written a warning against any man whose smile stopped before it reached the eyes — beware of that man. O'Hara was a tireless collector of impressions about such things as unfinished smiles and unmarked gateposts.

He had often observed, for example, the lack of posted names at the estate entrances as he bowled along Pretty Brook Road in one of his imported automobiles toward his own house at the Province Line crossing; and O'Hara knew why the names did not appear at the estate entrances. It was, in part, a matter of fashionable simplicity, an avoidance of ostentation that would serve as a signal to others in the know. And there was a second reason: These hills, with their thick stands of pine and cedar, were the foothills of the Sourland (originally Saarland) Mountains, and back up in there, in Somerset County, the Lindberghs had built the lonely house from which their baby was stolen one night by a man who carried him down a homemade ladder. Thirty-eight years later, in this April of 1970, the people who lived along Pretty Brook Road remembered the Lindberghs, and did nothing to advertise position and wealth.

The road curved in front of O'Hara's place, and his driveway led between iron eagles at the gate to a low white brick house which had two heraldic bronze peacocks, heads in air and tails spread, to set off each end of the parapet at its door. Linebrook took its name from the adjoining roads, and had been described in magazine articles as an elaborate mansion and even as a French château, bringing to mind.thoughts of George Washington Vanderbilt's Biltmore at Asheville, or something on the label of a wine bottle. Grandeur had not been the aim when O'Hara and his wife built Linebrook in 1966. One of O'Hara's characters had said, and it sounded like the author speaking, that nowadays the rich build small. This was true of Linebrook, whose charm lay in beauty and comfort rather than overpowering size. Beyond the entrance, the house opened on the ground floor into a spacious living room and a dining area with tall windows on a terrace where families of deer often appeared in fall and winter, seemingly aware that the O'Haras and their neighbors would protect them from the hunters who came out from Trenton and Brooklyn hoping to decorate their Buick hoods with bodies of dead animals. There was war between the estate owners and the hunters who cruised the roads with shotgun barrels protruding from car windows, leather coats buttoned across heavy bellies, and rum-hurt faces peering under long-billed caps. Men of this kind would shoot one deer on Linebrook ground and make off with the kill before the state police could get there at Katharine (Sister) O'Hara's call.

These sportsmen could have shot over the entire Linebrook estate from the road, for O'Hara's spread covered only three acres. But the lie of neighboring property was such that one looked into deep woods from the terrace beyond the living room, and from O'Hara's study at the end of a passageway in the wing of the house that opened to the left of the entrance hall. O'Hara spent a great deal of his time in the study; here he wrote his stories, articles, and novels late at night, usually from after midnight until just before dawn. He would write with the curtains closed, and outside there would be no sound in the forest except for wind when it blew, the occasional scuttling of a small animal through underbrush, or the distant howls of a dog. The curtains cut off the light of the green-shaded student lamp on O'Hara's desk so that from outside, all of Linebrook was dark. In the study, O'Hara would be writing with intense concentration, hunching his muscular shoulders, typing on yellow sheets in his office-size Noiseless Remington Rand, and when going well, drawing a rhythmic sound like muffled drumming from the machine, mostly absorbed by the sound-proofed ceiling and the draperies. The yellow paper was no affectation.

O'Hara used it because the slightly roughened surface gave off little reflected light, and his pale gray-blue eyes were sensitive to glare. He was color blind. Once when friends sent him a colored photograph showing them feeding a peacock, the gaudy tail vanished into a monochrome background, and he thought the bird a Christmas turkey.

Princeton lies far enough south to have an early spring, and the weather was fine on Friday, April 10, 1970. First green had come to the oaks, elms, and chestnuts, and a blue sky with clouds riding toward the mountains framed the fields and woods around Linebrook. That morning, O'Hara had stopped work between four and five o'clock, leaving page 74 of a novel, *The Second Ewings,* in the typewriter. Although he always worked late, O'Hara seldom structured one day like the day before; sometimes he stayed up in the morning to breakfast with his wife around seven A.M., and on other days he would go to bed before first light; in either event he would have taken time late at night for a long soak in the tub, which left water spilled on the floor of the bathroom he had designed for himself with the snug accommodations of an ocean liner in mind. He said space was wasted in bathrooms, and had stood over architect and builders to make sure this one was properly shipshape. When he got up to face the day, O'Hara would dress in country clothes, unless he put on pajamas and a robe. While writing a novel O'Hara might go for weeks without getting fully dressed or walking outside. During those periods his daily costume would be a fresh suit of the Brooks Brothers end-and-end madras pajamas, that classic item, in blue, tan, or gray, with a silk or light woolen robe, and Pullman slippers of fine leather, or a pair of those slippers that are made on a last like a dancing pump, with an embroidered monogram in front. It was the standard lounging costume for thousands of men who had attended eastern boarding schools and colleges during the first half of the twentieth century.

There were guests at Linebrook on April 10, and O'Hara, wearing a soft jacket and biscuit-colored flannels, emerged to lunch with them. He had always worried about his health, but today his color was good, and his manner, affable when there were guests in the house, seemed especially relaxed as he listened to conversation in the sunny living room. This room was large enough for two constellations of armchairs and sofas, and for a number of tables that supported lamps, jars of flowers, silver boxes of various sizes, cigarette lighters carrying the initials of New York and Philadelphia clubs, and twenty-one silver-framed photographs. O'Hara had reason to be at ease, for he was in good company on that April afternoon. The guests were C. D. B. Bryan, who was Mrs. O'Hara's son by her first marriage, and his wife, who had been Judith Snyder of Allentown, Pennsylvania. O'Hara knew about Allentown, for he had spent the first twenty-three years of his life in Pottsville, forty miles away, and the two small cities were centers of background in a large part of his work, the fictional creation of something that he had marked off as his territory before he started to write, under the private title of The Region. Anyone from The Region would engage O'Hara's interest, and his stepson's wife, who was known to her friends by the nickname of "Sam," inspired affection as well. Sam Bryan was a beautiful slender young woman whose dark eyes and soft voice conveyed a singular charm. When she first met her future husband and heard that O'Hara was his stepfather, Sam had exclaimed, "John O'Hara — we studied *him* in school!" O'Hara had written nine years before, in the preface to his sixth collection of short stories, that he had begun to receive "letters from students who are the sons and daughters of men and women who read my early short stories when they first came out. Thus, without realizing it, I was writing for posterity, and posterity is here."

O'Hara's stepson Courtlandt Dixon Barnes Bryan had already launched himself as a journalist and novelist. He had attended four boarding schools in preparation for Yale, graduating in 1958, and was a tall, easygoing man who gave the impression of looking on the world with benevolent curiosity. With "Courtie" and Sam in the living room was his mother, whom Charles Poore of the *Times* called "John's enchanting wife." Sister O'Hara had among her gifts the ability to make a roomful of people feel friendly and happy, showing themselves at their best without effort or strain. At the moment, however, there was no call for Sister to work her magic, for this was a congenial family gathering. The two younger people had shared with their hostess a good lunch preceded by cocktails or sherry. O'Hara ate some bland food that he reported to be lacking in taste, but his nervous stomach compelled the diet. Two years before, while walking up the ramp of a parking garage in Philadelphia, he had fallen, and sustained injuries that sent him to the hospital. He had not touched wine or liquor in the seventeen years since a bleeding ulcer had brought him close to death in New York City. O'Hara felt that he had done his share of drinking before the erupting ulcer made him a total abstainer. He had said that during a certain period in his life, he experienced "trouble with the sauce." And he had recently told Courtie Bryan about a recurrent dream of standing at the bar in "21," and the barman pouring a shot of his favorite St. James Scotch. O'Hara said, "I always wake up just as I get the glass to my lips, and I wake frightened." O'Hara had accepted the end of drinking as a place-mark in his life. When he could sit up in Harkness Pavilion after the ulcer knocked him out, he had written a letter to his nondrinking friend Joseph W. (Pat) Outerbridge, that made his position clear: "Dear Pat — Answering things in the order of their importance — yes, I am going to be up there on the cart with you. I will enjoy the company but it will take me a little while to get accustomed to the vehicle: but the only alternative is the glass-sided wagon with the six white horses, and where the hell can you find six white horses nowadays? My chief trouble is that the belly resists booze, and if I take too much of it I'm liable to fall over dead. A hell of a way for booze to treat me after I've been so kind to it. I used to watch Bill Fields put away the Martinis at Paramount, and say to myself, "That's what I want to be when I get big.' Well, I almost made it . . ."

Since the writing of that letter O'Hara's resolve to keep alcohol entirely out of his life had held as firm as his friendship with Pat Outerbridge. And now he looked forward to spending some time with his friend on the following day. If Outerbridge could come over from his house in Princeton on Saturday afternoon, they would watch the Masters Golf Tournament from Augusta on television in the living room; but perhaps Outerbridge would call in the evening, and if so, they would pass the early hours in O'Hara's study. The two men often sat there, sometimes in silence. When O'Hara spoke of Outerbridge, he described him as "my best friend." At times when O'Hara had been working for weeks without a break, Sister would telephone Pat Outerbridge: "John is getting stir crazy." Outerbridge would come at once. He was a man whose presence was soothing and calming, like that of a good clergyman or doctor.

There was no need for any ministering friend at O'Hara's side this Friday afternoon. As he joined in conversation, listening more than he talked, he was amused by the efforts of a small black poodle named Taxi to persuade him to throw a rubber ball. Taxi was a well-mannered, intelligent little dog, a gift from O'Hara to his wife, and he trotted in and out of the room with an engaging air of ownership. The conversation turned to the purposes and ambitions that people carried in life. Sam asked O'Hara what he now wanted to do, and he said, "I want to flood the world with my writing."

Later in the afternoon, O'Hara lay down for his customary second sleep of the day. As a general rule, he got up from this nap and took a light meal around eight P.M., and then pottered about the house, talking and smoking cigarettes, and searching for something to look at on television. In the latter part of the evening, he often found a movie that had been made in the 1930s, when he had gone to Hollywood for studio writing jobs. O'Hara enjoyed seeing the stars of the decade — Cagney, Crawford, Bogart, Swanson, Ladd, and the rest. Not all of them had lasted into the present. On this Friday of April 10, the late program offered a choice: an adventure film about an airplane lost in Brazil, and *Distant Drums,* a picture made in 1951 and starring Gary Cooper. O'Hara admired Cooper, who had played Joe Chapin, the unlucky hero, in the screen version of *Ten North Frederick.* Now "Coop" was dead, like Bogart, Bob Taylor, Gable, Sheridan, and Lombard. Once in the carefree days, O'Hara had played a small part in a movie starring Cooper and Madeleine Carroll, *The General Died at Dawn*. The director had been Lewis Milestone, a friend of O'Hara's, as was the author, Clifford Odets, who wrote in the bit part for a harmless joke. There had been additional entertainment when Odets named Cooper's character "O'Hara." Long after he turned in his script for *The General*, Odets had died with his achievements largely forgotten. That could happen to any writer, but O'Hara was determined that it would not happen to him. What he feared was loss of mental vigor. Ill health came with advancing age but one could fight it. Many writers had produced good work in an hour a day, even though they were invalids. The horrible bad luck would be to go stroke-simple, like H. L. Mencken, who had passed through hell in his last years at Baltimore, unable to write or read. John Wesley had thanked God with joy in his heart when tired and sick at eighty-five, "I can preach and write still." At sixty-five, John O'Hara in his own way would say the same. But the fall in the Philadelphia garage had been ominous. Joe Chapin had fallen on the stairs at 10 North Frederick Street, and after that he had been "like a magnet that is dropped and de-magnetized." A hideous death had come to George Lockwood of *The Lockwood Concern* when he fell down a secret stairway in a deserted house. Charles Kinsmith in a story called "The Flight" had fallen on an icy road and died three hours later. One must keep one's footing. Around twelve o'clock, O'Hara went to his study, hoping to settle down for a good night's work.

The study was immaculately kept, and O'Hara inhaled a familiar clean smell of woodsmoke, leather, and furniture polish as he went to his desk in the corner. On the desk familiar objects acquired over years lay under lamplight and gave him assurance that the work habits he had forged during those years would never change. At right angles to this heavy library desk, a sturdy typewriter desk formed what O'Hara's friend Don Schanche had called "a secure little six-foot-square open hutch," in which the author could "recline, swivel, think, and talk in the comfort of a castored executive chair." O'Hara took his seat and looked around the workroom. The study at Linebrook was exactly what its owner wanted it to be, and it said a great deal about O'Hara and his work, and what he thought of his work, almost as though he had planned the room as a record. It had been reported that O'Hara wrote his obituary for the files at the *Times*. He did no such thing, but he had worked on newspapers, and for Henry Luce's *Time* magazine, and had noticed that any item of fact, from a date to the spelling of a name, offered a chance for error, and that mistakes established themselves and paraded as unquestioned facts after generations of rewrite men had repeated them when the clips came out of the manila envelopes in the morgues. And so here on the desk and tables of the Linebrook study, on the shelves and walls, were *things* that could be photographed, or listed as if by an impersonal appraiser, for whatever impression they might make on an inquiring mind.

The first general impression of O'Hara's study, a room measuring thirteen by sixteen feet, was one of comfort and ease. A low door in the wall beside the big fireplace opened on a wall safe, and the fire irons included the Cape Cod lighter from which he had taken the title for a collection of short stories. There were three deep leather chairs, sinfully comfortable like those in the lounge of a men's club, and a wooden armchair bearing the seal of the Princeton Theological Seminary. On entering for the first time, a caller might feel that there was more to be seen than could be taken in at one visit. But the total effect was reassuring, for this was a good-humored room that made no attempt to be overbearing. And as O'Hara looked at the finished pages of *The Second Ewings* that lay at the left of the Remington Rand, the books and pictures and various other objects beyond the lamplight were as familiar to him as his hands and brain. Their presence was part of the ritual he needed to break the surface tension of each night's work. If he swung away from his typewriter, O'Hara could see over the door on his right the framed certificate of merit that the New Jersey State Teachers of English had conferred on *Five Plays* and *Sermons and Soda-Water*. Between these citations a horseshoe was properly hung with the open end up, to retain luck. Beside the door was a red American La France fire extinguisher in a holder screwed to the wall. Near this was a shield-shaped medallion over the electric light keys, and a button to ring a bell in the kitchen when O'Hara wanted a fresh supply of coffee. He did not expect this service throughout the night, and when he felt the need of coffee in the late hours, he would walk to the kitchen through the silent house. Back in his chair, he could run his eye over the bookshelves covering the two walls that paralleled his two desks. In the first wall of books stood the Eleventh Edition of the *Encyclopaedia Britannica*, Aldous Huxley's favorite, on India paper. This finest of *Britannicus* had come out in 1911, and described a world of certainty with entries on such subjects as Dreadnoughts, Wireless Telegraphy, Renaissance Architecture, Cavalry Tactics, Flying Machines, and Hydromechanics, together with critical and biographical articles by Swinburne, Viscount Morley, Thackeray, George Saintsbury, Andrew Lang, and Edmund Gosse. The Eleventh Edition on India paper, like bound volumes of *Chatterbox*, *St. Nicholas* and *The Youth's Companion*, was another of those private signals that the owner had been properly brought up. Beneath the Eleventh stood a more recent and less entertaining edition of the *Britannica*, and twenty-two scrapbooks for reviews, each bearing the gilt-lettered title of an O'Hara work. Attached to the bookshelf near these volumes was the framed manuscript of a school composition written by O'Hara's daughter Wylie at the age of nine; around the room were other souvenirs of Wylie, including a school-made pottery ashtray inscribed "To the Literary Father of 1956 and my father Always," a framed telegram from Ella K. Watkins, head of St. Timothy's School in Stevenson, Maryland, announcing that Wylie had been elected senior class president for 1963, a photograph of O'Hara dancing with his daughter when she was a graceful nineteen, in 1964, and the manuscript of a poem by Grantland Rice, celebrating the euphony of the name Wylie Delaney O'Hara. The daughter had been named for her mother, O'Hara's second wife, who had been born Belle Wylie, and his mother Katharine Delaney, and was now Mrs. Dennis Holahan of San Francisco.

The shelf to the right of the larger desk held a number of significant items. There were two cartoons by Frueh, showing the principals of *Pal Joey* at its opening in 1940 and its revival in 1952, and photographs of O'Hara with the composer Richard Rodgers and Vivienne Segal, female star of the piece. Close by were photographs of O'Hara holding a plaque with two unidentified men, and O'Hara talking to John F. Kennedy. Within easy reach was a wooden pig with a brass snout and a ball of twine in its belly, and two brass hunting horns, one circular, one straight, both beautifully polished. Sketches for the covers of *Hellbox,* a collection of stories, and *BUtterfield 8,* a novel, hung near the theatrical items. O'Hara's delight in well-designed artifacts was shown in a telegraph key and sounder, neatly mounted on a block of wood. Another example was the Stewart Speedometer, mounted on a slab of mahogany, perfectly polished like all the metal in the room, and registering five miles per hour and 4296.3 season miles.

On a shelf under the window at the left of the typewriter desk stood a Kamplite acetylene lantern in working order, and a brass steam whistle, polished, mounted, and displayed for the esthetic value of its sharp flanges, with the metal plate declaring it to be a piece of "Early American Abstract Sculpture." A cube of machined steel, four by four inches in size, stood on the large desk as a paperweight. A friend had given it to O'Hara on the eleventh (steel) anniversary of his marriage to Sister, in 1966. And it could be inferred that O'Hara was conscious of anniversaries and the passage of time, for he could see two calendars from where he sat. One was a round brass device containing the twenty-eight years from 1944 to 1971; the other was a "perpetual" register that could keep track of every day from 1900 to the year 2000. The annual Wafer diaries for 1942 through 1970 stood in two neat piles on the shelf near the Frueh drawings. These diaries, measuring two and three-quarters by four inches, were made in England. John got them every year at the MM Importing Company on Park Avenue. The leaves were thin gilt-edged light blue notepaper, the covers dark blue leather with the year in gold figures on the front, and the monogram JOH. These small pocket diaries, though not really of much use, were another private passport among people who considered themselves to be in a certain group, a common article with members of what O'Hara's friend Wilder Hobson had referred to as "the higher internal crowd."

It would be a mistake to pin significance on every item that lay in front of O'Hara on his larger desk, around the base of the student lamp. There was a small brass-bound mahogany chest, for example, with JOH on its nameplate. Perhaps this was meant to hold stamps or stationery, but it was empty, and its four secret drawers held nothing. The box had earned its position by having been there so long that O'Hara's eyes had become accustomed to seeing it in that place. And there was no symbolic value attached to the heavy brass key that served as a paperweight, or the small silver bell with the date of 1878. Stuck on the edge of one shelf at eye level to a seated person was a large celluloid button, "SAY HELLO TO AN OLDTIMER, O'HARA AND DELANEY FAMILIES, September 23–29. Pottsville Sesquicentennial." The birthday-cake-sized candle in the miniature iron frying pan had been provided to melt the wax if O'Hara had ever decided to make use of his seal ring to imprint the family crest on an envelope. A fatter candle mounted on a silver matchbox waited for the same purpose, but had never been lit, for he would have thought it an affectation to seal a letter with wax, and would have done it only as a joke for someone he could depend on not to rush out with a story about O'Hara putting on airs. Nevertheless, he liked the look of old-fashioned writing gear, the pen tray, the heavy inkwell with its silver lid, and the silver stationery holder with the two kinds of Linebrook notepaper, one with a conventional heading, the other carrying this insigne:

O'Hara sent out most of his letters on the typewriting paper and he used a stationery embosser from an accommodating firm in Peru, Indiana, to imprint the Linebrook address and "Rural Delivery 2" in raised letters on these yellow sheets. He was a good mail-order customer of such firms, and liked to order rain clothes and outdoor equipment for himself and Sister from L. L. Bean, Inc., of Freeport, Maine.

Keeping up his correspondence was no problem to O'Hara. He dealt with letters from cranks and strangers by throwing them into the antique leather fireman's bucket which served as a wastebasket. And he never had quailed before the "arrears overwhelming" that beset the writer-hero in Henry James's story of "The Great Good Place," to which George Dane escaped when "the old rising tide" of letters and engagements rose too high. Linebrook *was* the great good place in O'Hara's personal and professional life — the two lives were one. Professional care had assembled the reference books around the writing hutch, and the number of dictionaries alone would surprise anyone except another writer. In a commanding position stood the 2,515-page *Oxford Universal Dictionary*, concise in comparison to its thirteen-volume parent, the *Oxford Dictionary of the English Language,* which O'Hara did not own. But he had an unabridged Webster, and thirty other dictionaries in various languages. Macmillan's *Everyman's Encyclopedia* supported the two *Britannicas*, and a dozen histories of Pennsylvania showed O'Hara's interest in his home state. O'Hara was not altogether serious when he provided shelf room for the 102nd edition of *Burke's Peerage, Baronetage, and Knightage,* a book he seldom took down. But he felt different about *Who's Who in America*, and his habit of reading at random in this reference work was well known. *Who's Who* had listed O'Hara before he reached his thirtieth birthday, just as he had predicted to his father when he was nineteen years old and still a resident of Pottsville. At the top of the writing hutch and at O'Hara's back as he faced his typewriter stood the cast of a bronze portrait head of the author. Next to this, on a plaque of Peruvian mahogany, were incised the words of Joseph Conrad: "My task, which I am trying to achieve, is, by the power of the written word, to make you hear, to make you feel. It is, before all, to make you see. That — and no more. And it is everything."

Louis Vuitton of Paris was a luggage maker whose product had special appeal to persons of means and taste. He also was one of the first tradesmen to hit on the idea of making his customers advertise his shop, by means of the LV monogram, endlessly repeated in a sort of wallpaper pattern on the tan fabric with which he covered the durable boxes, bags, and trunks that he supplied at astoundingly high prices to members of a small clientele. O'Hara was an old Vuitton customer, and had used the LV monogram in one of his best stories, "The Ride from Mauch Chunk," which earned him more than the sum he had spent on fine luggage. In the study one could see a capacious pottery ashtray with the repeated LV monogram baked in, a present from O'Hara's brother-in-law Courtlandt Barnes, and on the window seat lay two envelope briefcases that had come from Vuitton. O'Hara also kept in his desk a Vuitton card case no larger than the Wafer diaries, and its contents were as interesting as its exterior was smart. In order from the top, the case carried Identification Card No. 7280 from the National Press Club in Washington; a credit card for Saks Fifth Avenue; a similar card for hiring automobiles at International Car House Limited of London; membership cards in the Writers Guild of America West, which was the screenwriters' union, and the Authors Guild of America, the book writers' organization; a customer's card for the First National Bank of Princeton; a card identifying O'Hara as an active member of the Marine Historical Association of Mystic, Connecticut; a membership card signed by the Commander-in-Chief, Sons of Union Veterans of the Civil War, Camp Abraham Lincoln No. 100, New Jersey (O'Hara was the grandson of a veteran); and a card showing O'Hara to be a Companion of the Military Order of the Loyal Legion of the United States.

It could be deduced from this evidence alone that O'Hara was something of a joiner. His biography in Who's Who listed eight clubs, and he himself had founded one of them, the Hessian Relief Society. This Society had fewer than twenty members, and met at the call of the Founder, who never called a meeting; it consisted only of its roster of members, which was secret, and its orange and blue striped necktie, by which the members could recognize each other. O'Hara had modeled this organization on the lines of a club called the Kew-Teddington Observatory, which Pat Outerbridge had founded some years before. The presentation of his Observatory tie, striped in black, red, and gold, had delighted O'Hara and started him thinking of the Relief Society, that would give help to any properly identified Hessian who appeared in full uniform and stated his case to the Founder's satisfaction. These two organizations were largely notional, but the club books on the shelves with the other reference works showed that O'Hara belonged to several institutions with identifiable buildings, and membership lists that were not kept secret. It could be said that if O'Hara had not made himself famous as an author, he might have been referred to as a clubman. In addition to the Press Club in Washington, he held membership in the National Golf Links of America at Southampton, the Leash and the Century Association in New York, the Nassau Club of Princeton, and the Philadelphia Racquet Club. Since filling out the form for his most recent entry in Who's Who, O'Hara had added the Savile of London to his list of clubs. And his propensity for organizing was shown by the small silver cup that stood near the typewriter table, and carried the engraving, "Quogue-Southampton Tuesday Lunch Club — John O'Hara, President." Giving himself a cup, as he had in this instance, was a joke that O'Hara played on O'Hara, and on three friends whom he also made presidents. Again, as with so many things that he observed in others or himself, O'Hara had used this idea for a story, "The Chink in the Armor," about a desiccated New York bachelor who has a silver box engraved as though presented to him by members of a club bridge team.

Silver boxes that served as marks of real achievement could be found at Linebrook, both in the living room and the study. The desk lamplight glinted, for example, on a silver cigarette box which was engraved "To John O'Hara in honor of the 1,000,000th copy of the Bantam Books Edition of *Ten North Frederick*." A similar box memorialized the millionth copy of *BUtterfield 8*. Other novels by O'Hara that had met with equal success stood in the set of his works, in a special uniform binding, that occupied most of a shelf among the reference books on the south wall above the typewriter. The reference material in this section of O'Hara's library had to do with automobiles, shooting and gunmaking, horses, golf, ocean liners, medals and decorations, the Army, the Navy, and the American Civil War. Here was the twelve-volume *Dictionary of American Biography*, along with several histories of the United States, and a rare book entitled *Historic Dress in America*. There was a copy of *Proud Are We Irish*, and *P. S. Wilkinson*, Courtie Bryan's first novel. The 1934 edition of *Tender Is the Night* had been inscribed, "Dear John: May we meet soon in equally Celtic but more communicable condition — Scott Fitz." *The Portable Scott Fitzgerald*, for which O'Hara had written the foreword, carried an inscription from its editor, "To John O'Hara — who here, as always, did what I cannot — with admiration beyond envy and love beyond words — Dorothy Parker." Scott Fitzgerald, Mrs. Parker, and John Steinbeck were among the writers of O'Hara's generation who had liked and respected him, and now they were gone. Nowadays more of his good friends were dead than living, and an ever-present sense of inevitable death had always put darkness and despair into O'Hara's work. He had said he did not expect to live beyond the age of thirty. Later on, O'Hara said he thought his life would not last fifty years, and the penetrating ulcer came close to making this prediction true. Now, since he had taken the fall in Philadelphia, O'Hara often felt that death was near him in the study as he worked. A wet leaf underfoot had received blame for the fall. But O'Hara was willing to ask himself if it had not been the result of a stroke. He had reduced his weight and brought his diabetes under control. Recently he had been swimming three times a week with a coach in the university pool, for strangely enough, O'Hara had not learned to swim in his Pottsville boyhood. What O'Hara had done was to allow his torso to grow too heavy for his ankles. On his last trip to England, in 1969, he had been moved in a wheelchair at the airports. In the past few months, he had gone with Outerbridge for an occasional walk around Linebrook. Outerbridge reported, "I think the walking helps John, but he does a certain amount of tottering." A man who did a certain amount of tottering was especially well aware that the possessions surrounding him would be there after he was gone. O'Hara's gloomy temperament made him draw comfort from that thought as he looked across the circle of light around his working space and saw such treasures as the early nineteenth-century purser's chest that he kept for its integrity of shape and the deep shine of its mahogany, the toy automobile, vintage 1914, modeled on the famous Mercer Raceabout that had been manufactured at Trenton, only twenty miles away, or the metal-sheathed sabers that stood against the wall, or the small red Presto fire extinguisher, another example of abstract American art in O'Hara's eyes. The Region had furnished the Astrolite miner's lamp, an antique sale had supplied the two handsome decoy ducks on the top shelf, and the two highly polished brass cuspidors up there beside them were things of beauty for their roundness and the sheen of heavy metal. Near O'Hara's feet and ready for his next trip to California or London stood a Remington Noiseless Portable in its case. It lined up beside a U. S. Army Paymaster's Field Chest that O'Hara used to store his shoe brushes, and a supply of Kiwi Polish and Old Meltonian Cream. Often when talking with Outerbridge, O'Hara would occupy his hands by polishing a pair of shoes, stowing the gear away in the solid, four-lock pay chest when he was through. Attached to the dictionary stand above this chest was a sign, PRIER DE JETER VOS PAPIERS DANS LA CORBEILLE. The window shelf in reach of O'Hara's left hand held a Derringer pistol of about 1850, unloaded but in working order. In the drawer of his typewriter table lay two loaded tear gas guns, the Penguin Potent Protector model, with three additional cartridges. The gas guns appeared to be as well made and functionally designed as any other object in the typewriter drawer, on the shelves, or on the broad desk where O'Hara's magnifying glass lay clean and ready in its leather cover, with the letter openers ranged beside it, the leather-covered library shears, the pencil knife, the memorandum pad in a morocco holder stamped JOH, all this on the clean red blotter bound in tan leather set off by black stitching.

In addition to the sabers and the Penguin Protectors, O'Hara might have used his Irish hockey stick — the hurley — for a weapon. The hurley stood behind one of the chairs, and looked like an ax handle with a broad end, seeming to protect the mandolin and violin that shared its corner. O'Hara was a self-taught violinist, and in younger days would sometimes scrape along with the Philadelphia Orchestra when he could get a concert on his radio. He pointed out that he shared an amateur interest in the violin with Sherlock Holmes, and this was the sort of thing that cheered him in lonely hours. And he could always look just past the typewriter and see the photograph of himself and Sister in Washington, with the dome of the Capitol looming through a big window behind them. It amused O'Hara that the picture looked like a fake, or what they called a process shot in Hollywood. The picture had been taken at the Senate Office Building in 1960, when O'Hara had lectured at the Library of Congress. Now ten years had gone by with incredible speed, yet in that time O'Hara had brought out six books of short stories, and had written six novels, one of which, *The Ewings*, was not yet published.* Had he

---

* Random House brought out *The Ewings* in February 1972.

sacrificed quality because he had the urge to produce, and the strength and self-discipline to satisfy that urge? Without exception, great authors produced large bodies of work; much production was part of an honorable effort to achieve greatness. And in any event, O'Hara might quote Henry James, who had said that one can but proceed in one's own manner. O'Hara's manner of work had always been as he hoped it would be tonight, an accomplishment in completed pages, after a period of pottering around, and at last settling to it. Looking to the right toward the fireplace from the Washington photograph, O'Hara could see one of the most diverting features of the room, a large low round table covered with books, magazines, cigar boxes, ashtrays, and bowls of matches in monogrammed paper covers. Under this table an equally ample shelf held more magazines, atlases, catalogues, and a folder of Picasso prints. It seemed almost as though O'Hara had developed will power by working night after night in the presence of those armchairs, reading lamps, interesting things to examine, new books from publishers, and magazines in their wrappers waiting to be opened and folded inside out so that one could read them. Not reading these tempting books and magazines during his long regular writing hours had put that row of O'Hara's works in their special binding on the shelf that he could see as he typed, estimating how much farther the row would extend when the manuscript now passing through his machine appeared as bound pages of print. He would light another cigarette and go on.

The nearest ashtray to the keyboard was the familiar heavy glass saucer in a square leather tray with wire netting across the top, made for office smokers of account executive rank who took things seriously and burned at least two packs a day. O'Hara lit cigarettes and let them go out, but almost always had one smoldering, and he invariably lit a cigarette before entering any room where people were waiting. He wrote in a syndicated column that nobody was going to scare him into giving up cigarettes, and nobody ever tried to. Besides the Vuitton and executive ashtrays, the study held half a dozen more, and seven lighters, including one from the National Golf Links, which had also supplied one of the working cigarette boxes in the room. Late at night voices could be heard in the study while O'Hara worked. There would be his own voice as he spoke dialogue aloud to test its rhythm, and from time to time the voices of news announcers on the radio. He would pull a completed page from his machine, lay it on the pile at the left, and put in another sheet, adjusting a second sheet under it because he liked the feel of typing on two thicknesses of paper. Then if the time was right he would hear five minutes of news. O'Hara used radio and television to soothe his nerves, and it is likely that the calm way in which newscasters report calamities was reassuring to O'Hara, alone in his writing hutch before dawn. In his longest novel,

From the Terrace — the title referred to the terrace outside the windows of the dining area — O'Hara had depicted the life of a colossal failure in scrupulous detail. Someone said to Noel Busch that it was an eerie thing to imagine O'Hara writing hour after hour in darkness and quiet on that old Revolutionary battleground by the Province Line Road. Busch replied, "It reads as though it was written at night, especially toward the end." In this novel a reader could identify the dark night of the soul, which Fitzgerald had said was always three o'clock in the morning. O'Hara had need of friendly and trustworthy objects around him as he prepared himself for work, but as his attention finally narrowed down on the pages in front of him, these things receded into soft focus in the background.

He might be conscious of the acetylene railroad lamp, another instance of high polish and satisfying form, or the long coach horn, the fly rod, and the buggy whip over the west window, the photograph of Pat Outerbridge in the Bermuda Race, the bulbed auto horn — one of a dozen horns in the study — and the photograph of O'Hara himself at the age of fourteen, mounted on a fine horse. This picture meant something, as did that of O'Hara at the wheel of a racing car, and two views of O'Hara's Rolls-Royce, one from the side, the other head on. Horses and automobiles had special significance for O'Hara, and often enough he had put these meanings into his work. The central figure of his first novel had been a Cadillac dealer, and O'Hara had looked into the tricks of that trade as carefully as Sinclair Lewis had examined the office routine of George F. Babbitt. What happened in O'Hara's mind as he fastened complete concentration on his characters was something on the order of the dissolve in motion pictures which ran the fade-out of one scene over the fade-in of another. The study at Linebrook, interior, night: DISSOLVE TO . . . whatever O'Hara was creating in his brain, perhaps the equal of his achievement in giving life and death to the Cadillac agent of *Appointment in Samarra*. He had spoken of reaching a state of "creative flow" in the substantial scenes or passages that made up his novels, blocked out in long paragraphs that met his theories of how the print on the page should meet the reader's eye. A writer had to go deep, and stay with what he found. O'Hara said, "When you're writing about the Armistice Day Parade of 1920, you have to get back there." His method might be called a form of self-hypnosis, and almost anything in the study could serve as the focus through which he made the dissolve: perhaps the last thing in the real world around him, before he went to the real world within him, might be the forty-eight-star American flag in the corner on the ten-foot pole surmounted by a silver spearhead. This was the size of flag that high bureaucrats rated, Assistant Secretaries and the like. But it was no joke — O'Hara was a patriotic man; he had once addressed a group of newly naturalized citizens, telling them how lucky they were to have become Americans. Or he might be looking beyond the long bay window at the shelves where the foreign editions stood — translations of O'Hara's work into Dutch, Spanish, Vietnamese, and seventeen other languages, or at the framed copy of one of Frank Sullivan's annual Christmas poems that mentioned John and Sister, or at the old print showing the northeastern view of Pottsville, or the framed Twenty-One hand which had been dealt O'Hara at 613 North Beverly Drive in 1939 — the ace of clubs, the four treys, and the deuce of spades, signed by the players present. Near this talisman of fortune O'Hara might rest his eyes on the storm-warning signals of the Coast Guard, or on the photograph of himself and Cardinal Spellman, which he had hung beside the fireplace although he had been away from the Roman Church for almost fifty years. On the other side of the fireplace, O'Hara might see an iris for the dissolve in a framed certificate of his membership in the United States Naval Institute, or the smaller frame which held a photostat of the check from a New Haven bank on the account of Yale University to John O'Hara for two hundred dollars, as payment for delivering the Bergen Lecture on May 4, 1955. Yale had paid in front, on April 21 — a touch of class. But it did not matter which of his curios and treasures held O'Hara's attention prior to the task at hand. When he was ready, he would begin by reading over what he had written on the previous night.

O'Hara's work in progress at this time was a sequel to *The Ewings*, and he had never written a sequel before. But having seen the Forsytes on television, he decided to build a saga on the family of a man named William Ewing, who lived in Cleveland, Ohio. O'Hara started the work he had titled *The Second Ewings* on February 13, 1970, typing the date as usual in the upper right hand corner of the first page. In the first novel, Bill Ewing had become chairman of the Cuyahoga Steel Company, and the sequel opens with a visit to Mr. and Mrs. Everett, the parents of his wife Edna, who live in Wingate, Michigan. The time is November 1924, and John Stuart Ewing, Bill's young son, is hoping to receive a .22-caliber rifle for his tenth birthday, which is coming in two months. Bill gives the boy the boxed rifle as they get on the train. At Wingate the Ewings are met by Mr. and Mrs. Paul Everett, Edna's parents. They all climb into the Everett Pierce Arrow, and on the way home it develops that John is to attend St. Paul's School and Yale instead of "Ann Arbor" (the University of Michigan), where his father was a member of Delta Kappa Epsilon. Next comes a description of the Everett sun porch, and the two women settle for a chat. Mr. Everett has gone to the hardware store to get ammunition for his grandson's rifle; Mrs. Everett is complaining about the family car. Her daughter says, "Let him keep the Pierce Arrow, mother. It's very fashionable to have an old car." There is to be a big party at the Everetts', Bill has not been warned to bring evening clothes, and Edna goes downtown to rent a dinner suit at Harry Jacobs' store. Jacobs is an example of the talkative, obsequious tradesman that O'Hara liked to depict, coming before the reader with remarkable conviction and economy. Since this is the town where Edna Ewing grew up, Jacobs uses her first name and eyes her figure as he bustles about, assembling the suit, shirt, tie, and Krementz studs. Back at the Everetts' house, it is revealed that the old man has a revolver, and Lloyd Sharpe, the Ewings' farmer, keeps a loaded shotgun handy; Edna has discovered a pistol belonging to Bill, and hidden it. With characters so well armed, there must be a fusillade ahead, but how it turned out we are not to know. We do have a dinner party scene — filet mignon with Béarnaise sauce, and hothouse straw- berries — with conversation about bootleggers and the Teapot Dome affair. In the morning John says he looks forward to showing the rifle to his friend Ted Wilmot when he gets home. The next passage of the book brings the Ewings back to their farm ten miles outside of Cleveland, where Bill Ewing invites Alva Harper, a Chicago steel executive, to stay over- night. Harper takes Edna to lunch at a speakeasy and suggests that they engage in an adulterous affair. Edna refuses, but meanwhile Bill Ewing has started an affair with Alicia Cott, meeting her at a hotel apartment that his company maintains. An associate named Walter Blake discovers Alicia in the apartment, but Bill is not there at the time, and he convinces Blake that Alicia's presence in a company bed was part of a joke to be played on another man. Bill Ewing then ends his friendship with Alicia, who says, "You're really a cold fish, aren't you?" As O'Hara read over this part, on page 72, he was satisfied that Alicia Cott spoke truth about Bill Ewing. And yet Bill could do decent things, as he had shown by advancing money for clothes to an office boy who wished to take the first step up by chang- ing his style of dress from cake-eater to collegiate. On page 74 Ewing was telling himself that he was in no danger, for "in any case, no harm had been done. Edna had not suspected him, and now his affair with Alicia was a thing of the past." Then came a line carrying the "#" used by O'Hara to indicate space on the printed page after a substantial passage. He usually left the last sentence in a stint of work unfinished, but as it happened, he had finished this one. His problem now was old and familiar and simple — to tell what happened next. O'Hara realized he would not do it tonight, he was not up to it. He felt pain in his chest and then in his left shoulder and arm. He put the plastic cover on the type- writer and page 74 of *The Second Ewings*, and walked out of the room. In the hallway leading to his bedroom he walked past photographs of him- self with Fitzgerald, with Hemingway, past the Thurber cartoon of O'Hara playing his violin, and his most prized citation, the award of merit conferred by the National Academy of Arts and Letters in 1964. It was one o'clock in the morning. O'Hara described his symptoms to Sister, and said he was going to bed. During the night Sister looked in on him and saw that he was asleep. Looking in again at about half-past eight, she noticed that he had turned on his side, and was sleeping quietly. At half-past one Sister went to wake him, and he was dead. The report was on radio in a few hours, and O'Hara's picture appeared on television news later in the day. There was agreement throughout the country that something important, which had come to be accepted as permanent, had gone. People who had not known O'Hara, or read his books, nevertheless got the feeling that there was a large empty space where he had been. No one could fill it, or attempt to supply what he had produced, for his work had been peculiarly his own, just as he had been, always and without question, his own man. Although a writer as successful as John O'Hara is a public figure, there was much in his life that he had not chosen to reveal, and he left to the world's curiosity the puzzle of high talent, and the mystery of genius.

TWO

THE
DOCTOR'S SON

ATRICK HENRY O'HARA, M.D., the father of John O'Hara, set up practice in Pottsville at the end of the year 1896. The Eleventh *Britannica* recognized Pottsville, locating the borough at Schuylkill Gap through Sharp Mountain on the Schuylkill River in the Pennsylvania anthracite mining regions ninety miles northwest of Philadelphia, and reporting a population of 20,235. Pottsville was more of a city than one would expect from that figure. It was the banking, trading, and professional center for a cluster of satellite towns including Lykens, Tamaqua, Coaldale, Port Carbon, Mount Carbon, Minersville, St. Clair, Mauch Chunk, Lehighton, Mahanoy (pronounced Mackanoy) City, Cressona, and Schuylkill Haven. Eighteen miles away over the mountain was Shenandoah, a grim place where the smoke from a subterranean fire that had burned for years could be seen within ten minutes' walk of the borough hall. Shenandoah added 25,744 people, many of them Lithuanian and Polish, to the metropolitan population around Pottsville.

Dr. O'Hara was familiar with Shenandoah, for he had been born there, the son of Major Michael O'Hara, a local magnate. Mike O'Hara had come to the United States as a small child in the early 1830s, settling with his parents in Reading, thirty-five miles southeast of Pottsville, the seat of Schuylkill County. When the Civil War came, Mike O'Hara rode into action as lieutenant of a local cavalry troop. He was promoted to the rank of captain, then to major. His sweetheart was Mary E. Franey of Shenandoah, and he married her on July 5, 1864. The Franeys were an established family, rated superior to the O'Haras; and Mary's parents were dubious about the match, although anyone could see that Mike O'Hara would make his way in the world. His first commercial venture in Shenandoah after the war was a livery stable, which he conducted in partnership with his brother Jim. Business became so good that the firm was able to lease three hundred horses to the John B. Robinson Circus. This

connection with show business made it logical for the brothers to buy the
Shenandoah Opera House on Main Street, which they renamed the
O'Hara Theater. And Mike revealed that he had sporting blood by building a private racetrack at his farm. In town Major O'Hara owned a large
house that still stands at the corner of Lloyd and White Streets, and here
his second son Patrick was born on December 26, 1867.

Patrick O'Hara grew up a privileged youth, marked, like his brothers,
for the college and professional education that his father was able to
provide. In Shenandoah, children often left school for permanent jobs at
the age of twelve, and although he gave his sons advantages, Mike O'Hara
saw to it that they did plenty of hard work. Idle hands, indeed, were
generally deplored in Schuylkill County, and Patrick O'Hara accepted
his chores as part of the unquestionable order of things. He drew heavy
duty when his father and uncle branched out into the undertaking business and made a success of it. They built an enormous barn for hearses
and funeral carriages, which Major O'Hara ordered to be drawn up every
night with the neatness of an artillery park. Patrick and his fellow workers
had to line the vehicles against the wall, shafts up, pulling them into position by lifting the front axles. In later life Patrick O'Hara said this exercise
had shortened his legs, while stretching his chest and shoulders. Mike
O'Hara wanted his sons to be absolutely unacquainted with alcohol until
they turned twenty-one, after which he hoped they would continue to
abstain from it. According to tradition, Irishmen had a special weakness
for liquor. The average Irish immigrant had to work long hours for low
pay, and he took the edge off his fatigue, and the bitterness from his
frustration, in the periods of release that he was able to get by drinking
in saloons. The horrors of the hangover on the morning after payday
night, with the grocery money gone and the woman reproachful, can be
imagined. But it was not headaches and empty pockets that Mike O'Hara
feared for his boys so much as loss of self-control. He knew what he was
talking about: he had been a two-fisted drinker in his youth. On one
occasion he had taken too much whiskey punch and injured a friend in a
scuffle. Then and there Mike O'Hara sent for the priest and took his
oath. Never again. The 1870s and 1880s may have seen the heaviest
drinking in our country's history, and Schuylkill County consumed its
share of booze: at the center of Shenandoah there were three or four
saloons to the block. Under these conditions, it turned out that Mike
O'Hara did not succeed in keeping his sons from learning the taste of
liquor. From this there came a tragedy that seemed to prove Mike O'Hara
right in his most solemn warnings. It happened that the bloods of
Shenandoah liked to go to the railroad station to meet the midnight train,
which was known as the "oyster train" because its manifest included sea-
food packed on ice in Baltimore. The young sports would buy and eat

oysters beside the tracks. One night a party that included Patrick's brother Martin came to meet the train; they had been drinking, and as the oyster train came in, Martin fell under the wheels. They took him home and laid him on the horsehair sofa in the formal sitting room of the house at Lloyd and White Streets, where he died in a few minutes from shock and loss of blood. Some time afterward, when Patrick O'Hara was home on vacation from Niagara University, word reached his father that the young man had been seen drinking in a saloon. Mike O'Hara summoned Patrick and pointed to the sofa. He said, "There's where your brother died because of drink. I won't see the same thing happen to you." Whereupon he produced the family Bible and administered the temperance oath. Patrick O'Hara considered himself bound not to drink until his twenty-first birthday. After that he didn't want to, as it might interfere with his main purpose in life, which was to become a first-rate surgeon. He had gone from Niagara to the University of Pennsylvania in Philadelphia, where he received his medical degree in May 1892. During that period Philadelphia was a stimulating place; for some time Thomas Eakins had been turning out his paintings of men and women, of racing shells on the Schuylkill, and other interesting things which he presented in clear unflattering light. Many people found Eakins disturbing, especially in such works as *The Gross Clinic,* which shows the eminent teaching surgeon Samuel D. Gross with blood on his hands as he demonstrates the bladder-stone removal to intently concentrating students in the dramatic light of the operating theater. Patrick O'Hara's hero among the noted surgeons of the time was Dr. John Blair Deaver, a brilliant operator who had graduated from the University Medical School in 1878. It was his example above all others that encouraged Patrick to continue, for Dr. Deaver was of Irish extraction, and showed by his impressive performance that the comic Irishman with his clay pipe, the rummy crying into his booze, and the cold-faced priest were not the only characters in the cast. Patrick O'Hara took the first step toward establishing himself as a surgeon by setting out after graduation on a trip to Europe "to see some of the big men operate." He came home by way of Ireland, and was pleased to find that the surgeons in Dublin were the best of all, or so it seemed to the newly graduated American doctor. The time now came for Mike O'Hara to die; and from the day of his funeral in 1893, there was a "feeling in the family" — a polite term for misunderstandings that grew like weeds, and dislikes that became incurable. One of the brothers had failed at the University of Pennsylvania Medical School, and Patrick said it was because he preferred social life to study. After Mike's death the O'Haras could not get along as a family, and Patrick gave up all ideas of starting practice in Shenandoah. He later told his wife and older children that the other O'Haras were happy to see him leave town and establish himself at

Schuylkill Haven, four miles south of Pottsville on the Schuylkill River, and twenty-two miles from Shenandoah, with a mountain between. Patrick O'Hara took lodgings and announced himself available for consultation. He also obtained the post of medical director at the county almshouse and insane asylum.

As medical superintendent Dr. O'Hara did what he could for his hopeless charges, but Schuylkill County provided only the necessities of life for paupers and madmen, and they had nothing in the way of comforts or amenities. Consequently Dr. O'Hara did not know what to make of it when he was asked to sign a voucher for "inmates' whiskey, thirty-two barrels." Since taking his post, the doctor had prescribed scarcely thirty-two ounces, and at that rate, one barrel would last the inmates thirty-two years. He summoned the dealer who supplied the county hospital, and was waited on by Joseph Nichter, a man of political influence who had grown rich selling wine, liquor, and beer. His card read Mellett & Nichter, Ale & Porter, but the partners got their best trade in whiskey, of which Nichter himself made liberal use. A smell of high-grade rye hung about him as he took a chair beside the doctor's rolltop desk at the asylum office. Patrick O'Hara's retentive memory recorded the scene: Nichter was overdressed, with flash jewelry and oiled hair, and he committed a final offense by lighting a cigar. The doctor was no smoker, and hated the smell of tobacco in his hair and clothes.

"What's it all about, Doc?" Nichter asked as O'Hara came back from opening a window.

"What's the meaning of this voucher?"

"Why Doc, that's what the inmates drink. You understand, the inmates."

Nichter's further efforts to explain showed that this whiskey order was a piece of time-honored county graft. A part of the barrel-whiskey delivered to the asylum was bottled and taken home by guards and employees. The rest was resold to the profit of Mellett & Nichter. With these facts established, the doctor declared the graft ended, tore up the voucher, and ordered Nichter out. Dr. O'Hara said if he heard of any more such knavery, somebody would go to jail.

"Don't you threaten *me*, Doctor O'Hara."

"Just get out."

At the door, Nichter turned and shouted, "You mark my words, O'Hara. I'm gonna get your job!"

Nichter brought all his political influence to bear, and found that the ousting of Patrick O'Hara was more than he could accomplish. All he succeeded in doing was to publicize the fact that Dr. O'Hara was a man of principle. The story of the whiskey reached Mrs. Charles Lee, one of Pottsville's leading citizens, and Mrs. Lee said to her friends, "I'd like to meet that Irish doctor." Within a week, Dr. O'Hara was taking tea at the house of this important lady, and listening to what she had to say with such interest that he could repeat it years afterward. Mrs. Lee opened the conversation by remarking, "I understand you told Joe Nichter off." The doctor replied, "I told him I wouldn't take part in a swindle." "That's what they're saying all over the county," said Mrs. Lee, "and it hasn't done you a bit of harm in Pottsville. What I want especially to tell you is this: I hope you settle here and start a practice. If you do, you just can't *help* being successful. We don't have an Irish Catholic doctor at present, so you will get all the Irish patients. I hope you'll give thought to what I've suggested to you."

Dr. O'Hara recalled in later years that the advice was sound, but he added, "Mrs. Lee was wrong if she thought the Irish alone would make it profitable. The poor Irish, oh, of course, they'd come hat in hand — and I'd help them. But the rich Irish are choosy about everything, including doctors." As it turned out, Dr. O'Hara's practice was to take in a socio-logical cross section of the Pottsville area, high and low, rich and poor, Irish, German, Slavic, and Anglo-Saxon.

The practice began with Dr. O'Hara's appointment as resident at the new Pottsville Hospital. Patrick O'Hara had brought from Schuylkill Haven a reputation for personal integrity and in Pottsville he soon began acquiring recognition for professional skill. Each week he went to Phila-delphia to see Deaver operate, and he took another European trip to keep up with developments in his field. With this background, the doctor in-spired further confidence by his authoritative manner when talking to patients. Though of medium height, Patrick O'Hara carried himself so well that people thought of him as a tall man. He wore conservative suits; his neckties were remarkable only for quiet richness of fabric and neat-ness of knot. A little less than half an inch of immaculate starched cuff with plain gold links appeared at his wrists, and Patrick O'Hara com-pleted the picture of a man of taste with his neatly trimmed dark mous-tache, like that of the gentlemanly actor John Drew. On horseback, Dr. O'Hara looked like an officer in the Brigade of Guards, visiting Schuylkill County on a trip around the world.

The ladies of Pottsville wondered who the doctor would choose for a wife, and the question was answered in the late summer of 1903, when Mr. and Mrs. Joseph Delaney of Lykens announced the engagement of their daughter Katharine to Patrick O'Hara. Mr. Delaney was a substan-tial citizen, owner of a general store and wholesale warehouse in Lykens, and a director of the bank. His family went back to pre-Revolutionary times and he had been born Protestant, entering the Roman Church when he married Alice Roark of Swatara. John O'Hara said his father took a step up when he married Katharine Delaney, for her family was the social equal of the Shenandoah Franeys. During a brief period as radio editor of the *New York Morning Telegraph*, O'Hara used the pseudonym "Franey Delaney." He had discovered that the founding of aristocracies among the Irish, as among any other Americans, depended on two factors: length of time in the country, and a reasonable degree of prosperity. Without the latter, people were not much impressed by the former. And there can be no doubt that Dr. O'Hara was aware of all this, when he brought his bride to Pottsville in December 1903. It was the sort of marriage that public opinion of those days held to be ideal: a pretty, accomplished, and "feminine" girl mated with a strong, handsome man who was about ten years older than his wife, and the dominating figure of the two. Mrs. Lee and her friends were pleased to see that the town had not only acquired a good doctor, but Pottsville society had gained a presentable couple for the suppers, dances, home-talent plays and concerts, treasure hunts, picnics, charades, and dinner parties that made life agreeable for members of the accepted set. Socially speaking, the O'Haras were among the saved. One has to mark this down as a significant fact because of theories advanced about John O'Hara's writing in relation to his place in the Pottsville scheme of things. It was true that pain drove O'Hara in his writing, but we shall see that it was not the pain of social rejection in youth.

John Henry O'Hara was born at 125 Mahantongo (pronounced Mackantongo) Street on January 31, 1905. It was a three-story brick house, which stood only a block from Centre Street and the business district of Pottsville. There was a street like Mahantongo in every American city of the early twentieth century: it was Commonwealth Avenue, it was Peachtree Street, it was Euclid Avenue in Cleveland and Summit Avenue in St. Paul. From the doctor's house, Mahantongo rose some sixteen blocks up a hill to the west, passing the Pottsville Club at No. 314, St. Patrick's Church in the five hundred block, and the town house of the rich brewer Frederick G. Yuengling at No. 606. Along here the town houses gave a metropolitan air to the street, built as they were to form a continuous façade with party walls, just as in London, Philadelphia, or Baltimore. A short distance further up, the town houses gave way to large free-standing structures, some with mansard roofs, conservatories, and driveways, on ample lawns amid magnificent trees. In good weather one could see gardeners, coachmen, and grooms at work around these houses, and ladies driving out in carriages to shop or pay calls. For these were carriage folk, families of established wealth and unassailable position. On its upper reaches, Mahantongo Street gave its message plain and clear: in this part of Pennsylvania, life followed an established course, and was quiet, dignified, and gilt-edged.

There was a profound difference between his father's birthplace and the little city where John O'Hara was born. Schuylkill County, where both places lay, had been since the early nineteenth century the center of anthracite mining, and supplied that hard variety of coal to markets throughout the world. The immeasurable pressure of the mountains, through an incalculable number of years, had packed into the anthracite an amount of energy that burst out in use with almost smokeless fires that gave intense heat. The energy also exploded in the form of money, and more of this money remained in Pottsville, the management town, than in Shenandoah, the working town. Pottsville was New York to Shenandoah in the role of Pittsburgh, and inevitable feelings of superiority on the one hand, and resentment on the other, played their parts in making it impossible that Patrick O'Hara and his Shenandoah kin should ever become reconciled. The final episode of family estrangement was an accompaniment of John O'Hara's birth.

It happened that Patrick O'Hara's sister Catherine had grown up an unusually handsome young woman. She was to be remembered as dressed in a white habit, riding a black horse over the fields and along the mountain roads. From her train of admirers, this spectacular beauty singled out a man named Gorman, of whom Patrick did not approve. He was convinced that Gorman was a rotter. Nevertheless, Catherine married Gorman about the time that Patrick married Katharine Delaney; and her first child, a boy, was born within a few days of John Henry O'Hara. The tragedy was that both Catherine Gorman and her baby were very ill, the illness resulting from a disease that Gorman had acquired, according to Dr. O'Hara's belief, during his career as a rotter. It was thought that the baby might be saved by giving him a wet nurse. Accordingly, Shenandoah relatives came to Dr. O'Hara and asked if John's mother would nurse her newly born nephew along with her son. The thought of it enraged Patrick O'Hara, and he ordered the supplicants out of his office. In a short time word came that his sister and her baby had died. Neither the doctor nor his wife ever mentioned this occurrence to their children, until more than fifty years later, when Katharine Delaney O'Hara told the story on her deathbed in New York.

John was the first child of Patrick and Katharine Delaney O'Hara; after two years, his sister Mary came into the world, to be followed at two-year intervals by his brothers Joseph and Martin. There were to be three more brothers and a sister — Thomas, born in 1914, James in 1916, Eugene in 1919, and Kathleen in 1920. A decade before this little sister joined the family, Dr. O'Hara bought Mr. Yuengling's house and moved his family into it, in time to celebrate Christmas of 1910 at 606 Mahantongo Street. There was nothing symbolic in this move toward the heights. It meant only that the doctor's growing family needed more room. He continued to keep office hours at 125 Mahantongo Street, and on most days went up the hill to take his midday meal at home.

When neighbors saw Dr. O'Hara marching along, or driving his carriage behind two well-groomed horses, they invariably commented that
he was a fine figure of a man. What the doctor saw in the neighborhood
and throughout the county was conditioned by his only physical flaw,
defective eyesight that he helped by wearing one pair of glasses all the
time, and mounting an additional pair for distant vision. John O'Hara at
the age of seven or eight would use the busybody in the middle window
on the second floor of No. 606 so that he could see his father coming up
the street and be at the door to meet him. A busybody was an arrangement of mirrors, something like the periscope employed by Tennyson's
Lady of Shalott, in which one could observe the street and sidewalk traffic, and prepare to be not at home for unwanted callers. As he approached
No. 606, and came into view on the right-hand mirror of the busybody,
Dr. O'Hara could see that his house was a good example of a successful
man's place of residence, its heavy stone walls enclosing three stories, and
a basement opening on an areaway. The doctor would leap up the steps
of the stone porch, pull open the heavy oak door, which was never locked,
and enter the tile-floored vestibule. The tile continued chest high; em-
bossed metal covered the rest of the walls. John would open the inner
door, his father would lift him for a moment, and then go bounding up
the stairs to drop his medical bag on a chest in the second floor hallway,
hang up his coat, put on a soft jacket, and hurry down to get the news of
what had happened during his absence. The American midday meal had
not yet begun its evolution into evening dinner, and in Dr. O'Hara's household, as in most others, it was an important family gathering, with everyone present except babies so small that they still inhabited cribs. The
doctor's family gathered at a long table in the paneled basement dining
room and there Katharine Delaney O'Hara fed them bountifully, with the
help of a German cook. Dr. O'Hara believed in general talk at mealtimes,
and the children were not under a rule of silence, as they might have
been in some households even as late as 1913. However, Patrick O'Hara
was the chief justice of the conversation, and did not hesitate to hand
down rulings on questions of fact and propriety. He did not propose to
be told the right of things by a pack of children in his own house, and he
conducted himself in a manner that would have caused the savants of a
later period to label him an authoritarian personality. This was not eccentricity on the doctor's part. Family men were supposed to lay down the
law and exercise unquestioned though presumably benevolent authority
in their homes. It was part of the eternal war between parents and children, that is fought under different rules today, but the same old struggle.
In one of his stories about Pottsville, O'Hara gives the frustrated housewife Bobbie McCrea a bleak remark: "'Children don't love you back.'"
But as a small boy, O'Hara worshipped his father. He wrote a gentle

reminiscent passage from his father's point of view in *A Rage to Live*, looking through the eyes of Sidney Tate:

Whenever I see Billy he smiles and I smile, and now, when I start to think of him, I smile. Now there's a child who's *all* reserve. "Hello, Billy. What you been doing?" you say to him, and he smiles before answering, "Nothing." . . . He'll keep his hand on the knob of the door, looking up at you as if you were God Almighty, or Santa Claus — no. No. Looking at you and smiling that way because you are Sidney Tate, his father. It is almost more than you can bear, to look at such free, happy love for you. "Don't do it, boy," you want to say to him. "Please don't look at me like that. I'm only me. I am *only* Sidney Tate, father of you." You turn away, to get that sun out of your eyes, and you want to be rough, to reject his offering because you know you cannot match it with something of your own. But he doesn't want anything. To think I can give such pleasure by no more than being. I never did anything to deserve this, but more than that, I never set out to earn it, to purchase it, to inspire it. I didn't know it was there, I hardly knew he was there, except as a baby. But then one day it *was* there, has been there — but of course it won't always be there. It will pass as he begins to leave the heaven he seems to be in. And the strange, unbelievable thing is that I can keep that heaven existing for him by no more than saying, "Hello, Billy. What you been doing?" and ruffling his hair a little, asking him to do me a favor by getting me something I could easily get myself. "Will you reach me those matches, please?" I say to him, and someone of an alien tongue might think, looking at Billy, that I had said, "You can stay home from school tomorrow," or "Here's a five-pound box of Huyler's for you and you alone." I am familiar with admiration-and-love and respect-and-love, if for no other reason than that I have felt them and sent them out. But Billy loves me freely, happily, wholly, trustingly, without my having to sing for him, bat a ball for him, jump a fence for him, do a trick for him, carry him, feed him, or even touch him. He will rub the back of my hand when it is resting on the arm of a chair, and he will kiss my cheek in front of the ear while I am eating my breakfast. But the gestures of affection must originate with him and he does not expect them to be reciprocated.

John O'Hara was still living in his private heaven in 1913 when the Pottsville Academy of Music burned to the ground. This auditorium and meeting place at Second and Mahantongo Streets, near the Reading Building and Dr. O'Hara's office, had been the scene of performances by symphony orchestras, opera troupes, and first-class plays with New York casts of the kind now referred to as national companies. Pottsville was a split-week town, but the best of the road attractions played there, and after the Academy burned, not to be replaced, the city lost something important. Over the mountain in Shenandoah, the O'Hara Theater was playing vaudeville, but not of the Keith or Orpheum "time," as the booking circuits were known among actors. As a theatrical manager, Mike O'Hara was known to be a slow man with a dollar. If an actor complained, Mike would win the argument by growling, "You're not on the Keith time now. You're on the O'Hara time."

In Pottsville John had other connections with the theater; his cousins the Higginses owned the leading movie house on Centre Street. He was given door privileges, and could pass in half a dozen boys to see the bathing beauty Annette Kellerman in *Neptune's Daughter,* or the early film dramas of D. W. Griffith. He had been too young to understand the cultural loss that came from failing to rebuild the Academy. To John the burning of the Academy had been a thrilling public event, but nothing more. He heard his father say it was the greatest destruction by fire that Pottsville had seen since the *Miner's Journal* building burned in 1893, a disaster that had removed from the local skyline the two hundred-foot *Journal* tower, an exact copy of that on the Bradford town hall in the West Riding of Yorkshire. The Academy left something valuable to John and all Pottsville boys, because for several years the burned site remained vacant, with catacombs where the cellars had been. The boys called this subterranean area "the ruins," and "Let's go play in the ruins" was a welcome suggestion when things got dull in other parts of town. John and his friends could also gratify their interest in caves and mysterious underground galleries in the subbasement at No. 606, where Mr. Yuengling had dug a wine cellar. One entered this thrillingly dark and cavernous place by a stairway under the kitchen. It would be fanciful to say that delving into the earth was instinctive for boys in the mining regions, and the days when a mine gallery had run beneath Centre Street were many years past by the time John was born. To John as a child, his native town was not a place of tunnel entrances, but rather a succession of spectacular views because of its site on the steep sides of surrounding mountains. Coming down from Shenandoah, one could see that Pottsville had a wild kind of beauty, with the Schuylkill County Court House on one side, the spires of the south side churches on the other, the business district lying between. In this matrix the city ran west up the valley to its suburb of Minersville. On sunny days the town had a sparkle about it because of close-ranked windows in the light where streets mounted and houses packed themselves closely together. Balancing the court house, an unforgettable building in the Richardsonian style, there stood on the opposite slope of Sharp Mountain rising above Mahantongo Street the Yuengling Brewery, dominating its part of town like the Castle at Edinburgh. Coming through the Lehighton Gap from the east, one saw scores of turnip-topped Slavic churches; they were all over St. Clair, Coaldale, and Shenandoah

— but not in Pottsville. This did not mean that Catholics were of no account there; for the tallest church spire in Pottsville was that of St. Patrick's parish. John's mother was a constant attendant there, and he started two years' service as altar boy when he was twelve.

Saint Patrick's had the tallest spire, but John had begun to notice, at who can say how early an age, that Trinity Episcopal Church on South Centre Street drew a glossier congregation than the one which came to St. Patrick's, or to any other church in the city. It was an important idea, not especially welcome, but something to reckon with. In his mature years, O'Hara wrote a story about Pat Collins, a newcomer to Gibbsville (the author's fictional name for Pottsville) and his friendship with Whit Hofman, a leading citizen. Hofman suggests to Pat that membership in the country club would be a good thing. Pat says he's Catholic. Whit says, " 'That's all right. We take Catholics. Not all, but some.' "

John observed that Trinity was not on Mahantongo Street. Trinity didn't *have* to be on Mahantongo Street, for there was an air of authority in those few blocks of South Centre Street near the church, and in the elegant building at No. 325, which housed the counting rooms for mining and banking interests controlled by the Sheafer family. No. 325 was an Italianate palace with an arched entrance suitable for a museum or a club of millionaires, and the impressive effect was not dispelled by a strange sight on the steep wooded hill above it, where a gigantic figure stood looking to the north, apparently sustained by levitation, or by some lofty perch in the thick forest growing there. This was a cast-iron statue of Henry Clay, and those who clambered into the woods could see that it stood on a column 150 feet high. A little farther up the mountainside was an old pillared house, mostly hidden by trees, the former home of David Bannan, who had founded the *Miner's Journal* in 1826, and used his influence to erect the statue of Clay in 1855, after the Kentucky senator's death. The statue and column were made of iron out of gratitude for Clay's aiding both the coal and iron industries by working for laws to establish high protective tariffs. When O'Hara grew older, he could reflect that while Pottsvillians were memorializing Clay, Southerners were cursing him, and the higher price for manufactured goods brought on by protective tariffs was among the causes of the Civil War. But whatever the verdict of economic history might be, many citizens of Schuylkill County had taken part in the Civil War, and Mike O'Hara of Shenandoah had been among them.

Although it thrilled John to be told about Grandfather O'Hara's achievements, the grandparents who exercised the most direct influence on his early years were the Delaneys at Lykens, thirty miles west of Pottsville. Nothing pleased him more than a visit to these indulgent grandparents: Joseph I. Delaney resembled Santa Claus—white-bearded, stout, and jolly — and Alice Delaney would always drop what she was doing to welcome the children. She gave them their favorite foods, organized trips and parties, and set them to playing games in the long side yard. The Delaney house fronted on the brick sidewalk of Main Street; mountains formed a backdrop across fields in the rear. Whenever John came here, he felt peace and happiness. Grandmother Delaney had a lovely voice, and she trilled a greeting to the children as "my t-r-r-reasures." In Lykens, no one made demands on John, and he could do as he pleased, and pass his time at leisure inspecting a large number of interesting objects that belonged to his grandfather in the Delaney brickyard, lumberyard, wholesale warehouse, and store.

There was a special satisfaction in the store, with its smells of spice and coffee, its reels of thread and trays of nails, its ranks of flat drawers that pulled out and revealed articles of merchandise precisely arranged by shape and size, and its shelves where bolts of cloth lay ready to come down on the counters with a soft thump for display to customers and measurement between brass tacks. The flat drawers had served as the first Lykens bank, when Joseph Delaney put away money for the miners, keeping it locked up over Saturday nights when the drinking was heavy. Mr. Delaney had befriended the miners during the strike of 1903, extending credit until the strike was won. All of this made Joseph Delaney an important and respected man, a condition of life which his wife constantly bore in mind. John O'Hara presented the town of Lykens under the name of Lyons in his writing, and he made his grandparents the McMahons, who lived in a house exactly like the one he loved to visit. He opened the novel *Ourselves to Know* with a paragraph that showed how things looked in Lykens:

As a boy and until I was sixteen I spent a large part of every summer at my grandfather's house in Lyons, Pennsylvania. We always sat on the porch on Sunday and my grandmother would hold court with the people on their way home from the Baptist, the Catholic and the Evangelical churches; and like all children I realized at an early age that older people did not treat each other as equals. A man and his wife were a little above you or a little below you. All the people who stopped to chat with my grandparents were a little below them, and they could not help showing it. In fact, I used to think it gave them pleasure to be respectful to my grandparents, even when my grandmother would sharply contradict them on matters of no importance. As a boy who was being brought up very strictly, I was often embarrassed by my grandmother's manner with older people. When they had said as much as she wanted to hear, she would turn away and chat with one of my aunts until the poor man and woman found the simple phrases to excuse themselves. "Guess we better be going along," they would say, and my grandmother would say, "All right. Goodbye." I did not know then, of course, that quite a few of those people were in financial debt to my grandfather. I did not even know that some of them lived in houses that were owned by my grandfather. There were a lot of things I did not know.

There were some things that did not remain long unknown. John sensed that his Lykens grandparents stood high on a ladder of status, and was able to locate his own position without much difficulty: he had no superiors among the children of Schuylkill County, and only a limited number of equals. He got this impression because his parents decided against both the public and parochial schools, and enrolled him in the select private academy conducted by Miss Katherine Carpenter on Howard Avenue. Miss Carpenter offered more than the social stamp of attending a school where only "nice" children were accepted: she was a gifted teacher who had her pupils reading at five or six, doing simple arithmetic with ease, and writing a legible hand. Like most Americans of fortunate background in his time, O'Hara benefited from the ideas of Maria Montessori, the first woman to receive a medical degree in Italy, who was then at the height of her influence as an educator of young children. The great Friedrich Wilhelm August Froebel himself had contributed to the excellence of John's instruction in the kindergarten that "Miss Katy" conducted in preparation for her graded school. O'Hara liked to say that Miss Katy taught him the virtue of the simple declarative sentence. He said he became a millionaire by using that kind of sentence, casting himself as a Henry Ford of literature who made his product from plain old materials at hand. O'Hara took the tone of that remark from his youthful reading of the *American Magazine* and the *Saturday Evening Post,* in which there appeared much praise of men who made valuable property from obvious things that ordinary people overlooked. The *American* and the *Post* seldom printed anything about an author, although they might run an occasional piece on a visit to the home of Dr. Henry van Dyke, or a photograph of Mark Twain's octagonal study at Hartford. So far as sentences went, O'Hara's were not always simple: the admirable thing about them was that they were always clear.

There was clarity of form on all sides in the world that opened around John O'Hara in his early youth. After he was ten years old, the doctor often took him along on drives around the county. What John saw on these trips instilled in him a fundamental feeling for shape and construction. The boy's color-blind eyes missed the bursts of gold and red on autumn hillsides: all the more striking was the contrast of black and white when deciduous trees stood bare against snow on the mountains, and the pine forests were dark masses in John's view. At these times in winter, the shapes of mountains came up clear in economical lines like the shapes of waves, or dunes on the desert. Blending into the sides of real mountains, John saw smaller mountains that men had created. These were the hills of slag around the collieries, waste material of the mining process that piled up as it fell, forming peaks and ranges. The force of gravity had pulled slag and culm into logical statements of the idea expressed when one said, I see a mountain. The shapes of exterior mining construction and machinery were logical too: the shed housing a breaker might run up a hillside twenty stories in weather-beaten silver-gray wood and corrugated sheet iron, sometimes with many windows that made a wall of glass. Running alongside, the "plane" or inclined railroad gave an uninterrupted line. No deliberate esthetic consideration had gone into the construction of mining works; yet if you had the eye to see it, they conveyed a beauty of logic and line, of shape and definition and hard truth.

Riding the back roads beside his father, O'Hara took in the peculiar beauty of the mine workings, in sensations that came to him mixed with respect and fear for the terrain itself. The wilderness was implacable. At some places, power lines went over the valleys on steel towers that seemed to be walking across hills like the Martians in Mr. Wells's story about the war of the worlds. In winter twilight the lines would be the only things in the long bleak landscape that indicated the presence of man. A turn of the road, the lines would disappear, and John could look across upland country that had not altered in four hundred years. No houses, no lights, and fifty yards off the road in winter a man could lose himself and freeze to death by morning. Wildcats and mountain lions inhabited the woods; in summertime, rattlesnakes crawled from their dens to hunt small animals. A rattlesnake would not attack a child or grown person who let it alone, but you could step on him by mistake, he would hit back, and the poison could be fatal. These snakes had magnificent skins that made up into fine leather, and the doctor had heard that their flesh was good eating, although he had never tried it and didn't intend to. His purpose in taking John along on these rides was not to instruct the boy in natural history, but to give him an idea of the interest, importance, responsibility, and authority of the doctor's trade. Patrick O'Hara was determined that his son should follow him in the medical profession, and there was much to be said for taking up a father's calling. One thing only was essential, the son's willingness to continue what his father had begun, and this element was missing in the case of Patrick and John O'Hara. John was aware of his father's importance as a good doctor, and admired the way Patrick O'Hara conducted himself, with his strong chest and shoulders carried proudly, his direct gaze, and the medical bag that signified his authority to cross any police line, or enter any doorway where people stood around looking scared and solemn: "I am Doctor

O'Hara." That was splendid. But John did not want to be a doctor. When he was twelve years old, Patrick O'Hara offered to deposit ten thousand dollars in a fund for medical education, if John would promise to pursue it. John refused the offer, although under high pressure for a twelve-year-old. After that, much pain was to come from the relationship between son and father, even though John grew to resemble the doctor in some ways, and to accept some of his basic views. Yet the boy could find no words to make his father see that where he differed from him was in the essential John O'Hara, the person that he had to be. Tom O'Hara observed that John and his father grew to have "a touching physical resemblance." Their gestures often were the same: Dr. O'Hara, for example, was a leaner, who liked to prop himself, still standing very straight, against a doorjamb or a mantelpiece. With his elbow on the mantel of the big second floor living room at No. 606, he would show his laundered cuff, muscular wrist, and strong graceful hand. John moved and stood in a similar way, not as an imitator, but because his inherited nervous system sent out the same reflex actions as those that governed the body of Patrick O'Hara.

Disappointment over John's refusal to bind himself to a career did not lessen the doctor's generosity to his son, or to the other members of the family. Among the advantages he had provided for his children was the opportunity to attend dancing school. Acceptance in the right dancing class meant that a child was "nice," and destined to receive invitations to balls and parties later on with the same boys and girls who were now learning to bow, circle the floor in a waltz or two-step, and say goodbye politely to the teacher when the class was over. Mothers gave dancing classes considerable importance wherever enough people had been around long enough for social stratification to take place. Most girls liked going to dancing school; most boys complained and acted as though they hated the idea, but the smart ones knew they were getting a ticket that might have value in the future. For the present, the dancing class came along with concerts and plays and books and magazines, and presents at Christmas that seemed to be radiant with love and wonder — for the boys such things as marvelous chests of Meccano parts from which one constructed models of the Brooklyn Bridge or the Flatiron Building, or made a stamping mill powered by a small steam engine that whirled its flywheel with a great deal of hissing and the smell of hot metal and burning alcohol. John's weekly appearance at dancing school, in his navy blue suit, and carrying his pumps in a green bag, was one among many privileges that he enjoyed as the son of Patrick O'Hara. The doctor also decided that his children should learn to ride, and he provided them with ponies, who were cared for along with the horses at his private stable on Second Street at Schuylkill Avenue.

Patrick O'Hara understood how children thrilled to the idea of a surprise. Accordingly he told John and the three younger ones to be at home on a certain spring day in 1913 for an event that he guaranteed to be of interest. Martin, Joseph, and Mary stood by, climbing on the granite hitching block that held the initials F.G.Y. so deeply incised for the previous owner that the children took them for granted like the tracing of a prehistoric fossil. On the second floor, John kept watch through the busybody. He rushed downstairs when he saw Arthur Woodruff, the doctor's groom, turning the Sixth Street corner in a brand new governess cart with a Shetland pony between the shafts. There were to be six ponies in all. The children named the first one Billy; Dot soon joined Billy, and as the O'Hara family grew, the pony troop increased with a tiny one named Midge, and then came Captain, Major, and Colonel. The doctor provided his children with a dogcart in addition to the governess cart. He also had a child's-size Conestoga wagon built at the Sieffert Body Works in Cressona for a four-pony hitch. This diminutive pioneer wagon was a popular entry at shows, and won several prizes around the county, where crowds delighted in the cargo of good-looking children, and the fine little ponies trotting along. Mounted on a pony at the age of twelve, John edged into the Centre Street parade of a Wild West troupe, hoping to be mistaken for a performer, but the people said, "There goes Doctor O'Hara's boy." The doctor spoke seriously to his children about the care of animals, and John appointed himself foreman, carefully repeating the instructions to his sister and brothers. To Dr. O'Hara, ponies for children were part of something that he called traveling first class in life. This concept had a certain magnificence, and applied to more than transport: land, houses, furniture, clothes, and musical instruments were some of the things that Patrick O'Hara considered to be important, in support of self-respect, integrity, dignity, good manners, and style. He found it emotionally rewarding to match his earning power against the demands of financing the first-class way of life for a growing family. One should bear in mind that Dr. O'Hara did not have to pay income tax until 1913, and the tax was still within bounds by the time he died in 1925. Moreover, the dollars that Patrick O'Hara earned in the twenty years following John's birth in 1905 were loaded with a purchasing power that can scarcely be imagined in the 1970s. The money was bursting with energy, like anthracite coal; and because of his skill and high reputation, Dr. O'Hara had sources of income aside from patients' fees. In addition to his salary from the Pottsville Hospital, Dr. O'Hara drew a retainer from the Philadelphia & Reading Coal & Iron Company, for services in tidying up after the mining machinery had chewed off arms and hands, or caved in chests, or separated legs from torsos, as happened almost every day except when work was slack. He did the same sort of repairs for the Eastern Steel Mill, where men were crushed, burned, torn, broken, and blinded in various ways. The doctor was present at so many scenes of horror that he developed a high degree of professional detachment, and correctly so, for a cool head and a steady hand in the emergency represented the victim's only chance. Patrick O'Hara performed well, and by one method or another he was paid well, so that his income grew bigger as each year passed. And he appeared to regard his earning power as a permanent material asset, quite the same as railroad bonds or first mortgages.

It was natural that Katharine O'Hara had moments of anxiety about family finances, for at times Patrick O'Hara seemed alarmingly relaxed in his attitude toward money. Her father could call in money when he wanted to, without having to give up a piece of himself in return. The magnates of Schuylkill County were men of the countinghouse, and they made money from money, scratching with their pens and clamping the weight of debt on other people. This was not Dr. O'Hara's way. He was on call twenty-four hours a day to industrial employers and his own patients: he earned every dollar that went through his bank account with physical work. The question was, what would become of the O'Haras if the doctor should be disabled, and where would they turn if he should die? In 1915, when John was ten years old, his father was forty-eight, and appeared to be thriving on long hours in consulting and operating rooms, hard travel around the county, and little sleep. The doctor was a Theodore Roosevelt sort of man: he believed in the strenuous life, keeping fit by means of cold showers, exercise, and boxing. He had received ring instruction at the University from William Muldoon, a trainer known as the Old Roman for his uncompromising rectitude. Later in life, Patrick O'Hara sometimes visited Muldoon's health camp, where he would undergo a severe program of exercise and dieting, which was of questionable benefit to a man in middle life. The boxing gloves hung in Dr. O'Hara's office, and he liked to spar a round or two with any opponent. On one occasion the doctor asked an instrument salesman if he would care to put on the gloves. The man hesitated, but agreed to go one round when assured that it was all in fun. They squared off, the doctor aimed a punch at the salesman's head, and immediately landed on his back looking up at the ceiling. The salesman said, "My apologies, Doc. I used to fight professional." The doctor reported this encounter to his sons, and told them, "Boys, this proves one thing — never box with a stranger." But Patrick O'Hara did not draw the line at *fighting* with a stranger. There were times when a man had to settle things personally, and one knew by instinct when those times came. At the corner of Second and Market Streets in Pottsville one day in early winter, a milk wagon driver thought that Dr. O'Hara's carriage stood in his way. The driver was a Pennsylvania Dutchman, and his traditional surliness apparently increased because the doctor was wearing the second pair of glasses. He yelled something about a four-eyed Irish bastard. Dr. O'Hara stepped down, pulled the driver out of his wagon, and hit that Dutch son of a bitch so hard that he fell unconscious in the gutter. The doctor then went to the office of the Alderman, as the chief town magistrate was called, and said, "I just knocked out a Dutchman. When he comes to, he'll be in here for a warrant. I'm due at the hospital and haven't time for formalities. So if you'll please tell me the fine I'll pay it now and be on my way." The magistrate said, "Get out of here, Doctor. I'll handle that Dutchman." When the milk wagon driver appeared, he got a reception like that accorded the top banana in the burlesque-show skit, "Irish Justice." And Dr. O'Hara heard no more about it.

At some time during this period Katharine Delaney O'Hara told her husband that he was the most intemperate man she had ever seen who didn't drink. The occasion for this remark was the doctor's announcement that he had bought Oakland Farm in the Panther Valley six miles southwest of Pottsville. He had acquired a large house, with quarters for a tenant farmer, barns, outbuildings, and 160 acres of land in rolling country, dramatically sited between wooded hills that framed the valley. The place would serve as a summer home and also for the breeding of cattle. To this end the doctor had paid three thousand dollars for a bull called Noble of St. Mary's. The news caused Mrs. O'Hara to open her silver vinaigrette and take a sniff of smelling salts to steady her nerves. She had not forgotten the shock a few months before when Dr. O'Hara had taken his wife and oldest son to a sale of blooded stock at Cressona; John had wandered away; spying him across the auction ring, Mrs. O'Hara waved to the boy, and the doctor said, "You've just bid forty-five hundred dollars." The auctioneer called for more, a stockman signaled the next bid, and Mrs. O'Hara sighed with relief. But it was evident that nobody had raised the O'Hara bid on Noble of St. Mary's, and Katharine wondered how they could sustain life in town and on the farm if spending continued at this rate. She had "something of her own" — certain inherited bonds, in what amounts the children did not know, but supposedly a substantial holding, and this the doctor never touched, for it was "Delaney money," destined to go, some day, to children and grandchildren. Whatever her financial worth might be, Katharine was giving her children many things of greater value than Delaney money. She had received a finishing-school education at Eden Hall, the academy for young ladies conducted by the Sisters of the Sacred Heart at Torresdale, near Philadelphia. Among her accomplishments was a sufficient facility in French to make her a leader in the Pottsville Cercle Française. Katharine also had a gift for music, and had studied at Eden Hall under the direction of Professor Zeyderheily, a pupil of Liszt. Mrs. O'Hara had learned to make her small hands stretch across an octave, and she played Mussorgski, Chopin, and other serious composers with pleasure to herself and her family. The children observed that their mother's books of piano music, published by G. Schirmer and Company, "had no pictures on the front." That was one way to tell important music from popular stuff, and from the semiclassical parlor music which Mrs. O'Hara also played on request. The doctor was musical too, though without training, and Katharine sometimes accompanied his singing when he came home for the midday meal. She would take off her rings, seat herself at the Brinckerhoff upright, and the doctor would stand leaning, one hand against the mahogany where the treble ended, the other on his wife's shoulder, as he sang "I'll Take You Home Again, Kathleen." The piano stood in the long back living room on the second floor: the front room held the harmonium (a small organ operated by three pedals), and Mary's harp, which came from Lyon and Healey in Chicago. Mary often played the harp for her father in this front room, where he would sit in a big leather chair near the window, leaning back with his eyes closed. Mary had inherited her mother's musical touch, and allowed herself to be persuaded to play the harp at a public concert, although she feared disaster, with her father in the hall. But Mary charmed her audience, and made Patrick O'Hara happy and proud. He also found it gratifying when his wife performed in a concert of sixteen pianos at the Academy of Music, one of the most spectacular home-talent shows ever given in Pottsville.

Katharine Delaney O'Hara belonged to the Outdoor Club, which maintained tennis courts and a simple frame building on a hillside above Howard Avenue, the street that paralleled Mahantongo to the south. The club was far from showy, but extremely "nice," and membership indicated acceptance in the best circles. Besides playing tennis at the club, Mrs. O'Hara and other ladies held card parties on the veranda, with ices from Imschweiler's candy store, and inexpensive prizes. In the opening years of the twentieth century, there was doubt in some circles concerning the propriety of traditional playing cards. To meet this prejudice, the game companies offered various four-suited packs, sorted in some other way than by diamonds, spades, and so on. Some of the ladies used these cards in games that were similar to auction bridge, with names like Flinch, Rook, and Five Hundred. After the First World War, the knaves, kings, and queens finally routed the Rook cards and other synthetic packs. Gone too were the simple, white-flannel dances with fruit punch and three-man orchestras that parents organized at the Outing Club, in its plain main room with walls unfinished and roof timbering exposed in summer cottage style. The new Schuylkill Country Club took its place, with dinner and supper served by uniformed attendants, and dance bands from Harrisburg and Philadelphia. The same thing was happening all across the country: at Charlevoix, at Harbor Point, at Mount Desert and Narragansett, an Arcadian simplicity had given way to complicated and expensive pleasures. O'Hara used his impressions of the Outing Club in the passage of *From the Terrace* where the poor boy Tom Rothermel attends a small dance, talks to the three young people there whom he knows, and goes home. By contrast, *Appointment in Samarra* presents a large and costly dance at the country club, during which Julian English begins his slide to destruction.

Sociologists may have failed to observe it, but the fact is that boys and girls in early adolescence tend to organize themselves in sets of three. These triads may take form because of the instinct that moved Horatius to put a trustworthy companion on his left and right sides; at any rate, an adult man or woman will usually recall *two* close friends of the same sex, acquired before the opposite sex became fascinating. On John's right and left after the age of twelve there stood Ransloe Boone, who was also a doctor's son, and Robert Thurlow Simonds, of an established Presbyterian family. These boys lived on Mahantongo Street a few blocks up from No. 606. Their families were in comfortable circumstances, though not wealthy, their mothers were on good terms with John's mother, and their fathers respected Patrick O'Hara. Dr. Boone was a gynecologist, and so not a direct competitor of Dr. O'Hara, which made it easy for John to use the Boone house as a second home. Ransloe (Beanie) Boone was a cheerful youth who had the gift of being able to make other young people laugh. They all laughed a great deal when they got together, but Robert Simonds has recalled that there was a serious undertone to the life of Schuylkill County that even young people were aware of, because of the frequent deaths in accidents at the mines. There are people in Schuylkill County today who mention the names of old closed mines in the same tone of voice that is used to mention battles. And the two doctor's sons got acquainted with death soon enough. A third of a century later, O'Hara wrote to William Maxwell of *The New Yorker*: ". . . in my boyhood, death was a commonplace. Every time the telephone rang there was a chance that death would be in on the call, especially late at night. 'He died on the table,' was an expression I heard a hundred times — at the dinner table. Also, I saw the dying in hospitals, and once I held a brakeman's hand as he died after my father had amputated both his legs. I did not grow up at the Schuylkill Country Club — or the Stork Club. I grew up one Christmas day, stopping to pick up the priest in my governess cart so that he could take the Holy Viaticum to Stink Schweiker's father who was lying on a railroad track with a leg smashed off. I grew up when I had to take something, I don't know what, to a Mrs. Murphy's house, a widow with one daughter a few years older than I, and I had to stand there and mutter to the girl, alone with her, and then a year or so later I heard that the girl had become a whore, but that day I was alone with the girl and her dead mother and I did not know what I was feeling till I got the same feeling reading *Dubliners*."

In Pottsville, the undertakers had set up shop next to the physicians' offices in Market and lower Mahantongo Streets, and the boys always knew who had died. John had grown big enough at fourteen to act as chauffeur for his father, and sometimes got out of bed before dawn to drive the doctor to the hospital or to the scene of a wreck. On one occasion he sat beside dying men and did what he could to let them know they were not alone. O'Hara said of this in later years, "They wanted somebody's hand to hold on the way out, and the nurses were busy." The death of a patient cared for by Dr. Boone usually left motherless children, something that the boys had trouble squaring up with the doctrine of God's infinite love and mercy. The Episcopalian Beanie Boone could throw no light on this, and Bob Simonds was unable to solve the problem with anything he had learned at Presbyterian Sunday School. Mrs. O'Hara was devout, and attended early mass every day. She was happy to see how well John served at the altar, and to hear the care and clarity with which he pronounced the Latin responses. She did not know that John had started smoking in the sacristy, and that he was beginning to question the spiritual authority of Monsignor McGovern. John and his two cronies debated the possibilities of atheism and considered many other questions. They wondered, for example, if a perpetual motion machine could be constructed, why the moon seemed to move with you when you walked up the street, and whether or not it would be possible to arrest a policeman. They also took delight in the possibilities of language. In this line something satisfactory came from the firm name of Arbogast & Bastian, competitors in the liquor trade to Melett & Nichter, Porter & Ale: Tom O'Hara recalled that few greetings to a friend could yield more joy than "Hello there, you arbogast bastian." The boys also liked "Good morning, you poor unsophisticated fragment of debased humanity," and John convulsed them by announcing that "Mortals who abide in vitreous edifices should not possess morbid propensities toward disestablishmentarianism."

We may tend to forget the intensity with which adolescents examine the world around them, and how closely they scrutinize the people claiming authority in that world. John and his friends discovered that if you looked at them carefully and steadily, grown people sometimes made sorry spectacles of themselves. Speaking about the character of Tom Rothermel, in *From the Terrace*, O'Hara summed up an observant boy's view of his elders:

. . . After some indeterminate point when he was ten or eleven he was never again to be impressed by age *per se*, and when he began to question that superiority he was unconsciously getting himself ready to question other verities. If a man was not your superior although he happened to be older, then another man might not be holy although he was a preacher, another man might not know everything although he was a teacher, a woman need not be considered a fine lady although she wore satin and exuded cologne. And he discovered the heresy that the possession of money did not make the possessors better people . . . Money was money, and people were people. He was still years away from the development of his eventual philosophical attitude toward people and money, but he had made a start.

On June 24, 1916, John saw the mayor of Pottsville ride a black horse up Centre Street at the head of a brass band which preceded Captain James Archbald's company of the 103rd Engineers, Pennsylvania National Guard, on their way to take a train for the Mexican border and the pursuit of a warlord named Pancho Villa. John had seen pictures of the commander in chief who had ordered out these citizen soldiers — President Woodrow Wilson, with his stern, thin-jawed face and long-tailed coat like the Lawyer Marks in an Uncle Tom troupe; and John had studied newspaper portraits of the iron-faced General Black Jack Pershing, who wore a tight-collared tunic hooked under his chin. The Pottsville soldiers had dressed for route march, with khaki shirts and campaign hats. The glory of it was almost unbearable as they swung by, Our Flag at the column's head and Captain Archbald marching at attention, looking straight in front. Captain Archbald was handsome, well-connected, and a graduate of Yale. His daughter Margaretta was five years older than John, and one of the most interesting and popular girls in town.

John did not spend all his time scrutinizing grown people. Music was one of his interests, and Dr. and Mrs. O'Hara took him to concerts and operas in Philadelphia, implanting a taste that made him a lifelong patron of the Orchestra. But in John's youth it was popular music that spoke to him most directly. O'Hara and his friends often made their own music around Beanie Boone at the piano, with John performing on the kazoo and banjo. Recorded music also was a big part of their lives in 1916 and 1917 just as it is for young people in the 1970s, because they had experienced the evolution of the phonograph record from cylinder to disc, and had become familiar with the reproducing machines in their mahogany cases, the Pathé, the Aeolian Vocalion, and the Victor Victrola, which stood in every prosperous living room and wicker-furnished sun porch. Boys and girls also treasured the Stewart, a portable phonograph shaped like a plum pudding, from which the sound issued through metal grilles around the circumference of the machine. But it is probable that the best-loved of all mechanical musical instruments was the pianola or player piano. The player attachment was built into the vitals of a regular piano, and the operator worked two pedals that forced air through the perforations of an unwinding paper roll, which activated the keys to give a performance exactly like that of the professional musician who prepared the master roll at the factory. The pianola had attachments to control tempo and touch, so that the operator could impose his own musical ideas on those of the recording artist, and some people became so expert that they gave concerts as interpreters of player piano rolls. Katharine O'Hara did not approve of the pianola, but Dr. Boone put a Cunningham player in his living room for the enjoyment of the young people, who could hardly get enough of Scott Joplin's "Maple Leaf Rag," "Nola," and W. C. Handy playing his "Beale Street Blues." John told Bob Simonds and Beanie Boone in 1917 that he had two ambitions, to lead a jazz band and to own a Mercer Raceabout.

It was easy to see why any spirited youth would like to own that car. From 1911 to 1915, the Mercer factory had turned out only a few more than eight hundred Raceabouts. But they made an indelible impression on those who drove them or saw them go by. The automobile historians, Griffith Borgerson and Eugene Jaderquist, recorded that "seldom had so much machinery been covered by so little sheet metal. The Raceabout had a wire-wheeled chassis, a hood strapped over the engine, and a dashboard from which a brass steering column jutted. There were two skimpy bucket seats with cushions about three inches above the floorboards, and behind the seats was a huge cylindrical fuel tank topped by a great wing-bolt-operated filler cap near each end. There were meagre flat fenders. Shift lever, hand brake, throttle pedal, hand pumps for fuel and oil, and even the flywheel — all hung out in public view. The total, practical effect of this nakedness was that these cars had little more than their own chassis weight to pull, and they did it in hair-raising style." The Raceabout's integrity and high functional style were understandable to any boy who had worked with Meccano and had grasped the engineering doctrine of eliminating what was not essential. So far as musical ambitions went, John O'Hara's Dixie Serenaders would have been playing "For Me and My Gal," "Smiles," "'Darktown Strutters' Ball," and "The Tiger Rag." They would also have offered "Goodbye Broadway, Hello France," and "Over There," for on the sixth of April, President Woodrow Wilson had led the country into war, and Our Boys were going overseas to stamp out Kaiserism and make the world safe for democracy.

Schuylkill County had a tradition of boasting about the exploits of local troops in the Civil War, and the flag-waving that accompanied preparations for Pottsvillians to fight Mr. Wilson's war failed to arouse John's skepticism. Like other boys he accepted the war as a glorious episode, although he may have wondered why we had to draft men to take part in it. For John and most of his fellow Americans of all ages, the war was a thing of reality only in the sense that a stirring melodrama in the theater is real. It was a righteous war, because the Germans had burned villages and killed civilians — something the soldiers of a civilized country would never do. Patriotism replaced religion in John O'Hara's developing mind, and the concepts of Uncle Sam, Our Country and Our Flag took precedence over Our Saviour, the Church, and the Mother of God. O'Hara remained an uncritical patriot as long as he lived. He was to draw attention to the misery and inadequacy of much that took place in American life, but never to look with distrust on the nation itself as a government and a political entity. He was to hurry to the White House in Lyndon Johnson's time, delighted to receive an invitation with other writers to make some contribution, by their presence, to the glory of the Johnsonian reign. Under the usual O'Hara analysis, Johnson would have proved to be merely another Texan of the objectionable kind, like Jack Tom Smith in *From the Terrace*. The conventional patriot O'Hara saw the presidency itself as something to be reverenced. O'Hara wrote, 'When the President of the United States invites you to the White House, you damned well go." He could not understand why Robert Lowell turned down the same invitation, and chided him for "bad manners." That was Pottsville speaking, with its ranting priests and preachers, its flags, bands, and parades, together with the battle honors of Major Mike O'Hara. All this had soaked into John's personality with the indelible print of things that touch our hearts when we are young.

In September and October of 1918, a mysterious disease overran the world, including Pottsville. It attacked the throat and lungs, and was called Spanish influenza. There had been a premonitory outbreak in May and June; in autumn it became an epidemic. Everywhere the symptoms were the same: aches throughout the body, pains in the head, fever, nausea, paroxysms of coughing. In a short time the victim either got well or died. Throughout the United States, authorities forbade crowds to gather, so that many a boy and girl enjoyed a serene and unexpected holiday, bicycling through quiet streets in mellow October weather. During that period John saw his father coming home at four o'clock in the morning to fall on the living room couch and go to sleep in his clothes. When the noise of the family getting breakfast wakened him, he went out and shut off the engine of the car, which had been running while he slept. Patrick O'Hara had gone for three days without sleeping more than two hours at a stretch, and John recorded that Dr. Malloy in "The Doctor's Son" had two ways to get sleep:

> At first he would get it by going to his office, locking the rear office door, and stretching out on the floor or on the operating table. He would

put a revolver on the floor beside him or in the tray that was bracketed to the operating table. He had to have the revolver, because here and there among the people who would come to his office, there would be a wild man or woman, threatening him, shouting that they would not leave until he left with them, and that if their baby died they would come back and kill him. The revolver, lying on the desk, kept the more violent patients from becoming too violent, but it really did no good so far as my father's sleep was concerned; not even a doctor who had kept going for days on coffee and quinine would use a revolver on an Italian who had just come from a bedroom where the last of five children was being strangled by influenza. So my father, with a great deal of profanity, would make it plain to the Italian that he was not being intimidated, but would go, and go without sleep.

There was one other way of getting sleep. We owned the building in which he had his office, so my father made an arrangement with one of the tenants, a painter and paperhanger, so he could sleep in the room where the man stored rolls of wallpaper. This was a good arrangement, but by the time he had thought of it, my father's strength temporarily gave out and he had to come home and go to bed.

The mines shut down, and the authorities finally went so far as to close the churches. James Malloy, the doctor's son in the story that recorded many of John's own experiences, feels the weight of one emergency measure when he discovers that if you want an ice-cream soda you have to take it away in a cardboard container, as it is forbidden to consume it at the counter from a glass. He sees the epidemic at close range when Dr. Malloy puts him on duty as chauffeur, and learns that "men who for years had been drilling rock and had chrome miner's asthma never had a chance against the mysterious new disease; and even younger men were keeling over." James drives his father to the mining villages, which are called patches, where the saloonkeeper marshals ambulatory patients into line for inspection by "Mister Doctor Malloy." At one patch the doctor's son hears a woman complain because the doctor has said he will go to a Polish cottage to see children too sick to line up at the saloon. Mrs. Brannigan says, "'To be sure, and ain't that nice? Dya hear that, everybody? Payin' a personal visit to the likes of that but the decent people take what they get. A fine how-do-ya-do.' "

Mr. Kelly the saloonkeeper says, "'You'll take what you get in the shape of a puck in the nose. So keep your two cents out of this, Mame Brannigan, and get back into line.' " The Polish family's yard is full of old wash boilers and rubber boots, tin cans and the framework of an abandoned baby carriage. The woman is so fat and blowsy that James keeps trying to think of the skinniest girl he knows. The baby coughs as they enter the bedroom. "The half-covered little girl got awake, or opened her eyes and looked at the ceiling. She had a half-sneering look about her

nose and mouth, and her eyes were expressionless." This child has diph-
theria, and dies as the doctor prepares for an emergency operation to
open the throat so she can breathe.

> The woman . . . did not need the English language to know that the
> child was dead. She was rocking her back and forth and kissing her and
> kept looking up at us with fat streams of tears running from her eyes. She
> would stop crying for a second, but would start again, crying with her
> mouth open and the tears, unheeded, sliding in over her upper lip.

Dr. Malloy followed Patrick O'Hara in such matters as urging his son
to be a doctor — saying that the boy had "perfect hands for a surgeon"
— and in objecting to his longing for a coonskin coat as a foolish desire
to appear in "one of those livery stable coats." Jim almost reached the end
of his endurance on the night drives, keeping up strength on coffee and
fried-egg sandwiches, with the doctor nagging:

> "Why, I do more good and make more money in twenty minutes in the
> operating room than you'll be able to make the first three years you're out of
> college. If you go to college. Don't drive so fast!"
> It was like that for the next two days. I slept when he allowed me
> to. . . . We drove fast, and a couple of times I bounded along corduroy
> roads with tanks of oxygen (my father was one of the first to use oxygen in
> pneumonia) ready to blow me to hell. I developed a fine cigarette cough,
> but my father kept quiet about it, because I was not taking quinine, and he
> was. We got on each other's nerves and had one terrible scene. He became
> angered at my driving and punched me on the shoulder. I stopped the car
> and took a tire iron from the floor of the car.
> "Now just try that again," I said.
> He did not move from the back seat. "Get back in this car." And I got
> back. But that night we got home fairly early and the next morning, when
> he had to go out at four o'clock, he drove the car himself and let me sleep.

The scene reflected the violence that could arise from the emotional
tension between John and his father in real life. Whether or not the tire-
iron incident actually took place, Patrick O'Hara sometimes lost his
temper with John, and during this period he went so far as to knock him
down and kick him as he lay on the floor. Tom O'Hara saw this encounter,
and the sight filled him with misery because these were the two people
he most admired in the world. The doctor was unable to make any
expression of regret. And if Patrick O'Hara found it impossible to apolo-
gize, it was almost as hard for him to utter words of praise. He expressed
his love for John by giving him presents — a shotgun, a rifle, shoes and
suits from the best stores in Philadelphia. His most splendid gift was a
beautiful five-gaited mare named Julia, which he brought back from

Kentucky. All over town people said, "What can Doctor O'Hara be thinking of to give such a fine animal to a fourteen-year-old boy?" The doctor did not care what people thought, for John rode well, and with the help of the groom kept Julia in show condition. One evening Patrick stood in the doorway of No. 6o6 as John came up the street on Julia, and said to Tom, "He rides like a trooper." But all he had to say to John was, "Get off."

When Dr. O'Hara did succeed in making himself praise John, it was something to keep in memory, and use in a story like "It Must Have Been Spring." The story told how after the arrival of Julia, the doctor ordered a new riding habit for John, who was then attending St. Patrick's School across the street from No. 6o6, and so was able to look out and see Wanamaker's delivery van stop in front of the house. After school the boy hurried home, put on the new riding clothes, and started for the stable eight blocks away, hoping his father would see him as he passed the office at Second Street. The doctor was out in front, ostensibly to enjoy the sunshine of what "must have been one of the very first days of spring." The boy saw that his father was "standing with his legs spread apart, while his hands sunk deep in his hip pockets and his tweed coat spread behind him like a sparrow's tail. He was wearing a gray soft hat with a black ribbon and with white piping around the edge of the brim. He was talking across the street to Mr. George McRoberts, the lawyer, and his teeth gleamed under his black moustache. He glanced in my direction and saw me and nodded, and put one foot up on the porch and went on talking until I got there. . . .

" 'You look fine,' he said. 'You really look like something. Here.' He gave me a five-dollar bill. 'Save it. Give it to your mother to put in the bank for you.'

" 'Thank you,' I said, and turned away, because suddenly I was crying. I went up the street to the stable with my head bent down, because I could let the tears roll right out of my eyes and down to the ground without putting my hand up to my face. I knew he was still looking."

John was no longer the trusting child described in the passage about Sidney Tate and his little son; he had started "wanting something." His need was to be assured that his father approved of him. But he gave no outward sign of his longing for encouragement as he rode over the countryside, waving to people along the road to the doctor's farm. Sometimes he rode up and down the sidelines at the high school football field, which was considered cheeky because he never attended that school. He would turn up almost anywhere, watching intently, not always talking as much as might be expected of a teen-age boy. There were some adults, including Dr. Boone and his wife, who said John was a youth of intelligence and charm. And John observed much from the superior position of a boy on horseback; but he always suffered from the fear that Dr. O'Hara would bring him down to earth. Everywhere, the doctor's standing was high: there were men and women all over the county who said they owed their lives to his skill. But an old friend recalling her experiences with Patrick O'Hara felt compelled to say, "There was never any question of talking things over with the doctor, or telling your side of things." Nevertheless, Dr. O'Hara could be helpful to colleagues as well as patients when he wanted to. Dr. Wallace D. (Buz) Drummond, the medical politician in "A Case History," said of Dr. Malloy — John's fictional name for his father — that he had given sound advice in the matter of signing on as panel physician for coal companies and lodges: "'You'll find out that for their God-damn fifty cent fees they think they own you, and as for the big companies, the surgeons are the only ones that make any money out of them.'" Later on Dr. Drummond said, "'I was never very fond of Malloy. Too brusque, too domineering. But he was nice to me when I first started out, and I remember his trying to get me to stop smoking. A doctor must rely on all his senses, he said, and one of the most important is his sense of smell. Smoking ruins the sense of smell, he said.'" John's father also opposed the drinking of Coca-Cola, and it is easy to imagine the vehemence with which he forbade his son to drink liquor. But John O'Hara began to experiment with alcohol about the time that Congress passed the act enforcing Prohibition in January 1920. It sometimes drove the doctor to distraction when he thought of John subjecting himself to the risks of alcohol and tobacco. He said, "Keep on this way and you'll be dead before you're thirty." John then made the retort, which he was fond of recalling in later years, that he would be listed in *Who's Who* before that date. And so he was. But Patrick O'Hara did not live to see it.

Although John felt that he got more reproaches than encouragement from his father, there was a strong tie of affection between them, and family life at No. 606 was based on love and respect. Nevertheless, John often walked up Mahantongo Street to warm himself with the unquestioning friendship of Dr. and Mrs. Boone. Their household included Ransloe's sister Arlene, and was a refuge in Pottsville like that of the Delaney grandparents in Lykens. John had become a bridge player, and would enter the house with his palms up for inspection. "They're clean," Helen (Nelly) Boone would say, "get out the good cards." Dr. Boone and his wife treated John with the informality they would accord an adult friend, and he called Mrs. Boone by her first name, but he always addressed her husband as Dr. Boone, and when the doctor asked why, John said, "I respect you, but I love Nelly." He might have added that Patrick O'Hara would explode if he ever heard of his son's addressing a medical man in an informal way. He insisted that the children be respectful to all doctors, though John knew of his low regard for some of them. John was to combine several Pottsville doctors into Dr. Buz Drummond, and Dr. William English of *Appointment in Samarra* and *Ten North Frederick*.

Patrick O'Hara did not get on well with all his colleagues at the hospital. He had an especially low opinion of one staff member whom he believed to be traveling under an altered name. The situation is reflected in "The Doctor's Son" when Jim says he thinks a miner named Terry Loughran has gone to another doctor: " 'He probably got Lucas.' " His father snaps, " '*Doctor* Lucas. Doctor Lucashinsky. Ivan the Terrible. Well, if he got Lucas, it serves him right. . . .' "

Some of Dr. O'Hara's patriarchal authority was entrusted to John where his sister and brothers were concerned. His parents placed him in full charge, for example, on a day in the summer of 1920, when the children drove in their pony carts from Pottsville to the Delaney house in Lykens. Mary, Joseph, and Martin drove the carts, while John rode in command on Julia. They started early, and before departure Dr. O'Hara gave John instructions as to the pace and resting of the ponies. The cavalcade moved on dirt roads, or the ponies could not have done the thirty miles, and reached Lykens in the late afternoon. The doctor had telephoned ahead to a number of places, and got reports on their progress throughout the day. John led his ponies past a dismal patch, and the mine children rushed out to see "the little horses." Mary said, "Please, John, may we give them rides?" John decided that was all right, but warned, "Don't go into the cabins." After the mine children had been returned to the patch, they asked, "Are you coming again?" Mary said, "We don't know when. But we'll be back." Three days later, John conducted his convoy on the return march. When they got to the patch, they found the mine children waiting on the fence beside the road.

John O'Hara was writing before he gained the advantage of surveying his fellow townsmen from the backs of ponies and horses. His recollection was that he wrote on the wallpaper with crayons during his earliest schooling with Miss Katy. After learning to use pencil and paper, he looked for subjects to write about. He began to study a tapestry that hung in the upstairs hall at No. 606, depicting the Great Seal of the United States, which may be examined on the back of any one-dollar bill. The seal features a truncated pyramid, surmounted by an enormous eye. John invented a story to explain this scene, and wrote it out on a sheet of paper which he hid behind the tapestry where he knew it would be discovered. John O'Hara's first public award for writing came in 1918, when he wrote the best composition in his class at St. Patrick's School, and received a German helmet from Monsignor McGovern as first prize. John was not a compulsive reader, but he worked his way through an encyclopaedia for young people called *The Book of Knowledge*. This was an early example of his respect for books of reference. His satisfaction in accurate detail would not be so great as the pain he suffered for his few inevitable errors. Pat Outerbridge said he had seldom seen O'Hara so disturbed as when a reviewer pointed out that the author had mistakenly placed the visiting crowd on the east side of the field at the first Yale football game played in Palmer Stadium. When O'Hara was writing the novel (*From the Terrace*), supporters of visiting teams at Princeton sat in the east stands; in the period he was writing *about,* they did not. As a child, he did not suspect that any such error could have crept into *The Book of Knowledge,* and in 1916 he found a different and unassailable kind of accuracy in a series of stories that appeared in the *Saturday Evening Post.* The pieces were written by a man who signed himself Ring W. Lardner, and they soon came out in a collection called *You Know Me Al.* They were unlike anything John had seen before. Lardner had presented his material in a series of letters from a professional baseball player named Jack Keefe, and as you read these letters, you heard Keefe's voice, and the living speech of his friends and enemies. Keefe had married Florrie, whose sister was the wife of Allen, a left-handed pitcher. It was obvious that Allen was the father of Florrie's baby, born eight months after the marriage, which had been preceded by a three-day courtship. The author revealed Keefe's dishonesty, greed, and vanity without comment, in such clear pictures that you would no more have called them literature than you would think of water as a chemical compound while drinking it. Lardner was an American original, who influenced all writers who were beginning to read when his baseball stories appeared. John O'Hara saw in Lardner the virtue of simplicity, and the power that was to be gained by letting characters speak for themselves.

It often happens that at some point about halfway through his second decade of life, a boy will fall in love with a girl four or five years older, and it is an experience that can cause great pain. The young woman with whom John O'Hara fell in love was Margaretta Archbald. He never forgot her. Margaretta was tall and slender, and though her friends thought her quiet and reserved, she was said to have a kind of "nervous charm" that was unusual. There was much life in her eyes: she was a girl who made you want to be at your best when in her company. She rode well, walked gracefully, and danced like Irene Castle. Margaretta was bright, and one of the things she liked about John was his mental quickness, and the common store of things they agreed were funny. At the time she first attracted him, Margaretta Archbald was attending Bryn Mawr College, and John had grown just old enough to start receiving invitations to the holiday parties. The opening passage in their friendship was to be written in a story called "Winter Dance": Ted and

Natalie try not to attract attention as they dance together at the country club, but know they will have to pay for their happiness in the mockery of supposed friends who think it amusing that a boy should feel mature emotion for an older girl. He has memorized every word of a postcard Natalie sent him that summer.

By the time John was old enough to consider himself a serious suitor for Margaretta, parental opposition had developed. Margaretta's father showed little enthusiasm for John, and Dr. O'Hara had no use for the Archbald family. He would say, "There's bad stock there — bad stock." The Archbald name is no longer to be found in Pottsville, but it was among the elect in the 1920s, and had been so established a good deal longer than that of Patrick O'Hara. The doctor was a member of the Assembly, a ball held twice a year which could be attended only by invitation of the committee. He belonged to the Pottsville Club, a venerable institution that served as Knickerbocker and Union for Schuylkill County. The O'Haras had gone into the new country club because of their standing in the town and their membership in the Outdoor Club, from which the larger organization came. What else could you do, in Pottsville, to show high social position? There was one thing more, which was to hold membership in the publicity-shunning organization that O'Hara identified in *Ten North Frederick* as The Second Thursdays. This group consisted of about twenty married couples, children or grandchildren of the founders, who met for dinner parties at each other's houses. The men wore red ribbons across their shirtfronts, and the first toast after dinner was to General George Washington, the second to the President of the United States. Doctor English was a member, even though his father had been a thief and a suicide. It was supposed that some day his son Julian, the Cadillac dealer, would enter the Second Thursdays. The thing was hereditary, like the Order of the Cincinnati, and not for Patrick O'Hara. He was, after all, a newcomer. Still, Pottsville was John's city just as much as if both his grandfathers had been born there, and he could see that his position was secure, so long as there was money to maintain it. But membership in the prototype for the Second Thursdays was something that money could not buy. The realization of this fact may have planted in John O'Hara's mind a feeling that always, somewhere, there would be an impenetrable inner circle, the higher internal crowd defined by Wilder Hobson. O'Hara did not altogether believe in its existence, and yet he never completely persuaded himself that it was not there. So far as his place in the world was concerned, O'Hara as a young man suspected that his Irish and Catholic background might have closed some doors to him. Even after he discovered in later life that this was not true, O'Hara sometimes gave the impression that he thought the best defense was attack.

The history of the Irish in Schuylkill County illustrates the problems these immigrants were called on to face. In the mining of anthracite there were many unskilled jobs to be done, and these fell to Irish and Slavic laborers, who worked as assistants to expert English and Welsh miners, doing a considerable amount of heavy lifting for light pay. Long hours and low pay for the Irish were not confined to the coal fields: Emerson found Irish laborers in Massachusetts working fifteen hours for fifty cents. In the anthracite regions, the better-paid Welshmen and Englishmen were professionals already trained to the business, whereas most of the Irish had been farmers. Now they were living in the patches around the shaft-heads, huddling together in a way that more fortunate people sniffed at as "clannish." Another adjective often applied to the Irish immigrants was "ignorant." It would have been more nearly accurate, as well as kinder, to have called them "unschooled." Back where these transplanted farmers came from, they had been exploited with almost inconceivable brutality by English and Anglo-Irish landlords. Famine struck in 1845, lasted through two years of bureaucratic efforts to relieve it, and killed half a million men, women, and children. It was to escape that famine, and not because they possessed any skill at the mining of coal, that Irish working families had emigrated to eastern Pennsylvania and settled in the patches where John O'Hara saw their descendants as he drove along the roads with his father. Later on John would learn nearly all there was to know about the American Irish. The most important part of his heritage was that a long time before, the Irish had taken over the English language and put their music in it. They venerated poets, orators, and storytellers. They respected learning; they tended to be puritanical in thought if not in conduct; they had beneath their politeness a vein of irreverence for the mighty; because of remembered injustices and betrayals, they were capable of quick anger; and their family feeling was strong because of hostilities encountered in the outside world. Their reaction to life had points of similarity with that of American Jews, and the white inhabitants of the American South. Since the defeat in 1603 of Hugh O'Neil, the Catholic Earl of Tyrone, through the centuries of guerrilla warfare, there had been night riders, informers, and assassins in the Irish countryside, as in Ulster today. The avengers took various names, and landlords sometimes received letters that said, "Molly Maguire is angry that you would turn out one tenant and give it to another. Molly Maguire and her children have been watching you . . ." Tradition held that there had been an actual Molly Maguire, who carried two pistols in her belt. At any rate, her name was recognized in Schuylkill County when it was rumored, in the late 1850s, that a secret society of Irish miners had been formed to terrorize the region, and that they called themselves Molly Maguires. By 1870 word was out that the Mollies maintained headquarters at Patrick Dormer's Sheridan House on

Centre Street in Pottsville. From time to time a shot from ambush killed a mine superintendent or policeman, the violence coming to a climax in the winter of 1873, when it was reported that terrorists had taken control of Schuylkill County. The Mollies had an implacable enemy in an Episcopalian Irish lawyer named Franklin Benjamin Gowen, president of the Reading Coal and Iron Company. Gowen planted a Pinkerton detective among Dormer's associates, and the agent gathered evidence which brought several men to trial. During his investigations, the undercover man had probably become accessory to at least one murder. Public opinion exonerated the agent, and the Commonwealth of Pennsylvania eventually hanged twenty men for so-called Molly Maguire murders that had been committed over a period of years. Six were hanged at Pottsville and four at Mauch Chunk on June 21, 1877. Franklin B. Gowen killed himself in 1889. The Molly Maguires and their unmasking fascinated A. Conan Doyle, who gave Pottsville its first appearance in fiction when he wrote *The Valley of Fear* in 1915. According to Doyle, avengers pursued the Pinkerton man to his death in spite of all that Sherlock Holmes could do. In Doyle's novel, Pottsville was called Vermissa, and the author imagined it as a dark, soot-stained place, an inaccurate conception that might have been closer to Shenandoah over the mountain.

The executions at Pottsville and Mauch Chunk remained in the memory of Schuylkill County, and for years it was said that one must be cautious in conversation about the Molly Maguires and the ringleaders' fate. John O'Hara knew of a family tradition that his Uncle Mike had refused an offer of membership in the Mollies. Whether or not he was called on to defy the terrorists, Mike O'Hara was a typically enterprising Irish American who prospered in business while paying some attention to a sideline of politics, and served a term as Chief Burgess, the equivalent of mayor, in Shenandoah. The full-time professional politician appeared in *Ten North Frederick* as Mike Slattery, a boss who moved on equal terms with the leading citizens of Gibbsville. The opening scene of this novel shows a group of big men from the county, the state, and the entire country gathered for the funeral of Joe Chapin, a Protestant lawyer of the highest standing: Slattery speaks familiarly and confidentially with the most important men in the crowd. During his life, Joe Chapin had possessed nothing that Mike Slattery coveted, and had been Slattery's inferior in anything that required a grasp of practical considerations. To portray Slattery triumphant over Chapin was in accordance with the truth of life in Schuylkill County. For all the success and power that came to Mike Slattery, O'Hara knew that being Irish in eastern Pennsylvania connected you with something that brooded in the past, an echo of resentment among people who had sometimes exacted violent revenge for their suffer-

ings, and who lived for clan and family — devil take the hindmost elsewhere. The Irish are sensitive about other Irish, whom they usually either
love or hate. In this O'Hara ran to form, with some dear friends who were
Irish, and some Irish enemies whom he never forgave. He wrote to his
brother Tom in 1963 that he cherished no great fondness for the Shenandoah relatives, "but you have to give them their due . . . The thing about
our grandfather and grandmother is that they were the top people of
Shenandoah, which is top of nothing much, but top . . . His money came
from contracting. For instance, in moving houses. He also did a lot of
business with James Archbald's family, which owned some mines in the
Gilverton area, and our James Archbald (Margaretta's father) greatly admired our grandfather for his industry and honesty. All the O'H boys
except Martin were sent to Penn, all the girls except Nell to Chestnut Hill
(Sisters of St. Joseph). There was always money around, and there were
always fights about money. Mike O'Hara had his finger in many pies, and
I daresay his ethics never bothered him much, in spite of Jim Archbald's
family's happy experience. His sons Mike and Jim were all larceny . . .
This Uncle Mike had a way with him. Very tall, eccentrically dressed,
rather unsmiling, he was actually very popular without being much respected. I often saw him come into saloons and roadhouses and restaurants alone, as though he owned the place, and he would sit down at a
table and immediately people would flock to him . . . What you must not
forget about Mike and Jim is that they were half Franey, and the Franeys
were the *gentle* Irish, like the Delaneys. The O'Haras were violent and
spectacular in contrast with the Franeys. But the Franeys were not flawless. Irene Franey, a little older than I, was quite a beauty and a wild one,
who was the only girl I ever knew whose slipper was actually used to drink
champagne out of — at a Snow Dance in the early 20s. Her sister married
Dr. Gallagher, head of the Locust Mountain State Hospital, who got into
some dreadful financial jam that our old man had to help him out of, but
the old man was so righteous about it that the Gallaghers never spoke to
him after that. Irene didn't like me much either. She called me a Pottsville
snob. Actually the Franeys did not approve of the O'Haras generally, as
far back as 1864, or whenever the first Mike married the first Franey. The
instinct for natural selection got Mike O'Hara to marry a Franey, and
his son Pat to marry a Delaney (and you a Browning and me a Wylie, etc.)
but I chose to believe that however unattractive some of us may be, the
stuff is somewhere there. You probably don't remember Uncle Jim, who
was actually our great uncle. He was Grandfather O'Hara's brother, and
one of a generation of giants. Dark, handsome, quiet and ineffectual, he
used to come to the farm and just sit until the old man gave him some
money and sent him back to Dunsmore, which is where the first O'Haras
settled. He was the only one of that generation I ever saw, but he helped

me understand the others. He had a brother who, according to Mother, invented the air brake. Uncle Airbrake, who worked for the NY Central in Elmira or some such place, had a naughty wife who walked out on him, taking with her the drawings for the new invention, which she turned over to the Westinghouse people. By a strange coincidence, Wolcott Gibbs once told me that his father invented the air brake and was screwed out of the royalties by Westinghouse. To paraphrase Betty Furness, you can't be sure if it's Westinghouse. Anyway, in that generation they produced an inventor, and they also produced Sister Lucy. Mother regarded her as a saint. Sister Lucy was a nun, a member of the Little Sisters of the Poor, which is a French order, originally. She and all the others were expelled from France and she ended up in Pawtucket, Rhode Island, as head of the convent there. Mother and Daddy went to see her in Pawtucket just before she died. I believe she is buried in France. Mother said she was very tall and beautiful and a fascinating conversationalist. She and Mother spoke French for three days, and I guess the old man sat there and nodded when he heard a word he could understand. Don't ask me how an O'Hara from Dunsmore got to be a nun in France. That's one of those missing links, forever lost to our generation.

"But I have always felt that we were something out of the usual run. The Delaney side we know about. They were pre-Revolutionary American. But I mean beyond that, on the O'Hara side. Do you remember William Wright, an old mining engineer who lived in Heckscherville and was a patient of the old man's? He had gout, was chair-ridden, and I often had the dubious pleasure of bathing his gouty foot, putting some kind of powder on it, and wrapping bandages around it. While this was going on he and the old man would talk, talk, talk. Well, he convinced the old man that the O'Haras of our line were descendants of the 9th Century kings, and he went to the trouble of authenticating our right to the coat of arms. Our papa pretended not to care about such things, but if you will look in the History of Pennsylvania biography of the old man, you will find that coat of arms right there. When Sister and I were in Dublin a few years ago my friend Geraldine Fitzgerald explained to me that the gentry were not so much in awe of me as an author as of one of 'the real thing,' O'Hara being one of the seven or eight ancient Irish names. Well, I believe that, if only for two reasons: whenever I am in the company of the Irish (and this has been true all my life) I instantly get a feeling of being a little bit superior to the other ones — and they in turn look at me as though whatever I had to say was going to be important. There is a sort of resentful respect to them, and I have sensed it since I was a small kid. I even got it with the late JFK, and I always had it with his father. I get it with Jim Kerney, the Trenton publisher, I got it with Tim Costello, and it is not mere egomania. It almost has nothing to do with me, because

I watched the same thing happening between Irish men and women and the old man. You never saw anyone get fresh with him, and do you know something? They never really got away with getting fresh with his brother Mike. If they said something fresh, he would look at them witheringly, pause, and then say something like, 'Is that so, now?' and they would squirm. It was the look that did it. When Geraldine asked me if I would like to meet Brendan Behan, I said I'd already met a thousand Brendan Behans, and she laughed, because she knew exactly what I meant . . . And even if it exists only in my imagination, it's what I face the world with."

O'Hara signed this letter, "As ever — John REX."

A semiserious belief in grand ancestry somewhere in the past marks the inherited personality of defeated peoples who have seen general injustice done and individual talents unrewarded. William Shannon, historian of the Irish in America, has recorded that the Irish who became prosperous in the good times following the Civil War had to face reproaches from less fortunate friends and relatives for having sold out to Protestants and English sympathizers. The successful ones refused to accept their Irishness as a sign of inferiority, but they needed to maintain a kind of exaggerated confidence in their merits, and they continually sought the "tangible signs of success and authority; titles, gold chains and robes of office or the silk hat and frock coat of the gentleman or material displays of affluence and generosity, so that they could manifest their acceptance in the highest places." John O'Hara recognized in himself this longing for marks of success. At the height of his career he said, "I always wanted the badges — they were very important to me." When O'Hara spoke as a literary artist, he sometimes gave the impression of being a touchy Irishman. When you belittled his work, you attacked O'Hara himself, Irish sensitivity and all; conversely, if you expressed disapproval of O'Hara as a person, you also attacked his work, for he and his work were inseparable.

One of the marks of position in Pottsville's upper middle class was sending children to boarding schools, and in 1919 Dr. O'Hara decided it was time for John to have this social and educational privilege. The doctor believed that the Roman Church could provide first-class preparatory education, and although he was willing to put John in a secular college, he wanted him to get there by way of a Catholic school. A priest suggested that the place for John was a school administered by the Jesuits as part of Fordham University in New York City. Fordham sounded very good indeed. It had been founded in 1841 as St. John's College, was chartered as a university two years later, and had taken the name of Fordham in 1905, from the section of the Bronx in which it is located. What impressed Patrick O'Hara most deeply was the awesome reputation of the Jesuits. It was an item of American belief, even among Protestants, that the trained minds of the Jesuits were the keenest article in the intellectual

hardware shop. Their brains were filled with learning beyond all calcula-
tion, so said the commentators in saloons, livery stables, and barber shops,
and they attributed to the Jesuits a special cunning manner of debate
that could tie you right up, no matter what the point at issue. When John
O'Hara came to Fordham Heights, he found the university and its preparatory department in a loosely related group of large stone buildings on
a wide campus. As for the famed Jesuit instructors, it seemed that they
had been reading their own publicity, and believing it, for they turned out
to be an arrogant lot. John also observed a good deal of hard drinking
among the faculty. He reported the drinking at home, but his father
refused to listen, and his mother could not believe that it was true. Mrs.
O'Hara thought that if anything went wrong for John at Fordham, she
would hear of it through her sister Verona, who was married to John J.
McKee, an official of the Immigration Service, and lived in East Orange.
It was presumed that their house at 538 Central Avenue would be a place
of refuge on the weekends that John was not allowed to spend in Pottsville. On these short trips between the Bronx and East Orange, John got
a few tantalizing glimpses of postwar Manhattan. He could look into the
softly lit, perfumed rooms where the hotel tea dances went on, and the
orchestras were playing a magical tune called "Dardanella." And like
almost everyone else in New York, he was humming "I Might Be Your
Once-in-a-While" from *Angel Face*, "Just Like a Gypsy," with which Nora
Bayes captivated the audiences at *Ladies First*, and two tunes from the
Ziegfeld Follies by Irving Berlin — "Mandy" and "A Pretty Girl Is Like a
Melody." Aunt Verona was a kind woman, but even more strictly religious
than her sister, and the atmosphere in East Orange could not be called
indulgent. Mary and her mother went to see John at Fordham and found
him subdued in manner and not enthusiastic about school. He failed to
distinguish himself, and after three terms, the authorities suggested to
Dr. O'Hara that John might do better somewhere else. From John's point
of view, the best thing he got from Fordham Preparatory School was the
privilege of being among those who came home for the Christmas holidays. That made up for a good deal of loneliness and boredom, for during
those two weeks the fact that one had gone away was more significant
than where one had been.

John O'Hara always remembered how a Christmas season would begin
on that December afternoon a few days before the twenty-fifth, when the
early arrivals from school and college would gather at Hodgson's drugstore to see and be seen. There would be four or five boys — including
Robert Simonds — in the long gray greatcoats of the Staunton Military
Academy. John wrote in a reminiscent *Collier's* essay that the uniforms
were "distinguishable only by certain marks from the uniforms of West
Pointers, but the boys themselves were markedly different because the

West Pointers always seemed to become a little more West Pointed in the presence of the younger lads from Staunton and the New York Military Academy. The same kind of difference could be noted in the manner of the college men as compared with the prep school men. The prep school boy tried to be as smooth as the guy who was home from State or Lehigh, Yale or Brown, Lafayette or Penn."

Some of the boys who were freshmen at college would be wearing small enameled lapel badges known as pledge buttons, indicating probationary membership in fraternities. This interested O'Hara, and it was a matter of grave concern to the freshmen: the early 1920s saw the American college fraternity at the height of its influence, the most important aspect of college life for many students. O'Hara observed that the young men wearing pledge buttons were to be congratulated, but "it was not considered good form to talk about the fraternity until one had actually been initiated — after midyears. For that reason the pledges, or pledgees, were somewhat restricted conversationally, and because they were expected to be a credit to the fraternity, their conduct was likewise under scrutiny." Curb conversations in front of Hodgson's usually began with "When did you get in?" Then there would be consideration of "When does Mercersburg (or Andover, or Princeton or Bucknell) get out?" O'Hara recalled that "the earliest arrivals sometimes would be at the railroad station to greet the later ones. It was a courteous gesture that I now realize was not appreciated by parents of the later arrivals, who would go to the station to meet Junior — and Junior would be off with the boys before even setting foot in the old homestead."

O'Hara penetrated to the heart of the return for the holidays with that observation. The boys and girls were a separate order of people, who would enjoy some fourteen gloriously selfish days devoted entirely to pleasure, and the satisfaction of displaying and recognizing the signals of their privileged group. Clothes were a serious matter: not everyone held with Brooks Brothers, although this fashionable New York and Boston firm took advertising space in most of the college magazines. A New Haven tailor named Arthur M. Rosenberg also had a large following. One could identify a "Rosey" suit by its curved lapels, wide trousers, and coat collar high on the neck, as may be studied today in contemporary drawings by John Held, Jr. Nat Luxenberg of New York was a reasonably priced tailor who sent salesmen to college towns, and did a large business for some years. O'Hara observed and recorded that Frank Brothers and Whitehouse & Hardy were the preferred shoemakers, supplying the heavy, thick-soled brogues that "smooth" collegians affected. All these items had their significance and grades of merit, but the finest thing an undergraduate could own was an overcoat made from the matched skins of raccoons. A few of the boys from the larger cities understood the elegance and comfort of a fur lining inside a black or tan cloth shell, but in O'Hara's set, the young bloods wanted the furs outside where they would show and a majority of college youths in other towns agreed with them. The "coon-skin" was worn with anything, including evening dress, when it was topped with a derby hat and a neckcloth of colored foulard. At dances, the bulky coats overflowed the cloakrooms, or covered the floors of retir-ing rooms in private houses with carpets of fur, and there were piles of fur on the beds like the warehouse of a Canadian trapper. O'Hara longed for a coonskin coat, but his father insisted that such garments were fit only for undertakers' hostlers. In 1924, John's mother used some "Delaney money" — cashing a Pennsylvania Railroad bond — to buy him a coat made up from a fine set of skins. John did not have this impressive over-coat for his first appearance as a member of the gathering in front of Hodgson's, but he had some trumps to play that were not in every social hand. This became evident after the fashion inspection, when the next conversational phase began with " 'Are you going to—?' A certain delicacy in human relations was observed in this phase: all the boys who were going to the Assembly — and the Bachelors, and the Modern Maidens — knew which other boys would be going, and which would not. The same was true of the country-club Christmas dance. But there were other parties to which the invitation lists were not known beforehand, and some of the boys whose families were not club members were invited to those parties."

John had no problems about invitations, but like most of the young men he felt the need of cash in the days leading up to Christmas. He recorded that this period was fairly quiet, with no major party on the schedule before the twenty-fifth, and that most of his group had not been given their Christmas money. He continued in his *Collier's* memoir, "But on Christmas night the balloon went up, or, for some of us, it was Christmas afternoon. With the crisp new fives and tens from relatives we would forgather at the poolroom for pocket billiards and dice. There was always one boy who blew his Christmas stack before eleven o'clock. And there usually was one boy who had passed out before that hour."

More than forty years later, O'Hara compressed the emotions of return-ing for holidays, and the selfishness of the young people, only faintly realized by the most sensitive of them at the time, into a magazine story, still unpublished in book form, called "Christmas Poem." In this tale he introduces Billy Warden, just home from Dartmouth and eating dinner with his father and mother and sister. The father says, " 'I suppose this is the last we'll see of you this vacation.' " Billy assures them that he will be seen around the house, but it develops that he wants to borrow the family Dodge from the twenty-seventh to the thirty-first for a houseparty at Montrose, which is " 'up beyond Scranton.' " The party is being given by a girl named Henrietta Cooper, and it seems that her family is above the one-Dodge Wardens. Having arranged for the car and wheedled ten dollars from his mother, Billy leaves, not without a twinge of regret, "but this was his first night home and he had his friends to see . . . *They* all had families too, and *they* would be at the drugstore tonight . . . He would like to have a talk with his father, a chat with his sister . . . Oh, what was the use of making a lot of excuses? What was wrong with wanting to see your friends? . . . The starter in the Dodge seemed to be whining 'No . . . no . . . no . . .' before the engine caught . . ." At the drugstore, Billy runs into a rich boy named Teddy Choate, who says, " 'I hear you're going to be at Henny Cooper's houseparty.' " Billy wants to know where Choate heard this, and is told, " 'From Henny, naturally. Christ, I've known her since I was five years old. She invited me, but I have to go to these parties in New York.' " In a few more lines from Choate, we learn that the Coopers have a swimming pool, a private golf course, and " 'God knows how many horses.' " Choate continues, " 'Very hard to get to know, Mr. Cooper. But he was in Dad's class at New Haven and we've known the Coopers since the Year One . . . They have an apartment at the Plaza, just the right size, their own furniture. I've been there many times, too . . .' " Without question, the Coopers will prove to be too much for Billy Warden. He goes to a poolroom and loses his ten dollars. Next, he walks down a cold street with his friend Andy Phillips, home from Penn State. He refuses Andy's offer to bear the expenses of a beer-drinking bout, and they part. "He watched his friend, with his felt hat turned up too much in front and back, his thick-soled Whitehouse & Hardys clicking along the sidewalk, his joe-college swagger, his older brother's leather coat." As he walks home, Billy realizes that Andy is headed for a life of contented mediocrity. At home, he finds his father in shirt-sleeves working at some papers in the sitting room. It turns out that Mr. Warden is writing a poem in which he is trying to express his appreciation of Billy's mother. It develops that Mr. Warden has been doing this every Christmas for twenty-six years. Billy is "kind of tired," and shows no interest in the long-distance call that has come by way of the Scranton operator while he was out: " 'I know who it is. I'll phone them tomorrow.' " Lying awake, Billy "wondered if Henrietta Cooper's father had ever written a poem to her mother. But he knew the answer to that."

There were thrilling contrasts in the holidays: outdoors, the mountains stood in their arrangements of black and white, and along the streets of Pottsville the blue arc lights came on at four in the afternoon; indoors, there were lamplit rooms, flowers, wreaths of fragrant evergreen, fireplaces going, logs popping and crackling in a friendly way, or what was even better, the glow of hard coal in iron basket-grates, everything radiating emotional and physical warmth as the elders beamed with pride at the good looks of the boys and girls who trooped in with the smell of cold air on their clothing. The homecoming delegations were beneficiaries of a worship of youth, and also, in most cases, of parental ambitions to see children go higher in the world. Not everyone could make casual reference to " 'Dad's class at New Haven.' " But with the money from the 1917 war gathering strength to burst out booming in the 1920s, almost everyone had become aware of something the sociologists called upward mobility, and young people at "good" schools and colleges were helpful to parents on the move. O'Hara's holiday reminiscences included "a great deal of calling in the afternoons, paying calls on the parents of our friends, and that usually meant a glass of wine and a piece of fruitcake or sand tarts and other Pennsylvania Dutch sweet cakes. Sometimes instead of wine it was a cup of tea, and sometimes, if Father was home, it meant a straight slug of Canadian Club. You can be sure, as you are, that we were punctilious about calling where the Canadian Club was served." On some calls there might be time for a dance or two to the Victrola on the sun porch, and during the holidays of 1920 there were some wonderful new songs to be heard on records. John memorized the choruses of "Avalon," "I Never Knew I Could Love Anybody," "Japanese Sandman," "When My Baby Smiles at Me," "Rose of Washington Square," "Whispering," and "Margie." In the holidays of the following year, the Victrolas and the dance bands added such numbers as "Second Hand Rose," "I'm Just Wild About Harry," "The Sheik," "Wabash Blues," and "Wang Wang Blues." All the young people had taken to their hearts the tune and words of "Ain't We Got Fun," and as they slid their feet over the smooth sun-porch tiles, men and girls sang to each other with great glee about how *The rich get richer and the poor get — children, but in the meantime, in between time, ain't we got fun?* After that you pulled on the rubber boots known as galoshes, invariably leaving the metal catches unfastened so that they made a clacking noise as you crunched through snow to the car, and so on to a tea dance with a real orchestra, and then home to dress for the night's dinner dance at the club, and then to anything that might suggest itself in the way of an informal party at someone's house, taking some of the musicians along, or a visit to a roadhouse, almost leaving the earth and flying over the bright icy countryside on a mixture of youth, alcohol, and gasoline. The girl in *Appointment in Samarra* was speaking truth when she said everyone agreed that Gibbsville — the fictional Pottsville — was the peppiest place in the country at Christmas.

There was danger in the holidays: the Dorts, Marmons, Cunninghams, Stutzes, Packards, Pierce Arrows, Dodges, and Buicks did not always stay on the road when the dances ended and the young people set off in search of further entertainment. There was nothing about this that John O'Hara did not know. Indeed, anyone who lived through the period could tell stories of narrow if not miraculous escapes from death in the ditch, or head on, on the highway. O'Hara remembered that "wherever you went, you had the snow to contend with, shovelled and drifted high on the sides of the streets and roads, and if you were going anywhere off the heaviest travelled path you first called up to ask how the roads were . . . Two of the most attractive girls in our crowd lived in a town not more than a dozen miles away but several hundred feet higher above sea level. If you had a date with one of those girls you left home an hour before the date, just to make sure: the road in those days was just barely wide enough for two cars moving slowly, and if you happened to be on the east side of the road you could skid down into a ravine deep enough to be your semifinal resting place. . . . The cold air was exhilarating . . . But the air and the snow were potentially as dangerous as they were pleasant to feel and to behold; it never happened to anyone I knew, but no winter passed without the finding of the body of someone who had frozen to death on the mountains."

The new ballroom dance, descended from something called the one-step, was known as the fox-trot. The young man put his right arm around his partner's waist, extending his left arm, and the girl laid her right hand in his left hand, resting her other hand on his shoulder. The close contact of the dance was a new thing: there were girls who gained the reputation of pushing themselves against the boys as though they meant to go right through them. Such tactics could mean many partners for a plain girl with an interesting body. A good party had to have plenty of boys who came without girls, "stags" who ranged the floor or herded in the middle of it, and cut in on the girls as they danced by. At the height of the party, a popular girl might go only a few steps with each cutter-in, and if she went all the way around with one partner, she might doubt her popularity. Every stag got a welcome whether he was a schoolboy or a man of thirty or thirty-five, and to extend the welcome, girls used a flow of collegiate slang and society chatter known as a "line." A girl had to dispense her line continuously, and it must have become hard labor by four or five in the morning, even for young women who had acquired stamina by climbing the hills of Pottsville-Gibbsville. The success of dancing as a performance to music was entrusted to the man, who improvised variations on a basic step, and the girl followed him. There was disapproval of girls who unconsciously tried to lead. Most girls were amazingly light on their feet, and sometimes appeared to be floating a few inches above the floor when in the grip of an awkward partner. John was known as a first-class dancer who had the ability of showing off his partner and giving her a chance for some graceful whirling. He looked especially good as partner to his sister, and to her friend Augusta Yuengling, and to Margaretta Archbald and a number of other good dancers among the girls. He always danced with Mrs. Boone when she appeared among the chaperones at a party. It may be well to explain that chaperones were older people who attended parties where young unmarried women were present, to assure propriety. In the early 1920s, chaperones had to contend both with the new close dancing, and another hitherto unheard-of social custom, the appearance of openly tipsy young men at parties. John Held's drawings that show bottles and flasks partly hidden under the coonskins are not exaggerated: O'Hara's holiday recollection stated that "we drank everything we could lay a lip on, from boilo, which was a Polish whisky that derived its name from the fact that we drank it while it was still-hot, to champagne that prudent men had laid down before Prohibition went into effect. We also drank a great deal of beer. The word would get around that some speak-easy was serving 'good' beer and away we'd go before the Feds, those who were not taking graft, made their raid. In a section that was populated by German farming families who liked their beer, and Italian laboring families who liked their wine, and Irish and Slavic and English mining families who went for the hard stuff, Prohibition was in effect but ineffectual. We grew up in an atmosphere of complete contempt for the one law that affected the rich, the middle class, and the poor . . ."

The most convenient place to get a drink at a holiday dance in the Schuylkill Country Club was the smoking room adjacent to the lockers, where members could keep ample quantities of liquor. Efficient and trustworthy bootleggers saw to it that supplies would not run low on a big night. The established leaders of the young married set, like Clinton Sheafer of the family that owned the countinghouse on Centre Street, would establish themselves at accustomed tables and act as liberal dispensers of drink. The easygoing, good-looking Clint Sheafer, Yale graduate and war veteran, was an acknowledged symbol of Pottsville aristocracy, and John O'Hara as a youth thought him admirably poised and high-toned. Sheafer either lost his poise or invoked aristocratic privilege at a Christmas dance when he threw the contents of a highball glass in the face of Bill McQuaid, the club bore. The incident impressed O'Hara strongly, and he still had it in mind next morning when he looked into the busybody and saw Mahantongo Street rising up the hill in "cottony" whiteness and silence. He heard a loose tire chain thumping along, "cack, thock, cack, thock, cack, thock . . . Then it came a little faster and changed to cack, cack, cack, cack-cack-cack-cack" and he saw an acquaintance pass by — Mort McDonald, a bootlegger who had made an early delivery of champagne. As McDonald drove away, he expressed his opinion of Mahantongo Street customers by shouting, "Merry Christmas, you stuck-up bastards! Merry Christmas from Mort McDonald!"

John attended holiday dances from the age of fifteen, and he learned the fundamental lesson that young people travel in packs. Although girls now attracted him in a powerful way, he still felt the need of membership in a male clique. The original trio of O'Hara, Boone, and Simonds had increased to six with the addition of Fred Hoefel, George (Deacon) Deischer, and Robert (Lem) Root. They formed a separate faction within the group of about a hundred youths who received party invitations. In this main crowd there were fifteen to twenty subgroups like the one that formed around O'Hara. The small sets met a need for sharing transportation and liquor, pooling funds, driving off interlopers, seeing that their girls had a good time at parties, and making sure that a friend got a fair deal if he challenged someone to a fight. Nobody was good enough to go it alone: the main pack could turn hostile and destroy a straggler or nonconformist. O'Hara recalled that "our group-within-a-group was called the Purity League. The name was hung on us by the father of one of the boys, a man with a sense of the sardonic. Although I was the only one ever to do time — I passed a night in a city-hall cell — we had an unwritten record, and certainly a local reputation, for fractures of the law that were by no means limited to our protests against the Volstead Act. . . . One Christmas Eve we collected a large quantity of empty gin and whisky bottles and deposited them neatly on the porch of a gentleman who abominated the Purity League. We always enjoyed thinking that the rows of dead soldiers must have delighted the devout on their way to the five-o'clock Christmas Mass. . . ."

With your own coterie to back you up, if you were a young man in the middle reaches of Pottsville society, you learned how to make an entrance at a party, with shoulders hunched high, and legs swinging in the joe-college swagger that Andy Phillips had mastered at Penn State. You looked around as though you owned the place, and it was an act of condescension to stay. You greeted allies and friends with much cordiality, glanced with marked coolness at rivals or inferiors, and smiled agreeably but without any air of presumption at people like Clint Sheafer or Woodward (Woodie) Archbald, Margaretta's handsome brother. You were polite to all girls and women, including the evening's hostess, but attentive to no more than half a dozen. Sometimes a mild delirium set in after a long day and night that began at five in the afternoon at the tea dance. A renewal of energy, like that promised by William James at Harvard to those who would work through fatigue came to those who played through fatigue, fought off the weariness of two or three A.M., and pushed through till daylight when they found themselves in perfect possession of their faculties and seeing things with what appeared to be an unearthly clearness of vision. A new unit of reality had been created, something that took the name of The Party, and all connected with the mystic occurrence would know that history was being made. The morning would go by in about fifteen minutes, and to their amazement and delight the members of The Party would find themselves lunching on gin and whiskey, still in evening dress, still making sense, or so they thought. And they were saying and doing terrifically funny things — or so they thought. With his intense acceptance of experience, young O'Hara absorbed the doctrine of the great historic Party and put himself into an onlooker's role in the story called "The Strong Man," where he shows the New Year's Day reception, a fixture in the Gibbsville calendar, that is given by the rich widow Arielle Stokes. An element of the younger set arrives when Mrs. Stokes hears a commotion in the front hall and sees four young men in coonskin coats stamping the snow off their arctics. She asks her friend Mr. Widmer if he can identify "the boy in the Tuxedo."

" 'That's Bruce Bayer, Bob and Kitty Bayer's son,' said Widmer."

" 'Whoever he is, he's intoxicated,' said Arielle."

Bruce stands in the hall and yells, " 'Happy New Year. A hap-py, hap-py New Year. Merry Christmas cried the warden and the prisoners shouted balls. Hap-py everything.' " Everybody watches Bruce, who at his sober best could not have been an attractive young man:

"Hello, Mr. Wilson, Mr. Evans. Hello, Mrs. Evans. Wunnia looking at me like that for? Din't you ever see anybody plastered before?" He took a large silver flask out of his jacket pocket. "Mr. Wilson, you know who ga' me this for Christmas? You don't? Well, you paid for it, old boy old boy old boy. Givena me by none other than Miss Barbara Wilson, that's who gave it to me. The lease I can do is offer you a drink out of it. It's g, i, n, gin. No, I beg your pardon, it's applejack. Berks County applejack. The gin is all gone. No? you won't take a drink out of Miss Barbara Wilson's flask? All right. Suit yourself. No skin off my rumpletilskin. There's my hostess! Mrs. Stokes. I'm so glad I could come to your party."

Mrs. Stokes manages to say, " 'Good afternoon, young man,' " and Bayer mimics her. " ' "Good afternoon, young man." Here, take a swig of apple. That'll put hair on your chest.' " Several men rush to Bayer and grasp his arms. He gets loose:

but now George Singleton, age forty-five, who played tackle for Lehigh, punched him in the jaw and he went down. The other men picked him up and carried him to the driveway and dropped him in the snow. A girl screamed and two of the young men in the coonskin coats made a rush at Singleton. He threw his left shoulder at one of the young men and punched the other. Two maids clung to each other in the front hall and all the men gathered in the vestibule. The father of one of the unpunched young men in the coonskin coats was heard to say, "Leave this house. You'll hear from me later."

Mrs. Stokes sits down crying, the cellist picks up his instrument and runs for the kitchen, and there is general confusion. O'Hara wrote that "the entire disaster, from the entrance of the young to the scuffle with George Singleton, took only a little longer than an earthquake." In a few days it turned out that the dreadful scene had been something of a social triumph for Mrs. Stokes after all, for as "the principal victim of the misbehavior of young Bayer and the other young people, she became a symbol of the right people of the town, whose dignity had been attacked . . ."

John O'Hara felt inner tension from trying to do what his conservative and somewhat puritanical father wished, and at the same time gain the approval of his friends. After parties in the holiday season, or on a week-end in summer vacations, a crowd would often go to Clint Sheafer's house to drink, listen to recorded or live music, or sit around and talk. Sheafer was rich enough to travel a good part of the time, and since he could live anywhere he liked, his preference for Pottsville as home base endeared him to his fellow townsmen. He did everything quietly and well, excelling at gentlemanly games, and his face was tanned during every month of the year, an effective setting for his blue eyes. Clint Sheafer was a charmer of all who met him, except for an occasional unfortunate like Bill McQuaid in the episode of the thrown highball. It was true that Sheafer had committed exogamy, or marriage outside the tribe, by bringing home a wife from Long Island. But it is no wonder that John much preferred Sheafer's genial tolerance of various follies to Patrick O'Hara's constant laying down of the law, and felt that on most matters of importance, the doctor did not understand his son. The doctor thought he understood as well as need be, and gave orders that John must go to work, and that the work must be hard enough to knock the nonsense out of him. This attitude was an inheritance of the hand and mind of Mike O'Hara, who had administered the terrible temperance oath and decreed that his boys must experience the rough side of life in Shenandoah. John signed on as helper in the railroad yards at St. Clair, the largest coal-loading facility in the country at the time. The town was about halfway between Pottsville and Shenandoah; more than twenty Slavic Catholic churches raised their bulbed turrets over streets surrounded by railroad tracks leading into yards that covered hundreds of acres. John would come home exhausted from the long dangerous hours among the switch-engines and dump-cars, his face drawn with fatigue and streaked with grime. Although she had been disturbed by the failure at Fordham, Mrs. O'Hara thought that her husband had not meant to send his son to an early grave, and would welcome a chance to relent if she put her opinion in forcible terms. She said, "I hope you understand that you're just slowly killing your son." John had accepted the job among dangerous locomotives as a test of his will power against that of his father. The county was full of

legless men holding watchman's jobs because of accidents at work for the
Reading and the other railroads and coal companies; and well did Patrick
O'Hara know it, for he had done the surgical tidying up after many a
maiming. This was not what he wanted for John. Accordingly, he decided
to put his son into the preparatory department conducted by the Keystone
State Normal College at Kutztown, fifty miles from Pottsville. The purpose of a Normal College being to train teachers, John was in the position
of laboratory material, not necessarily a bad thing from the educational
point of view. Since Dr. O'Hara had now retreated from the decision
that John's secondary schooling should be under Catholic auspices, it is a
matter for some speculation that he did not now attempt to enter John at
a New England boarding school — Exeter or Andover — or at one of the
Episcopalian "church schools," with the names of saints, that were highly
regarded. But evidently the doctor's mind did not work that way. In
later years, John O'Hara sometimes said he was expelled from Keystone
Normal. His departure was not so drastic as that: what happened was
that the people in charge told the doctor, after two terms, that John would
not benefit from coming back. Years afterward, on a trip with Pat Outerbridge through eastern Pennsylvania, O'Hara drove past the grounds of
the Normal College. He said, "For a time this was Alma Mater. I was
sent here to do penance." Outerbridge recalled that O'Hara did not
seem bitter about it, but was calm and relaxed at the wheel of a Mercedes
touring car of the highest mark.

O'Hara had begun to think that he ought to become a writer, and he
saw the possibilities in going on to college and getting experience on an
undergraduate magazine. Bob Simonds had entered Dartmouth, and
John wrote to him in April 1923: "I've often expressed a desire to write
things — and still do — but you haven't, and yet your vocabulary has
been developed to a far greater degree than mine. Apropos of vocabu-
laries, here's something that may strike you as incongruous — tho' it's quite
possible that you've discovered the same thing: I read Robert Benchley's
criticisms of the drama in 'Life' and while he writes in a semi-cynical,
-sarcastic, -satirical vein, he nevertheless has helped my limited vocabulary immensely. For example, I can't recall ever having seen the word
'protagonist' before, yet he used it last week and I knew what he meant.
Too bad he's a Harvard man else I might suggest a cheer . . ."

In this letter, O'Hara also dealt with a project for which he needed the
support of friends. He had been planning to found a convivial Greek-
letter fraternity which would enroll his Pottsville cronies, and Simonds
had advised that he suspend operations until everyone was home from
school and college. O'Hara wrote that the "suggestion to let the club matter ride until summer meets with my hearty approval. Root was home last
week-end and didn't bring the matter up, so I shall wax indifferent and

allow the whole thing to ride as far as I'm concerned. Yes, there is visible
a merger of two or possibly three gangs into one, yet our gang of last summer was constituted of factions. Perhaps a tolerant attitude extends only
as far as there is no tangible form of organization. As to the drinking part,
I'm going to continue to get drunk just as much as I can, club or clubless.
The beauty of a drinking club is the identical spirit that actuated the first
cave-dweller in opening up a bar. What I mean is that since drinking is
patently a 'social vice' (a man who drinks much alone is dangerous) there
is always a feeling of comfort in knowing that there is at least one good
frater in urbe who will respond to the call of one of his fellows and go out
on a bat. I daresay I have boozed a little more than anyone else in the
gang — though Fred seems to run me a close second this winter — and I
know that I don't get as much kick out of drinking to get boiled and *then*
going to a saloon and making up with a bare acquaintance or even absolute stranger and getting fried as I did on our last summer's parties when
someone would suggest something and we were off. Verily, ah verily,
them was better days!

"I have often felt like appealing to my grandmother to send me to
school, but there's the hitch that you recognized in my make-up. For purposes of classification, I have created a name for myself; it is 'the Psi U
type.' I say Psi U because almost invariably the Psi U's are snakes — they
dance, drink, dress and dawdle, yet, though I never expect to strut with a
Phi Bete key dangling carelessly but ostentatiously from my chain, I mean
it when I say that I'll do less dawdling than I would had I not worked this
year. When I get to college, I want to rate a good national social, a drinking club, a minor varsity letter, varsity play, and 'The Lit.' I would also
like to be a political boss. There's a peculiar attraction in politics for me.
Perhaps in the future years the wielding of my masterful pen will spell
defeat for more than one seemingly likely candidate. (Opposing candidate, of course.) I would like the minor letter to show my son as he
matriculates at my college. I crave athletics for the fun I get out of them.
I don't deny that I'd not refuse a tennis or golf cup, but I start out by
liking tremendously both sports. I would like the place in a play or something because of the trips involved. I would like 'The Lit' because it's an
honor and because I like 'Lit,' and the only sincerely unselfish feeling I'd
have would be the fraternity spirit (in its campus sense). All the other
'points' I have spoken of are inspired by a motive purely for '*me*' and not
'for the good of the college.' Frankly . . . I think the man who flaunts *that*
flag to the breeze is either old Joe Athlete who is sure of his letters and gold
footballs or he's Joe's brother, Tom Politician, who for himself or one of his
clique is sending thrills thru' the freshmen's spines and incidentally
thereby getting said frosh vote. (I don't claim that juniors and seniors are
immune to that applesauce.) I hope I'm not being iconoclastic and smash-

ing any cherished ideals of yours, but when one says 'frankly,' one feels that almost anything is permissible.

"Bob, you're deserting me. I can see that I'll be the only genuine failure in the gang. The passing of your exams was the turning-point in your life and you can now sit back and decide what to call your three children while you cogitate over just how much a failure I'll turn out to be. Mark my words, Bob.

"Well, old boy, I mustn't run out of material for my next letter. In the next I shall dwell on psycho-analyses I have made. Always your friend, Doc."

One month later, O'Hara again unburdened himself in a letter to Bob Simonds at Dartmouth College: ". . . My father and I are off again. This time he has good and sufficient reason to become perturbed; someone has told him of my boozing. He told me about what he had heard and made several dire threats which aren't even interesting; he hasn't the nerve to carry them out, but nevertheless, life henceforth will be a veritable hell for me. He has made it so before and he'll use every means he can to make it hell, because of all things he hates, liquor receives double its share — he had a brother who, when drunk, fell down a flight of stairs and died from the effects of the fall.* As I told you and Lem, our relations have been anything but amicable since August 1921. This discovery of my intemperance may eventually culminate matters. Anticipating such culmination, I have begun tentative bag-packing. I'll probably hang around here for a month or so, but when Marg returns from the Vineyard after Labor Day, I think that she'll find one less persistent snake. (Very poorly put, but you know what I mean.) If war were to break out, matters would be simplified, but one can't order wars overnight.

"Another thing that adds greatly to my discomfiture is the fact that I may lose my job. No job means no money and one can't go very far without money. I have made up my mind to get out of Pottsville but when, I can't say. If the Deacon is in earnest about going to Europe, he can count on me as a companion, but there is to be considered 'the drama of the emergence of an idea.' Perhaps *you* may feel the urge. A job as night clerk in a large hotel appeals to me. When I say large hotel I don't mean in New York especially, but some place the *size* of New Haven, or Los Angeles. I don't think I'd crave New Haven because I might not like to take hooey from some half-boiled freshman and I'd probably reach over the counter and tap him with the register. Los Angeles is quite the nice thing — but pardon me for raving on this way . . ."

Another letter to Simonds in this period showed some of the things that troubled John O'Hara's mind: ". . . If I carried a notebook and jotted down

* John O'Hara's version of the oyster train tragedy; see pp. 24–25.

some of my thoughts there'd be a continual stream of mail pouring into 305 Topliff, but some of the thoughts might land me into either Federal prison or a home for the violently insane — and inane. I'd likewise be excommunicated from the Catholic Church. (Pardon, I just saw E. Fox pass; he must be week-ending in town.) I have arrived at what amounts to a second childhood. Sounds ridiculous, but look: a child plays with a mechanical toy and after a time he will want to see what makes the wheels go around. After a time he destroys the toy in his eagerness to get at the spring. My toy has been about everything one can imagine: the study of behavior; the change in lines of a Packard car; the loopholes in certain laws. Every damn thing imaginable has come in for a share of inspection by me, and this may sound queer, but one thing I blame it on is learning to arrive at the meaning of a word by recalling its Latin root. Bend that!"

The founding of a club or fraternity in Pottsville again engaged O'Hara's attention as he went on, "I'm so glad you mentioned my remark about working on a sort of outline for a constitution. I'll take you up on your suggestion immediately. For some time past I was going to ask you and Lem to act as a committee to draw up a constitution but I was afraid you might think I was electing myself president pro tem, but now you have relieved me of what to me, was the hardest part of establishing this thing as a fact. Go right along old man, and thanks for the suggestion and offer to help. I do hereby rescind any prior right, so there! I picked out you and Lem because you two have one or two brains in your heads and have had experience with college fraternities, which, if I may say so, are the only real fraternities. A prep fraternity is usually wrong, being founded on the desire of a certain coterie to become exclusive. I know. But I digress. You could also write the boys and let them know that if the gang goes in its entirety, then you're all for it . . . Your influence means something. As I have often said, everyone is all for the idea . . . It only remains for you to spread the propaganda with Lem and Deac, who, upon seeing you're with the idea, will readily acquiesce.

"I've been invited to a party at Doc Kenney's on Monday. Joe Dewitt is going to furnish the oil, so I expect to take on something for a battle.

"Now that you're bored to tears I'd better lay off for a time. Write soon again. As ever, Doc."

Two years later, O'Hara was still going out with Margaretta Archbald from time to time, and still working on the idea of founding a fraternity. And he continued to have trouble with liquor, which he referred to as "oil." These matters came up for discussion when he wrote to Bob Simonds: "On Saturday, the entertainment committee came out of their trance and gave a dance at the club. Marg and I and Jack & Alex went down for dinner. We had with us one (1) quart of lubricant. It was Dougherty, and just about as good as I've had for a helluva spell. Well, as the evening progressed, our (editorial plural) pep began to wane, where-upon the bottle was brought forth. The women failed to function as re-gards absorption of the oil and Jack held out on me with the very natural result that I got drunk as a skunk. All well and good but as near as I can figure — and conservatively withal — I downed 1½ pints, which is noble, but is also ½ pint beyond my present capacity, so that at closing time I was though by no means raucous, still visibly moved. Jack had to take the wheel but unfortunately I had imbibed some White Rock but not at the same time as I inhaled the hootch. To this I attribute the later occur-rences. Anyhow, Jack had to stop the car 5 (five) times between the C.C. and Pottsville so that I might get out and act seasick. It's the first time I've ever done that with women on the party and so help me, I hope it's the last. I think that it's disgusting, etc. Well, L'Envoi would be nothing more or less than I'm off until 'the boys come home.' Needless to say, there were two nice apologies to make. However, all is well . . . Now for some-thing of a different character. About this club. You and Lem, and possibly the Deacon, are the doubtful prospects and your grievances, if I may say that, are basically identical. Although you and I have several faults in common, you possess a virtue to which I never laid claim: said virtue is conscientiousness. The point of that is this: I personally, and I might say the four who seem to wax most enthusiastic about the fraternity, did not notice any friction in the old gang at Xmas. I will concede that it was damn hard to get any enthusiasm about a meeting, but remember that between two parties to Reading; Joe Haight's visit, and numerous dates by individuals, it was a case of try and find a nite to get organized. As to the Deac, I don't know what to say. He was invited to Boone's on two occa-sions and turned down both bids. Likewise he had a chance for the Assembly and one of the club dances, which also he turned down. Well, one can't force him to go along. So I rest my part of the case with you. The others are writing to me and asking me about organizing and getting the keys. Well, I feel as you do; I want to see the gang go in en masse. Secondly, I have had Clawson send away for better estimates on the chain-weights.° I've even drawn up a tentative constitution. Of course, we'll bear a greater resemblance to ΘNE or KBφ than to ΣX or φΓΔ.† It's a kick in the can to find that after spending a little time on this thing, the enthusi-asm I tried to put into it has not touched *everyone*."

° Small keys or seals to be worn on watch chains, highly regarded in collegiate circles at the time.
† The first two organizations mentioned, Theta Nu Epsilon and Kappa Beta Phi, were burlesque fraternities whose main purpose was to hold drinking bouts. Kappa Beta Phi members sported a key purposely resembling that of Phi Beta Kappa, whose insigne was conferred only for the highest scholastic standing. O'Hara's other two Greek letter combinations referred to Sigma Chi and Phi Gamma Delta, regular fraternities with chapters in many colleges.

O'Hara then informed his friend that "good beer" was again available in Pottsville, ironically adding "we'll soon have prohibition." Then he turned to the proper mode of dress for a smart young man: "I've up and bought me a norfolk suit. A dark herringbone. Not really *very* dark, but it's darker than the run of norfolks. Cheaper, too, but that's alright. (No, it's not whipcord.) I've also accumulated some Foulards and a dotted scarf, a suspicious cough and a tougher beard." The matter of the Norfolk jacket was important. This garment was a kind of high-buttoned shooting coat with deep pockets under pleats in front, which somehow or other had become a symbol of refinement and worldly wisdom, or at least a desire to attain these qualities, among young college men.* He continued, "Did you ever read any of John Galsworthy's thrillers (?) I've finished 'In Chancery.' Liked it immensely. Also read two other English authors — Beresford and Frances Hodgson Burnett. The more I read modern English authors, the more I think that we Americans are sadly lacking in pen-wielders. I've assayed Balzac and am compelled to admit that he held no interest for my temperamental nature. Christopher Morley amuses me with his one act plays. (Yes, I've acquired a taste for plays.) By the way, did you read 'Brass'?† If you didn't, don't. I saw something quoted from it and thought, 'Lord God, I gave up that book over a year ago; I must have missed something.' As a result, I've learned not to trust my passions when in search of reading . . ."

O'Hara's interest in founding a Pottsville club with Greek letters and a watch charm did not mean that he felt college organizations would be unattainable. Provided he cleared the hurdle of getting into college, O'Hara thought himself fairly sure of social recognition. He believed, however, that his father had met with anti-Catholic prejudice as a student, and still held this opinion in 1960, when he wrote to Courtie Bryan that "along about the beginning of the 20th century a man's being a Catholic did not automatically disqualify him from such social acceptability; it remained a consideration, but the automatic blackball existed in less force than it had a generation earlier. As an example: my father was blackballed for DKE at Penn in 1890††; in 1922 I was given a sub-freshman bid to Delta Phi, a socially much better fraternity, at Penn. That's exactly one generation difference, less two years. And in the same year I was bid DKE at Amherst and Alpha Delta Phi at Wesleyan, Phi Gamma Delta at Lehigh and Penn State, Sigma Nu at Lafayette and Cornell, Theta Delta Chi at Lafayette, etc. At Yale I probably would have made Bones (and wanted

---

* In 1953, O'Hara was to give a full explanation of the Norfolk in an article for *Holiday* magazine.
† A novel by the Californian Charles Cilman Norris.
†† No chapter of DKE existed at the University of Pennsylvania in 1890, according to *Baird's Manual of American College Fraternities,* the standard reference work.

Keys) on literary accomplishment, and with little or no consideration of my being a Catholic, which I was then. Not one of those bids would have been forthcoming in, say, 1890, and yet in 1900 my father was a member of the Pottsville Assembly, and the Pottsville Club, the two most exclusive social organizations in that part of the State. My point is a chronological one: the change occurred almost overnight, but a little too late. From here I could go into a really long one about Jack Kennedy and his candidacy for the presidency, but that will be another essay at another time."

On the completion of John's Kutztown penance, Dr. O'Hara returned to his original idea of Catholic secondary education. This time he decided on the preparatory department at Niagara University, his old college in upper New York State, where he placed John in the fall of 1923 as a member of the top form, which corresponded to senior year in high school. Once again Dr. O'Hara had succeeded in getting his son into a preparatory school that was not a separate entity but an appendage to something else. The doctor felt that this would make no difference in the long run, provided John redeemed himself on the campus near Niagara Falls. The Vincentian Fathers, who ran the place, were less intimidating than the Jesuits of Fordham. John profited by what the Vincentians had to offer. He made a good record in class and received the appointment of valedictorian for the graduation ceremonies of June 1924. The doctor found this immensely gratifying. At last "Johnny boy" was showing some sense of responsibility, and an appreciation of what had been done for him. Patrick O'Hara returned to his old campus for the June exercises in a mood of happy pride and optimism. But graduation day proved to be a disaster. The night before, John went out with some classmates to celebrate with a few drinks in a speakeasy. They considered their school days over, and the ceremonies of the following day a formality. John returned to school, tipsy in broad daylight, and encountered the proctors, who reported him to the dean. The authorities stripped John of his honors: he was not to deliver the valedictory, and must leave at once. If John had planned a revenge on his father for a lifetime of strict authority, he could hardly have hurt him more. Dr. O'Hara's state of mind is painful to contemplate. One can imagine that among his feelings were a sense of personal shame before the school authorities, an almost blind rage at his son for causing the disgrace, and a terrible fear that in spite of all warnings John had turned into a drunkard. As for John, his load of guilt was partially lightened by a sense of youthful defiance, and the knowledge that he was building a reputation as a notable free spirit among his contemporaries. But there was no escape from the fact that he had let his father down. Back in Pottsville, the only thing to do was lie low and try to keep out of the doctor's way. There were days of strain at No. 606; and then, as they must, matters righted themselves, at least on the surface. Patrick O'Hara told John he had been inclined to rule out the idea of Yale. From what he heard, New Haven was the last place in the world for a young man with a weakness for liquor. But he was going to offer one more chance: if John would work for a year, keeping away from alcohol and out of trouble, the doctor would allow him to seek entrance to Yale. It would be a matter of tutoring and passing examinations. Assuming that John tutored in the summer of 1925 and gained entrance at New Haven that fall, he would be in the Class of 1929, but considering the methods of the College Entrance Examination Board at the time, John would have been more likely to go through with the Class of 1930. In either event he would have been old for an undergraduate, which might have been to his advantage. But the important thing was to become a part of eastern American life, at any age, as a product of Yale.

John O'Hara had become aware of something that was far from unsound when he planned to be a Yale man in the early 1920s. In those days Yale as a concept permeated the national mind, with various degrees of meaning related to wealth, social position, natural leadership, and the achievement of worldly success. The big block "Y" had the effect of a Chinese ideogram, signifying all those things, wrapped in a romantic aura of ivy-covered walls, secret societies that met in windowless stone buildings, the music of close harmonizers, and the longest list of football victories in America. John seemed to have little interest in what might be taught in the classrooms at Yale. What he had seized upon was the dramatic impact of the place, and anyone who first saw New Haven in the 1920s can testify that this American university city could exercise a powerful effect on a visitor's emotions. Yale came at you strongly through the sense of sight, because after seeing the Old Campus and the Green, you walked along University Avenue to the Bicentennial Buildings, completed in 1901 and 1902, which told the story in one word: money. Memorial Hall was a circular building that connected the Woolsey and Dining Halls, all handsome and assured in the magnificent metropolitan banking style of the period. From 1903 to 1906 the Vanderbilt Scientific Hall (Van-Sheff) and other buildings for the Sheffield Scientific School took shape, and by 1921, the Harkness Memorial Quadrangle and Tower stood over all in great and picturesque effectiveness. One might get into town on the night before the Harvard or Princeton game, and come across a band of Negro fiddlers and guitarists in battered top hats, strolling up Elm Street as they played and sang "Bingo" and "Bulldog" by Cole Porter, who had graduated in the Class of 1911. When you have a Cole Porter to write your football songs, you are going to make a distinct impression on anyone who has considered a game of football important enough to warrant a trip to the Yale Bowl. After all, the crowds had not come in search of music, and so the early works of Porter in praise of the Yale eleven were a premium, so to speak, a mark of extra quality in the college itself. The complicated Yale social system of clubs and fraternities also gave the outsider something to marvel at, for it appeared to provide enough paneled barrooms, hung with portraits, team photographs, and sporting prints, to accommodate hundreds of well-dressed young men. The world outside believed that most of these youths, for all their genial manner, were engaged in hard and even bitter competition within the system of undergraduate Yale. Popular belief had it that the offices and societies the young men achieved by senior year indicated the leaders not only of Yale College at the time, but of the entire country, a few years in the future.

In the early 1920s, O'Hara had the opportunity of meeting a number of Yale graduates in Pottsville and surrounding territory. *The Alumni Directory of Yale University* for 1923 showed fifteen names within the city limits, mostly on the upper reaches of Mahantongo Street — Sheafers, Thompsons, Archbalds, and Ellises — and there were two in Minersville, twenty-one in Reading, and fifty-seven in Harrisburg, the Fort Penn of *A Rage to Live*. In this novel, O'Hara was to ask his readers to believe that a man named Reichelderfer got into Yale and belonged to Death's Head, the name a coinage from Skull and Bones, the oldest senior society, and another called Wolf's Head. A glance at the 1923 *Directory* establishes O'Hara's credibility when one notes that the Reading delegation at New Haven included men named Maltzberger, Kuntz, Ermentrout, Gerhard, Keppelman, Stauffer, Hendel, and Womelsberg. One of the best-known Yale men from Pottsville in O'Hara's youth was Conrad Hock, the hero of a dormitory fire. "Cooney" Hock had shown courage and unselfishness in this emergency, his conduct summing up the collegiate ideal of that period: those who were to be given privileges and advantages must be prepared to behave well when trouble came. O'Hara had seen it in the outpouring of college volunteers for the 1917 war. And he felt that a year's hard work was a small price to pay for entrance into that chivalrous company at its most desirable rallying ground, in New Haven, Connecticut. O'Hara's reputation as a Yale fan or buff was increased by the sharp tongue of Ernest Hemingway, who said to Vincent Sheean and John Lardner, when some unexpected payment came in, "Let's use this to start a fund for sending O'Hara to New Haven." The cruelty lay in the fact that John O'Hara by that time was thirty-seven years old and a famous established author.

In the probationary year John obtained work at various jobs, none of which impressed his father. He found employment at Lakeside Amusement Park, at the end of the trolley line, where his duties included renting rowboats and keeping an eye on the owner's property. Out of this experi-

ence came a story called "Yostie," in which the proprietor of an amusement park in the Gibbsville region hires a stranger named Ed Smith to
look after boat lockers, but thinks better of it in a few hours: " 'Here's for
the whole day. Now you can go, and I don't want you hanging around no
more. You can get the next trolley back to Gibbsville.' " It had become
evident that Ed Smith had done time in the penitentiary and was as
dangerous as a predatory wild animal. Mr. Yost the proprietor was not
thinking of himself, but of Mildred, a dimwitted farm girl who worked
for him. "She was only twenty-seven and he was past sixty, but it came
over him now that before the summer was out he would ask her to marry
him and she would accept." The story O'Hara built around this plot
showed how completely he had taken into his memory the details of
running a rural amusement park — the icing of the pop bottles, the
demands for various goods and services at different times of day, the
amounts of money the factory workers and farmers would be able to
spend on their outing. When he was done, O'Hara had given the reader
all that, plus three people — Yostie, Mildred, and the sinister Ed Smith.

For a time John worked as a checker at the Eastern Steel Mill. A fight
with a fellow employee was the most dramatic event on this job. It was
customary to hold grudge fights outside company property, and they met
on a nearby vacant lot, each man accompanied by a train of seconds and
coat-holders. O'Hara's record as a fighter was not by any means a string
of victories. He usually lost because he tried to fight while drunk. But
on this day he was sober and he won by a technical knockout when the
other fellow could not continue the fight after an O'Hara punch on the jaw.

Patrick O'Hara had known for some time that his son wanted to be a
writer, and that the recognized apprenticeship to this trade was served
on newspapers. And the doctor knew nothing would be gained in the long
run by keeping John at work in factories or amusement parks, or reading
gas meters, or serving sodas, as he did for a time at Rensler's Pharmacy.
So in the early fall of 1924 Dr. O'Hara asked H. I. Silliman, publisher of
the *Pottsville Journal,* to give John a trial. Mr. Silliman interviewed John
at his office in the traditional atmosphere of pipe smoke and printer's ink,
and told him the only way to find out whether or not a man had the
makings of a reporter was to give him a trial at the actual gathering of
news, for the business required inborn aptitudes that one either did or
did not possess. A short trial run would tell, and Mr. Silliman was prepared to offer this opportunity out of respect for John's father. He then
advised John to read Shakespeare and the King James Bible, and turned
him over to News Editor David Yocum. When O'Hara asked about
salary, he learned that for the time being he was in the position of
Dickens's young man who enjoyed an income of nothing a year, paid
quarterly. Earn while you learn was not the policy of the *Pottsville*

Journal. The paper was the direct descendant of the famous *Miners'
Journal;* it had prospered until the railroads put on fast mail trains in the
early 1900s, and made the Philadelphia and New York morning papers
available at breakfast time in Pottsville. When he took over in 1914,
Silliman made the *Journal* an evening paper in competition with the
strongly entrenched *Pottsville Republican.* At the time O'Hara joined the
staff, the *Journal* was offering its readers eight-column pages closely
printed in small type, so that local stories were expected to run long.
O'Hara's first assignment was a case of manslaughter, at the nearby town
of Tamaqua. This was a difficult hurdle for a brand-new reporter, but
O'Hara went at it and questioned everyone he could find who knew anything about the case. His story appeared in the paper with a few minor
editorial corrections. David Yocum's comment was "Pretty good — but
we could have used more details." That criticism would never again be
used about any writing by John O'Hara.

In a short time O'Hara began to draw a salary from the *Journal,* although
at first it was only six dollars a week. His friend Beany Boone also came
on the *Journal* staff. Along with Katherine (Kit) Bowman, a mine superintendent's daughter who had recently graduated from Mount Holyoke,
O'Hara and Boone gave the city staff a look of youth and modernity, for
they all three owned coonskin coats, in which they set out every morning
in cold weather, stopping for hot chocolate at Hodgson's before starting
the day's legwork. The three young journalists sometimes used the office
floor for the execution of a spirited, hopping, pigeon-toed dance called
the Charleston, to the astonishment of Mr. Silliman, who would peer from
his private room to see what was causing the commotion around the city
desk. These were the first high days of a tradition of bibulous, irreverent
newspaper people in Chicago and New York, a tradition that was echoed
in Pottsville. The role to be played was that of a man on the inside who
knew everything about everybody. Printing everything was another
matter. The hat on the back of the head, the cigarette between lips even
while talking, a bottle of bootleg gin with a spurious Gordon's label in
one coat pocket, the latest *American Mercury* in the other — all were
stage properties of the character. While making his first attempts to play
the part of a young newspaperman, O'Hara took careful note of his older
colleagues on the *Journal,* starting with Mr. Silliman, from whom he drew
certain characteristics of Bob Hooker, the editor who waits on Edith
Chapin, the recently bereaved widow, in the opening passage of *Ten
North Frederick.* The editor in the novel was obsequious before Mrs.
Chapin, a local great lady, which may reflect O'Hara's feeling of discomfort as a newspaperman more than the actual character of his employer.
O'Hara respected the paper's daily general columnist, Walter S. Farquhar,
who was also a sports editor in the style of Grantland Rice, and capable

of writing a good set of verses, especially when inspired by the Pottsville
Maroons, a football team composed of rock-hard mercenary athletes. Like
the Green Bay Packers, Providence Steamrollers, and Canton Bulldogs,
the Maroons represented a small city in a big league. They were to win
the National Football League championship in 1926 by defeating the
Chicago Bears. O'Hara put in overtime as Farquhar's assistant because
of his interest in sports. A year or so before, he had been at home one
Sunday afternoon when a party of coaches and hangers-on brought an
injured member of the Frankford Yellow Jackets to No. 606 for emergency
treatment. His brother Tom stood unnoticed in the front hall and saw
John watching his father as Dr. O'Hara cut off the muddy red and yellow
jersey, felt the dislocation, and pulled the shoulder into place while the
player's face went gray with pain. "Just send your bill to the team
office, Doc." The mud they left in the hallway was all the payment Dr.
O'Hara ever got. Walter Farquhar could have advised Dr. O'Hara to
insist on cash, but that was something the doctor would never do when
emergency help was needed. The doctor respected Farquhar and another
of John's colleagues, a veteran reporter who made his knowledge of news
sources in Schuylkill County a matter of pride and craftsmanship. O'Hara
made this man's craftsmanship and integrity the material for a powerful
story, "Claude Emerson, Reporter." The middle-aged Emerson showed
skill and courage in getting the facts about a fatal laboratory explosion at
a large plant even though the company had more than enough influence to
suppress the truth, and nobody did anything, or even considered doing
anything, when a company cop hit Emerson so hard in the stomach that
he had to take the rest of the day off and go to bed. The city editor says,
"'Listen, I'll get one of the boys to drive you home. The circulation
department has a car.' 'Any other time, but today I'd rather take a taxi.
This is the first time in thirty-two years I wished I'd been a bookkeeper.'
'Not you, Claude,' said the city editor."

Not all of O'Hara's fellow workers on the *Journal* had the qualities
of Claude Emerson. A woman feature writer went into *Appointment in
Samarra* under a light disguise applied with noticeable malice as Lydia
Faunce Browne, a sob sister whose treatment of the news was both pretentious and superficial. O'Hara ranked considerably below the original
of Lydia Faunce Browne on the staff, and spent a good part of his time
at the telephone gathering high school basketball scores around the
county, or taking down accounts of church suppers for the editor of the
religion page. All cub reporters did this sort of desk work, and on small
papers they also learned to write headlines and prepare copy for the com-
positors under the pressure of a deadline only a few minutes away. Later
in life O'Hara liked to say that he could earn his living as a deskman if
his literary talent burned out. But he detested the telephoning that went

into the production of a daily newspaper. Few people knew that John O'Hara was a very shy young man. He was happiest when he could observe some human situation, without openly seeking to find out its inner workings, but finding out all the same. And in spite of the emotional stress of telephoning strangers, he preferred newspaper work to anything else available to him in Schuylkill County; he enjoyed the comradeship of the *Journal* staff, the comfortable clutter of its newsroom, and the feeling of accomplishment that came when heavy machinery in the basement shook floors as the first edition went to press.

At home, things went along fairly well. In the years after O'Hara became famous and newspaper and magazine people began turning up in Pottsville looking for material about him, the old friends went to a good deal of trouble to emphasize their memories of John as a gregarious young man who had friends and saw them frequently, by no means a solitary or melancholy figure. There was affectionate family life at No. 606; John and his father were capable of disagreement, but this was "because they were so much alike." The storming, frightening sort of conflict came less often now: Patrick O'Hara was slowing down.

One night John and Mary came home from a dance, and found a bat in Mary's room. They were startled but not astounded to see this creature, for a bat family had lived for years in the O'Hara backyard pear trees. Wearing his dancing pumps and dinner jacket, and hilarious from drinks at the party, John thought it overpoweringly funny that he should be picking up a golf club and pursuing a bat while his sister took refuge under the bedcovers in her party dress. When John abandoned the golf club and seized a tennis racket, their shrieks of laughter awakened Dr. O'Hara, who made an entrance, wearing a long robe. Time was when Patrick O'Hara would have upbraided John at sight for leaping about with a tennis racket at three o'clock in the morning. But all he said was, "What's going on?" Mary said, "Get out, Daddy, there's a bat in here." And the doctor withdrew, pausing to utter his strongest domestic oath: "By — *George!*" Next morning, Dr. O'Hara made no comment on his son's pallor at the breakfast table, and asked, "Did you get the bat?" Yes, John had killed the thing and disposed of the corpse. The doctor said, "Never fool around with a bat. They're full of vermin." The young people said they would keep this in mind. The remarkable thing was that the doctor had nothing to say about his son's hilarity of a few hours before, or the lateness of the disturbance.

Patrick O'Hara's family and friends believed that the influenza epidemic of 1918 had taken a serious toll of his vital forces. Those forces had also been drained by the stress of a medical quarrel in 1922, when Patrick O'Hara had led a faction of doctors out of the Pottsville Hospital. His chief enemy was a doctor he believed to be working under an altered name, whose conduct was such that Dr. O'Hara decided he could no longer practice in good conscience at an institution that tolerated this man. Knowing how doctors cover for each other, we can judge the intensity of feeling that caused Patrick O'Hara to take this stand.

There were meetings at No. 606. Mrs. O'Hara served no alcohol, but the doctors emptied many plates of apples, and their pipe and cigar smoke permeated the house for weeks. These councils resulted in the founding of a new hospital by Dr. O'Hara and those who left with him, under the patronage of Mrs. Lee and other substantial persons in the town. This institution grew to be the Good Samaritan Hospital that rises on the heights of East Norwegian Street today. Dr. Boone did not get into the fight, and remained at Pottsville Hospital; Dr. O'Hara did not openly hold this against his colleague, but their friendship cooled. In his earlier days, it would not have been Dr. O'Hara, but his adversaries, who left the established institution and launched out on something new. Late in 1924, Patrick O'Hara's barber stopped John on Centre Street and said, "I'm worried about Doctor. He wakes up slow under the towel and his skin feels slack to the razor. He's not a well man."

The Gibbsville barbers of "Good-by, Herman" and "The Cellar Domain" owed something to this friend of Dr. O'Hara who had felt in his face the touch of approaching death. And the prediction began to fulfill itself in early 1925, when Dr. O'Hara found that he was going to bed exhausted and rising still tired after a night's sleep. The doctors he consulted found evidence of Bright's Disease, and recommended a Florida vacation. He went to St. Petersburg with hopes of recovering his tone, but alarming news came back in the first week of February. The news was sent by a friend, Alice Maddock Diemer, who had been a crack surgical nurse in Pottsville, often working with Patrick O'Hara. Now she visited the doctor at his hotel and saw that he needed more than a stay in St. Petersburg. Friends put him into a stateroom on a northbound train, with a special porter in attendance. John met the train at the Pottsville station and saw his father helped down from the car, wearing a polo coat and tweed cap. He looked like any prosperous important American man returning from a trip, until John came close and saw that the doctor's face was bright with fever and that he did not know what was going on around him. Patrick O'Hara thought he had been locked under guard on the train and was suspicious of his son, but allowed himself to be driven home and put to bed. Tom O'Hara was frightened to see his vital, dominating father a stricken man, and it disturbed him when orderlies installed a hospital bed in the front room on the third floor. Then came a lucid interval, and Tom in the hall downstairs heard his father say to his mother, "Katharine, I'm going to die." She said, "Who will take care of the children?" The doctor's voice echoed in the stairwell as he answered, "The world will take care of them."

The doctor had come home on Thursday, March 12, 1925. On the morning of Wednesday, March 18, his physicians told the family that death was near. John and Patrick O'Hara still had power to hurt each other, but the doctor had the last word, and it was a word of kindness, when John came to the bedside and saw that his father was trying to say something. He bent close and heard a faint whispering: "Poor John. Poor John." They called Tom to the vigil at ten A.M., and he saw the gathering of relatives in a room darkened by drawn curtains, and John in his characteristic leaning pose, so like their father's accustomed stance, in a corner by an open door. Dr. O'Hara became unconscious and began to take deep snoring breaths. The devout were praying quietly and waiting for The Time, which came at one P.M., when the snoring stopped. Patrick O'Hara had died at the age of fifty-seven, leaving eight children and his widow.

All the doctors and many of the citizens of Schuylkill County attended the funeral of Patrick O'Hara. After services in the church, the doctors formed a double line of honorary pallbearers outside, then followed the coffin to the cemetery. In maturity, Tom O'Hara thought of this delegation of doctors at the graveside, and remarked, "I dimly recall that this was not necessary nor especially desired but I do remember that when they were lowering Daddy's body into the grave — an awesome sight for me — a small, spare doctor from north of Pottsville burst into uncontrollable tears. He was a man some of the family knew, but they did not expect him to break down in sorrow at our father's death. I believe the thought was that he must have had more than one tough diagnosis and Daddy had helped him, as he did other doctors, sometimes without insisting that they call him into formal consultation."

The city of Pottsville knew that an important man had died, but the family remained in shock for some days after the burial. When the shock wore off, the younger children still found it hard to realize that their father was gone, and that they had lost the family breadwinner. It was impossible for John to undertake the upkeep of No. 606 and the support of his mother and seven brothers and sisters. The change in the O'Hara fortunes was dramatized three weeks after the doctor's death, when the children learned that their ponies had been sold. The new owner was the Stonewall Jackson Riding Academy of New Jersey, and on a cold clear morning in early March, the men came for the ponies and carts. Tom followed the cavalcade to a freight yard on the edge of town, where he saw the men take the wheels off the governess cart, the dog cart, and the little Conestoga wagon, and stack the carts and wheels in one end of a boxcar.

Then they lowered a ramp, and put web harnesses on the ponies to hold them during the trip. The ponies went up the ramp; the men pushed the door on its grooves across the opening in the side of the car and clamped it shut. And Tom told John that only then did the fact of his father's death at last sink into his mind.

In addition to ponies, one of the things that make children feel privileged and special is a summer place. It was not long before the young O'Haras learned that Oakland Farm was soon to pass from their family's ownership forever. Patrick O'Hara had made some money in the stock market, but on opening the doctor's safety deposit box, John and his mother got a shock: the box was crammed with worthless German marks. John said to himself, "Daddy was a fine surgeon, but a lousy businessman." Katharine O'Hara now settled to the struggle of keeping the family together and educating the younger children. Mary graduated from Eden Hall, which had been her mother's finishing school, and then, like Booth Tarkington's valiant Alice Adams, took secretarial training and left Pottsville to make a career for herself at the *New York Daily News*. All the other children had the opportunity of attending college, and Katharine O'Hara retained ownership of the house at No. 606 Mahantongo Street until 1940, when she sold the property and moved to New York, to live with Mary until her death in 1967.

Shortly after Dr. O'Hara's death, John wrote to Robert Simonds about things that were close to his heart: "My father's death had a sobering effect on me. I have given up all hope of seeing Europe or anything like that . . . I don't know much about the governor's estate. I don't think any of the children will have to sell papers or have to rely on my small stipend for sustenance, but I have, nevertheless, begun to plan to live economically . . . My ambition is to get a job on The World. To be able to say, 'Yes, I worked for the N.Y.W.' is open sesame." O'Hara then broached the idea of publishing a newspaper in partnership with Simonds: "A couple of years experience and a desk somewhere as city or news editor, then your own paper, OUR own paper! We could get a paper in some small town and see what a go we could make of it. Nanticoke, I hear, has a paper that has been defunct several times and it always comes back when someone else starts it. The only thing is this: how about money? Of course the idea would be to make money and lots of it. My smokiest dream would be to have you, Beanie and me run a paper: You, the editorials, Beanie, the news — for he has good news sense — and I the features: sports, humor, and human interest stories, as well as a colyum. I shall take up the matter with the board . . .

"I had one pleasant surprise when the governor came home from the dear old Southland. He heard me cough and it prompted him to tell me or reveal to me (I haven't found out which) that I have two spots in the

pulmonary apparati. Since then, I have been taking mighty good care of
myself: No liquor and lots of milk, vegetables and the like, and even cutting down on my lone vice, Madame Nicotine . . . No one knows better
than I what sort of life the governor led. Hard work, a clean life and so
little pleasure. No one can tell me that he derived a lot of satisfaction
from the knowledge that he was doing good and that alone. It's all out of
proportion. He never took vacations and he had very little real pleasure.
And it's awfully unsettling to the predestination idea, my boy, is this death
affair. I was inclined to believe in predestination but when it strikes like
a thief in the night, when it strikes near YOU like a thief in the night
you say, 'This sort of thing can't be predestined; why does he linger until
just this moment?' One can readily presuppose the argument which will
follow these questions but in the calm hysteria of the moment one seems
awfully close to God and God doesn't seem like the kind of man who
would predestine that a man should die without having had some enjoyment in life, a proportionate enjoyment to the amount of hard, thankless
work he has done . . . Always your friend, Doc."

At work John had his rounds to make, picking up routine Pottsville
news. He also had some telephone chores that he did not object to, as
they involved nothing more onerous than friendly calls to reporters of
equally low rank in the surrounding towns, for county items such as
industrial-team bowling scores and freight loading statistics. The young
journalists relieved the tedium of transmitting this material by discussing
the features in that morning's New York World. Those were the days
when the early mail trains threw off a bundle of Worlds at every tank
town within two hundred miles of New York City. It was the paper for
progressive-minded people who cared about literature, art, and an inde-
pendent approach to the news. In each small city and town, the World
readers — teachers, ministers, a few lawyers, and the newspaper staffs —
looked fondly on the gothic lettering of The World nameplate each morning as a sign that a powerful and articulate organ of metropolitan civiliza-
tion was still in business. The front page often carried stories in the
left- and right-hand columns signed by the star reporters Dudley Nichols
and Oliver H. P. Garrett — each of whom was to achieve success in Hollywood — and often, too, a humorous piece by Frank Sullivan, who had a
marvelous way of culling absurdity from the news. The Sullivan piece
was an almost daily miracle, greatly relished by John and the other
reporters; but the thing that pleased them most in The World was a
column called "The Conning Tower," conducted by Franklin Pierce
Adams, who signed it with his initials, F.P.A. Good literary usage and
style were important to F.P.A., who terrorized pedants and slovenly proof-
readers in a campaign for clear, idiomatic English. He pointed out such
errors as that committed by a reviewer who seemed to think Ring Lardner

should have titled his book *You Know Me, Al* and not as Lardner had written it, *You Know Me Al*. Adams took an interest in what authors had to say as well as their manner of saying it, and a brief favorable mention in "The Conning Tower" could help a new book as much as an entire review in the *Times* or *Herald Tribune*. All this was interesting to provincial apprentices like John O'Hara; but to him the most fascinating thing about "The Conning Tower" was its hospitality to contributors: on some days the "contribs" filled the column with verses, parodies in prose or verse, and satirical comments on topics in the news. John sent a number of contributions to F.P.A., and after many rejections, Adams began to accept an occasional item. O'Hara was less successful at *Life*, which was still a humorous magazine and not yet sold to the Henry R. Luce organization. The *Life* editors rejected a burlesque of Luce's new *Time* magazine:

Another Wedding, as Time Would Write It

As every schoolboy knows, when six young women of various sizes, heights, be-hatted, be-flowered, bedecked, followed by six men, bespatted, befuddled, march up the aisle of a church, there will be a wedding. No exception was the parade in St. Vitus's Church, 14th & Broad Streets, Philadelphia, last week, when 12 young men and women marched, officiated as bridesmaids, ushers.° Miss Mary Featherstone Myriyam Doe became the bride of Tareyton Edgeworth Chesterfield, 3d. She is the daughter of John Sebastian Doe,† famed warrant officer, onetime (1926–1926) Port Commissioner of Tallahassee. The groom is a vice-president, billing-clerk of the Corn City Bank, Manhattan. Potent William S. ("Bill") Vare, senator-elect, was not among the guests. He was not (see Time, August 11, et seq.) invited. Of the bride was said, "She looked . . . darling." One Vernon Gibson Hennessey,†† usher, tripped, fell, caused consternation, ushed himself out. Abe Bishop Meriweather Merry-wether, noted divine, performed the ceremony. Society attended, prominent being the hounds of the Astigmatic Hunt Club. The bridal couple, happy as is often the case, planned to honeymoon in the Maine woods (See Catastrophe).

— JOHN H. O'HARA

° Six bridesmaids, six ushers.
† Not to be confused with Actor John Do, to whom George ("Rhapsody in Blue") Gershwin wrote a song.
†† Yes, that's the one.

This bit of early unpublished work shows its author's alertness to current journalism, an interest he continued all his life. It also indicates O'Hara's knowledge of smart metropolitan society in the reference to the Astigmatic hounds, the joke apparent to those who knew that the Myopia Club near Boston was a fashionable hunt. There was nothing ignoble or abnormal about O'Hara's consciousness of a structured society, with money, education, and "family" among the materials from which it was put together. There were persons around the older towns and cities who traced ancestry to the earliest times, and considered themselves practically of noble blood. Many houses of by no means overpowering exterior had a coat of arms neatly framed and hanging in the front hall, usually next to the closet where one put wraps and overshoes. Pride of real or fancied descent could thus be inexpensively shown, but there were additional grandeurs to be observed, from St. Louis eastward, wherever the Civil War money had flooded in. This was the money that had twice rebuilt Yale College, each time with greater magnificence, and at New York City it would seem to have thundered across Central Park and crashed in a two-mile surf of stone mansions on the east side of Fifth Avenue. High society! It was a romantic conception for any inquiring young man, and also a subject of keen anthropological interest because it offered so many aspects of humanity to analyze and classify. Emerson had said, "We honor the rich because they have externally the freedom, power, and grace which we feel proper to man, proper to us." And most of the rich who considered themselves to be living in proper style could not march on without the aid of a supply train in which the sutlers were a strong and numerous detachment of dressmakers, tailors, milliners, barbers, bishops, games coaches, cooks, maids, butlers, chauffeurs, preachers, doctors, lawyers, headwaiters, headmasters, portrait painters, decorators, wine merchants, college presidents, fortune-tellers, band leaders, hotelkeepers, architects, jesters, and the society editors who acted as public relations officers for this fashionable army.

The *Pottsville Journal* followed other American newspapers of the time in promoting a society page under the direction of an editor who specialized in reporting upper-class activities around town. John saw that the trivial doings of established people had importance in the eyes of his publisher, and he also observed that the ladies of exclusive circles did not encourage the society page in its beginnings. The tradition of their mothers and grandmothers had been that a decent woman's name appeared in the paper only at her birth, marriage, and death. O'Hara's colleagues on the *Journal* helped to kill that tradition, and it fascinated him to see them going to work on it. The first *Journal* society editor was Eve Garrett, a graduate of Wilson College, who came for her employment interview wearing a tricorn velvet hat, unbuckled arctics, her brother's tweed topcoat, a red fox scarf, and white gloves. Miss Garrett was hired because of her family connections, but soon discovered that Pottsville ladies did not like the idea of her new society column. She had to dig for news in the department stores, where salespeople told her who had been buying party dresses, and at the railroad stations to see who was coming and going. It also was important to make a daily stroll up Mahantongo Street, and to visit the country club at lunch time. Kit Bowman inherited this routine, and found the socialites still reluctant to supply details on their lunches, bridge teas, and dinner parties. But the publisher was convinced his readers wanted such items, and O'Hara saw how Kit Bowman worked all night to describe the gowns worn by women attending the New Year's Eve Assembly. It was said in Pottsville that this dance had been organized prior to the founding of the Philadelphia Assembly; during the Prohibition years the ball took place at the leading hotel, and various subgroups reserved suites where the dancers retired to drink whiskey and champagne. Clint Sheafer was notably generous in his hospitality at the Assemblies, and at a certain time in the evening would take over the drums in the orchestra until the leader said, "Clint, if you don't mind — we're supposed to be doing a job here." The genial Mr. Sheafer would then return to the dance floor, or to his suite. After the ball he liked to bring members of the band to his home to play for breakfast guests, a procedure that O'Hara recalled when he wrote a story of threatening tension called "In the Mist." The Pottsville mountains turned into the Hollywood Hills for this tale, which expressed the same old anxiety of refusing to let The Party come to a natural end.

It was believed in the 1920s that reporters had front-row seats for the spectacle of American life, along with the privilege of examining the machinery that produced the stage effects. This was the doctrine of H. L. Mencken, who held that newspapermen should wake up each day grinning from ear to ear at the thought of the frauds and follies they would witness as they gathered that day's news. It was true that newsmen were allowed behind many false fronts: O'Hara knew a politician, for example, who burlesqued his own flag-waving speeches for the amusement of reporters in barrooms. The great company of Pottsville-Gibbsville characters in O'Hara's work, however, came as much from his social contacts and boyhood memories as from anything he saw purely as a newspaperman during his last three years in town. An unpublished article among the papers of his estate gives an idea of the teeming population of remembered humanity in O'Hara's mind. Under the title "*Character in Search*," O'Hara said, "I had to become a writer. All my life I have been rebellious. My father and mother were well educated people, and I am not. Put those items into an International Business Machine and out comes a card marked Writer. As a small-town boy who was sent away to (and from) second-rate schools I have come across quite a few characters in my lifetime, but I haven't done much about them." O'Hara then listed some unused characters, starting with an aunt "who was around one hundred and three when she died." In his youth O'Hara had acted as bootlegger for this old lady, selling drugstore gin at 100 percent markup. Then there was an Italian known as King Philip who lived down the hill. The name came from his resemblance to a commercial picture of the famous Indian chief, and children would follow him yelling, and scatter like quail when he turned in pursuit. O'Hara recorded that he fell down the coal chute at Schott's grocery when running away from King Philip after they had baited him. A joke among the boys was to ask if anyone had heard about the terrible murder at the corner of Second and Mahantongo: George Schott the corner grocer. The unpublished article also recalled Miss Rinehart, a Sunday school teacher who reproved the boys for tormenting a moron called Schwartzy, who had an obsessive fear of scissors. Schwartzy reacted with hysterics when boys ran after him making scissoring movements with their fingers. Another eccentric recalled from O'Hara's adolescence was a young gardener known as Eggy, the Boy Engineer, whose clothing was hand-me-down but of noticeably good quality. His recollection of Dory Sands, a street cleaner who ran for mayor, brought to mind a terribly earnest man without a chance of rising in the world. Then there was Jack Kantner, "a lush who touched my father, a dry, for five dollars." That night O'Hara and Kantner treated each other in a speakeasy and drank toasts of respect to the doctor: " 'Your father is a very fine man.' " This drunkard was locked up so often that some people called Schuylkill County Prison the Hotel Kantner. O'Hara remembered a young gangster called Screendoor, a Dutch hoodlum called Unie, and "a fat little tart who called herself Dardanella." On a mountain near town lived the family Dombrowski, who collected snakes, "fine healthy live rattlers and copperheads." Perhaps the oddest of these unpublished characters was "the inveterate first nighter" of Pottsville, a man known as Violets, who was always in his accustomed seat on Monday and Thursday nights when the vaudeville bill changed. One night the town boys saw him sitting in his car, and hailed him by nickname. Violets got out of the car and came over to them under the arc light. He said in his pansy voice, "You better thtop calling me that." The crowd quieted down in a hurry when Violets pulled a .45 Colt automatic and let them have a look at it. A few weeks later, Violets used the pistol to kill himself after accountants uncovered shortages at the factory where he was bookkeeper.

The newspaper job gave O'Hara a chance to look into the Schuylkill County underworld. What he saw could be frightening: One day he followed up a tip that someone had left the body of a murdered man beside a mountain road, north toward Shenandoah. O'Hara and a *Journal* photographer were the first to reach the victim; his throat had been cut, and not very long before, by the look of things. The county underworld lived by the same law of silence that big-city criminals observed: Pottsville gangsters murdered a prostitute who had threatened to complain to the district attorney about conditions in the trade. They beat the girl to death, soaked the corpse with gasoline, and left it burning in the woods. O'Hara and Bob Simonds knew an apprentice gangster called Peanuts McCormick, and acted as his seconds in an alley fight. Not long afterward, a speakeasy proprietor remarked to O'Hara, "They filled your friend Peanuts full of lead. He talked too much." The police had picked up McCormick's body on a back road, another unsolved homicide in Schuylkill County.

The murder of the prostitute was to figure in "The Gunboat and Madge" — about a bold man and a tough woman — and life in the Pottsville underworld also produced a story called "The Bucket of Blood," one of O'Hara's best. There was an actual speakeasy having that name, which O'Hara used in the tale of Jay Detweiler, a drifting, alcoholic ex-convict and carnival man who collapses of acute appendicitis shortly after he arrives in town dead broke. Jay has enough pride and integrity to take a job as orderly to repay the hospital for his emergency operation and the care he received while helpless. Then, through an arrangement with crooked police, he becomes houseman in a gambling joint, where he saves his earnings in order to better himself, and eventually puts aside enough money to take over the Bucket of Blood from its retiring owner. Soon "there was a noticeable improvement in the class of people coming in. The old customers stayed, but now the place began to attract the low-salaried white collar men who could not do without their booze; the artisans who had to have cheap whiskey; the pensioners who had nothing more left in life but the conversations and long silences they could share with other pensioners. The word had got around that Jay Detweiler served the cheapest decent drink in town." When better-class customers came to Jay's on a trial visit, they found that the place, "though bare of beautifying features, was scrubbed clean and smelt clean; in among the beer and whiskey smells was the smell of strong soap, and the smell of disinfectant in the toilet was almost overpowering, but reassuring." Jay had his meals brought in, and put the tray "at the end of the bar where he would eat the food standing up . . . he ate only because he knew how important it was for a drinking man to get some food in him." Jay believes that the booze will not destroy him so long as he just drinks with the customers — accepting a "steam," his private name for a drink, whenever asked to — and never takes a drink alone. At the end of the story, Jay quarrels with his girl, a whore named Jenny. He forbids her to solicit trade in the speakeasy: " 'No dice, Jenny. The whole place'd change.' 'It's nothing much now,' she said. 'Not to you, maybe.' 'Well what the hell are you so stuck up about it? They call it the Bucket of Blood, for God's sake.' 'Not any more. They used to, but not as much.' " The quarrel rises and Jenny leaves in anger. "There was no one else in the saloon, and he was pleased that that was so. He poured himself a steam and raised his glass and faced the door. 'Good luck, Jenny,' he said."

The sporting life of Pottsville centered at the Alco Restaurant, an all-night establishment on Norwegian Street near the Reading Station. Close at hand was the alley back of Centre Street, where some of the cellar doors were entrances to speakeasies. In this neighborhood O'Hara saw his Jay Detweilers and Ed Smiths, and the terrifying police officers like Charley Paxton who "gave it" to a thief in "The Victim." What he gave was a bullet in the head. The food at the Alco was pretty good; one could get a solid meal there at any hour, and be served on the late shift by a waiter known as Loving Cup because of his projecting ears. Disorderly conduct occurred from time to time in this haunt of night owls; O'Hara did not record what happened when the police detained him, but it was the result of some disturbance like the one he caused when he baited Loving Cup by dropping a succession of water glasses on the tile floor. Bob Simonds heard the night manager telephoning the cops, but O'Hara refused to leave until the sound of the siren drew near, and he ran out the kitchen door and into the car, which was parked in the alley. Playing the thankless role of the noisy drunk's friend, Simonds covered O'Hara with lap robes and drove away, letting his pal come up for air when they reached a place of safety. One night a girl in the Alco took O'Hara for a member of a visiting professional football team, a mean end who had made trouble that day against the Pottsville Maroons. O'Hara liked being taken for an athlete, as any young man would; the incident came up years later in "Fifty Minutes to Broadway," which told of a reporter who escaped from a small-city newspaper to Philadelphia and New York. The Maroons and their opponents at the Minersville field had the swagger of really tough men. They worked for low pay, and the club owners in the National Football League would have collapsed in apoplexy at any suggestion of hiring separate teams for attack and defense. The fans in the wooden bleachers at Minersville saw some remarkable play: O'Hara was a witness when Les Asplunth, formerly of Swarthmore College, kicked a football 105 yards, helped by the wind. In 1925 O'Hara accompanied sports editor Walter S. Farquhar to Providence for the Maroons' game against the Steamrollers, and to Chicago when Pottsville played the Cardinals for the national professional championship. Farquhar's account in verse told how

On to Chicago to win and fight went the proud little Queen of the
    Anthracite.
On the 6th of December in '25, a date to remember while you're alive,
As the zenith of Pottsville football might.

By the third quarter the Maroons had gained a 14-7 lead, and stopped a Cardinal rally:

Now yell, ye fans, with all your might, for the proud little Queen of the
    Anthracite,
For the turning point has come and gone and our day of victory is at
    dawn!
Far down the field rolled French's punt, and the peerless Berry has done
    his stunt,
Nailing the Cardinal's shifty back on his 30-yard line, right in his track.

Walter Farquhar recorded that "when the game was over and Potts-ville had won, the Maroons were hailed as champions in all the news-papers everywhere." A week later, the Maroons won an exhibition game against Notre Dame at Shibe Park, Philadelphia. At this the Frankford Yellowjackets (still owing a bill to the estate of Patrick O'Hara) claimed that the Maroons had invaded their territory. The president of the National Football League ruled this a just complaint, and penalized the Maroons by making their championship void. This he accomplished by scheduling post-season games for the Cardinals, so that they came out ahead of Pottsville in the revised averages. O'Hara agreed with Chris O'Neill, the Chicago manager, who said he did not want a championship which had not been won on the playing field. Walter Farquhar's verses proclaimed that

Pottsville's Chicago game is done and our rightful place in the sun is won.
Honor to those who spread her fame where ne'er before was heard her
    name.
And honor to those who forced the test that, sometimes, things at home
    are best.
Far in the future, looking back, when the day seems dull and the prospect
    black,
Inspiration we'll gain from the day that unfurled a champion team to the
    football world:
For 'twill always prove that there's one more fight in the little old Queen
    of the Anthracite.

O'Hara used the situation of a provincial editor covering an important sporting event in a large city when he wrote "Pilgrimage," in which he contrasted the decency and almost boyish enthusiasm of the small-city journalist with the malice and ugliness of the regular patrons at a sport-crowd chophouse in Manhattan.

Life continued at No. 606 as though there had been no change in the family finances. After the evening meal, Tom O'Hara liked to open the discussion by intoning: "Good evening, ladies and gentlemen. Now that we're in such a friendly group, let us discuss the important matters of the day." Then they would talk and laugh for half an hour or more. John was protective toward his brothers and sisters, and he worried about the effect of too much adult knowledge on the younger ones. Tom offered a witticism: "The widow's mite and then again they might not." John looked grave and said to his mother, in local "Dutch" diction, "This one knows too much already."

During this period, O'Hara sometimes stayed at home in the evenings, or came back early. On these occasions he would sit by a large table in the north end of the sitting room which opened out of the front parlor. The doctor's favorite leather armchair still stood in this front room, along with Mary's harp, the harmonium, and Mrs. O'Hara's desk. On the walls were some well-loved pictures, including a battle print by Meissonier, and a reproduction of the painting called "The Challenge" which showed a lion guarding a desert moraine. Another picture worth looking at was the famous Victorian posed photograph called "Fading Away," in which a dying young woman is propped in bed with sorrowing relatives at hand, while the baffled physician stares out the window in defeat. About half-way down the west parlor wall stood a boxlike chair in which John liked to take shelter. It was covered with heavy fabric having alternate stripes in two tones of green. This cloth had fascinated the children because it would change from dark to darker when you rubbed it and back again when you rubbed it the other way. With its three straight sides this chair gave a sense of refuge. In the sitting room, John created the feeling of a workshop around the long heavy library table. He had acquired an office model Remington typewriter with a carriage and cylinder of "billing" length, and found he could forget disappointment and frustration as he hammered this formidable machine in the lamplit room. Somehow he had already learned the professional's stratagem of sending suggestions to editors before writing an entire piece, but failed to draw an assignment or even an expression of interest. He suggested an article on what it felt like to vote for the first time to Scribner's Magazine, and got turned down. He wrote a number of sketches which he submitted to The New Yorker without success. When she saw these manuscripts returning in the mail, Mrs. O'Hara would say, "This will break his heart." Instead, the rejections made John keep at work, and stay with his campaign to crack The New Yorker, Scribner's, and Life. He could take comfort from the thought that although he had yet to appear in a national magazine, he was a working newspaperman. For besides the encouragement of an occasional acceptance from F.P.A., he read in "The Conning Tower" that "in spite of the fact that there are many persons in the trade of journalism who do their jobs poorly, or at best perfunctorily, there are still many who put a great amount of art into their work, and there are few newspaper jobs in which beautiful work is not possible." F.P.A. was a good model for O'Hara or anyone else, and he held up to provincials the light of New

York and *The World*. He pretended to be a curmudgeon, but was in fact a generous, civilized man. And so over his typewriter at home and at work on the *Journal*, O'Hara took pride in being a practitioner of F.P.A.'s trade, though still a novice, and on some days he must have felt reasonably happy. But at other times O'Hara had to deal with the emotional pain that came from lack of money, and because of his unsatisfactory relationship with Margaretta Archbald. After graduating from Bryn Mawr, this young lady began going abroad, and making trips around the country on projects of her own. She was frequently out of town and always out of reach, although both Margaretta and John were conscious of their interest in each other, and the value of their friendship. They discussed marriage, and may have considered themselves engaged, or on the brink of it, at one time or another. When Margaretta Archbald went to Montana to help the Flathead Indians as a social worker on their reservation near Missoula, O'Hara wrote to Martin J. Hutchens, editor of the *Daily Missoulian and Sentinel,* asking for a job. Hutchens sent back a letter, expressing regret that he had no job to give, and encouraging O'Hara to stay in newspaper work. The letter meant a great deal to a young man struggling through a low period in his life. During the time immediately after Dr. O'Hara's death, John suffered additional pain because he could not solve his family's problems — although nobody expected him to in the circumstances — and because he had seen how rapidly the lack of money could erode the dignities and even the decencies of life. Hawthorne had said it long before in *The House of the Seven Gables:* "In this republican country, amid the fluctuating tides of our social life, somebody is always at the drowning point."

The struggle to stay afloat as a Pottsville newspaperman was especially hard for John because the *Journal* came out in the afternoon, which meant that the staff had to be in the office and ready for work by seven o'clock in the morning. John had established his habit of working at night when not attending a party or talking with friends, which made it hard to arrive in the *Journal* office on time. John's direct boss, David Yocum, carried a burden of writing and copyreading in addition to the task of deploying a small staff to cover the city and county. Although he liked O'Hara, Yocum could not overlook his chronic lateness, which sometimes extended to half a day. At last Yocum reported to Publisher Silliman that he would have to let O'Hara go. Mr. Silliman said, "Dave, I was a great admirer of John's father. Would you consider giving him another chance?" The reprieve was granted, but O'Hara still found it impossible to keep office hours. The *Journal* management tried shifting John to the Tamaqua *Courier*, an allied paper in the nearby town of 12,000 population. After a few months, O'Hara returned to the *Journal*, and then left for good in early 1927, when it was said that he decided he

preferred to take a girl to a party rather than cover a dull evening assignment. Whatever the precise circumstances, he was not discharged in
anger: what it amounted to was that O'Hara had become tired of the
Journal, and the paper's management felt the same way about O'Hara.
He liked the *idea* of being a newspaperman; in those days, thanks largely
to F.P.A., daily journalism was a fashionable occupation for young people
who felt they had talent to develop, but it was never really O'Hara's work.

All the surviving companions of O'Hara's Pottsville youth have joined
in testifying that he took satisfaction in the company of friends. His male
cronies were mostly the members of the Purity League that had dismayed
the elders during Christmas holidays a short time before. O'Hara also
admired Edward Fernsler (Baar) Beyerle, who once had impressed him
by an act of courtesy at Joe Tomanio's speakeasy. A group of young men
had gathered there when a Negro woman came in and sat at a vacant
table. It became obvious that the proprietor was deliberately neglecting
this customer, whereupon Beyerle went to the bar and ordered a shot of
whiskey, which he set before the woman with the remark, "I think this is
what you want." That was the sort of thing that Julian English, the hero
of *Appointment in Samarra,* would do when so disposed.

There was serious talk at these gatherings, and Robert Simonds recalled
that "John, most certainly, commanded the moderator's position and
would put forth ideas for discussion." When John argued any point with
his friends, he could be "somewhat caustic, but never nasty." Though
fond of tavern debates, O'Hara was no sedentary barroom philosopher in
the making: he frequently was the first to suggest adjournment to the
Lakewood Amusement Park, or to one of the county roadhouses — the
Amber Lantern, the Stage Coach, the Log Cabin, and Papa Turin's. These
roadhouses fascinated O'Hara with their facilities for mysterious and sinister doings, and the possibility of providing rooms for the love trysts of
men and women who wished to be unobserved. Papa Turin was an interesting figure: he had the exotic quality of a Frenchman in a region
where Frenchmen were seldom seen. This roadhouse proprietor's face
seemed to be made of some hard kind of wood, and he served as physical
model for Foxie Lebrix, the Manhattan exile and maître d'hotel of *Appointment in Samarra*. O'Hara also took note of the roadhouse bartenders and
their skills. He found out that a first-class barman could work all over the
country, moving on when he wanted a change of scene, and that an alert,
intelligent man could augment his pay by serving drunks inferior liquor
for the price of good stuff and pocketing the difference, by short-changing
customers who were drunk or had their attention on women, by stealing
liquor to sell outside, and by falsifying the cash register. They had chances,
too, for adventures with women customers, and sometimes made extra
money by acting as agents for prostitutes. This was the retail liquor busi-

ness on a different level from the trade at the Bucket of Blood; O'Hara squirrelled away his knowledge and used the type of seasoned, worldly bartender against the roadhouse setting for "Trouble in 1949," and some time after that as a big-city character in one of the stories of his closing years, "It's Mental Work."

The members of O'Hara's group often enjoyed dancing at the pavilion in Lakewood Park, and they patronized another place of the same kind that was called Lakeside, especially when famous bandsmen like Paul Whiteman or George Olsen appeared with their musicians. The men and girls would crowd around the bandstand, undulating to "Blue Room" or "Moonlight on the Ganges" while colored lights played over them. It was during this period that Clinton Sheafer gave a dance at his house with music by the entire Olsen orchestra. The traveling bands fascinated O'Hara, for he perceived that the sidemen, as the musicians called themselves, led lives completely different from those of average Americans, or even from troupers on the Keith time or the Columbia burlesque circuit. He knew their consumption of marijuana, alcohol, and cocaine, and understood the dedication that some of these tired young men carried within themselves to a music, indescribable and perhaps unattainable, that went far beyond the commercial product they delivered to their leaders and their public. In the early 1960s, O'Hara would bring such a doomed and haunted traveling musician to mind when he wrote "I Spend My Days in Longing," which dealt with a suicide-bound bass player who was listening for a note so low he could never reach it, and " 'gave himself' " until his thirty-fifth birthday, " 'number thirty-five in the old book.' " He says to a pal, " 'Maybe I'll be playing Harrisburg. It would save me a lot of trouble. What the hell is that river? The Susquehanna?' "

One evening O'Hara and some friends were waiting in intermission time at Lakeside when Paul Whiteman approached them and asked how he could draw the crowd back onto the pavilion floor. O'Hara said, "Play 'Kamenoi-Ostrow.' " He was referring to a semiclassical piece in the band's repertoire, the sort that used to be played from behind potted palms in hotel lobbies. Whiteman looked at him closely, and decided the young man was serious. He then mounted the podium, called to the sidemen, "Number twenty-three in the book — medium tempo," kicked the platform twice, and they sailed into it. One minute later, a respectful audience stood forty deep around the bandstand.

O'Hara's circle of intimates ranked Whiteman and his band as the most popular, followed by the Dorsey brothers — who had been born in Shenandoah — Benny Goodman, and Red Nichols. They admired Olsen, Count Basie, Gene Goldkette, Ted Lewis, Fletcher Henderson and the Casa Loma Orchestra. The Scranton Sirens also drew enthusiastic crowds. At the end of an evening they would play a waltz for two minutes in complete darkness. Then lights up and they hammered out a fast number, known as a flag-waver, to send the dancers off the floor in a good humor. The Sirens featured an Irish singer named Jack Gallagher, who had lost an arm in the war. Gallagher was a natural musician with a fine voice, which he used to great effect in such numbers as "I Know That You Know," "What'll I Do?" and "Remember." O'Hara wrote of a singer who resembled Gallagher in "The Pioneer Hep-Cat." The narrator of this story is the hep-cat, an elderly editor trying to speak the language of a high-school audience and interest them in recalling the days when big bands came to Gibbsville. The singer he tells about lost his arm in a mine accident instead of at war, and the story comes to a logical conclusion in an empty dance pavilion.

The dance pavilions of Schuylkill County were crowded all summer long in the late 1920s, but when winter came, the center of attraction for many young people was Patrick J. Maher's Hall in Shenandoah. The half a dozen Pottsville youths for whom O'Hara served as moderator would often increase to fifteen or twenty and set out in four or five cars for the weekly dances at Maher's establishment. A lady who had lived in Shenandoah as a girl recalled that "the Friday night dances at Patty's were unique, as was his whole place, for it was far more than a dance hall. It occupied a four-front frontage on North Main Street and was three stories high. On the left of the entrance was Patty's saloon and a long mahogany bar where the boys sipped their beer. To the right was an ice cream parlor where the ladies used to congregate to exchange local gossip. In between was the entrance to the ballroom, at the top of a wide stairway down to the dance floor itself. This gave the girls an opportunity to make some effective entrances. I'll never forget those moments at the top of the stairs, when, if you were popular enough, you held up both hands, indicating that you were already fully engaged for the evening."

Years later, Patrick J. Donovan of Shenandoah recalled that Mr. Maher's wife Elizabeth, "a charming and beautiful lady," acted as "a sort of unofficial chaperone" for the dances. Mr. Donovan remembered that "the winter social season started with the annual Snow Dansante which was held on the Monday following Christmas." With two bands alternating, the ball started at ten P.M. and continued until six o'clock next morning. Some delightful girls attended these dances. The most startling beauty among them was Mary Shuck, a girl of Slavic background who had shortened her last name from Shuckeleitis. Mary Shuck was recalled as "the Zsa Zsa Gabor type, only more so." Eventually she went to Europe and married a French count. In Shenandoah, O'Hara made one in Mary's train of admirers, and he later used her as a model for a Wanamaker department store salesgirl of fatal beauty in his unproduced play *The Way It Was*. There were other pleasing girls at the Maher dances: still to be recalled with admiration are Isabelle (Izzy) Muldoon, Helen Elliott of the dimples and sparkling eyes, Kitty Coogan, Peg Graham, Honey Meluskie, Peg Walsh, Mary Serocca, and Kitty Cuff. Among the young men who danced with these girls were Marty McGuire and Ed McGrath, Bucky Cox, John (Lemon) Moon, John Garrity and Barney Wentz. From Coaldale came Tommy Boyle, Bob Rudner, Jim Sharp and Ken Miller; from Girardville came Bill (Irish) McDonald, Berny Ginley and Cyril Kilker; Ray Pepper and his sisters Anna Mae and Mary came from Ashland; Frank and Adrian Donohue and their sister Helen drove over from Mahanoy Plane; and one would also see on many an evening such smooth dancers as Red Kirk, Tippy O'Brien, Jim Coogan, Johnny Kitlock, Frank (Puss) Kleta, Syl Sylvester, and popular Mike O'Hara, John's uncle who was the original Michael's son and the doctor's brother. All these people and many more enjoyed coming to Maher's, and John with his group of Pottsville friends spent hours in their company.

Although they found the music and the girls so much to their liking, the members of O'Hara's delegation did not always receive a unanimously warm welcome in Shenandoah. Some said the visitors were "nothing but a crowd of country club sports," while others called them "Pottsville snobs." Robert Simonds recalled that "in all honesty I must state that many of the young men in the county resented O'Hara because he got along too well with the young ladies. The ladies found him most attractive." Not all the ladies — the same popular girl who remembered her ballroom entrances also had a clear recollection that "John carried a chip on his shoulder toward the entire world. There were those who indulged him, but I did not. I'm sure that didn't bother John." This lady remembers O'Hara turning up "slovenly and unkempt" at the Shenandoah dances. The impression came from the prevailing "collegiate" style, which John may have carried to excess. It was a manner of wearing one's clothes that called for socks falling around the ankles and hats battered into shapes that would frighten a dog. On one occasion O'Hara bought a hat at McMahon's in Pottsville, took it outside, and began to jump on it. "Please, John," said Mr. McMahon, "if anybody asks you where that hat came from, don't say you got it here." It was believed that the wearing of a coonskin coat transformed this beaten-up appearance into high style. O'Hara never deposited his coonskin in Maher's checkroom, but always left it hanging in the bar. Critics of his conduct said this was to avoid paying a dime, but it seems more likely that O'Hara wished to keep the garment on display. The bar patrons were unfavorably impressed, and one night the waiters had to throw out a drunk who swore he was "going to piss on that God-damn coat of O'Hara's." On another occasion, someone "spoke out of turn" and a number of local young men followed the Pottsvillians as they left the hall. Robert Simonds hurried his crowd to their cars, while Patty Donovan of Shenandoah stepped in front of the pursuers. He called out, "Don't spoil the evening, fellows — go back inside," and the local lads turned back.

Not everyone in Shenandoah took umbrage at O'Hara's style of dress, or wanted to run his crowd out of town. There were men and girls over the mountain who found him "considerate, charming, witty, and understanding." And O'Hara was not always in the depths of depression about his inconclusive friendship with Margaretta Archbald. There were times when he played the field, and along with other young men he danced attendance on Mary Shuck and her almost equally dazzling sister Adele; on "a beautiful brown-eyed blond from Frackville," Jean Taggert; on a girl he called "the Captivating Creole"; and on another young lady who was referred to in honest admiration as "the Wonderful Wench." Like other young men, O'Hara made an impression that varied according to the temperament of each girl to whom he paid attention. Some took him more seriously than others; one girl O'Hara sometimes escorted home had the idea that her house was not grand enough, and always got out of the car at the Lutheran parsonage, where she could enter the vestibule, which was never locked, and wait until O'Hara drove away. He was much too observant not to be aware of this, and it struck him as a bleak sad thing. On the way back to Pottsville, having picked up his car-pool passengers, O'Hara would give them a thrill by taking the car out of gear and coasting six miles of twisting road, and they sang a great deal on the way home. John was partial to a fraternity song that Fred Hoefel brought from the University of Virginia, about "D.K.E., the mother of jollity, whose children are gay and free." This was to be sung by Sam Ainsley while taking a bath in "The Next-to-last Dance of the Season," which O'Hara wrote sixteen years later. They also found it amusing to sing a combination of words to the same tune from Mercersburg Academy and Dartmouth College, in honor of Simonds: "Dartberg, our Mercersmouth we'll sing to thee, fairest of colleges," and so on. But according to present memories, O'Hara's favorite song in those days was "When Hearts Are Young." In 1971, Mrs. Maher held a reunion for surviving patrons of the Shenandoah dances, and gave each of them a crystal prism from the cut-glass chandelier that had illuminated the ballroom.

Now that his dominating father was dead and sincerely mourned, John was not always entirely comfortable in his relationship with his mother. It was true that they could talk in a friendly way, as they often did with the others over the supper table. Mrs. O'Hara could delight John with her reports on people and things in Pottsville, and he listened with pleasure when she told him about the meetings of the woman's club. But no more than the doctor himself could Mrs. O'Hara tolerate intemperance, and it was impossible to live in the same house with John and not be aware that he often stayed out late, and patronized the bootleggers. If Mrs. O'Hara failed to observe this, people were willing to tell her. There was an anonymous letter, for example, with a Shenandoah postmark, reporting that John was drinking in that town. Scorning the anonymity, Mrs. O'Hara still knew that the accusation was correct. This was in August 1927, and O'Hara wrote to Robert Simonds toward the end of that month that, "You missed a friendly little reunion on Sattidee night. R. Boone came home for the weekend, so Fred, Baar and I obtained two quarts of Dusel oil and repaired to the country club where we did injustice to it. The occasion was more or less of a reunion for me also, I having been in Lykens for two weeks. I got home Thursday with $10.55, which my grandmother had given me. After a vain attempt to get a ride to the lake I gave up and Jim Bailey and I proceeded to do the town. We did. After getting a good base of Scotch at Mart Motley's* we went places, all places, until five a.m. An interesting feature of the proceedings was a high Mass which was sung at St. Joe Brennan's church, corner Norwegian & Logan, by Father Bailey, Cardinal O'Hara, the Rev. Dr. McCarthy and one unidentified person. It must have been great. Fortunately we knew all the Latin. I went home in a taxi, with the 55 cents and one cigaret in my pocket and was greeted by the mater. The conversation:

— Where have you been?
— Nowhere.
— What have you been doing?
— Nothing.
— Who was with you?
— Nobody, now lemme go sleep . . ."

O'Hara liked to refer to Margaretta's father as A'chie, mimicking his manner of speech. But the same letter showed that Mr. Archbald was a friend to the unhappy young man who meant something to his daughter, as John continued, "I tried admirably to get in Yale. Had A'chie write to the Dean, who was a classmate of his. The result was some very pleasant correspondence for all concerned and the information that my chance of going to Yale was about as good as my chance of going to Heaven . . ."

The problem was how to get out of Pottsville, even if for only a brief time. A chance for temporary escape had come through John's uncle in the Immigration Service, as the same letter related: "Had a letter from the purser of the Leviathan asking me to make formal application at 45 B'way for a job on that boat. That is the extent of my job-getting thus far. I'm mad at the world and if I had the guts I'd Take the Cowardly Course and jump in the lake. Disgusted and disillusioned at 22, that's me . . . when you're broke and tired of it all we'll hit the highways for the south

---

* A Pottsville speakeasy.

. . . Marg's uncle, Albright Archbald, the one from Buffalo who made a couple of million out of gold mines, is one of about 50 men who have bought this island and developed it for themselves only. They all belong to a club and in order to live on the island one must belong to the club. Try and get in. My idea is, there must be at least two jobs at a place like that. Certainly there is a lot of dough. But the talk is off if I can get on the Levi or with the United Fruit. Bumming is the third alternative, but I really mean it. If you'll go, we'll be off whenever you say. A loaf of bread, a jug of wine, and how! . . ."

Shortly afterward John made his trip to Europe, though not on the *Leviathan*. He recorded what happened next in a letter to a friend, written in September 1968: "In September 1927, having recently returned from a trip to Germany (I was a steward on the old Washington of the U. S. Lines), I went up to Penn State to visit a friend of mine and go to a football game. This friend was half owner of a restaurant, and fed me, and was a member of Phi Gamma Delta, which gave me a bed. One word led to another and I found myself headed for the Great West with $5 in my kick, thumbing my way and sponging off people until I landed in Chicago. There I took a room at a fleabag at 600 West Madison Street and began looking for work. I got no work. I hung around Chicago until it got too cold — me without an overcoat — and I thumbed my way back to Pottsville, Pa., having spent my $5 and another $5 my mother sent me, and forming a lifetime impression of Chicago as a very cold place to be without an overcoat . . . The low point was Chicago. I even applied for a job as groom, and the guy who had the job to give said, 'What's a young fellow in a Brooks suit trying to get a job as a groom for?' 'To eat,' I said. He didn't believe me, and wouldn't hire me. The only friend I had in Chicago was in the insurance business, and he was no help except that he and his wife supplied the free booze. It was fun, but no fun, if you see what I mean. I was just as broke in New York a year later, but Chicago was a totally unfriendly place to me, and it was awfully cold. In New York I once went for three days with nothing to eat, but I didn't lose hope. In Chicago I never had any hope, and though I have often been there since, in the chips, it is not my town. I am too much of an Easterner for it . . ." While in Chicago, John spent $1.65 for admission to a lecture by Richard Halliburton, whose adventurous travels were of interest to a large public at the time. O'Hara's comment on Halliburton was, "He speaks in English, which is different from speaking English."

Back in Pottsville, John was now fully determined to break away. He wrote to Robert Simonds in Allentown, inquiring, "Do you want to go to Central or South America with me?

"There, in words of one syllable (for the most part) is the question.

"To be more explicit: I think I can land a job with the United Fruit

Company as overseer in one of their Latin American plantations. With the possibility of inducing you to come along I told my uncle, who is trying to get me the job, to make it for two . . . There's always a hitch and here's the hitch to this prospect. While the Plantations are made as liveable as possible, still they are not to be confused with the estate of T. Suffern Tailer at Newport. There is a constant stream of Americans going back and forth from the plantations: quitting, accepting jobs, dying, living and whatnot. The jobs are kept in circulation, and no mistake.

"A year ago I don't think I'd have considered the possibility of taking such a job. Now, however, since I've made the original break, I'll go lots of places I would have passed up heretofore. For one thing, I've decided I'll roam the world (or as much of it as I can) over until I'm twenty-five. Three years on the high seas and in the low valleys doesn't seem to me to be a bad idea. It would be at least as good as college, I believe. Everyone goes to college; not everyone leaves the comparatively good old U.S.A. . . .

"There is still another possibility — and that's all it is. The Firestone people want men to go to Liberia, on the west coast of Africa, to take jobs as overseers on the rubber plantations. They pay more money and offer a better trip, but God knows why they ought to. The weather in Liberia is o-u-t as far as white men are concerned and the family has done a lot of putting-down-feet at the idea of my taking such a job. However, if worst came to worst, it wouldn't be the very first time I didn't entirely acquiesce to the family's desires . . .

In October, John wrote some figures to show how he, Bob Simonds, and "Baar" Beyerle could set up an apartment in New York if each earned a salary of $30 a week. He submitted the estimate in a letter figuring one-third of: $100.00 rent, $48.00 to a cook for dinner and cleaning, $8.00 for laundry, and $90.00 for food as $81.66 2/3 "total pro rata share" per month by O'Hara's arithmetic. Take this from $120.00 salary and you had left $38.33 1/3, divide by four and the result is "$9-plus for cigarets, carfare, liquor, etc., per week." He added, "The thing to do is go, no matter how. I simply must get out of Pottsville, or I'll buy a gun and use it. Yes, it's come to that. I've never been so unhappy, so little enthusiastic about life, and it's all the fault of this place, or of myself . . . Once we've made the break we'll be better off. We'll at least have the satisfaction of knowing we did make the break . . . Now is the time for all good men to come to the aid of this certain party . . . "

In December 1927, Mr. Archbald put O'Hara's name on the list of job seekers at the Yale Placement Bureau in New York, and a few days later, O'Hara had news for Robert Simonds: "I have to report that I am about to go to Mammon. That is to say, I am about to go to work. The Yale Club wired me last week, and asked if I wanted a job on the New Yorker —

'Manhattan smart-chart,' Time calls it — at $35 a week. The job is reporter. So I wire the Y. club for an appointment, then received a letter telling me to write a letter of application to a Mr. Ingersoll and ask him for an appointment. It is too early yet to make any positive predictions, but it looks as though I will be drafted into the great army of the employed. But have no fears, my boy. What I will write will be the type of thing I like — impressionistic, satirical, interesting, not humdrum . . ."

There was further news in this letter: "I have fallen in love again. It all happened this way — strengthening my alarming tendency to accept Determinism. Mary O'Hara, Fred, Reilly and I went to Reading last night to a Junior League show and dance. I didn't want to go but the family practically insisted. We got all lushed up on the way down and were in fine shape when we got to Rajah Temple. Well, whom did I see but a girl I met only once, years ago, but who always has been an inhibition of mine . . . She's beautiful and I fell. I danced with her no less than 10 times and when the thing was over she invited me to a dance at her house on the 29th. [Her mother and father] are Mr. and Mrs. Reading — the kind of people who give $10,000 to community chest drives. In other words, if my feelings are requited I will be just where I was but 35 miles away! Apropos, wouldn't it be fate-freighted if I were to work in New York and Marg there and me calling her up once a week or so, and saving my pennies for visits to Reading! Thank God I can still laugh, for I'd otherwise go crazier . . . I'll be famous in two years — not world-famous, of course, but at least well-known — but I'll need you to prod me along and laugh at me . . . More later . . ."

Nothing came of the suggestion that John apply for a staff job at *The New Yorker*, and like the boy in "Christmas Poem" he abandoned his dreams about the great family in Reading. But he did not give up his determination to get away from Pottsville. He had been talking for a good while now about leaving, and the time had come to roll or pass the dice. O'Hara decided that the place to be, with or without a job, was New York City. At Christmas 1927 his sister Mary said she was ready to leave for New York and start her career. John asked when she planned to go, and Mary named a date in January 1928. John said, "I'll be there ahead of you." And he was, by one week.

THREE

MALLOY IN MANHATTAN

O'HARA TOOK SHELTER with his aunt and uncle in East Orange, and started to look for work in the city. New York air in those days was bracing and stimulating, especially for young men just arrived from the provinces with the intention of becoming "at least well-known" through some kind of journalism. Nine newspapers came out every day, plus the excellent *Brooklyn Eagle* at the other end of the Manhattan Bridge. Two new national weeklies had fought their way to solvency after some tentative introductory months, and an electrifying aura of success pervaded the offices of *The New Yorker* under the editorship of Harold Ross, and *Time, the Weekly Newsmagazine,* which had been started by two young Yale graduates, Briton Hadden and Henry R. Luce. In the new Graybar Building on Lexington Avenue, one could find the offices of *Vanity Fair,* a monthly magazine conducted by Frank Crowninshield, who looked like a distinguished elderly character man in a British drawing-room comedy while he got out a publication dealing with books, the theater, the arts, sports, politics, and metropolitan life as the expression of a civilized attitude. And once a month, H. L. Mencken came up from Baltimore to join his colleague George Jean Nathan in editing another issue of *The American Mercury,* a magazine that encouraged new writers, and welcomed controversial pieces from established ones, while it ridiculed pedants, boobs, politicians, and bad writers in Mencken's uproarious slapstick style. Mencken and Nathan had made an important discovery: the German language is comical. It appealed to the low humor of their readers when they denounced the eminent Professor Paul Elmer More as a *blutwurst* and a *katzenjammer,* and one could never again take the victim seriously. Those who set themselves above Mencken, or attempted to patronize the editors of *Time* or *The New Yorker,* did so at their peril. Irreverence toward dignitaries and high officials was in the spirit of the day, and nobody feared even the President himself, for it was known that Calvin Coolidge was happy to mind his own business and would certainly never order anyone blown to pieces from the air.

O'Hara had been trying to get his name into the correspondence page of *Time,* with as little success as had greeted his offerings to *The New Yorker.* He now took occasion to answer a woman who had chided *Time* for referring to the size of Charles A. Lindbergh's feet. This made the letter column on January 23, 1928:

> Sirs: Says Grace Gordon Cox, of Boston, under LETTERS in the Jan. 9 issue of TIME ". . . there will never be a man on your staff big enough to stand in Lindy's shoes." Why not give Robert Emmet Sherwood a job?
> — JOHN H. O'HARA

The editors added: "Robert Emmet Sherwood's feet fill size 13 shoes. He is editor and cinema critic of *Life* and author of *The Road to Rome,* successful comedy." It was O'Hara's first appearance in a New York magazine.

Scott Fitzgerald had written in "May Day" that "never had there been such splendor in the great city, for the victorious war had brought plenty in its train." Splendor was the precise word for the midtown area that had burst out with a profusion of elegant shops, tall business towers, and palatial hotels. O'Hara noted the new Commodore, the Biltmore, and the Roosevelt, and at 50 Vanderbilt Avenue the Yale Club rose in twenty-four stories, handsome and assured, with its dining room windows at the top surveying the entire city. Nearby and just around the corner from F. R. Tripler & Co. was the Béarnaise Restaurant, whose proprietors had dealt with the Prohibition law by disregarding it, except that they moved their tables into the basement, and it was here that Jay Gatsby of Long Island entertained Nick Carraway and Mr. Wolfshiem under "the Presbyterian nymphs on the ceiling." One block to the west, Fifth Avenue traffic obeyed lamps that glowed from bronze towers of admirable design, each having a windowed compartment high above the pavement from which an officer could look down the street to his colleague two blocks away. There was only one drawback in the general scheme of things for O'Hara, and that was the difficulty of getting into Manhattan from East Orange. As they still do, railroad passengers coming in from north Jersey had to make the last stage of their journey by way of the Hudson Tubes. It was even more inconvenient going back at the hours O'Hara liked to keep. More than once he went to sleep on a late train and went all the way to Summit, where he had to wait for the next train down. Nevertheless, O'Hara came into the city every day in search of work, making his first attempt to find a job at the World Building on Park Row.

In 1928 it would be impossible to believe that *The World* and the golden dome of its building were to disappear within a few years, for the paper still justified its reputation for high quality, editorial courage, and zeal in exposing frauds and rascals. These were expensive virtues, but it was supposed that the paper had sound financial backing from its sister publication, *The Evening World*, which shared department store and national advertising with *The Evening Post, The Sun, The Telegram,* and William Randolph Hearst's flamboyant *Journal.* For an out-of-town news-paperman looking for work, there was no question that *The World* was the first place to try — and it was surprisingly easy to do this. All you had to do was walk past the lobby guard with an air of knowing what you were about, and get off the elevator at the local news floor, which was high up under the golden dome. Only a few steps from the elevator, at a desk on a raised dais, sat the city editor James W. Barrett, with an arched window at his right looking out over roofs and towers. And you simply approached that desk and waited for Barrett to acknowledge your presence, which he would do by putting down his pencil and looking at you with an air of courteous patience. The great city editor and ruler of journalistic fortunes was a tired-looking middle-aged man; like those of Walter Pater's Mona Lisa, his eyelids were a little weary. He would wait for the aspirant to speak, and the dialogue would go something like this:

"Mr. Barrett?"

"Yes?"

"I wonder if you need a man on your staff. I have put in four years with the *Toledo Blade* (or the *Norfolk Virginian,* or the *Salt Lake City Tribune,* or whatever). I can handle general news, write heads, and read copy."

"I'm sorry, I have nothing for you."

"Thank you, Mr. Barrett. Perhaps I could try another time."

There would be no answer to this as the editor turned back to his work, but the applicant would go away feeling oddly elated: at least one had tried, and spoken to the great man, and set foot in the city room of *The World.* Men with longer service on larger papers than the *Pottsville Journal* were turned away. And yet, if Barrett did need a man, he would sometimes put a chance applicant to work on the spot. But he did not do so with John O'Hara. O'Hara also visited the office of Paul Palmer, who edited the Sunday feature section of *The World.* Mr. Palmer was not much older than John, and gave him a sympathetic interview, but no job.

On March 7, 1928, O'Hara wrote to Robert Simonds in Allentown that he expected to start on the following day as a reporter on the *Evening Post.* It had resulted from a recommendation by F.P.A., who had invited O'Hara to come in and talk to him after a telephone conversation about possibilities of working on *The World.* Having been turned down by Palmer and the city editor, O'Hara was glad to accept the suggestion that he visit F.P.A., and found him "editing the weekly diary and [he] said as I entered 'Hello. Sit down.' Then forgot about me in the excitement of editing. Suddenly he began to read aloud, that stuff about the power of print. We discussed that and then he said 'How'd you make out.' I told him no soap. He said, 'Sunnovabitch! Isn't it hell?' So we talked some more and abruptly he halted, picked up the phone and demanded a connection with a Mr. Mason or Mr. Renault at the *Post*. 'Julian? This is Frank Adams. Say Julian I'm sending a boy up to you and I want you to put him on, hear? He's probably better than anyone you have there now anyway . . . Oh, a perfect gentleman . . . Can he *write?* What a question! Very well, three-thirty, thanks.' Then he turned to me and described Mason: Yale, about 40 and inclined to be snobbish but a good fellow really. So he asked me more questions: Where do I send my stuff? Where *is* Pottsville? Had I tried the New Yorker? 'What? Oh, hell! *I'll* talk to Harold Ross. Don't worry. *I'll* get you somewhere. Now get the hell out of here and come back Monday. I'll see Ross tomorrow and Sunday.' So I saw Mason and he wants me on, but doesn't do the actual hiring himself. 'Come back Monday and I'll take you to Renault. I'm sure everything will be all right.' So this time tomorrow I may be . . . [O'Hara's dots]

"How about F.P.A., huh? Never saw me before and did more for me than anyone but you would do. With him cheering for me I'll get along. Remember what I told you about 1927 or 1928? This time next year I'll *be* somebody.

"Now plan to come to N.Y., Bob. I'll need your snicker to keep me from getting a swelled head and I'll need your solace when things break not to my liking. Why not be a newspaper man? You have a better supply of gray matter than most and the rest isn't hard if you can learn to feel that way. To *that* degree Harry Silliman was right. The above address [the McKees' in East Orange] is correct. — Doc."

A sudden change of plan, not unusual for that period, put O'Hara to work on the following day, but at the *Herald Tribune* instead of Julian Mason's paper. F.P.A. had arranged a fast interview for John with Stanley Walker, the bright young city editor of the *H T*, who thought John looked and talked like a man who had the makings of a metropolitan reporter. O'Hara was pleased to accept the offer, for while each paper was steeped in tradition, and a good place to begin, the *Herald Tribune* came out in the morning, and the hours would be easier for John to keep. That at least was his thought, but Walker assigned him to day rewrite, a desk job that would require his presence at nine A.M. on working days. The *Herald Tribune* had an ironclad Republican editorial policy which did not prevent Walker and his staff from producing a knowledgeable, civilized, and well-written sheet. When John reported for work, he found that the *H T* city room was like the *Pottsville Journal*, only larger. There were the same cigarette-scarred desks and their clutter of proof sheets and clipped-up newspapers, with paper ripped from the teletype and streamers of ticker tape casually tossed in the direction of gigantic wastebaskets. O'Hara felt at home, and wrote to Bob Simonds in a state of euphoria. His friend replied in a satirical vein, and O'Hara immediately answered on *Herald Tribune* stationery: "Did I sense faint sarcasm in your being glad to know the great O'Hara? I grow cynical as the number of my days decreases, being now 23 years old and so forth.

"Of course I'm going ahead. A year from now people will be glad to have loaned me money and proud to have insulted me and, a few, rewarded for calling me friend. Right now I am a little happy. My pay check was for nine dollars above the salary agreed upon. Shall the morrow bring an adjustment and disillusionment? I have got drunk, slightly, with the city editor and the asst. c.e. went to the trouble of coming down from his desk to congratulate me on a story, but nine dollars! . . . Through F.P.A.'s kindness I am a potential contributor to the New Yorker once more. This time I have more to base my hopes on. I have been told to write a profile of Al Smith, Jr., and asked to contribute other stuff. It will be at least a month before I am able to call myself settled, so far as selling stuff is concerned. But I keep prodding myself with a remark the city ed. made the other night; 'In this town the sky's the limit for you.' Please pass the size 10 Herbert Johnson . . ."

The extra that O'Hara thought he saw on his paycheck was a fortnight's advance of the $4.50 expense money that the *Herald Tribune* granted all reporters. Though welcome, the additional money made it all but impossible for a man to file an account for more, unless he could produce a chit signed by Stanley Walker himself. The editor was thirty years old, always kept a fuming pipe clenched in his bony Texas face, and had come to the paper in 1920. His observations of New York furnished material for two popular books, *City Editor* and *Mrs. Astor's Horse*. He would have been the man to make a star New York reporter out of John, except that the motivating works inside O'Hara were not sending him in that direction. At the *Herald Tribune*, John was like the young men who go to college for the friendships rather than the course of study, and like most of those young men, he soon flunked out. Before his dismissal, which came in a little over two months, O'Hara found his way to a speakeasy called the Type & Print Club, upstairs in a loft building near the *H T*, where editorial and composing room employees mingled every night from eleven P.M. until they felt like leaving. O'Hara was standing at the bar in the Type & Print when he heard someone say, "Mr. Hutchens," and an intelligent-looking young man made reply. This was John K. Hutchens, starting on his career as a literary critic, and son of the Montana editor who had written kindly to John. Introducing himself at once, O'Hara began a lifelong friendship. In his stay at the *Herald Tribune*, O'Hara also met Joel Sayre and Richard Watts, Jr., at that time the paper's cinema critic. When it came to the working part of the job, O'Hara proved himself a tidy hand at the desk chores of daily journalism, and he showed interest in the "stringers" or part-time correspondents in small cities and towns throughout the country. He could readily imagine what those people had to contend with, and spoke of them sympathetically to Joel Sayre, who like Donald Ogden Stewart and James Thurber had come to New York from Columbus, Ohio. Sayre was a man of enormous talent, from whom charm radiated like heat from a fire in an open fireplace, and he further impressed John because he had attended Williams College and taken an Oxford degree.

The writing required of O'Hara was easy, for it involved nothing more complicated than paraphrasing items of the previous day's news so that they could get by one more time on the inside pages. This O'Hara could do, but he failed to rouse Walker's enthusiasm with his performance as a reporter outside the office. He did have a moment of glory when he went to cover a fire on a cold March afternoon, wearing the coonskin coat, and was mistaken at the scene for William Randolph Hearst, Jr. Later on a legend grew that O'Hara began ordering the *Journal* and *American* men about with imperious directions, you take the back, you cover the front, and so on. The story goes that senior reporters from the *Herald Tribune* arrived while O'Hara was marshaling Hearst forces into line, and astounded them by dispatching the supposed publishing heir to a nearby lunchroom for coffee. Whether or not he actually took temporary command of Hearst reporters, John O'Hara was not to remain much longer at the *Herald Tribune*. But he was still there when he at last managed to land a contribution in *The New Yorker*. On April 9 he received a check in payment for a two hundred-word sketch called "The Alumnae Bulletin." O'Hara cashed this draft for fifteen dollars at Bleeck's, the lunch and dinner speakeasy favored by the *Herald Tribune*. The German proprietor handed over the money without hesitation, but was heard to ask another bar patron, as he put the check away, "*The New Yorker* — what in hell is *that?*"

O'Hara was justified in the satisfaction he felt at making this sale: it was his first step in the right direction. Magazine and contributor were made for each other, and each had appeared at precisely the right time in the other's life. O'Hara wrote about it to his brother as soon as he was told of the acceptance. Tom was almost fifteen, and beginning to experiment with writing, and so he took special interest in John's experiences. The letter said: "I have sold a piece, at last, to The New Yorker. I mentioned it in Ma's letter so you've probably heard about it by this. I don't know how much money I'll get for it and as a matter of fact I don't really care an awful lot. The point is that I've broken in. The idea in this willitch is to get yourself known; the rest will follow after that. I had a long interview with Harold Ross, editor of the N.-Y.-er, on Friday and he sounded very encouraging. He's a queer duck. Funny stiff German hair and a long gap between his two front teeth. Like F.P.A. he swears all the time and when I say swear I mean swear. I saw F.P.A. the other day. We had a nice chat about this and that. Needless to say I think he's quite the boy.

"I am feeling rather vague at this writing. Last night I was on a party with Dick Watts, the movie critic, Frank Sullivan, The World humorist, Don Skene, the boxing writer for the H.T.* and later, Noel Busch of *Time,* Lynne Segal of *Time* (a girl) and many others. We started at the Artists and Writers club [Bleeck's], which is really a speakeasy near the H.T., and then went to Tony's, another speakeasy where all the celebrities go. There I met Frank Sullivan, whose stuff you may have seen in *The World.* He gave me a big howdedoo and congratulated me on my stuff, etc. From there we went to Chez Florence, a night club, and had much fun. I met lots of celebrities, near-celebrities, and people like myself. Among the former was Tommy Guinan, Texas Guinan's brother, and Charles Brackett, who does theater reviews for the *New Yorker.* It was great fun and I had a lovely time. Only a few venial sins, too.

"Well, this must come to an end. Not long, of course, but it's something. Be a good boy and don't forget your morning prayers and don't ever kick your mother. With love — John."

In the sentence about Frank Sullivan congratulating him on his "stuff," O'Hara achieved an uncanny resemblance to Ring Lardner's Jack Keefe writing to his friend Al about receiving praise from seasoned players. Frank Sullivan was the kindest of men and undoubtedly gave cordial encouragement, but unless he recalled items in "The Conning Tower," he could hardly have seen any of O'Hara's writing at this point, for John had received no by-line in the *H T*, and the *New Yorker* sketch was not to appear until almost a month later, on May 5, 1928. By this time, O'Hara and the *Herald Tribune* had parted company.

John wrote to Robert Simonds on the twenty-fifth of April, urging him to apply to Walker for a job, although he had been "fired from the Trib by this same Stanley Walker, because I was drunk most of the time and was never very punctual, but we are still friends. He's young — about 30 — and very intelligent. He's a Texan and inclined to be querulous . . . Write to Stanley, mentioning that I told you he and I had been conversing about you. Confirm (within whatever modest bounds you like) the nice things I said about you. Tell him you've done a little reporting with me (he thinks I'm swell and had tears in his eyes when he fired me) and that you've lived off and on in New York, know the streets, the location of important and

---

* Skene maintained that the most beautiful words in the language were, "We can sleep all day tomorrow."

semi-important places. (They're sick and tired of kids who don't know where the police station is.) Be brief, but not too brief. Be snappy, but not too snappy. Above all, just merely dash off the fact that you went to Dartmouth. (They're griped with nice young Rosenbergers-Frankers* who made D.K.E. at Yale.)

"In the meanwhile, read the Trib. Notice that instead of saying 14 W. 46th St. it says 14 West Forty-sixth Street. Although it *does* say 14 West 146th Street. Notice the absence of Mr. except on the editorial page or in dealing with Coolidge or some other personage. Notice that you don't say secure when you mean obtain — all things which I shall point out to you if Stanley says come ahead. Stanley knows that I couldn't have a friend who would be dull or nit-witted, and I really would not be a bit surprised if you got a job. But don't expect any money. $25 is what you may count on. $30, if you're lucky. We can live together and keep down expenses."

There was a touch of Jack Keefe in this letter, but even more interesting is its revelation of O'Hara's inner anxiety which he was attempting to cure by giving advice to a friend in the provinces. He had sent instructions in college politics and fraternity lore from Pottsville while that friend was a student at Dartmouth. Now we find John giving directions on how to succeed at the *Herald Tribune*, a paper from which he had been discharged after failing in his probationary period. O'Hara closed this letter by revealing the true state of affairs: "I have just come off a three-weeks' bender, during which I fell down a flight of stairs, was punched in the face, had a mild attack of d.t.'s and spent about $400 . . . maintaining a residence (if such it may be called) at 107 West 43. I expect little difficulty in getting a job and if I should land somewhere this week, I'll try to rope you in too. Things aren't at the best for me just now, but I'm hoping I'll land this week on some daily rag so that I can tell the family that the reason I won't be home for Xmas is because I'm a new man on a paper and will have to usher in the newborn in back of a typewriter. I am expecting a New Yorker check this week, which will carry me over . . . My best to Coaldale† and always to you. I told Stanley you're my best friend. — Doc."

Whether or not his description of the three-week debauch and its expenses was entirely accurate, there is no question that O'Hara experienced violence just before Walker separated him from the *Herald Tribune*. A few years later, O'Hara gave an account in *BUtterfield 8* of the trouble that overtook Weston Liggett at the hands of a policeman and a bartender in a speakeasy that was located, like the Type & Print, up the iron-trimmed

---

* Referring to the Rosenberg tailoring firm and Frank Bros., New York shoemakers.
† Home town of Simonds' fiancée.

stairs of a loft building. In this scene Liggett talks when he should have
kept quiet, the cop slugs him, the barkeep trips him up and they kick him
downstairs. Outside in the street, Liggett

> had no hat, he could hardly see, his clothes were a mess of dirt and phlegmy
> spit that he had picked up on the floor, he was badly shaken by hitting his
> coccyx when the cop pushed him, his nose was bleeding, his body was full
> of sharp pains where they had kicked him.
>
> To be deprived of the right to fight back when you have nothing left to
> lose is awful . . . The only thing was, he was facing the street now, and it
> was too damn much trouble to turn around, and inside of him he knew he
> did not have the strength to climb the stairs. If he could be transported up
> the stairs and inside he could fight, but the stairs were too much. He heard
> the door upstairs being opened, then closing as his hat landed at his feet.

Although that description came from experience, Weston Liggett was
not modeled on John O'Hara. The author put himself into this novel as
James Malloy of "The Doctor's Son," now a young reporter in Manhattan
who likes to drink and stay up late, isn't greatly concerned about getting
to the office, and makes a point of being sensitive and Irish:

> "We're Micks, we're non-assimilable, we Micks. We've been here, at least
> some of my family, since before the Revolution . . . I show a sociological
> fact, I prove a sociological fact in one respect at least. I suppose I could
> walk through Grand Central at the same time President Hoover was
> arriving on a train, and the Secret Service boys wouldn't collar me on
> sight as a public enemy. That's because I dress the way I do, and I dress
> the way I do because I happen to prefer these clothes to Broadway clothes
> or Babbitt clothes. Also, I have nice manners because my mother was
> a lady and manners were important to her, also to my father in a curious
> way, but when I was learning manners I was at an age when my mother
> had greater influence on me than my father, so she gets whatever credit is
> due me for my manners. Sober . . .
>
> "Well, I am often taken for a Yale man, by Yale men. That pleases
> me a little, because I like Yale best of all the colleges. There's another
> explanation for it, unfortunately. There was a football player at Yale
> in 1922 and around that time who looks like me and has a name some-
> thing like mine . . . The people who think I'm a Yale man aren't very
> observing about people. . . . In fact, I just thought of something funny."
> "What?" "Most men who think I'm a Yale man went to Princeton them-
> selves."

The prospective *New Yorker* check that O'Hara mentioned was for his
second sale to the magazine, a sketch called "Overheard in a Telephone
Booth" which appeared in the next issue after "The Alumnae Bulletin."
Between them the sketches contained the germ of O'Hara's method, and

indicated the point of view that he was going to hold throughout forty-
two years of writing. In "The Alumnae Bulletin," which was signed John
H. O'Hara, a young woman is talking as she reads about the doings of
her classmates, for whom she hasn't one good word. The piece came to a
point which was almost imperceptible, but the writing had a virtue of
naturalness that made the reader hear a speaking voice. The telephone
booth sketch, also signed John H. O'Hara, was twice the length of his
first contribution. Again we hear a voice, this time that of a young man,
who is upbraiding a girl for going out with someone else: "Such a banal
ending to a grand affair. A telephone conversation. Why, it's funny. It
really is funny. But of course this won't be the ending. You know it won't
be. You said so. You said, 'You'll call again?' But will I? Will I? I wish
to God I didn't know." That was James Malloy talking and the
effect of bitter jealousy and resentment stayed in many readers' minds.
In those days the prosperity of the 1920s was approaching its crest, and
The New Yorker carried so much advertising that the editors needed
many short pieces to fill what they called the back of the book. An editor
named Wolcott Gibbs had been marking O'Hara's contributions "Possible
B," meaning back-page filler, and "The Alumnae Bulletin" finally got in
on page 101, along with the advertising of a tearoom that offered home
cooking, fifty cents for lunch and one dollar at dinner. The telephone
booth sketch started on page 77, next to an advertisement for the Sherry-
Netherland — "Entirely removed from rumbles and vibrations . . . These
tower apartments are truly New York's most delightful way to live" — and
continued on the next page beside some copy for the Roosevelt Grill.

Shortly after the publication of "Overheard in a Telephone Booth,"
Frank Sullivan suggested to John H. O'Hara that he drop the middle
initial as excess baggage. It was gratifying to hear Mr. Sullivan talking
as though he felt sure O'Hara's work would be seen frequently in the
future, and less than a month later a third contribution to *The New
Yorker* carried the author's name with the middle initial omitted. It was
to appear on 264 more *New Yorker* pieces during O'Hara's life, the last
one a story called "How Old, How Young," on July 1, 1967.

The first sketch signed with no middle initial was entitled "Tennis,"
and it fell short of being a story, or even an anecdote, yet its 250 words
again gave the impression of a living voice. It was a monologue without
quotation marks, and made one conscious of a self-satisfied hearty type
congratulating himself in a locker room. We are told that tennis is the
game, nothing like it:

Course the best part of any sport as near as I can make out is the
shower. A good sweat and come into the locker-room all hot and bothered and step into a warm shower and get it gradually to real, needle-

point cold — Boy! there's nothing in the world like it. . . . No, not even
that. [O'Hara's dots]

So I'm getting in my tennis now, while I'm young, because the pace
I live you can't expect to have the same kind of heart when you're forty
that you do now. Time enough for golf when I'm forty or so. Course I'm
not implying it's an old man's game . . . [O'Hara's dots]

The suggestion to write an article on Alfred E. Smith, Jr., was one that
New Yorker editors made to all new writers, and it produced no results.
O'Hara continued to submit short pieces to Gibbs, who ran them in the
back of the book with encouraging regularity. Two sketches appeared in
June, one of them an echo of Pottsville Christmas parties. It was called
"Do You Know —?" There is no description of any kind as the characters speak: " 'Did I hear you say you went to Yale?' 'Uh, yes. I was at
New Haven,' " and so on until the young man and woman have laboriously
reached the identification of a common acquaintance. This brief scene
depended for interest on naturalness of speech and unspoken comment
on the dullness of the speakers. Sinclair Lewis had published *Babbitt* six
years before, and had fascinated the country with the conversation of
George F. Babbitt and his friends, which was taken by some readers
to be an accurate reproduction of common speech; but it was not, for
Lewis deliberately heightened the absurdities and burlesqued the attempted profundities of the characters' talk. O'Hara was working in a
lower key, very close to actual speech, as he would continue to do in his
career. His special gift was an ability to make readers feel that he must
have been standing by with recording equipment. He produced that effect
by a finely tuned ear for what Gibbs called "the broken and inconsecu-
tive rhythms of living speech, and the shrewd detail that suggests the
whole." On September 15, *The New Yorker* published a longer effort, "A
Safe and Sane Fourth and the Part Played by the Orange County Afternoon Delphian Society." The piece ran over a thousand words and earned
O'Hara sixty dollars, which was gratifying, for that sum could go a long
way in 1928. Gibbs's support had enabled this contribution to appear in
September, although its subject was a bridge party held to raise money for
the encouragement of safety on the Fourth of July. We hear a woman
giving an account of the proceedings in the manner of Robert Benchley's
"Treasurer's Report":

Well, the bridge netted us a total of — let me see. I have it here somewhere. A total of fifty dollars. No, that was the bill for the rental of
the hall. Oh, here it is. After deductions for all expenses were made,
including thirty dollars for cards; five dollars for Mrs. Kelly, who sweeps
up the Masonic Temple, two dollars tip to Moriarty, the policeman, who
so ably directed traffic and let us park in front of two fire plugs at either

end of the Temple; eighty-five cents for a window pane which we broke when someone bumped a ladder against it while fixing up the decorations; five dollars for Miss D'Andrea, of the high-school art department, who made that big cardboard firecracker and painted the sign, "Death to the Deadly Firecracker"; eleven dollars and sixty-four cents for stamps and telegrams, and fifty dollars for the hall; after all deductions were made, we found we had cleared, all profit, over and above *all* expenses, forty-eight dollars and eighty-five cents. (Applause.) Mr. Symthe, when he heard about how much we had made, said he would gladly give us the dollar fifteen to make it an even fifty dollars. (Laughter and applause) . . .

O'Hara was drawing from life, from his mother's mimicry of bores at her ladies' club in Pottsville. All told, O'Hara wrote fourteen Delphian sketches for *The New Yorker,* enthralling Gibbs and Harold Ross with "the beautiful precision of his ear." But the editors at last perceived the danger of tiring the readers, in the accurate representation of a complacent bore haranguing a captive audience. However, there was no question about publishing "The Cannons Are a Disgrace," in which the indefatigable Delphian says that:

we might well hang our heads in shame [over] the condition of the cannons in Memorial Park . . . There's something funny and yet at the same time grotesque about a bird's nest in the mouth of a cannon. Of course, there are some, I suppose, who might hazard the conjecture that it is a good symbol: a sign of peace when the birds build their nests in the mouth of a cannon. But it doesn't appear that way to me. Those cannons were loaned to us by the government after the war. They didn't give them to us; they just loaned them, and it's up to the community to take care of them. If the community as a whole neglects them, then it's up to the more public-spirited individuals or organizations to see that we are grateful to the government for the use of those cannons . . . [It develops that] when we first got those cannons from the government, they still had the camouflage painted on them. It was very attractive at the time, because we were used to it, but when we decided to have a World War group at the monument, it didn't look quite nice to have a splashy cannon here and there with the formal bronze statues, so to properly harmonize everything we gilded the cannons. They look very nice and neat that way, just like the statue of General — uh, that general on horseback at the Plaza. But time's ravages had their effect on the gilt and it's peeling off in many places . . . The statues have lasted — look at the Civil War group. But the gilt on the cannons just hasn't been able to withstand the elements. So we ought to do something about *that,* too.

This high point in the saga appeared on October 19, 1929. By that time, O'Hara had demonstrated his mastery of the Delphian material. Indeed, he had written a perfectly controlled piece, which *The New Yorker* had published on October 20 in the previous year, called "The Coal Fields: Being a Report on Actual Conditions in the Pennsylvania Coal Fields, Read Before the Orange County Afternoon Delphian Society." O'Hara's terrible woman is informing "Madame President, and sister-members" about a fact-finding expedition which "began with a rather silly little mistake. Not knowing the difference between hard and soft coal or anthracite and bituminous coal, I set out for Scranton and remained there two weeks, investigating conditions in my own humble way. There were conditions aplenty in Scranton, but it seems that the center of activities was not Scranton, but Pittsburgh. Scranton is in the anthracite or hard-coal district, and Pittsburgh is in the bituminous or soft-coal district, so I eventually took a train for Pittsburgh . . ." Banalities pile up as the lady tells how she then "accepted the offer of a Mrs. Conklin to stay at her home. She is a very charming person and has a lovely home. We soon found out that we had something very much in common, for believe it or not, both of us had boys at the Culver Military Academy Summer School in 1923! And in her boy's room — his name is Walter — there was a group photograph, just a snapshot, and both of us picked out our boys . . ." The investigator talks "with none other than Mrs. Clarence J. Yocum, whose husband is assistant to one of the vice-presidents of the Allegheny County Coke and Coal Company . . . The things Mrs. Yocum told me were almost unbelievable! The arrogance of some of the coal miners in refusing to leave their homes when they were evicted, and their strikes and so on. Really, dear friends, it is astounding . . ." Inanities are poured out until the speaker ends, in the manner of Robert Benchley, with some remarks about her satisfaction at having in her humble way done something "to clarify the doubt that surrounds the general impression of conditions in the coal fields." This piece landed with deadly precision on its victim, and produced the speaking voice with touches like the visit to Mrs. Conklin's "lovely home." The next O'Hara piece in *The New Yorker* was "The Boss's Present," which appeared on December 1, 1928, and introduced a new set of characters, the clerical staff at the Hagedorn & Brownmiller Paint Company. Again we hear a single voice, which is that of the office manager, who reveals himself as a company toady of the most repulsive kind: "The little trouble and effort that I go to in making this annual purchase is worth it because after all F.W. is one of the best little bosses in the world even if we do have our little disagreements now and then about matters of policy. I've been here twenty-two years and I hope I'll be here twenty-two more. That's the way I feel about F.W. and I'm only too glad to go to any little trouble I can, just to make him understand that he's got a loyal bunch of helpers around here . . ." There was a touch of Lewis in "one of the best little bosses in the world," and a suggestion of Lardner in the utter baseness of the office manager. But the total effect was O'Hara's own, which he achieved by his plain, lucid approach to the unnamed manager, which made readers feel that there was no author concerned with the sketch. The editors understood what O'Hara was trying to do; they might have derailed his career if they had insisted on some concluding point. But they allowed O'Hara to let his piece run down into absolute vacuity as the manager bumbles on, "If you fellows will authorize me to go ahead, I'll just collect the five dollars pro rata from each of you next Friday, which I guess everybody knows is pay day (at least we married ones do with families). Then after I've collected the money I'll go out and buy a lighter like I have described. I'll get it from a perfectly reputable firm, you may rest assured, so that if we aren't satisfied, why we can go back and get something else of equal value or even have our money refunded in case there is nothing equally desirable in stock at the place I have in mind. We'll have at least two more meetings before this is finally settled . . ." By this time many readers — some of them professional writers — were aware of these pieces signed John O'Hara, and were fascinated to watch the unfolding of a noticeable and individual talent. The theatrical producer Jed Harris said that here we might have the greatest natural playwright in America. Harris was known to emphasize his opinions to the point of overstatement, yet it was true that O'Hara had begun to create characters, though as yet he involved them in little or no conflict. Something could be done dramatically with the woman talking at the club, and the office manager in "The Boss's Present" speaks of Mr. Fessler, a miserable drudge, and Mr. Cleary, who is feared because of his family connection to the owners. The tension betwen Cleary and the manager is felt throughout the subsequent Hagedorn & Brownmiller sketches, the manager never daring to bring the enmity into the open. It was a fine picture of mean business politics and rivalry, especially well indicated by "The New Office," in which the firm moves to Park Avenue quarters and Cleary commandeers the desirable room that the manager had marked for his favorite, Mr. Auchmutty. "The New Office" ran in *The New Yorker* on May 17, 1930; O'Hara's first sketch that might be called a story had appeared as early as January 12, 1929, under the title "Fifty Cent Meal." Using the monologue of a young man eating at a lunch counter, O'Hara here introduces two other characters — the man's old girl and her husband, "a guy named Walter J. Morgoff" — and tells the story of the girl's unsuccessful attempt to break away from the dreariness in which life has trapped her. The story is told with such economy that one might take it to be merely another sketch, but it is more. And at the end, the narrator has no sympathy: "Funny how you get over a girl like that . . . [O'Hara's dots] Oh, why yes. Just let me have another cup of coffee and some of that pie a la mode." The cadence in this ending resembled that in the close of Lardner's celebrated "Haircut."

O'Hara made a significant advance in *The New Yorker* when a Hagedorn & Brownmiller sketch called "Halloween Party" put him for the first time in the front of the book. The piece — presenting the horrors of office social life — filled page 36 except for twelve lines of verse and a small cartoon. The date was October 26, 1929. O'Hara then returned to the position of a "B" writer until October 18, 1930, when he again came to the front, sharing page 28 with twenty lines of verse by Ogden Nash. This O'Hara contribution, which he called "Old Boy," described a former Yale athlete: "Six or seven times a year his name gets into print with the names of Snake Ames, Ted Coy, Pudge Heffelfinger, Eddie Mahan, Walter Eckersall, Jim Thorpe." It develops that the man earns only twelve thousand dollars a year, and does not seem to be completely alive except on the big football weekends. He experiences his keenest satisfaction when Grantland Rice asks his opinion in the lobby of the Taft Hotel in New Haven prior to a game. The piece represented something new in O'Hara's work, for the narrative is not carried by a conversational voice, but in the impersonal tones of an omniscient author. On March 29 of the same year, O'Hara had departed from monologue to do some scene setting in "Conversation with a Russian." He shows two girls and four young men at a table in a nightclub. The girls and their partners get up to dance, leaving two of the young men, one of whom is a Russian. The American is a pretentious fool, the Russian talks sense. And the girls come off the dance floor in the most extended movement of characters on scene that O'Hara had so far permitted himself except in "Fifty Cent Meal."

In the week of March 22, 1930, preceding the publication of "Conversation with a Russian," O'Hara had presented a character study called "On His Hands," first of the magazine pieces to be later appraised as worthy of appearing in a book. "On His Hands" had the assurance of O'Hara's mature years and the economy and certainty of touch that distinguished his best work. Here we meet "Tod" Sloane, a Princeton undergraduate who is telling his friend Blakeley about how he spent the holidays. Sloane is of the same kidney as Teddy Choate in "Christmas Poem" — he knows the rich and great better than anyone else does. "Not only Elinor though. The whole family. My Old Man and Mr. Tucker went to college together, and I went to prep school with Brick Tucker . . .'" But instead of visiting these important friends in Chicago, Sloane says, he detoured to Dayton, Ohio, where he was interested in an attractive girl, but found himself baffled in trying to determine whether or not her family was socially okay. He reports that he decided not to encourage this girl, for fear of having her "'on his hands,'" and continued his trip to

Chicago. " 'Don't let anybody kid you about Chicago. It's a swell Princeton town. Naturally I played around with Elinor Tucker while I was there . . .' " In the end, Sloane's vanity is completely revealed when the reader learns that this little monster is not going to encourage Elinor, either. No use getting these girls on your hands.

O'Hara had written to Bob Simonds that by approximately the ninth of March 1929 he would be established to such a degree that people would take pleasure in having loaned him money, that some would feel that they had gained a kind of distinction from having insulted him, and that he would be in a position to reward certain discerning ones who had called him friend. When that date came, it could be said that O'Hara had achieved much, though not what he had predicted as to insults and personal rewards. But he had created the Delphians and the odious office manager of Hagedorn & Brownmiller, he had written "The Coal Fields" and "Fifty Cent Meal." A year further on, in early March 1930, the *New Yorker* pieces had reached the level of "Conversation with a Russian." And in one year more, by the spring of 1931, *The New Yorker* had carried five more pieces that merited publication in his first book of collected stories. These included "Mary," which had its origins in Shenandoah, and "The Man Who Had to Talk to Somebody," about a member of the Class of 1898 at Yale: ". . . the richest class they ever had at New Haven. Huh. You've heard of Payne Whitney, of course? You've heard of Payne *Whit*ney." Unfortunately Mr. Whitney's classmate has served a penitentiary term and is always fired when the bosses find it out.

Convincing though they were, the Delphians and the paint company people began to tire their author; Gibbs said that O'Hara was "bored to madness with the Delphians long before he got through with them, and continued to write about them only when he needed money which, in those precarious days, was practically all the time. Even while he was turning out Delphians as briskly as a doughnut machine, he was meditating the next step." O'Hara took the next step in the issue of May 7, 1931, when he introduced Mr. Duffy, chairman of the Greens Committee of the Idlewood Country Club. Duffy is contentious and complacent, a male version of Mrs. Uhlein, the Delphian voice. O'Hara's growing *New Yorker* public found promise of good things in "Revolt Among the Women," in which Duffy tells the club governors how to deal with the protest from Mrs. Yangst of the Women's Golf Committee about a recently posted notice, "Women are requested not to use the golf course on Saturday afternoons, Sundays and the afternoons of legal holidays, unless they are playing in mixed foursomes." Duffy's harangue shows him to be a pompous fool and an envious, gossiping vulgarian. Readers were pleased when Duffy came back two weeks later, this time to lay a complaint before the House Committee, in "Ninety Cents For a

Sardine." Duffy says that what he is "chiefly innarested in is the welfare of the Idlewood Country Club . . . Bluntly, then, and wasting no words on the matter, our restrunt prices are entirely too high for a family country club — entirely too high — I tell you frankly I have heard plenty of unfavorable comment about the restrunt charges . . ." We learn that when the members of a visiting golf team were entertained:

Practically all of the Minnawasket crowd ordered fillay minyahn for dinner. Now last year I remember distinctly that fillay minyahn was two dollars, and you got side dishes of two vegetables with it for that price. This year it's fillay minyahn, two dollars; peas, forty cents; Julienne potatoes, forty cents. And are the portions any larger, even if the price is higher and you're charged for every vegetable? No. The portions are the same . . . Ice cream. Neapolitan ice cream, about as big as a pack of Luckies. Twen-ty-five cents. Let me see. I have some other items written down here that I copied from my bill. Oh, here's one. Aw derve, consisting of a bedraggled sardine, half a hardboiled egg — plain hardboiled egg like they have at Easter; nothing fancy — and some kind of thing I never saw before but tasted like some kind of anchovy paste with a toothpick ground up in it. That's what they call aw derve, and for that, ladies and gentlemen, you and I and all the rest of us are billed ninety cents.

Elaborating his grievance, Duffy says he might as well join "one of those ritzy places if we're going to pay the same prices . . . I've sounded out a lot of the others and they feel the same way about it . . . Ninety cents for a lousy little sardine just because it goes by the name of 'aw derve' — I'll eat at home before I pay those prices again."

On June 6, Duffy made another appearance in "Help the Younger Element," protesting the extravagance of the "younger marrieds" who had raised $650.00 because "they wanted to get this Bobby What's-His-Name's orchestra from some New York night club" for a holiday dance. Duffy thinks $150.00 is enough for any orchestra, and he suggests the balance be invested in rain shelters on Number Four and Number Sixteen. Three weeks later, the same voice is heard coordinating the activities of the "chairmen and chairladies of the various committees" for the Fourth of July festival at the club where "we golfers have seen to it that the skyrockets will be aimed away from the golf course, so we won't have to worry about the fairs and greens being littered up with debris. The skyrockets will be aimed at one of those farms east of the fourth fairway." This sort of thing was already being recognized as prime O'Hara, and the Idlewood Country Club could have had a long *New Yorker* run, but the author wrote no more about its dances and its Greens Committee.

The piece in which Duffy talked about fireworks was O'Hara's sixty-

eighth appearance as a contributor to *The New Yorker*. For the past three
years up to this June of 1931, O'Hara had been in the magazine almost
every other week. Those were years on *The New Yorker* when such
consistent exposure of a name in its pages was enough to make its owner
a moderate celebrity. Granted that the O'Hara contributions were mostly
brief, and sometimes slight, even the lightest had his individual mark.
It was true that somehow or other Yale continually appeared, like the inevitable intrusion of King Charles's head in the writings of Mr. Dick.
Nevertheless, O'Hara's editors and many of his readers decided that he
was a serious writer working toward a consistent view of life, and developing a method peculiarly his own. It might well be admitted that in
the beginning he owed something to Lewis, Lardner, Benchley, and Sullivan. But it was also clear, after his first few months of *New Yorker* contributions, that O'Hara was expressing himself, by speaking with many
voices. He had found and followed this method by instinct, working at
it in the face of rejections from the time he started sending sketches to
magazines from 606 Mahantongo Street. Speaking of his consistent production, John had said to his brother Tom, "Instead of keeping a diary, I
write stories." He saved some rejected pieces, but almost always destroyed unfinished work. A few of the false starts can be found among
the papers in his estate, and on reading them, one wonders what it was
that caused the writer to lose interest. For that was his method in composing stories, to start and keep on to the end unless for some reason he
felt that the people talking were no longer worth listening to. O'Hara did
not classify his stories, like Scott Fitzgerald, as having varying degrees
of merit, from merely commercial up to serious work. On the contrary,
O'Hara regarded everything he wrote as part of one statement. And
in the early work up to June 1931, he had composed some of the basic
themes of that statement: much of life was grotesque; decent people
were few and almost always flawed; wherever you looked in the world,
you found that fools and bullies had managed to take control. It was not
a comforting view of life, but it sustained O'Hara, and he needed something to help him hang onto sanity during those first three years in New
York. It was a period of struggle, and sometimes of trouble, in which he
suffered a great deal of emotional distress, and caused a considerable
amount of it in others. Even today one can feel the strength of O'Hara's
determination to gain success in the "willitch" of New York. His approach
differed from Scott Fitzgerald's first attack on the city: Fitzgerald had
taken a dreary apartment far uptown, tried to support himself working
at an advertising agency, and for a while was one of his own "young
nameless men" consumed with longing as he walked the streets. O'Hara
had done his anonymous walking of Manhattan streets while he was a
schoolboy at Fordham. And now, because of his acceptance at *The New*

Yorker, he had achieved a name during his first year in town. The problem was to reach working terms with life itself and the other people in it. Through James Malloy, O'Hara showed that he recognized his acute sensitivity and his tendency to go on the defensive, at times, when there had been little or no attack. Pulling back today for a long shot of O'Hara's first years in New York, one thinks of Conrad's man who said, "I've had to strike and fend off. I've had to resist and attack sometimes — that's only one way of resisting — without counting the exact cost."

After leaving the *Herald Tribune,* O'Hara looked into the possibilities that *Time* magazine might hold for him, and found that the prospects were good. He had met Noel Busch at Tony's, as he reported in his letter to Tom. In the late spring of 1928, Henry Luce asked Busch to recruit some writers for the magazine; one of the first applicants was O'Hara, who came in at the suggestion of the Yale Placement Bureau. Busch was interested to hear that O'Hara had not, in fact, "been at New Haven," and introduced him to Newton Hockaday, a *Time* editor recently on the board of the *Yale Daily News.* Hockaday said, "You're the man who wrote in about Lindbergh's shoes." John said, "I wondered how you found out the size of Sherwood's." Hockaday answered, "It was easy. I called him on the telephone." Busch thought O'Hara would be able to write for *Time,* and offered him a trial at sixty dollars a week, with substantial raises in prospect if all went well. Among other things, Busch was concerned with the magazine's sports department, which he hoped O'Hara could take over. O'Hara liked what he heard, and agreed to give it a try, for the regular salary would be welcome.

Trying out for *Time* put O'Hara into a separate community of people whose most demanding work came on Saturday and Sunday, with days off on Tuesday and Wednesday. Nothing much happened on Thursday except making up the preliminary story list, so that the *Time* schedule gave those who worked it an odd feeling of leisure when everyone else was busy, contrasted with a bout of work over the normal weekend. The offices of *Time* were in the Bartholomew Building on Forty-second Street east of Third Avenue, and the neighborhood was quiet and deserted through the long laborious Sundays. Noel Busch gave O'Hara one piece of advice: "Go easy on *Time* style." This startling manner of writing was largely the invention of Busch's cousin Briton Hadden, the magazine's co-founder, who had picked up the use of classical epithet from Homer, and the double-barreled adjectives from Carlyle. Having attempted to burlesque the style at 606 Mahantongo Street, the new writer accepted his instructor's advice: the identifiable *Time* items by O'Hara are sober, factual, pedestrian. John found his desk at *Time* a convenience for writing letters and *New Yorker* pieces; he shared an office with two women, Lynne Segal and Priscilla Hobson. Lynne Segal married Wells Root, a *Time* editor who went to Hollywood and a long career writing movies; Priscilla Hobson married Alger Hiss.

O'Hara's mentor at *Time* was a young man who personified a number of things that O'Hara believed to be important. The son of Briton Niven Busch, who had made a fortune downtown before he was thirty, Noel Fairchild Busch had come up to Princeton from St. George's School, and gained election to the editorial boards of all three major undergraduate publications in his freshman year. Three years before, his brother Briton Niven Busch, Jr., had arrived in Princeton to light up *The Nassau Literary Magazine* with the most accomplished verse and prose ever to appear in that publication. Niven Busch had gone to the infant *Time* and *The New Yorker*, and Noel followed him, not waiting to take a degree, like a college athlete who turns professional before playing out his last season on the varsity. The Busch brothers were tall, handsome, and assured in manner, apparently looking on the world with kindly tolerance or benevolent contempt. The attitude was precisely that of *Time*, and to some extent that of *The New Yorker*; O'Hara made careful observations of each brother, and learned to do a lifelike imitation of Noel's genial drawl, and Niven's incisive enunciation. Harold Ross had told James Thurber that he found something disturbing in Niven's walk; the fact was that Niven Busch had a secret job at *Time*, while also writing between two and three thousand words a week for *The New Yorker*, and so was constantly on the move. Niven Busch wrote stories, fact-pieces, and "profiles" for Ross like an immensely efficient and dependable machine, putting some touch of excellence and individual distinction into everything he did. He set O'Hara an example, if one was needed, in the production of high-grade copy and the meeting of deadlines. But his final example John did not follow: after writing enough *New Yorker* profiles to be published in a book called *Twenty-One Americans*, Busch went to Hollywood and entered on a serious moving-picture career. He also wrote such successful novels as *Duel in the Sun* and *California Street*. At the time they met, neither young man had any particular interest in the cinema, and O'Hara might not have been pleased if he had known how Niven Busch sized him up: "He looked as though he had cultured his appearance to represent a Yale grad, Class of '27, fast going to seed, the J. Press suit was stained and spotted, shirt slightly frayed, never quite a clean shave, deliberately uncured or early-morning-acquired hangover stance. He had one great piece of luck at *Time* — Henry R. Luce detested him." Niven Busch further recalled: "My mother had a pad in East 72nd Street, to which I had a key. I used to use it in the summer months when she was away and I was living in the city. My brother Noel used it too. In a fit of generosity, hearing that O'Hara was without a flop, he had a key made for John. O'Hara used to sleep on the living room couch. Several keys were made for him. He kept losing them. Finding them gone, he devised different ways of getting in. One way was to pile a crate on top of a garbage can, then leap up and grab the bottom of the fire-escape ladder, pulling it down to street level. Then he would climb up the ladder and bang on a window. Another method was to press the bells of tenants sleeping in other apartments. They would press the buzzer letting him in. Noel and I would not. However, we were used to his ways, we left the front door unlatched. Once in the building, he could get to his couch. The arrangement seemed a strain for all concerned. After a week or two, it came to a natural termination."

By the early autumn of 1928, it appeared that O'Hara was going to establish himself at *Time,* where Briton Hadden thought well of him, even if Henry Luce did not. O'Hara had begun to learn how to protect himself on the magazine, and he could count on the help of Busch and Hockaday, even though he did not like his frequent assignment to stay up and put the new issue to bed at two A.M. on Tuesdays by teletype to the printers in Chicago. No one ever thought of coming to work before ten o'clock in the morning, but even so O'Hara had trouble checking in, until he discovered the Charles Wertenbaker method: "Wert" left a hat and topcoat permanently hung up in his office, and bought an extra pair of spectacles which he placed on his desk every night, setting the scene of an office whose occupant has just stepped down the hall. After work, John often enjoyed going out with Hockaday, a sprightly fellow who had a vein of irreverence. It was Hockaday who took a girl into the bar at the Yale Club, up to that time a masculine stronghold; the girl was a model, wearing a hat and suit supplied by O'Hara, who accompanied his friends on this expedition. The disguise was penetrated, all three were asked to leave, and Hockaday heard from the board of governors.

On November 5, 1928, O'Hara received important recognition at *Time* when his name appeared as a "weekly contributor" in the masthead. Inclusion on this list meant that the writer's job was secure, with a chance to qualify for editorial responsibility and good pay. Henry Luce in person was one of the most intense bores of his generation, but it had to be admitted that he was all right about money. He did not suffer the traditional publisher's anguish at the thought of staff people drawing high salaries, and it appeared that the way at Time, Inc. lay clear before O'Hara if he chose to take it. Within a month, his name was off the masthead, and he was no longer writing for the magazine. It was the *Pottsville Journal* situation: a framework of deadlines was not what John wanted for his life. Some of his colleagues said they envied his freedom, but John remarked a few months later, as he returned a thirty-dollar loan, "Don't ever knock that regular check."

There followed what Mary O'Hara called "the period of jobs that didn't last." Forced on the market again after leaving *Time* when his money ran out, O'Hara worked briefly at the *Daily Mirror*, at *Editor & Publisher*, and on the *Morning Telegraph*, a paper that dealt mainly with racing and was edited in a tumble-down, barnlike structure on Eighth Avenue. As his list of contributions shows, O'Hara was writing all the while for *The New Yorker*, but the checks for his short pieces, coming in about twice a month, were not sufficient to keep him, between the jobs that he found easy enough to get and impossible to hold. For a time, O'Hara attended the night switchboard at a dubious hotel in the West Forties, an experience reflected in *BUtterfield 8* when Eddie Brunner takes the night desk of a hotel whose patrons will not bear inspection. O'Hara told his sister Mary never to call for him at this hotel, never to set foot in the place. Later on he tried moving-picture publicity, serving for two periods as a staff member in the eastern promotion department of Radio-Keith-Orpheum, a production and distribution company recently formed with the backing of the Radio Corporation of America and the Keith and Orpheum theatrical interests, and usually referred to as RKO-Radio.

A man who saw O'Hara at RKO has recorded his recollection of the meeting as follows: "When O'Hara worked in the publicity department of RKO-Radio Pictures, I was at the National Broadcasting Company, which was also under the ownership of the Radio Corporation of America. The two companies were supposed to work together, especially in the matter of promoting RKO films and NBC programs. One day they told me to go and see somebody called O'Hara about an NBC project to publicize an RKO picture, *The Phantom of Crestwood*. I must explain that *The Phantom* was a screenplay by Bartlett Cormack, who had written a successful Broadway melodrama called *The Racket*. In Cormack's script, the characters are isolated on a mountaintop by an avalanche, someone is murdered, the question is who did it, and the movie handled this sure-fire situation pretty well. The contribution of the brains at NBC was that we should make a six-part radio drama out of this script, getting up to but not including the denouement, and that we should broadcast one part per week for six weeks, whereupon we would invite the audience to attend the nearest RKO-Radio theater to see how it turned out. Also, there would be a prize contest for the most ingenious solution of the mystery by anyone in the radio audience. I was to describe this scheme to O'Hara and appoint him liaison man at RKO. Accordingly I went to their offices about eleven o'clock one morning. I don't know if you are acquainted with the New York offices of Hollywood movie companies. In those days they inhabited second- and third-rate West Side office buildings (except for the Paramount Building), had a gloomy and almost furtive air, and posted the most surly and uncommunicative type of office help at their outer doors. When you got past those receptionists, you found yourself wandering down hallways lined with open doors through which you saw large paneled offices with stained glass windows, fake fireplaces of baronial size, and dyspeptic-looking elderly men sitting at huge desks with cuspidors alongside. O'Hara used this cuspidor bit in one of his stories, I forget the title.* The office they had assigned to O'Hara was small, gloomy, and dingy. When I entered I saw at a desk of unimpressive size a vaguely collegiate-looking young man who appeared to be unwell. I mentally diagnosed his illness as serious need of the prelunch martini, being acquainted with that trouble myself in those days. My recollection is that his manner could be called just adequately civil to the representative of a sister company, and the thought that came to me was, 'O'Hara is not a permanent member of the team around here. This one is just passing through.' I claim only that much prescience. The rest is soon told: O'Hara was not successful in concealing his aversion to the scheme I described to him, and it was obvious that he meant to do nothing, or as little as possible, about it. Hoping to rouse some enthusiasm, I told him that the NBC production department planned to take pains with the radio drama, and that they had engaged a fine actor, Ned Wever, to play the lead. At this news, O'Hara warmed up slightly and said, 'Ned Wever, Princeton Triangle Club, 1921.' "

New York City had two good periods, which may still be called modern, before it fell apart following World War II. The first good period may be identified as the time of Prohibition, starting in 1920 and ending with Repeal in December 1933. Two years less than a decade followed in the second good period, which ended not on any particular date, but in a decline of decency as the country's war effort got under way. It vanished in the spring of 1942, when young men in new naval uniforms danced at Larue's with girls who had a look of softness to them, and shoulder-length hair. These girls had red hair, and black hair, and various shades of blond, some of it making one think of honey, or of amber; but the dark-haired ones were also very nice to see, and touch. Back in the first good period, the stock market collapsed in October 1929, when billions of dollars in notional money suddenly vanished into the surrounding air. This money had never in fact existed, but its reported disappearance caused distress, most of which fell on people who had never had anything to do with the stock market. But the disaster had no effect on O'Hara: he said to his friends, "For what it was worth, I had the advantage of being already broke." In any event, the noise of the Wall Street crash was muffled to those who spent their leisure time in the midtown and Greenwich Village speakeasies. It must be borne in mind that from high to low, every speakeasy operated behind a heavy

* "Mr. Sidney Gainsborough, Quality Pictures."

metal door, usually the basement entrance of a brownstone house, whose front windows were always heavily curtained, and once the customer was inside and seated at a table or propped against the bar, he might as well have been on an ocean liner so far as the rest of the city was concerned. Who can say how the ventilation was managed? Employees and customers alike throve on whatever it was that passed for air in these sealed premises, cool in summer and warm in winter. Though speakeasies had closed fronts, they otherwise varied as widely as restaurants today: Niven Busch labored to catalogue and describe them all in his sketches called "Speakeasy Nights," which appeared nearly every fortnight in *The New Yorker* during the first years that O'Hara was writing for the magazine. Wolcott Gibbs published a parody of the "Nights" in which he imagined a speak concealed behind the doors of a bank vault, about the only place where clandestine liquor service did not establish itself in those days. Peter Arno drew a scene that actually occurred at the Waldorf, with Busch asking a popeyed bemedaled general if he was a Shriner. High spirits of this kind made Niven Busch an enjoyable companion for O'Hara on the occasions when they would take out two young ladies. John also enjoyed the company of Noel Busch, and made several trips with him to sessions of New Haven and Princeton football practice, in an open, seagoing old Cadillac touring car that Noel drove at the time. Busch recalled that on these trips O'Hara talked a good deal about Pottsville and its people: he seemed to have an extraordinarily clear and detailed memory of the years he had spent there.

Routine office duties had little attraction for O'Hara; he already knew that the writer of fiction must practice his trade by seeking a variety of experiences and writing them up into stories that are all the more true for not being precisely true, and all the better as fiction for their grounding in fact. At this period, O'Hara had absorbed what he needed for "The Doctor's Son" and *Appointment in Samarra*, and those unwritten works were waiting to be put on paper. Some of the experiences through which O'Hara now passed were to be material for the adventures of James Malloy in *BUtterfield 8*, and also in two sections of *Sermons and Soda-Water* that would be written almost forty years later. And so, going from job to job, and spending time at parties and in speakeasies, O'Hara was doing what he was born to do — living a life of intense emotional stress, and observing himself and others, to lay a true foundation for his writing. It was inevitable that a feeling of guilt should spring from this use of life, and at times it made a heavy burden for O'Hara. His drinking caused some terrible awakenings: the honesty with which O'Hara portrays Malloy shows that he became aware of how truculence and undue sensitivity could be heightened by alcohol. One can understand how O'Hara must have felt, on occasion, waking up on some stranger's couch, broke, sick, jobless, and recalling with the hideous photographic clarity of such moments a regrettable scene, or even a series of them, that had taken place a few hours before. But O'Hara was by no means unique in sitting up all night around the speakeasies of Manhattan. Men and women of proved talent and established position did it all the time. It was customary, on encountering friends early in the evening, to make a later engagement, say two o'clock at Lou Richman's Dizzy Club, a never-closing upstairs resort in the West Fifties that featured a small Hawaiian band. The Busch brothers introduced O'Hara to this place, where he saw, standing at the bar, a small woman of striking personal style and melodious voice, wearing a purple dress and a great mad hat. Her name was Dorothy Parker, and her companion was a man whose frequent hearty laughter indicated his appreciation of other people's jokes, which was especially pleasing when one recalled that Robert Benchley himself was a great American humorist. Mrs. Parker and Benchley accepted O'Hara as a friend from the time they first met him, and continued so to regard him as long as they lived. Like most people of high talent they were liberals, and John absorbed from them his early political viewpoint. The Dizzy Club was too noisy for extended discussions of anything, and O'Hara began to frequent Tony Soma's speakeasy at 57 West Fifty-second Street, where Mrs. Parker, Benchley, Wolcott Gibbs, James Thurber, Heywood Broun, and other writers found the atmosphere congenial. Soma was a distinguished-looking man with a neat Van Dyke beard, and he was sometimes introduced to strangers by waggish patrons as Admiral Balbo, the Italian Fascist leader and aviator. Tony would then sing an aria from Verdi or Puccini while standing on his head, a feat he had mastered in studying the science of Yoga. Up two flights nearby at 35 West Fifty-second Street, John discovered the Onyx Club, a hangout of house musicians from the network studios. There were talented men among them, such as Dick McDonough and Carl Kress, the guitarists; Miff Mole, a fine trombone man; the trumpeters Mannie Klein, Phil Napoleon, and Max Kaminsky; the drummer Ray Beauduc; Johnny Mercer, who wrote "Blues in the Night"; and Jerry Colonna, the horn man who became a comedian. Early in the morning at the Onyx, Colonna would scream out a burlesque of Al Jolson's serious rendition of "Sonny Boy" that reduced the musicians to helpless laughter. John had little contact with Negro jazzmen, although he heard Thomas (Fats) Waller at a fashionable place called the Fifty-second Street Yacht Club, where that talented musician appeared as star entertainer.

A headliner of Fats Waller's class would go on at ten o'clock, midnight, and two in the morning. But music and entertainment of some sort was always in progress somewhere. At Dan Healy's Broadway Room, a revue featuring singers, comedians, and a chorus line went on at four A.M., and a sinister speakeasy called the Owl, behind a cigar store in the West Forties, catered to patrons who liked to come in at five A.M. and find a crowded bar with a piano going. One left the Owl anywhere from ten o'clock to noon, in mild delirium from fatigue, and drunk into a strange lax rigidity that bore some resemblance to being sober. This was like The Party of Pottsville days, except that few customers of the Owl had in them the sense of prankish adventure that had given a kind of fun to lunches in evening dress at the country club. There were people in the Owl who drank fast, said little, and had pistols under their coats. Others were there only because they did not want to interrupt their consumption of alcohol, except when unconscious, until they died. One was a young man who had announced that he intended to drink himself to death. He said he had just enough money to do this comfortably. He took no nourishment except peanuts from the free lunch counters, and paced himself on Scotch and plain water. All he asked of a bar, other than that it be open for business, was a mirror in which to stare at his reflection, and he always ended his nights at the Owl. Back to his hotel at noon: up and into Tony's by midnight. He lasted nearly a year and was found in his room, dead from undernourishment, with money for a few weeks' drinking left in his bank account. This kind of self-destruction showed that while alcohol might be a socially accepted narcotic, it could tear down a reputation, a personality, a nervous system, and induce death. John O'Hara studied that side of metropolitan life with fascination and fear.

O'Hara had the McKees in East Orange to fall back on at any time the problem of shelter became insoluble, but his desire for his own place was not hard to understand. He lived for short periods at various addresses, the usual thing for a young man getting a foothold in Manhattan. All through Greenwich Village, along Bleecker Street or in Patchin Place or MacDougal Alley, one could find adequate apartments at low rents with no lease required. Similar accommodations were available from Forty-second Street north to Central Park South, in a civilized district that had Sixth Avenue for its main street and appealed to O'Hara, and other young people, because of its nearness to the theatrical district and the Grand Central area with its editorial offices and hotels. People walked the streets at any hour, and O'Hara sometimes took a stroll in rain or snow, trenchcoat belted around him and hat pulled over his eyes. He enjoyed riding on the tops of double-decked buses with his sister Mary, and they once sat in the rain all the way uptown and back, which surprised the conductor. Mary gave her brother companionship, sympathy, and also some practical help in the form of breakfast or lunch at the Chrysler Building Schrafft's, near her office at the *Daily News*, when she thought he needed a good meal. Mary worried about John when he looked under the weather from too much night life, and sometimes started to tell him so in forcible terms, but could never keep on scolding when he said, "Do I have to pay for lunch by listening to a lecture?" Even when funds were low, John often took his sister out for an evening, or laid a present on the table at Schrafft's: a new book, or a pair of gloves from Saks Fifth Avenue. After Mary O'Hara established her apartment on University Place, John could see his mother there in soothing surroundings when she visited in New York. In a few years, it would give O'Hara pleasure to provide opera tickets for his mother and her friends, and to arrange for them to dine at the Algonquin. But early in 1930, when the newspapers recognized the problem of unemployment as a national emergency, O'Hara was thankful for friends like his sister and Heywood Broun, who had the imagination to see where help could properly be offered. Broun was a public figure: for some years he and F.P.A. had been top stars of *The World*. The management had dismissed Broun after a row over how far he could go in defending Sacco and Vanzetti and attacking their judge and prosecutors. O'Hara met Broun at Tony's shortly after arriving in New York, and followed his newspaper writings, as did most of the intelligent people in town. Broun was alarmed at the spread of unemployment, and started a "Give-a-job-till-June" campaign late in 1929 through his column, which was now in the Scripps-Howard *Telegram*. Writing to Broun's biographer Dale Kramer, O'Hara recalled: "I was out of work myself, so I wrote and asked Broun if there was anything I could do to help. Right away he called me up and said there were a lot of chores I could help out with. Such as handling his mail and contributions from his daily WMCA broadcasts and some interviewing. I ate lunch at his penthouse every day the first week I was with him, and incidentally it was usually the big meal of the day for me. At the end of the week I was genuinely surprised to receive a pay check for $35, which he gave me all the time I worked for him. And I know it came out of his own pocket, because I knew, through my job with him, quite a lot about his current financial situation, his checking accounts, and so on. Until I got a regular job he kept me on his personal payroll (I may say there was plenty of work to be done) and also he used to take me out at night, always, of course, picking up the tab wherever he went." Broun set an example of industry as well as generosity; in spite of the time he spent at restaurants and speakeasies, he turned out large amounts of writing in his deceptively easy style. His method when confronted with the problem of producing his daily column was to write it straight off at the typewriter, sometimes with people talking in the room. O'Hara assumed, and no doubt correctly, that this gift of concentration came from Broun's years in newspaper offices. John observed also that when his employer left a speakeasy, there might be two or three derelicts waiting for him, as the word would spread that he was inside, and he was known to be a good touch. Broun explained to John, "If a man looks down and out I give him something. That way I can't go wrong." Heywood Broun was conspicuous on the night side of New York because of his large size and a kind of senatorial dignity, combined with a carelessness in dress that drew from somebody the famous remark that he looked like an unmade bed. Broun could write stories when he wished to, and he impressed John with "Death Says It Isn't So" in which he presented a sick man about to breathe his last in a hospital bed. When Death appears, it turns out he is nothing more terrible than an apologetic fat man in a Palm Beach suit. But the dying man is alarmed and Broun has Death say, " 'I'm kind. That's my business. When things get too rotten I'm the only one that can help.' "

It was during this period that O'Hara made a trip back to Pottsville in the grip of depression and anxiety so deep that his brother Tom became alarmed. Tom O'Hara recalled the visit as a time when John seemed defeated: "I think he may actually have given thought to the idea of self-destruction. I watched him sitting in that big square chair, the one with the upholstery that changed its shade of green when you rubbed it. He seemed to hunch down as if he wanted, more than anything, a feeling of shelter. I couldn't do anything to help except by trying to make him aware of my love and admiration. Somehow he found inside himself what it took to get well, at least enough to go on with the walking wounded. There were New York friends who helped. They would call on the telephone, and somebody sent phonograph records, music by Lecuona, the Latin-American composer. I remember those records, good solid acetate of the Brunswick label, and John listening to 'Siboney' and 'Karabali.' When he got over this depression he went back to New York. I doubt if he ever felt any worse, except at the death of loved ones, in the rest of his life."

Although he had kept death constantly in mind since his boyhood as a doctor's son, O'Hara was in the midst of life while he tried to find identity for himself, and direction for his talent, during the speakeasy period in Manhattan. And he was in and out of beds as often as jobs, looking for a girl with whom he could have a permanent relationship. He wrote in his letters to friends about some of these girls, but did not mention names. In January 1929 his report to Robert Simonds gave a bleak picture: "I have taken up my abode with the little girl I told you about at Christmas, but I'm afraid it won't last much longer. Too bad, too, because we have a very comfortable place. Well, if you come to N.Y. we'll get ourselves one just as comfortable. I got very drunk last night on a party out at Kew Gardens with some friends of my sister's, to which the little girl was not, of course, invited. When I came barging in about five-thirty this morning her only comment was You can sleep in the other room. Which

I did. When I called her this afternoon (she works on the Trib) she was very polite and aloof and told me she wouldn't go to the theater with me tonight. Has a date. Well, that's O.K. with me, except that she's probably going out with a guy whom she likes . . ." That romance ended as O'Hara predicted and left him like James Malloy, on the alert for the next girl or woman to whom he might say, half believing it, or believing it all the way, that she had smitten him with love at first sight.

Cole Porter was to write that a New York romance, carried on partly in public, might prove to be just one of those things, with the lovers separating in style and politely hoping to meet now and then. Lorenz Hart, who later served as O'Hara's lyricist, wrote for another libretto that falling in love with love was falling for make-believe, and learning to trust was just for children in school. Malloy lived through emotional difficulties like these in *Sermons and Soda-Water*, a product of his author's maturity, in which O'Hara looked back on the 1930s and the pain that men and women inflicted on each other. In the last of the three stories in *Sermons*, Malloy encounters a former sweetheart, the actress Julianna Moore. They think there is a chance to revive the feeling they once had for each other, and they speak of the wonder of this "second chance at love." But Malloy marks it as "a synthetic romance that served well in place of the real thing," and after a couple of months there comes the time when "there is no love in the love-making." Julie packs a bag and asks, " 'Haven't you one nice thing to say before I go?' " Malloy as narrator recorded:

I thought of some cruel things and I must have smiled at the thought of them, because she began to smile too. But I shook my head and she shrugged her shoulders and turned and left. The hall door closed and I looked at it, and then I saw that the key was being pushed under it. Twenty-three crowded years later I still remember the angle of that key as it lay on the dark-green carpet. My passion was spent, but I was not calm of mind;* by accident the key was pointed toward me, and I thought of the swords at a court-martial. I was being resentenced to the old frenetic loneliness that none of us would admit to, but that governed our habits and our lives.

Throughout his early Manhattan career, O'Hara often brought Margaretta Archbald back to mind. He told a friend he wished they had said goodbye forever in 1928, but that would not have removed Margaretta from his thoughts. It now appears that O'Hara was looking for what he believed Margaretta might have had for him, as he sought out

---

* One of the few literary tags in O'Hara's work. He refers to the last line of *Samson Agonistes*.

girls in New York. And still, although it gave him occasional pangs of
sorrow, O'Hara had no intention of pining away because of his old friendship with Margaretta Archbald and its emotional echoes. Early in 1931
he thought he had found the permanent love of his life, when he went to
the Equity Ball and met a young actress named Helen Ritchie Petit. She
was one of the talented girls, on the order of Edna St. Vincent Millay,
who came out of the eastern women's colleges in the 1920s to write, go
into publishing or designing, or find careers on the stage. Helen Petit
had graduated from Wellesley in 1928, then taken an M.A. degree in
English at Columbia. Having starred in college dramatics, Helen played
the ingenue opposite Eddie Albert in *Room Service*, a successful Broadway farce. A writer in the *Wellesley Alumnae Magazine* said that "those
of us who knew Helen in College remember her gold hair to her waist,
her deep blue eyes, her delicate features and her Alice-in-Wonderland air.
She remained a great beauty all her life, but beneath her child-like manner
was a brilliant, highly imaginative mind." Her friend Elizabeth Hart recalled Helen Petit as "a blonde with the warmth and animation usually
attributed to redheads and brunettes. She had a beautiful bone structure and a Grecian nose, so her face in repose was, I think, what people
called classical. Only it never *was* in repose except in a few cabinet
photographs. After John met her he said that 'she had a shine all around
her' which was so intense that it took some little time for him to notice
the particulars. I can well believe it. When she was excited and gay, she
did give off this sort of irridescence." As soon as O'Hara recovered his
senses after being exposed to the shine that came from Helen Petit, he
began to court her. Although friends called her "Petey" (rhymes with
"Sweety"), O'Hara gave her the name of "Pet," and while telling her of
his own origins and ambitions, began to find out the background of his
new love. Pet was one of the first people O'Hara had run into who might
well be called an O'Hara character in her own right. She had a dragon of
a mother, who seemed to have been preparing for years to step into the
part of the suspicious, interfering mother-in-law, and a rich bachelor
uncle who had made a fortune in the 1920s from an engineering patent.
This uncle, David Mahood, had bought a house at 540 Ocean Avenue in
the conservative Flatbush neighborhood of Brooklyn, where he lived with
his sister and niece. Pet went to nearby Erasmus Hall, at that time a
crack public high school, descended from an academy founded in 1787,
which sent girls to Radcliffe, Wellesley, Vassar, and Bryn Mawr. In the
middle 1930s, David Mahood moved Mrs. Petit to a Park Avenue apartment in Manhattan, and established himself in a suite at the Plaza. "Uncle
Dee" was generous, but is remembered by Pet's friends as "a dull uneasy
man." For Mrs. Petit, they employ such terms as "monstrous" and "odious," and the evidence indicates a hysterical, incurably unhappy woman.

Pet's father had deserted his wife and daughter shortly after she was born somewhere in the farther depths of Brooklyn, in one of those regions of endless anonymity that fascinated Thomas Wolfe. David Mahood's fortune, and Helen's talents, had brought the irridescent girl to circles where she would meet a man like John O'Hara. But in spite of her independence as an actress and holder of a Columbia graduate degree, Helen Petit was still much dominated by her mother. Elizabeth Hart has testified: "After a nightmarish trip with Mrs. Petit through Central Europe, Petey and I refused to lunch at an American restaurant in Budapest called the Maple Tea Room. Unfortunately we took our stand literally in the Corso, crowded with local citizenry. Mrs. Petit said, 'If you walk away from me, I'll scream.' We did — and *she* did, with the lung power of a hog-caller. Everyone stared, a cop came up, and — well, we were in our late teens and horribly self-conscious — so we trailed ignominiously back. I cite this incident as an illustration of the kind of blackmail Petey was up against."

John O'Hara was not the type of man this formidable woman had in mind as an ideal husband for Helen. His personal charm failed so far as Mrs. Petit was concerned, and she had no interest in the possibilities of his talent. This was not entirely unreasonable; as we know, O'Hara's employment record was wretched. However, Helen Petit was a grown woman, and her abilities, combined with John's, made enough in the way of earning power to manage life in Manhattan, at a time when fifty dollars would rent a snug apartment and landlords would concede a month for tenants of any kind. One sure way to make Helen take John seriously as a suitor would be to oppose him: and Mrs. Petit did this so vehemently that she refused to take messages from John for her daughter. He employed a code, "This is Dick Watts. Please ask Helen to call me at the office," and Pet knew this meant to call John. They got married on February 18, 1931, at the registry office in City Hall, to the distress of Mrs. Petit and O'Hara's mother. Mary O'Hara found them an apartment on East Fifty-second Street, and in July they took a cottage in Bermuda.

It was a yellow cottage in Paget East, on the road to Elbow Beach, beside the first downhill slope after climbing the hill from Hamilton. Inviting Robert Simonds and his fiancée for a visit, O'Hara wrote: "We have a swell cottage. Living room, two mahster's bedrooms, maid's room, dining room, kitchen, electric refrigerator, and about ⅛ of an acre of woodsy ground, all for $50 a month. Food is comparatively inexpensive (although we haven't got the bills yet). The drinking question is by way of being an exclamation: we just don't drink. No resolutions or anything of the kind. It just doesn't seem to occur to us. We bought a bottle of gin when we got here, and we still have it, two weeks and one day later. Pet reads, and I have done a lot of writing. We eat and smoke, and at night we sometimes knock off a bottle of ale and a bottle of porter, and that's just about our life. I bike to Hamilton (about twelve minutes going, fifteen coming back on account of a hillock) once or twice a day to mail letters and buy the papers and magazines and cigarettes, and I haven't even got a sunburn . . .

"So far I have resisted the impulse to buy a pith helmet, but I do wear linens or flannels all the time. The only possible objection to the place is the insects, which are quite harmless but annoying, and will, I am told, decrease in number soon. Otherwise, the place is perfect, and I'd like to be able to buy this house and live here always. Go to NYC twice a year for the theater and new ideas, etc., etc., but have my home here. The Mrs. doesn't cotton to that idea, but as I said to her the other day: 'Sweetheart this is so heavenly that we must spend most of our time here, and if you don't like it I'll knock your God damn block off, sweetheart.' So we are not going to stay. We are going to remain here until September 15, however, so it looks pretty much as though you two'll have to spend your vacations with us. Remember, we're chaperones now . . ."

When Robert Simonds and his fiancée Catherine Melley of Coaldale arrived they found O'Hara and his bride leading an idyllic life. O'Hara was working well: his Pottsville material had started to line up in usable order, and he had begun to release some old tensions about his father in writing "The Doctor's Son." He also had in progress a story called "The Hofman Estate," which dealt with Whit Hofman, a leader in the society of Gibbsville. The Hofman estate resembled the Sheafer family holdings, and the Clinton Sheafer of real life was similar to the fictional Whitney Hofman who was destined to live in O'Hara's writings even though this first long story about him was not published and the manuscript has disappeared. O'Hara was writing with Schuylkill County in his head and the landscape of Bermuda before his eyes, each aspect of reality heightened by the contrast. Taking time off to entertain his guests, O'Hara had a startling reminder of The Region when the four young people attended a dinner party given by Mrs. Gosling, a member of the reigning mercantile family, on the roof of the Hamilton Hotel. Robert Simonds noted that "the sky was so clear it seemed that one could reach out and pick a star." And the band played "Star Dust," by Hoagy Carmichael. It was a perfect moment, and they sang in the open victoria on the way home. Just as they reached the crest of the hill outside Hamilton, another victoria drew alongside and passed them, and a voice called, "Hi, Cathy! What are you doing here?" The accent was unmistakable Schuylkill County, and the voice belonged to a girl from Catherine Melley's home town. As they drank their nightcaps on the veranda, the young people laughed and told each other that The Region had a long reach — there was no getting away from it.

In his working hours O'Hara completed "The Doctor's Son" and "The

Hofman Estate." He planned to submit the stories in a prize contest sponsored by *Scribner's Magazine,* and later to combine them into a novel, regardless of success or failure in the competition. On September 15, John and Pet returned to New York and a reckoning with Mrs. Petit, who had not been given full information as to her son-in-law's current business activities. By October 1, 1931, The O'Haras had managed to get an apartment at 19 West Fifty-fifth Street. In response to a letter of thanks from Robert Simonds, O'Hara wrote on October 17: "Candor, and all that, compels me to admit that I got your first letter. I then was in the throes of something which, I daresay, was a bit more immediately troublesome than your own problems in Coaldale. I was having mother-in-law troubles, which can be all that the comic supplements reveal. You see, Pet's mother found out, from a tactless friend of Pet's, that I was not on leave of absence, as she had been given to believe, but that I had quit my job, and would have none when I returned to New York. The result was simply hell. We had to live in Brooklyn with her family until I got together enough dollars to take an apartment in Manhattan, which we finally did a fortnight ago. But between the time of landing and the moment of apartment-taking there was enough on my mind to heighten my native neuroticism. On at least one occasion I got so drunk that I passed the evening in a speakeasy and did not return to Brooklyn. But finally I got some sort of job on the New Yorker: a drawing account of $75 a week, to be charged against whatever I wrote for them. That lasted exactly two weeks, until an officious son of a bitch decided to be efficient and called a halt to that.° Had I not last week sold a piece to Vanity Fair for $100 Mrs. O'Hara and I might well be worse off, by a week, than we are now. I have no job, and no source of income. I have written a lot of stuff for various publications, but the New Yorker particularly seems to be having manuscript trouble (excuse it please, this 'trouble' trouble). Right now, however, they seem to be on the verge — on the verge, my dear Simonds — of buying a piece which I called Screendoor, and if they do buy it I shall consider that the O'Haras are eating on R.T.S. this week. I told it in the first person, combining the character and the dog part of the Screendoor anecdote with an experience I once had in Llewellyn, which happened while I was wearing that state police raincoat.

"Ah, the novel! [Ogden] Nash read it (Scribner's having turned it down

° B. A. Bergman, the *New Yorker* editor who dismissed O'Hara, was not being officious, but carrying out instructions from Harold Ross. Years later, Mr. Bergman recalled that O'Hara produced several good pieces in his four weeks as staff writer, and that his account of a dirigible ride over Manhattan was "especially charming." Mr. Bergman said, "The unpredictable Ross would have none of O'Hara and rejected every piece I passed on to him. Evidently he didn't want O'Hara around from the day he came to work. Why, I never knew." When Ross realized that O'Hara had drawn three hundred dollars in staff salary, he ordered the firing over Bergman's protests.

insofar as giving me money while I rewrote it was concerned) and liked it. His words were that there was no monkey business to it, but that it seemed a shame to keep it so short, to overlook the opportunities for writing about a swell, small-town aristocracy. He told me to write him a synopsis and hand it to him so that he could take up with Farrar & Rinehart the matter of paying me so-much a week while I rewrote it (which is the only way it will ever be rewritten). I did the synopsis today, and he will have it tomorrow. Then the prosecution rests, so far as the novel is concerned, except that I am going to see one other publisher, William Morrow & Co., this week. Meanwhile I have taken a ride in the Goodyear dirigible Columbia, getting dope for a New Yorker piece, and I have tossed off various other pieces against the December 1 wolf . . ."

O'Hara constantly encouraged any of his friends who expressed interest in writing; Simonds had spoken of it, and John now went on to discuss some problems of composing fiction: "I find that my coal region memory is slipping in favor of new information on more recent visitations and abodes. I bought a Republican [newspaper] the other day, and there was a list of schoolteachers arranged by townships. I find that I forget where Hubley Twp. is, and things like that. I have to stop to remember where Duncannon is, and Rock. I forget many important facts about some of the County's most important people, such as Dory Sands and Puss and the Bolichs and the Moselines. Write a novel while you're more or less on the ground, and rewrite it when we go to Nassau next summer or before that. Read your Scribner's, which I humbly believe has the best short stories now being published in magazines. I don't like all their stories, and if I hadn't written it I probably wouldn't like the story I have coming out in the December issue.* Nevertheless, it's the only place I can think of where they are giving us newcomers a break, and publication in Scribner's does give some sort of stamp of approval. I like to think so. Keep writing, no matter how badly or how bad you think it is, because you'll never forget what you set down in writing or on a typewriter. Make it your own, as an old English teacher of mine used to say. Or file and forget, as Ross of the New Yorker says. But write like hell all of the good copy you can think of. Between us we might make Winesburg, Ohio, take a back seat. Imagine the vote of thanks we'll get from the Chambers of Commerce at Pottsville and Shenandoah! People like the half breed and so on, if written about in intelligent fashion, can be made to fit in with the brolies and the Irish and the dirty black Protestant Welsh of Sch. Co., and we'll create our own market. I don't know the principles of a good essay: vaguely in my mind has always been a theory, perhaps inaccurate, that a good essay form

---

* The story was "Alone": a young man has married a girl older than he, she has drowned, and he faces the ordeal of the funeral.

is the syllogism. This I truly believe, is a little too conclusive a form for the modern novel or short story. My half-baked theories on these forms of literature arrive at the ultimate opinion that life goes on, and for the sake of verisimilitude and realism, you cannot positively give the impression of an ending: you must let something hang. A cheap interpretation of that would be to say that you must always leave a chance for a sequel. People die, love dies, but life does not die, and so long as people live, stories must have life at the end. When there is no longer life, then is time for the Happy Ending, or any ending in the narrowest sense. . . . [O'Hara's dots] Horseshit yourself, Simonds.

"I cannot entirely resist the temptation to stick my nose into your trouble with Kate. I think you are now where Marg and I were at several points in our lengthy battle. That is, you have arrived at a sort of cul de sac, with two ways out: you can get married, or you can call it quits. But I sincerely feel that you ought to do one or the other and spare yourselves the anguish I had with Miss Arch, and which I undoubtedly caused her. If I had had sense enough to break it off early in 1928, or if she had had sense enough to have let me alone in 1929, we'd have been spared 1930, the worst year in my life . . .

"Mrs. O'Hara and I have done a good deal of drinking since Bermuda, you will not be interested to know. We have a nice enough apartment; two rooms, this time, and an elevator and various flunkies at the door, who very likely will look very lupine when the rent comes due, which is Dec. 1, thus leaving me flat for Christmas, which is as it should be. It will be something not to have to be sorry about not giving Christmas presents this year. I've been sorry so many years that I almost spoiled my holidays. Come and see us."

O'Hara ran into doldrums over the holidays at the end of 1931, and reported some of his troubles to Simonds: "We caught our colds on New Years Eve and have had them since: just the amount of time that has passed since I lost my most recent job. Well anyhow, the rent was taken care of by Mrs. P. (and I don't by any chance mean Mrs. P. H. O'Hara),* and day before yesterday Helen's uncle decided we needed a change of air to help us get rid of colds, and supplied the funds necessary for a weekend in Atlantic City. We left yesterday, Friday, and this afternoon I began figuring: $14 a day hotel bill, and dollars here and there for incidentals, and said: 'Look here, you, who the hell are we to spend this money this way, even if it was intended to be spent this way?' So we checked out and came home on the next train, thereby saving $14. . . .

"It really is a good thing the depression is catholic — the happiest catholicity I have come upon in quite some time! For since the depression *is*

---

* John's mother.

so universal the state of mind of the individual depressed is less morbid than it might be. And thus roundaboutedly I come to my comment on the Irony of It All. The telephone has been disconnected — and a press agent gives me a $20 hat for Chistmas. That sort of thing. We eat a cheap table d'hote dinner — and proceed to a first-night. We buy two quarts of cordial shop gin — and four people drop in (one of them, an artist named Strater, a boxing companion of Hemingway's) and the evening turns into a swell party. I try without success to get a $50 a week job, and a few minutes later am promised tickets for the Beaux-Arts Ball. Maybe this isn't a depression at all. Maybe it's just L-i-f-e. Of course I say that with all awareness of my sympathetic interest in, and vicarious knowledge of, the waywardness of Packard shares. . . .

"If I get any kind of money within the next six months I am going to return to Pennsylvania, Pet notwithstanding. My plan on that is this: I have quite forgotten altogether too much of what I once knew. For instance the other night I was writing a gruesome little piece about the South Penn explosion, and I discovered that the word 'slope' made me wonder. I never was a mining engineer, exactly, but Lord! I knew more about a mine than, say, my father. Tonight I honestly can't define a drift. Of course on the other hand I can describe the Breakfast Club at Delmonico's, but I want to get somewhere in The Region — Schuylkill Haven, Tamaqua — and be able to find out by telephone accurate information about mining, local history, geography, etc. I am now going out before the drugstore closes and get toothpaste so I can enter a radio contest and win $200. . . ."

On his birthday, January 31, 1934, O'Hara gave Simonds news of work in progress: "I haven't had a drink in exactly one week (the longest spell, and quite unintentional, since you know when). We've been so broke that we haven't dared, and I've been slaving away at the rewriting of The Hofman Estate . . . I am twenty-seven years, three hours, old; and God! I hate it." O'Hara's nervous system was tightened like the strings on a banjo because of his efforts to arrive at final arrangement of the Pottsville material that would eventually be sorted out to make *Appointment in Samarra*. Of all trades the writing of serious fiction must be, short of digging ditches, the most fatiguing. There is always too much material: selecting is what wears a novelist down. At this point in his development, O'Hara was seeking economy of means, and the effort to "write short" exhausted him and made him hard to live with. He also thought of himself as a man out of a job, writing in that same letter, "I am still among the idle. The only remarkable event in my life has been staying on the wagon for a week." O'Hara went on to tell about a member of the Pottsville Purity League who came to call at 19 West Fifty-fifth Street and failed to exercise the old convivial magic: "Robert, he can't take it any more. He had no more than six shots of gin, and when he left he was talking loud and — you know — confidentially. How the mighty have fallen! [Another former friend] dropped in a couple of weeks ago, and I got tight and let him have it. Not with my fist, but with words of abuse. I told him all the things, or at least quite a few of the things, that I have been waiting to tell him for a couple of years. I scored his social climbing, his attitude toward his old playmates, etc. When he left I refused to shake hands. But he called up the next day, and he and Lesher and two girls and Pet went out to dinner together. I was absent."

Pottsville was on O'Hara's mind, and in this letter he wrote of how he was thinking his way toward the organization of material for his first novel. As he had feared, neither "The Doctor's Son" nor "The Hofman Estate" had won a Scribner prize, and the linked stories had not found acceptance as a short novel, although there was interest at Farrar & Rinehart, where Ogden Nash had offered some encouragement. But O'Hara knew, because of the discomfort in his nervous system when he thought about it, that something more was needed: "My idea is this: make a few changes in both stories, that is, give them a definite common locale (such as referring to Pottsville by a fictitious name, and using the same name in both stories), and writing a third story, also with the same locale and putting them in one book together. I would write a third story, about someone like [two men from Maher's in Shenandoah] to complete what might inaccurately be called a trilogy. It would be a post-war picture of The Region, from the standpoint of the three classes: the Sheafer aristocrats, the middle class O'Haras, and the Schwackie gangster type. You'd have the three classes and the predominating races in just about the right periods. Don't you think it sounds good? All I'd have to do would be to make the simple changes in the stories I have and write the third. . . ."

The long letter continued as O'Hara thought at the typewriter, stirring and sifting Pottsville in his brain: "Pet gets bored when I talk about The Region, and I get sore when she gets bored, and so on . . . You see, I would like to sit around and chew the fat, sort of to refresh my memory about the roundheader boys, and to study Conditions. You and I might even go for a spin in the general direction of Pottsville, although not in it, to be sure. I honestly think there is a good book out of such a 'trilogy' and I'm pretty sure I could get it published. I have plenty of time on my hands, and the will to do, and so forth. Also, I could use the money. I could use any money, down to, and including a dollar . . . As is always the case with me, prosperity is just around a couple of corners. I'm not even looking for a job. What's the use, when shoe leather costs so much? And why go out and deliberately put myself in a position which ultimately will be only disheartening? In the book about the Sheafers, I brought them up to about the time of the crash, but, of course, did not refer to it. The

Doctor's Son was left hanging, as it were, at about the age of 14, just after the war. Now the third story, about the Schuylkill County gangster, could be built around a sort of hanger-on at the roadhouse which was occasionally visited by the Pottsville country club set. I would bring the doctor's son up to date, as of 1930; a drinker, roustabout, etc., playing around with the Sheafers. The roadhouse could be either a place like Turin's, or like the Log Cabin. The third story most likely would be told through the eyes of the gangster, whose job would be that of assistant manager (at a place like Turin's), or, if we decided on a lower-scale dump, the gangster could be just one of those mysterious pimps or bootleggers, whose source of income is never very definite, so far as you and I can be sure. He would be attractive, in a common way, and we could have the girl falling for him, the doctor's son either picking a fight or being a pal, and Clint being friendly but superior. In the first two stories there would be only slight relationships between the two: a common locale, and the names of the towns and streets and people would appear now and then in both stories, but in the third story the people would really get together in the same roadhouse barroom. It might be effective to have the whole story take place over a period of one night; from the time the gangster comes around, early in the evening, to "go to work," until dawn the next morning, when the night's festivities had ended. This would give me an opportunity to give a complete picture of the roadhouse, with a lot of behind-the-scenes stuff, such as the arrival of the liquor in a Reo speed wagon (Turin, I really think, would be the best place), and a few unimportant people having dinner, and Papa and the gangster talking business, and a small orchestra setting up their instruments, getting ready for the nightly brawl, etc., etc. If you and Kate could have us for a week-end, or even if I could come over alone, and you could tell Papa in advance what I have in mind, I think the atmosphere would be all set. You and I could go up there in the evening, or late in the afternoon, and just hang around and watch things. You could assure Papa that I have no designs on his place, that I'm not a Prohi agent, and that I would not libel him . . ."

O'Hara kept on with his ideas about a research trip to Schuylkill County and concluded, "We would guarantee not to be expensive guests, because through lack of wherewithal, we have forgotten how to spend money. As a matter of fact, if you *should* decide to have us, the trip would have to wait until I get enough money to cover the rock-bottom expenses, such as railroad fare. We have felt lousy about not crashing through with a wedding present, but if you knew the sales talks I've been giving the landlord, you'd understand. I'm sure you do anyhow. The truth is, we've been living on Pet's allowance of $100 a month, and just not paying the rent. We pay 'something on it' when I sell a piece. I've rewritten one piece three times, which the New Yorker is now considering, and in the last seven weeks I've sold two, for a total of $95. Well, I never expected to own a yacht . . ."

On the same day O'Hara mailed a long letter to his brother Tom, who was preparing to take the college entrance examinations. John gave instructions on writing to the Dean of Admissions at Yale, Mr. Archbald's classmate: "You plan, of course, to enter Yale College, not the Sheffield Scientific School . . . Be ready to take the actual examinations in June, and if you flunk them then you will have another chance in, I believe, September. But don't think of September, it is decidedly to your advantage to pass in June, inasmuch as Daddy was not a Yale man, because the September exams are understood to be held as the last chance for sons of alumni to get in . . . Later on, if and when you have more definite plans, I will be able to tell you some Yale lore, tradition, social custom and legend . . ." Tom was inclining toward Brown, which he entered that fall (1932), but in April John was still thinking of Yale, and wrote to urge against steering away from the place on any grounds that it was for rich men only. John wrote that he had met Ralph D. Paine, Jr., an editor of *Time,* who was recently graduated at New Haven, where he had been elected to a senior society. It turned out that "Del" Paine owned no riding boots, and had explained to O'Hara, "I sold them so I could pay for my diploma." John saw a lesson from this which he sent on to Tom: "Well, if a man can make Skull & Bones and has to sell his riding boots to buy his diploma, you need have no fear that Yale is strictly a rich man's college." He went on to give Tom the news that a job was now available at the Associated Press, and another at Radio-Keith-Orpheum: in all probability he would take the latter, as it offered higher pay. John informed Tom that he had been eliminated in the first round of the National Ping-Pong Tournament at the Algonquin Hotel, but "the guy who put me out later was a semi-finalist." O'Hara closed this letter with a social rating of American colleges. After Yale he listed Harvard and Princeton. Then he set Brown at the head of the second flight, followed by Williams and Amherst running as an entry, then Penn, Cornell, Virginia, Michigan, Stanford, Illinois, Southern California, Hamilton, and Wisconsin. (A noticeable omission from O'Hara's list was Lafayette, where Julian English of *Appointment in Samarra* belonged to D.K.E.) In October, with Tom a freshman at Brown, O'Hara wrote from the RKO offices to tell his brother that he had sold a *New Yorker* profile of a typical chorus girl, "Of Thee I Sing, Baby," and that the entire payment of $175.00 would go to the landlord, who would still have $25.00 due him. John was in a good mood as he went on to list, for his brother's guidance, "the best frats nationally." His ratings were: D.K.E., Alpha Delta Phi, Psi Upsilon, Zeta Psi, Beta Theta Pi, Delta Upsilon, Sigma Chi, Delta Phi, Chi Phi, and Delta Tau Delta.

Charges that O'Hara was guilty of snobbery have been founded on his interest in college fraternities, and those charges are unjust. In his youth and early maturity, American college fraternities had prospered to such an extent that they owned thousands of houses in college towns, and furnished the living and boarding quarters for more than 800,000 undergraduates throughout the country. Add to their attractions the secrets of rituals and closed meeting halls, which were similar to the pleasures of lodge membership to the public at large, add the beautifully machined and jeweled badges of enamel and gold, add the satisfaction of being *in* while others were *out*, add the belief that membership might give advantage in the competition of life after college, add the fun of flocking together, partying, singing convivial songs — and you have totaled up some powerful folkways. The Philistines were in command at American colleges, and fraternity houses were their strongholds and bases of operation. Many people, including O'Hara, were aware of this, but few spoke of it as bluntly as he did. It was an accepted mannerism to make light of fraternity membership, especially if one had been elected to a "good house," whether at one of O'Hara's approved colleges or elsewhere. One could hardly say, "Yes, I had money behind me at college, and connections, and, in fact, I made an advantageous sale of myself on the personality market." O'Hara understood this, and he startled some of his friends by labeling them in social introduction: he would say, "Jim Hart, a D.U. at Columbia, this is Harry Wales, a Phi Delt from Cornell." He presented Richard Watts as "a Sigma Chi if ever there was one." O'Hara was studying human groups; he was not saying the exclusive organizations were ethically admirable or right, but that they must have importance or they wouldn't exist on so large a scale. He made this statement in stories such as "Graven Image," with its outsider risen to power and his indelible hostility toward one of the former elect, now down on his luck and seeking a job, which he almost gets, then loses with one unguarded remark. The dictionary says that a snob is one who crawls before those he regards as his superiors. O'Hara felt himself the equal of anyone he met: some had "the badges" and some had not. If O'Hara had presented his world of social ladders in the jargon of sociology, academic critics would have hailed him as a great investigator and invited him to join their councils. On the whole he did as well with Pottsville as the authors of *Middletown* with Muncie, Indiana. Those writers received praise because their book was hard to read, and full of statistics and circular charts cut up like pies. Only the interest of the subject matter saved *Middletown,* and its authors did not have to suffer reproach for suspected snobbism. The pie-charts cleared them of any such accusation. O'Hara, in his Pennsylvania work, delivered enough sound data on the forms and functions of human groups to have merited

Katharine Delaney O'Hara, John's mother

Patrick Henry O'Hara, M.D.,
John's father

Dr. O'Hara on a house call in
the west end of Pottsville

With his brother Joseph and
his sister Mary in Atlantic
City, July 1916

John O'Hara, fourteen,
on Julia

With Helen Petit O'Hara in Bermuda, July, 1931

Ernest Hemingway, Sherman Billingsley,
owner of the Stork Club, and O'Hara

O'Hara and Belle Wylie at the West Side Tennis Club,
Los Angeles, 1936

With Belle in Palm Springs, 1939

With Scott Fitzgerald,
Hollywood, 1938

With Budd Schulberg,
Hollywood, 1936

1938

All Terms Strictly Cash

JOHN O'HARA
52. CHESIL COURT
MANOR STREET
LONDON. S·W·3
FLAXMAN 3909

SPYING   LIVE BAIT (Blood Worms)   WRITING

CESSPOOL CLEANING   FREE AIR   INSTRUCTION

Hay, Grain & Feed   Fried Chicken   Notary Public

Night Telephone Bryant 9-8200
Refs.:

To Mr.: *Harold W. Ross & Co.* ...Dr...

		$	¢
2	Rewritings	90	00
	Brt forward	3176	50
	Total	3266	50

Past due
Please Remit

Nonsuch PREFF

An O'Hara joke: A "bill" to Harold Ross of *The New Yorker*

O'Hara in 1943, bearded for OSS training

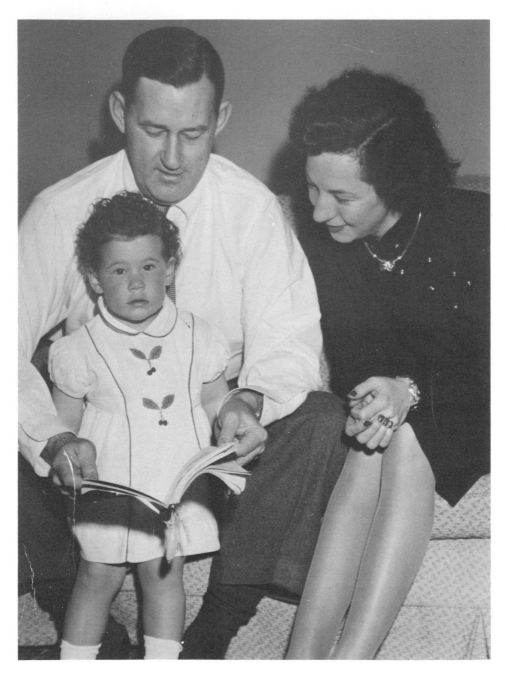

John and Belle O'Hara
with their daughter Wylie, 1948

With Frank Sullivan and Russel Crouse at dinner for Sullivan at the
Worden Hotel, Saratoga, December, 1959

With John Steinbeck at Quogue

Katharine, John and Wylie O'Hara in foul-weather gear at Quogue,
1958

Katharine and John at Quogue, 1958

John Hersey presents an Award of Merit to O'Hara, 1964

Katharine O'Hara with her son
C.D.B. Bryan, 1965

John and Katharine with C.D.B. Bryan, 1965

John and Wylie O'Hara, 1965

Katharine and John, 1965

Linebrook: the entrance and study

half a dozen degrees of Ph.D. in sociology. But he did not try to present a final answer to the central mystery of status by association: does the organization confer standing on the members, or is it the other way around?

In 1932 O'Hara did not spend all his time pondering sociological riddles, or observing the New Haven senior society men in the employ of Henry R. Luce, himself a member of "Bones." During this year O'Hara sold eleven stories to *The New Yorker,* and one to *Scribner's.* Nine of these twelve were published later with his first compilation in book form. The pieces for *The New Yorker* included three that were as effective as any he would ever write. There was "Frankie," a sad little episode involving a barber and a manicurist — no smart collegians here; "Lombard's Kick" is remarkable for the economy with which it presents three characters; and "Mr. Cass and the Ten Thousand Dollars" is a study of loneliness. The story that came most directly out of O'Hara's life at the time, however, was the contribution to *Scribner's,* called "Early Afternoon." The situation is simple: there is something wrong with the marriage of the Grants, and the young husband's loss of his job is not going to improve matters. We get a dusty, hopeless feeling from the story, a sense of defeat when the young man comes home in the early afternoon. O'Hara felt that he had brought this off successfully, and wrote to his brother Tom that "Dorothy Parker told me I would never be happy because I am a genius, and that she'd bet if Hemingway saw the Scribner's story he'd want to cut his throat. I am sorry to be compelled to add that Mrs. Parker was tight. But I understand she told other people the same about me . . ."

"Early Afternoon" appeared in *Scribner's* for July 1932. O'Hara was working for RKO at the time, with his plans for the Pottsville "trilogy" on the shelf, and a good deal of social life going on with writers, actors, and the varied assortment of people in speakeasies during the late watches. For the year O'Hara earned at least five thousand dollars, a respectable income for a young man at that time, and the money had purchasing power. Pet received funds from her uncle and her mother. The financial problems rose from their expensive manner of living, almost always eating in restaurants or speakeasies. Tony's, Michel's, the Basque's, and other places the O'Haras favored were not cheap, and his favorite speakeasy was frankly expensive. This was the establishment that had originated in Greenwich Village under the ownership of Jack Kriendler and Charles Berns, which O'Hara had begun to patronize when the partners moved it uptown to 42 West Forty-ninth Street and then to 21 West Fifty-second Street, where it became the Manhattan institution generally called "21." John and Pet were barely able to keep up with the expense of dining and taking supper after the theater at such places, and they suffered the anxiety of having to juggle the charges for rent, utilities, clothes, and personal items. The drink supply at 19 West Fifty-fifth Street came from the so-called cordial shops where liquor was sold openly during the last year of Prohibition, which ended on December 5, 1933. But many young people have lived this way: Becky Sharp, for example, after she married Rawdon Crawley. Neither John nor Pet was consistently unhappy; her friends thought she was in characteristic good humor most of the time, and they remember John as frequently in tearing good form, "amusing, amused, in tune with the world." But this was a doomed marriage, with the causes of its failure mostly beneath the surface of their lives in 1932. One cause of anguish was John's jealousy of Pet. He seemed to have an ingrained belief that all women will betray the men who love them if they can. He would upbraid Pet, and accuse her of making plans to sleep with any man she spoke to out of his hearing at a party or around the table at Tony's or Michel's. Pet complained to her friends and used the word "unendurable." Sympathetic friends said that one reason for John's jealousy was his vivid imagination, for in those days he had cast everyone he knew in a melodrama that went on in his head, and he had a theory that he needed to study people under stress. If there wasn't any stress, he appeared, often enough, to be trying to create some. He did not add to his popularity with the women in his circle by warning their husbands of fancied interlopers, wildly improbable partners in adultery for the ladies concerned. Undoubtedly liquor had much to do with this attitudinizing, but the jealousy of Pet and the obsessive fear of disloyalty was part of John's personality. All who knew him observed it, and all who admired John wished most fervently that he did not feel this way, for at times he was in obvious psychic anguish, and causing pain for others, thus building up a load of guilt that he could hardly carry around without continuous and crippling emotional discomfort.

Not to attempt anything in the way of Freudian analysis, it is permissible to say that in his childhood O'Hara had absorbed Roman Catholic puritanism, a powerful brand of that medicine. The effects cannot entirely wear off, hence guilt, fear of betrayal, and "frenetic loneliness." The hope and supposition of young people in the 1930s was that men and women would meet and mate in gallant, graceful, stylish love, as expressed in the dancing of Ginger Rogers and Fred Astaire. It might also be said that these attempts at grace and elegance had a way of failing in the realities of bed, or never reaching them, so that nothing was left but the effort to make a smooth exit with a good parting line at the door. It is a wonder that any young people in the period managed to stay married and many — in O'Hara's circles, most — did not. To make his marriage certain of failure there was, in addition to jealousy and fear of humiliation, the watching presence of Mrs. Petit, world's champion bad mother-in-law. And this lady, who may have been forced to admit that O'Hara did pretty well in 1932, saw the welcome reappearance of possible disaster in early January 1933. As he often did when troubled, O'Hara thought at the typewriter, and composed a letter sending bad news to Bob Simonds on January 8: "Today was my last under the happy sign of RKO, or the sign of the viscera. They fired me, pardner; they ousted me, and only because I missed, on the average, a day a week from hangover trouble. My boss is an old pal, and whatnot; but he insisted that pal or no pal, opal or diamond in the rough, I didn't belong in that p'ticular setting. I always was the last in the office, insisting on that as the prerogative of late-sleeping (albeit not latent) genius. But the others couldn't see it that way, and there was Talk; there were mumblings and murmurings about special privilege and teacher's pet. So today was my last as a publicity man for RKO. And am I glad! Now I have no excuse for not doing some decent work, and really I do feel a writing jag coming on. I don't know whether I have anything much, or important, to say, but I'm going to do a deal of writing, friend. I have two plays to write, which have been sithering (how's that for a word?) within me for some time past. One of the ideas you'll be liking. Do you remember the old Christmas tree parties at the Boones'? Well, I would start my play with a sort of reunion of such: a wealthy guy decides to get the old bunch together, after ten years, just as they were in 1922; that is, the same people, the same furniture. The play would be an exposition of what had happened to them all in the intervening decade, and what would happen the night of the reunion. I think it's a hot idea — and a lousy one if it doesn't come off. But we must watch and pray. The other play is much in the Philip Barry tradition, and is too New Yorky for words. I don't want to start it till I've spoken for Katharine Hepburn and Pat O'Brien, whom I see in the leading roles, and no one else do I see. In addition there is the item known as Novel, which I did want to get over and done with . . . We remain at 19 West 55 and in view of the fact that I have just received that 100% cut in salary, it is just as well we took no more roomy quarters. The owners voluntarily knocked $20 off the rent, so we have had as much as we could ask for. The only trouble is that while Helen's maw formerly paid $25 a month toward the rent, now that we had the cut she no longer contributes. A pity. A great pity. But we shall somehow weather it all . . . I'm pretty well fed up with myself at this juncture. I wish I could take a vacation from myself. I have, of course, taken quite a number of overnight vacations; getting so cockeyed drunk that twenty hours elapse before I recover. But that's just the trouble. A change of scene is what I need more than anything else. Even so short a trip as the one [to see Tom at Brown] made me realize that New York is licking me. I couldn't help thinking that the other day in a street car. A few years ago — say seven or eight — I could go to a town like Philadelphia, stay at a hotel, and get a swell kick out of listening to the city noises. I could get a kick out of uniformed delivery boys, and electric motor trucks, and elevated trains and orchestras unobtrusively playing at luncheon in the hotel dining rooms; mounted police and shops that sell $20 shoes. Maybe I could recapture that swell feeling in another city. Chicago still seems to me more of a city than New York, because I know New York so well. God, to think that I recognize the faces of scores of cops and doormen between 42nd Street and 59th! Waiters in speakeasies and the Algonquin and Sardi's and B-G sandwich shops know me by name better than the same craftsmen at George's or the [Pottsville] Plaza — and in essence I don't like it. Perhaps that's the reason I liked Chicago. It was so completely foreign and strange, and I was so completely an outsider. And yet it isn't that I am really an *insider* here. I have few enough friends, and a lot of people who speak to me really hate my guts. The spurious attentions, if you can call them that, from waiters and the like are entirely the result of 15% tips. All this is rather familiar stuff, I am aware. Well, when I write like that it certainly is time to call a halt . . ."

The marriage took its final blow when Pet discovered she was pregnant, and listened to her mother's arguments that she must have an abortion. Mrs. Petit's reasons were all aimed at O'Hara and his supposed lack of dependability. O'Hara gave his consent. He later told his daughter Wylie that he never stopped regretting that he had done this. But the abortion was performed, and O'Hara said he felt this betokened the death of the marriage. He knew something about the emotional shock and the deadening of love that comes from an abortion. Years later, he wrote a story based on something that had happened years before: in "Zero" he showed the reader a man from Gibbsville and a girl from Mountain City who are tortured by the awful coldness at the end of unwanted pregnancy and unsuccessful love. By June 15, 1933, Pet was in Reno; O'Hara also had left Manhattan, supposedly for an indefinite time. And the country's financial depression seemed to reflect the emotional bankruptcy, in Scott Fitzgerald's phrase, that troubled the spirit of John O'Hara.

In spite of the money panic and depression, certain journalistic ventures were prospering in 1933. The success of *The New Yorker*, with its sense of place and emphasis on good writing and drawing, had encouraged other local publications, most of them frankly imitative and leading off with a department of short items resembling Harold Ross's "Talk of the Town." Los Angeles, Cleveland, Chicago, Philadelphia, and other cities had magazines of this kind, and in Pittsburgh it was called the *Bulletin-Index*. The publisher had taken the title of a paper that had been part of the Gannett chain, and planned to give his readers the editorial approach of *The New Yorker* put together in the departmentalized style of Henry Luce's *Time*. Through Manhattan contacts he hired John O'Hara as managing editor, starting in May 1933. It turned out that John stayed with his job only a little more than three months, but the time in Pittsburgh had moments of interest.

O'Hara found that his living quarters were provided through a due bill on the magazine, in a room on the twelfth floor of the William Penn Hotel. Here he installed his typewriter and golf clubs, and was pleased to note that the *Bulletin-Index* offices were only a few blocks away, in the Investment Building. Pittsburgh was wallowing in the depths of depression, but the rich people kept up their hunting, polo, and party-giving, all sources of copy for the *Bulletin-Index,* which liked to stress the high-society aspect of the local scene. O'Hara had a staff of two young men, Frank Zachary, and Burtt Evans. Zachary got eight dollars a week, his colleague seven. At a later time Zachary was art editor of *Holiday* in that magazine's great years, and after that, an eminent consultant in his specialty of graphic journalism. But when he met O'Hara, he was nineteen years old and had never been far from Pittsburgh. He looked up to O'Hara as a young sand-lot ballplayer might admire a major league star, since John's name was familiar to all who read *The New Yorker,* and he was qualified to get out the *B-I* in the image of *Time*, for his name had appeared in the masthead of that magazine. Thirty-nine years later Zachary said, "As a boss, John was decent, considerate, and encouraging. I recall him warmly and kindly." O'Hara and his two reporters would write the entire magazine, send it to press in the early hours of Tuesday morning, and take the rest of Tuesday and Wednesday as their weekend in the manner of *Time* itself. Zachary recalled that "John had knowledge of social details, and while he played golf at the public links, he also spent time with Sewickley Heights people and seemed to understand their ways. He wrote a piece about a polo player named David McCahill III, which we ran as a cover story. There was a good deal of talk after this because McCahill had gone to Brown University, and John finished the piece with a reference to the traditional scatological doggerel about the color of horse manure. Among other things that impressed me was the way John would come in and take off his coat, loosen his suspenders, swing a leg over the back of his chair in front of the typewriter as though mounting a horse, and start tapping out copy for the *B-I*, or what was really exciting to me, a piece for *The New Yorker*. It seemed to me he could finish one of these before going out for lunch."

While in Pittsburgh, O'Hara wrote "Mr. Cowley and the Young," and "Never a Dull Moment" for his usual outlet. A better story than these, also written in Pittsburgh, was "Hotel Kid," which appeared in *Vanity Fair* for September 1933. O'Hara had observed the sad waif of this story in the halls and elevators of the William Penn. And it was in that hotel that O'Hara suffered an almost fatal moment of anxiety and guilt. His friend Gibbs had said that things were never easy for John, not even the writing that he made to seem an almost effortless flow: "His private desperation I know has often been about as much as he can bear." On July 4, 1933, that private tension came close to the unbearable. The Fourth of July had been a dramatic date in John's childhood, partly because of the marching bands and patriotic oratory, and the noise of cannon crackers that started before dawn. That was the exciting part of the holiday: there also was a frightening part, for which Dr. O'Hara prepared like an army surgeon getting ready for battle. Always present in his memory, "The Fourth" had appeared in two of O'Hara's published sketches. Now in Pittsburgh the holiday coincided with news from Pottsville that Margaretta Archbald was going to marry an Episcopal bishop's son. There was something about this news that gave O'Hara a desolate feeling, and made him wonder if he could go on — indeed, he asked himself if he *wanted* to go on. There was no solvent for this anguish in the holiday drinks. It got worse, and in a sort of panic, at some time on the Fourth, O'Hara went to his twelfth-floor room at the hotel, flung a leg over the windowsill, and prepared to jump. Perhaps the breathing of fresh air diluted the alcohol in his bloodstream and lowered the level of his self-pity. At any rate O'Hara realized how far he had gone and how close he had come to ending his troubles by destroying his life. He dropped back into the room and resolved to stop drinking for a while.

Frank Zachary further recalled, "I took John to Plush Alley, the North Side vice district, and he wrote a long piece for the *B-I* entitled 'Plush and Velvet,' referring to the velvet, or graft, that the panders gave the authorities for the privilege of doing business. This caused amazement and consternation in Pittsburgh. All the time John was with us, Burtt Evans and I were fascinated to observe that he was getting letters from Wolcott Gibbs, Harold Ross, Dorothy Parker, and Frank Sullivan. Our publisher couldn't resist opening these letters, John took umbrage, and there were very harsh words spoken. John left the *B-I* then and there, or very shortly thereafter, and I went up to his room to help him pack. I was impressed by the way he had dug in and made himself comfortable. There were good coats and ties hanging up, a businesslike typewriter, books, and a bottle or two on the dresser. John offered me a drink but we were both on the wagon. He seemed grateful for my company, and insisted that I take some shoes and neckwear as parting gifts. The books were to be boxed and sent on. It didn't take long to pack him up." O'Hara went to the window and looked out over Pittsburgh, which was big, tough, and ugly-beautiful. "Well, goodbye Frank." "Goodbye John." Frank Zachary did not see O'Hara again until twenty years later, when he ran into him at Brooks Brothers in New York.

While in Pittsburgh, O'Hara had talked to Zachary about a novel he intended to write. When he walked away from the *Bulletin-Index,* and shook the city of Pittsburgh — never to return — the novel had almost reached final form in his mind. He had at last decided to eliminate the trilogy idea, and to build his story around one person; any character strong enough to rival this central figure for the reader's attention should be used somewhere else. Accordingly, O'Hara took "The Doctor's Son" out of the plan, and let it stand alone, bringing its narrator James Malloy through adolescence, to appear later as a young reporter in New York. O'Hara still had a decision to make about "The Hofman Estate," which was obscuring his view of the material that finally went into *Appointment in Samarra.* The manuscript of this story, rejected like "The Doctor's Son" in the *Scribner's* contest, has been lost, but there can be no doubt that it contained an account of Whit Hofman and a description of his advantages in life. Much of this comes through in *Samarra* and "Pat Collins." Whit Hofman also turns up elsewhere in O'Hara's fiction, as an arbiter in Gibbsville, and a valued patron at "21" in New York. He stands just outside the central action in *Samarra,* along with Ed Charney, bootlegger and gangster, who was to have been the hero of the third story linked in the projected novel. This story did not get written, for O'Hara realized that the gangster, too, must be a supporting character and not the hero. That leading part must go to a doctor's son: but he was not to be James Malloy; and his father bore no resemblance to Patrick O'Hara. While these plans for what proved to be the organizing point of his life matured, in the fall of 1933 O'Hara took a room in the Pickwick Arms at 230 East Fifty-first Street, and began to earn his principal income by writing the football department of *The New Yorker.* He filled this space four times, attending games at the Yale Bowl, Harvard Stadium, and Palmer Stadium in Princeton. He sat in press boxes with the famed gentleman sports writers of the time — the courtly Georgian Grantland Rice; the old Princetonian Lawrence Perry, who reported only on amateurs in his syndicated column "For the Game's Sake"; and George Trevor, who wrote his weekday copy in the library at the Yale Club and sent it downtown by messenger to the *Evening Sun.* O'Hara also met Damon Runyon, the star of the Hearst papers, who wore a belted polo coat and a velour hat the size of a coal scuttle. O'Hara's attendance at the Big Three football fields was not because of any snobbish notions of his own. In those days the games played there had national importance on the sporting scene. O'Hara's writing on football was perfunctory, and in the following season of 1934 he took over the department only once. By that time he was no longer just a fairly well-known writer of magazine pieces and third-line restaurant celebrity around town, but a famous author whose reputation had rushed up like a rocket from the explosion of one book, the novel on which he began serious writing in December 1933. O'Hara did not work with peace of mind, all passion spent: He had felt death in his marriage to Pet, and she had returned to New York on August 12 with a Reno divorce, but he could not rid himself of the feeling that there was unfinished business between them. Perhaps there could be another chance. Writing to his brother Tom at the end of October 1933, O'Hara described the situation: "I am not working but am getting by with pieces for the New Yorker, which have been selling well enough to keep my belly provided for, but not so well that I don't dread the coming of colder weather. I have an overcoat and a fur coat at Macy's, in storage, but I owe two years' storage on them, so I haven't tried to get them, and even so when I do try I may find that they have been sold. I have no plans except to live until I die, which may be for weeks, and may be (though God forbid) forever. As I daresay you know (though how, I cannot tell) I was divorced in Reno in the first week of August. Pet and her mother went out there. Then I got thoroughly fed up with Pittsburgh and my job there, and quit. You may have heard some story to the effect that Pet went to Pittsburgh with me and did not get the divorce. It was untrue. She did not go to Pittsburgh with me. Well, I got fed up with the job at about the same time that Pet was to return from Reno, so I quit and came to New York and saw Pet the day she got back and have been seeing her ever since. That was about August 12, when she got back. I want her to marry me again, and this time make a go of it, and she says she will if I get a job and make some money. The money is necessary, because in the first place, she is living with her mother and uncle, and they don't even know I'm in New York, let alone suspect that she is seeing me, and if she marries me again she'll never get a cent from them. So I am looking around for a good job. I dream of going to Hollywood and making large sums there, but I don't suppose that ever will come true, so I am on the make here. That is a resumé of my life, except to add that since July 4 I have been a sober citizen. I got good and drunk, I mean good and drunk, the night of July 3, and then went on the wagon . . . I am leading what is called a life, but there isn't anything to it. I am staying at a place called the Pickwick Arms Club Residence, above address, Eldorado 5-0300, because my room costs $8 a week without bath. Still I don't miss the bath, as I am not in favor of pampering children the way these modern parents do. I usually sleep all day, get up and have breakfast, meet Pet and go to the movies or something, sneak her home, and then go to Tony's and talk with Dottie Parker, who is by way of being one of my best friends at this point. Or else I go to the Gershwins', Ira and wife, and play backgammon for a cent or a dime a game. I come home late — around three — and try to write something, and read the morning papers, and then take some aspirin for my cold and then go to sleep. I have a feeling that all this is time-out preparatory to something terrible happening to me, but I almost don't care . . . It is quate daylight now, quate, and I ought to get some sleep as I am going to two very dull parties tomorrow, and I want to be at my dullest. Write me at length. How tall is Genie? I was wondering about him today, and according to my figures he ought to be 15 in March, and in freshman high school, the idol of the ladies and a hot-cha-cha. I suppose he never asks about the picture that's turned to the wall. Now spread yourself, son. At ten cents a word this is valuable letter . . ."

One night shortly before Christmas 1933, O'Hara rolled a sheet of yellow paper into his typewriter in the room at the Pickwick Arms and wrote, "Our story opens in the mind of Luther L. (L for LeRoy) Fliegler, who is lying in his bed, not thinking of anything, but just aware of sounds, conscious of his own breathing, and sensitive to his own heartbeats." O'Hara was started at last on his novel, which he planned to call *The Infernal Grove.* Luther Fliegler was a member of the chorus which would surround the hero, Julian English, and observe his fate. Emotions connected with his former wife formed part of the psychic energy O'Hara summoned up for the story, and he wrote hard until the middle of January 1934, when he paused with the book a little over one-fourth finished. On February 12, O'Hara answered a letter from Tom with an account of work in progress: "I ought to wait, I guess, until I get into the right mood to write you, but what I usually recognize as the right mood hasn't come over me since your letter came, so I might as well write now. I keep forgetting that there is no way except by a letter from me by which you can hear what has been going on in this lovely life of mine, and that may be a good thing at this point, because without it I'd have little enough else left to write about.

"The most important news, so far as I'm concerned, is that I've sold a novel. Just before Christmas I started out to work on it, and I did 25,000 words without taking time out to write a single magazine piece. Then I began to get little notes, then bigger notes, from the proprietors of this Work of Art,* reminding me that the most important rule of the place is Payable in Advance. So, with no money coming in, I did take time out to write to three publishers: Harcourt, Brace; Viking Press; Wm. Morrow & Co. I told them all the same thing; that I was doing a novel, and wanted to finish it without having to interrupt my writing streak, if you could call it that, to do stuff for the New Yorker. I told them I would show them what I had written, providing they would agree to read it with the thought in

---

* The reference is to *Work of Art,* Sinclair Lewis's novel about a dedicated hotel-keeper.

mind that if they liked it they would pay me a subsidy to live on while I finished it. I mailed the letters, and the next day all three publishers phoned me (at one time or another all three had asked me to do a novel). I took the one that phoned first. I showed Harcourt, Brace the MS., and they kept it over night and the next day phoned me to find out if I would come in and tell them what I was going to do with the characters, how long I expected the novel to be, what further action was to take place. I went in and told them these things, and they signed me a contract: $50 a week for eight weeks. That was three weeks ago, and the novel is now about half finished. The $400 counts as advance royalties, to be charged against the book if and when it begins to sell. It is to be completed by April 1, and will be published in the fall. Harcourt himself said it was the most promising part-manuscript he'd ever read, and so far we are all pleased. But now that it is half finished I am suffering from what Dorothy Parker says Ernest Hemingway calls 'the artist's reward' — in other words, I think what I've written stinks, and I just can't seem to get going again. I gave the MS to Mrs. Parker, who took it away with her over the weekend, and has promised me an opinion. I have worked like hell on it when I've worked, and the two people who have read it (besides the Harcourt Brace people) like it. I refer to Mary March, whose family our parents met in Kentucky, and to Helen P. O'Hara, who has the best taste of anyone I know. What I am doing now is stalling. I work in jags. I work like the devil for days at a time, and then suddenly I dry up or get stale, or get physically too tired to go on.

"The locale of the novel is Pottsville, called Gibbsville in the novel. Mahantongo Street is called Lantenengo Street. All points in Schuylkill County are given fictitious names — Taqua, for instance. And others you will recognize. Points outside of Schuylkill County — Hazleton, Easton, Reading, Wilkes-Barre — are mentioned by their right names. The plot of the novel which is quite slight, is rather hard to tell, but it concerns a young man and his wife, members of the club set, and how the young man starts off the Christmas 1930 holidays by throwing a drink in the face of a man who has aided him financially. From then on I show how fear of retribution and the kind of life the young man has led and other things contribute to his demise. There are quite a few other characters, some drawn from life, others imaginary, who figure in the novel, but the story is essentially the story of a young married couple and their breakdown in the first year of the depression. I have no illusions about its being the great or the second-great American novel, but it's my first. And my second will be better. All I care about now is getting it finished, written. I'll be able to edit and polish off etc. after I've done the labor of setting down what I have to tell. I have done no rewriting up to now and very little editing. From now on, when I get the MS back from Dottie, I will have to work much harder than I have done, but I know where I'm going. God help me.

"I see I keep referring to Mrs. Parker. Right now I think she is the best friend I have in the world. You append a little note to your letter, a question asking how I got along without an overcoat. I couldn't have. Just before Christmas I was going to go away for a weekend with Helen and then I got a rejection from The New Yorker which put the kibosh on the weekend, and I mentioned it to Dottie. Without a word she got up and wrote a cheque for $50 so we could go away. I couldn't refuse it, even if I'd wanted to. Then Helen got afraid (her people think I'm still in Pittsburgh) and the weekend was put off, so I took the money and got my coats out of Macy's storage. I had that football job which kept me going all fall, and I sold a piece now and then by which I managed to keep going afterward. I sold a story to Harper's Bazaar, for instance, for $125, which came in the nick of time, whatever the nick of time is. So I have not frozen. In between times, when I managed badly, I skipped a day now and then without a meal, I mean I had a day — *you* know . . . I told Harold Ross I would like to have a job for $250 a week and he said what for and I said so I could do something for my relations, and he said, 'Yes. And make them unhappy.' He pointed out his own case and the case of his mother, who was happy in Aspen, Colorado, until son Harold made money and began to spend it on her. She came east, and hasn't been happy since then. I don't agree with Ross. If I ever amount to anything I'm going to owe a lot to a lot of people who paused to do me small favors — F.P.A., for instance, to whom I am dedicating my novel. I say if I ever amount to anything as though I had all the time in the world, when I know nothing could be much farther from the truth. I have been on the wagon seven months, but even with that I don't give myself more than five years to live . . . I'm twenty-nine years old now and I don't see as good as I used to. I went all the way to New Philly the other day, thinking I was on the Minersvull car. If I hear anything I'll let you know, but I probably won't hear anything but the banging of this noiseless portable (anyhow it's portable) and the 2nd Ave. L. for the next couple of weeks. If I had a radio now I could turn off Father Coughlin . . ."

In February O'Hara spent a weekend with the Simondses in Allentown. When they urged him to return soon for an extended stay, he thought this might be just the thing for his tired nerves. Back in New York he saw it differently, and wrote to these friends on February 21: "If I were to leave New York — which is to say the vicinity of Pet — I wouldn't be able to work, and right now the only important thing in my life is work, this novel . . . I think that if I came to stay with you now I should become jealous of your happiness — a lousy thing to admit, but I'm afraid it's true. I thought it over, and I told myself I could get a girl in Allentown, to use her for an anodyne, but my real self told me how impossible that was —

and I found out how completely impossible it was when I saw Pet last night.

"I do think I am in for some unhappiness, a complete set of the same. She is opening in this damn revue in a fortnight or so, and I hate the very thought of it. I think all actors are terrible people. As Benchley once said, scratch an actor and get an actor. As Percy Hammond said, The better you treat an actor, the more it hates you. The thing that makes actors of intelligent people is something I refuse to understand. However, there it is in Pet, one of the most intelligent people I've ever known, so I have to take it, and I am afraid it's going to cause trouble. I have many friends in show business, and if this revue closes soon, she'll get another job — a friend of mine offered her a job through me yesterday. So I think we'll have that to contend with. I have one chance of sanity, and that is to finish the novel and make it good. To have done that will enable me to keep my self-respect and not only my self-respect, but Pet's respect; she still will believe that a good novel is better than the best performance an actor can give. In order to finish it, I've got to have conditions right in my mind: I don't want to be pining for her, worried about money (I find that I have only three more payments coming on my contract, not four as I'd hoped), and feeling, as I inevitably would feel, that I was causing you inconvenience. What's worse, I suppose you have both noticed that there have been changes in me, and the changes aren't entirely for the better; when I am in one of my moods (what Dottie Parker calls a Scotch mist) I am unfit for human consumption, and it is best for me to be here in this two-by-four cubicle, alone, where I cannot snap at little children and aged couples, and can frighten my pet cobras, Audrey and Louise . . .* I want to come and visit you when I have finished the novel — or before that; at the current glacier-like speed the novel will be ready for publication in the Spring of '38, although my contract calls for April 1 [1934]. That's another thing: I'm going to try to put over a book of selected short pieces and get the advance on that, and that's going to mean I'll have to work on it for the next week or two, drumming up trade and breaking down sales resistance.

"Well, here I am. I thought on Saturday night when you invited me that that was an automatic solution of many of my problems, and late that night, when I missed Pet so horribly, I thought it would be all right in the morning, and it was all right in the morning and on Sunday night, but when I got back to New York and saw her I knew that missing her Saturday night was just a sample of what I could expect. So you see we rich people have our troubles too. . . .

"Here is the passage from Spectre and Emanation:

* O'Hara was not serious; he owned no snakes.

Let us agree to give up love
And root up the infernal grove,
Then shall we return and see
The worlds of happy Eternity.

And throughout all Eternity
I forgive you, you forgive me.
As our dear Redeemer said:
This is the wine and this the bread . . ."

O'Hara abandoned his first title for the novel some time during the final "writing streak" that began after his visit to Allentown. He had intended to use the lines by William Blake as an epigraph to *The Infernal Grove*, but Dorothy Parker showed him something, after reading his first section of manuscript, that lit up on the page like an electric sign as he realized that he saw here an extraordinarily apt and evocative title for the story he was writing. What Mrs. Parker had passed on was a play with an Oriental setting by Somerset Maugham, in which Death is characterized, and delivers a speech:

There was a merchant in Baghdad who sent his servant to market to buy provisions and in a little while the servant came back, white and trembling, and said, Master, just now when I was in the market-place I was jostled by a woman in the crowd and when I turned I saw it was Death that jostled me. She looked at me and made a threatening gesture; now, lend me your horse, and I will ride away from this city and avoid my fate. I will go to Samarra and there Death will not find me. The merchant lent him his horse, and the servant mounted it, and he dug his spurs in its flanks and as fast as the horse could gallop he went. Then the merchant went down to the market-place and he saw me standing in the crowd and he came to me and said, Why did you make a threatening gesture to my servant when you saw him this morning? That was not a threatening gesture, I said, it was only a start of surprise. I was astonished to see him in Bagdad, for I had an appointment with him tonight in Samarra.

The title *Appointment in Samarra* had a quality that haunted the reader after he finished the story. It might well be compared to other famous titles that helped their stories with lingering aftereffects — *This Side of Paradise, Gone with the Wind, For Whom the Bell Tolls*. O'Hara also was to use the blunt, noncommital sort of title, as in *The Instrument* and *The Ewings*. But he was fortunate in starting his career with a memorable title that enhanced the novel on which he placed it.

O'Hara opened his novel by displaying a sureness of touch that let the reader know what to expect. We have Lute Fliegler in bed. It is early on

Christmas morning, and outside there is "cottony silence" on Lantenengo Street. Lying beside Lute Fliegler is his wife Irma. They turn to each other and share the comfort of sex. This was startling, because in 1934 the realistic fictional portrayal of sex between married people conveyed greater surprise than accounts of intercourse between unmarried partners. The omniscient author now gives us some of the thoughts in Irma's mind after Lute has gone back to sleep. Her anxiety over having "taken a chance" recalls her distaste for a neighbor woman who "screamed all through a summer evening" while "having a baby." We are in a real world where sexual intercourse can lead to agonizing consequences. Irma thinks "it was awful to have those screams and have to make up stories to tell the nice children ... It was disgusting." We learn that the Flieglers are members of Gibbsville's middle-middle-class. Irma doesn't mind that, for she was a Doane and her Civil War grandfather "had been a member of the School Board for close to thirty years." Lute is a salesman at the Cadillac agency owned by Julian English, who belongs to the country club, of which Irma says, " 'We'll join when we can afford it.' " Right now, at twenty past three A.M., Irma knows the country club dance "would just be getting good," and she wonders if Julian and Caroline English are having another of their battle royals. We dissolve to the smoking room of the Lantenengo Country Club, and find Julian English smoldering with hostility, but not toward his wife.

The object of Julian's displeasure is Harry Reilly, a rich, self-made man who glories in his acquaintance with the Englishes, the Hofmans, and the Froggy Ogdens of the inner circle in the smoking room. Not yet a governor of the club, Reilly has made himself useful in doing minor chores — he is in some ways like Duffy of the Greens Committee in "Help the Younger Element" — and he has made himself extremely useful to Julian English, by lending him twenty thousand dollars. Julian at the age of thirty has run into economic trouble in the depression, and social-climbing Harry Reilly has been glad to help him out. Tonight the usual people are to be seen, including the alcoholic hanger-on Bobby Herrmann, whose credit is suspended. This has not prevented Bobby from showing up in a business suit, "gloriously drunk and persona grata at the inner sanctum." Herrmann is the official jester for the Hofmans and Ogdens, and renowned for having said, on seeing the golf course without a person playing on it, "The course is rather delinquent today." Now he is explaining to the wives and fiancées of his friends that he would like to dance with them, but cannot because he is posted. Harry Reilly also fancies himself as an entertainer, and at the moment, he is beginning "a dirty story in an Irish brogue." The self-satisfied performance is almost more than Julian can endure. Reilly told his stories in paragraphs, and when he came to the end of a paragraph he would look quickly over his shoulder, as though he expected to be arrested before finishing the story . . . It was funny to watch people listening to Harry telling a story. If they took a sip of a drink in the middle of a paragraph, they did it slowly, as though concealing it. And they always knew when to laugh, even when it was a Catholic joke, because Reilly signaled the pay-off line by slapping his leg just before it was delivered. When everyone had laughed (Reilly would look at each person to see that he or she was getting it), he would follow with a short history of the story, where he had heard it and under what circumstances; and the history would lead to another story. Everyone else usually said: "Harry, I don't see how you remember them. I hear a lot of stories, but I never can think of them." Harry had a great reputation as a wit — a witty Irishman.

This is where Julian English decides to throw his drink in Harry Reilly's face. He thinks about it for some time while people come and go, and Reilly congratulates himself: " 'Didn't you ever hear that one? Mother of God, that's one of the oldest Catholic stories there is. I heard a priest tell me that one, oh, it must of been fifteen twenty years ago. Old Father Burke, used to be pastor out at Saint Mary Star of the Sea, out in Collieryville. Yess, I heard that one a long while ago. He was a good-natured old codger. I remember . . .' " Through several pages O'Hara makes suspense mount as to whether or not Julian will commit the uncivilized act. Then, instead of the climax, we get a brief scene out on the dance floor where the stag line has scattered while the band is working on a second chorus. We have previously met a sixteen-year-old punk, Johnny Dibble, who has been hanging around the smoking room, and has had his tail kicked for stealing liquor. Now O'Hara uses the classic device of the messenger: the punk rushes out to the place where his cronies customarily stand, and " 'Jeez,' he said. 'Jeezozz H. Kee-rist. You hear about what just happened? . . . Julian English. He just threw a highball in Harry Reilly's face. Jeest!' "

Al Greco the bootlegger has made a Christmas delivery and he sees Julian English go by in the Cadillac demonstrator, the big sedan job, fighting the wheel, abusing the car, and taking chances on the icy road. Al follows the Englishes all the way home, knowing that his boss Ed Charney approves of Julian and would not like to think of him lying under a wreck. After the Englishes go inside, Al backs into Twentieth Street and drives down Lantenengo Street, addressing the prosperous houses that he passes with " 'Merry Christmas, you stuck-up bastards! Merry Christmas from Al Greco!' " The howl of contempt, like the silence that followed it, came from O'Hara's memory of Mort McDonald.

On the morning of Christmas day Julian wakes to "a pretty good hangover." It is "a pretty good hangover when you look at yourself in the mirror and can see nothing above the bridge of your nose." Julian gets back on good terms with his wife and manages to fight his way through the day. On Christmas night Julian and Caroline return to the club for a party like the one the night before at which the Reilly incident occurred. Julian enters the smoking room and heads for the Whit Hofman crowd's table.

Many men said hello and hyuh to him, and he said hyuh and hello back at them six or seven times. He didn't have an enemy in the place. Then he heard someone say, "Hello, socker." He looked to see who it was, although he knew who it was. It was Bobby Herrmann.

"Hello, Rum Dumb," he said.

"Yeah, Rum Dumb," said Bobby in his slow difficult way of speaking. "Jesus Christ. You have a nerve calling me Rum Dumb, I'll say."

"Nuts," said Julian. He was taking off his coat and hat and putting them in his locker.

Everyone seemed to think that the job of kidding Julian was being taken over by Bobby. "Jesus Christ," said Bobby. "I've done a whole lot of things in my life, but by Jesus if I ever sunk so low that I had to throw ice in a man's face and give him a black eye. My God."

Julian sat down at the table. "Cocktail. Straight liquor. Highball. What'll you have, Ju?" said Whit Hofman.

"Cocktail, I guess."

"Martinis in this shaker," said Hofman.

"Fine," said Ju.

"Trying to ignore me," said Bobby. "Trying to give me the old high hat. The old absent treatment. Well, all right. Go ahead. Ignore me. Give me the old high hat. I don't care. But the least you can do, English, is go in there and pay for an extra subscription to the dance."

"Huh?" said Julian.

"You heard me. You're responsible for there being one less man here tonight and the club needs the money, so don't forget, you sock out an extra five bucks when you pay your subscription."

"Who is this man?" said Julian to Whit. Whit smiled. "Did he come here with a member?" . . .

"Not driving you away, are we?" said Bobby.

Julian looked at Whit, deliberately turning his back on Bobby. "Something wrong with the can, Whit? Or don't you smell it?"

Whit gave a neutral smile. "Going in?" he said.

"Let him go, Whit," said Bobby. "You know how he is when he has a drink in his hand. Of course you're safer when it's a cocktail. There aren't any lumps of ice in a cocktail to give you a black —"

"Well, bye bye," said Julian. He walked out of the locker room, but as he left he heard Bobby say in a very loud voice, loud enough not to be missed by Julian: "Say, Whit, I hear Harry Reilly's thinking of buying a new Lincoln. He doesn't like that Cadillac he bought last summer." The locker-room loved it.

Julian and Caroline have arrived at the party in a mood of tender love for each other, but as the evening progresses, Julian's anxieties begin to grow heavier and more menacing. The friends of the inner table had not reassured him with their neutral attitude while Herrmann was tearing at him, and a talk with Monsignor Creedon, as representative of the Irish and the Catholics, does nothing to relax Julian's tensions. He fights with Caroline, gets thoroughly drunk, and roars away in the Cadillac to the Stage Coach, the roadhouse outside town that is managed by Foxie Lebrix. Here he makes a spectacle of himself before Lute and Irma Fliegler and their guests, and offers public advances to the singer Helen Holman, who is known to be Ed Charney's property. After some hours Julian collapses, and Whit Hofman drives his car home for him.

Next day is December 26, the last of Julian's life. He starts it by quarreling with Mrs. Grady, the cook. At the office, he has an angry telephone conversation with Caroline, who is displeased because of his attitude toward Mrs. Grady. Caroline says they will have to cancel the party they were scheduled to give that night if his vile mood does not improve.

" 'I'll simply call up every person we've invited and call off the party.'

" 'You'll simply, huh?'

" 'Oh, shut up!' she said, and ended the call."

By the time Julian gets to the Gibbsville Club for lunch he is in a mood of desperate irritability. In recent years the club has admitted some Polish lawyers from up the mountain, and Julian notices a number of them at a table as he enters the dining room. He is joined by Froggy Ogden, who is an unassailable member of the inner circle, Caroline's cousin, and a war hero minus an arm lost in battle: " 'Listen, Julian, I didn't come here for a friendly chat.' " A ghastly scene follows in which they quarrel, Ogden throws a glass in Julian's face, they stand up, Ogden strikes at Julian, the club steward intervenes, and it appears to the fascinated lawyers that he is protecting the one-armed man from attack. A lawyer tries to interfere, ugly words are exchanged, and Julian hits him a terrible blow in the mouth. The man falls backward choking on bridgework. Ogden protects Julian from another lawyer who has picked up a bottle — the gesture of basic loyalty comes too late — and when Ogden tries to pull Julian away, he is accidentally hit on the chin by Julian's shoulder, "and then Julian rushed Froggy and punched him in the ribs and in the belly and Froggy lost his balance and fell over a chair." Julian dashes from the club and into his car, driving "as fast as he could to the quickest way out of Gibbsville. The worst of that drive was that the sun glare on the snow made you smile before you were ready."

The final quarrel with Caroline takes place outside her mother's house, where she has gone to calm herself, but cannot remain so when she comes out, finds Julian waiting in his car, and one word leads to another. He can go home if he wants to: the party is off, she won't be there. Back at his house, Julian sets out the whiskey and asks himself, " 'Is there anything I haven't done? Anyone I haven't insulted, at least indirectly?' " The reader has a feeling of approaching doom when darkness has fallen and one hand of the clock is on ten, but Julian cannot be sure whether it is the little hand or the big hand, and doesn't care. He's been asleep — the doorbell is ringing. He goes to the door and admits Miss Cartwright, a reporter. She has come for the guest list of the party, and is surprised to hear of the "postponement." Julian asks her to come in. She does so, sits down, lights a Spud, and accepts several drinks. After a while they are on the couch.

" 'Just kiss me,' she said, but she put her hand under his coat and opened his vest and shirt. 'No,' she said. 'Just kiss me.' She was terribly strong. Suddenly she jerked away from him. 'Whew! Come up for air,' she said. He hated her more than anyone had ever hated anyone."

Miss Cartwright leaves, remarking that if she stayed any longer they know what would happen, and Julian is " 'married to a swell girl.' " He foresees a life in Gibbsville, divorced, and no girl willing to "risk the loss of reputation that would be her punishment for getting herself identified with him."

He recalls a piece of collegiate chatter, "Don't buck the system; you're liable to gum the works." How badly has he gummed the works with Caroline? He does not want to go back, and he does not want to proceed into the future. The author puts thoughts in Julian's mind between quotation marks:

"She's only twenty, and he's thirty. She's only twenty-two, and he's thirty. She's only eighteen and he's thirty and been married once, you know. You wouldn't call him young. He's at least thirty. No, let's not have him. He's one of the older guys. Wish Julian English would act his age. He's always cutting in. His own crowd won't have him. I should think he'd resign from the club. Listen, if you don't tell him you want him to stop dancing with you, then I will. No thanks, Julian, I'd rather walk. No thanks, Mr. English, I haven't much farther to go. Listen, English, I want you to get this straight. Julian, I've been a friend of your family's for a good many years. Julian, I wish you wouldn't call me so much. My father gets furious. You better leave me out at the corner, because if my old man. Listen, you, leave my sister alone. Oh, hello, sweetie, you want to wait for Ann she's busy now be down a little while. No liquor, no meat, no coffee, drink plenty of water, stay off your feet as much as possible, and we'll have you in good shape in a year's time, maybe less."

Julian sprawls on the floor with his favorite phonograph records around him. He has taken the flowers from a vase, poured out the water, and "made himself the biggest highball he ever had seen." For some time he plays records, falling on some and breaking them. He uses "the vase for resting-drinking, and the glass for moving-drinking." He finds that he has two cigarettes burning, one in the ashtray on the floor, and the other getting stuck in the varnish on the edge of the phonograph. "He half planned a lie to explain how the burn got there and then, for the first time, he knew it would not make any difference."

Here O'Hara took Julian English, by now a living person in the reader's mind, to the edge of death. O'Hara's depression in Pittsburgh had brought him to a window ledge: the method of suicide to be a twelve-story drop. Because he was breathing normal air, O'Hara could pull back in time, and fall on the safe side. Julian English, with his car-bound manner of life, chose suicide by Cadillac, which has a point of no return. He went into his garage, closed its doors, windows, and roof ventilator, climbed in the front seat and started the engine. The Cadillac did not sound a *no — no — no* like the car in "Christmas Poem." Instead, the demonstrator "started with a merry, powerful hum, ready to go." Smoking and drinking, Julian English waited for carbon monoxide to kill him. Twenty minutes before the end, he decided he did not want to die, and tried to get up. But "he had not the strength to help himself, and at ten minutes past eleven, no one could have helped him, no one in the world."

The suicide of Julian English, from which he tried to withdraw, is one of the most convincing in fiction. It left O'Hara facing a technical problem at his portable typewriter in the Pickwick Arms. He must now prepare a concluding passage in which the loose ends of the story would be tied up and the composition brought to a harmonious close. Into this coda he put the discovery of Julian's body, the reaction of his father — mostly resentment at the thought that the town would recall his own father's embezzlement and suicide — the surprise of Harry Reilly, who was prepared to forgive and forget, and the grief of Caroline. O'Hara wrote a paragraph to describe her pain:

It was a lively, jesting grief, sprightly and pricking and laughing, to make you shudder and shiver up to the point of giving way completely. Then it would become a long black tunnel; a tunnel you had to go through, had to go through, had to go through, had to go through, had to go through. No whistle. But had to go through, had to go through, had to go through. Whistle? Had to go through, had to go through, had to go through, had to go through. No whistle? Had to go through, had to go through, had to go through.

The oxymoron of the gay grief, jesting and laughing, is interesting as one of the few rhetorical devices to be found in O'Hara's work. It owes its effect not only to the startling contrast of joking and grief, but to the plainness of the writing throughout the rest of the book. This lack of ornament was to characterize O'Hara's style, perhaps the literary equivalent of what Mies van der Rohe was getting at when he said "Less is more." And Caroline tried not to think about Julian that first day. "For the rest of her life, which seemed a long time no matter if she died in an hour, she would always be ready to cry for Julian. Not for him. He was all right now; but because of him, because he had left her . . ."

O'Hara began this closing chapter with the sentence, "Our story never ends." From Caroline in her grief he moved to a Gibbsville newspaper office, to Reilly on an overnight trip getting the news in New York, and then to "21" where a young man and girl are sitting at a table. It is revealed that he comes from Scranton and she from "a little town you never heard of" near Gibbsville. He says, " 'Sure I heard of Gibbsville. I've visited there often . . . Do you know Caroline Walker? That's right . . . she married Julian English. Do you know them?' 'I know him,' she said . . ." They talk of other things, she refuses to go away, " 'not this week,' " with the young man, and these characters disappear from view. It may be that this beautiful and sophisticated girl, whose name is given as Mary Manners, owes something in her creation to Mary Shuck from up the mountain. At any rate it is plain that neither she nor her friend has the slightest interest in Julian English dead or alive. News of his suicide may never reach them. The story closes as it opened, with Lute and Irma Fliegler relaxing at home. They will have to be careful with money until they find out what Dr. English intends to do about the Cadillac agency. And it turns out that Irma Fliegler doesn't know that the head of General Motors is named Alfred P. Sloan.

After writing the last of *Appointment in Samarra,* on April 9, 1934, O'Hara typed out a letter to Tom: "I've just written the End at the middle of a page, and that means The End of my novel . . . I have exactly $5.55 in the world. . . ."

FOUR

THE BIG LAUGH

THE VIRTUES of *Appointment in Samarra* far outweighed its faults, and the book achieved one of the rewards of skillfully executed fiction when it became evident that Julian English would exist outside the story. People discussed his suicide as if they had known him; and those who said the author had not explained *why* Julian killed himself were refuted by more careful readers who found the reasons set down in the book. All agreed that it was an unnecessary suicide, for the worst that could have happened to Julian, had he managed to struggle out of the death-dealing Cadillac demonstrator, would have been a suspension from the Gibbsville Club and a settlement for damages to the man he hurt in the fight. But he had his appointment in Samarra, and the title haunted the mind as one thought about the story.

A set of proofs went to Paramount Pictures, where the script department noted the strength of such scenes as the verbal attack by Bobby Herrmann and the fight in the Gibbsville Club, with particular attention to the naturalness of the dialogue. They did not buy the novel, but they had a job for the author, and on June 4, 1934, O'Hara let Tom know that he was about to leave for Hollywood: "I'm so excited about the trip, and the prospect of being able to buy a Ford phaeton of my own, and a new suit, and some razor blades . . ."

On August 16 O'Hara was living at 370 North Rossmore Avenue in Hollywood. When it crosses Santa Monica Boulevard, Rossmore becomes Vine Street, an artery of downtown Hollywood, but the neighborhood around No. 370 had no special character and resembled the district inhabited by Harold T. Graham, the engineer who falls in love with a movie star in "Natica Jackson," a story O'Hara wrote thirty-one years later. It was Hollywood, but not the stunt-man, bit-player, set-dresser, assistant-director Hollywood that O'Hara was to explore on subsequent trips to the coast. The date is significant because it was publication day for *Appoint-*

ment in Samarra, and O'Hara had much to say about that in a letter to his brother Tom: "By the time you get this the fat'll be in the fire and I'll be officially the promising young novelist. The book is published today, and so far I've seen reviews by Kyle Crichton (a friend of mine, a Communist), who said my talent was too big for my theme; and by Donald Gordon, who does the SEPost and American News Co. bulletin reviews. Gordon praised the book and regretted the sex passages, one or two of them, because it would keep it out of the small public libraries, but said 'the man has what it takes.' . . . I'm very much afraid of Isabel Paterson, and the likes of her, but a few good reviews, which I expect, will offset the bad ones. I'll believe the good things they say about me, and assure myself that the bad ones are written by people who Missed the Point. I expect the book will have the curtains drawn at 606, but why should it? I certainly have been repudiated there for 3½ years, so help me. The advance sales are very encouraging, especially here, and tonight Helen and Herbert Asbury gave a party for me out in Beverly Hills. I'll try to think of some names: Dorothy Peterson represented the acting business; Nunnally Johnson, Joseph Moncure March, Douglas MacLean (who used to be an actor; you probably wouldn't remember), and a lot of other people whose names don't mean anything outside Hollywood were there. Oh, S. J. Perelman, who is a good friend of mine and a Brunonian, he was there. It was a nice party . . . The book had had good sales here, as I said, and the total advance sale is about 3500 copies, as far as can be estimated, and if the reviews are fairly uniformly good the thing ought to top 5000. I hope so. The League of Decency probably will scare off the movie producers who may be tempted to buy the book, which makes me no happier. The L. of D. is something that a few half-assed laymen and publicity-seeking priests put over. . . .

"I am no happier here than ever. I bought a new car; traded in my Ford roadster for a new 1934 V-8 phaeton, sand color. I got $355 for the roadster, and the rest I am paying off $50 a week. The insurance, etc. run into money, but what doesn't? Buy now, kid. Inflation aplenty is just around the corner, and not the corner where prosperity has been taking that long squirt. Paramount has taken up my option, which freely translated means I stay here another three months at the same salary. Then I go back to New York to get to work on my next novel, some more defamation of character. I have another book coming out either late fall or winter; a collection of short ones, most of them from The New Yorker. It'll probably sell like hotcakes in a cemetery, but I mustn't get bitter.

"I'm going nuts with a headache, which has lasted just one week. I've had to go to the doctor about it, and am going again tomorrow. It may be sinus, and it may be Brights, and it may be that concussion I got tobogganing years ago. I'll know more after x-rays etc. and washing my hands, as

the saying goes, in a bottle. Heart and lungs are okay, so it isn't throm-
bosis. Whatever it is I hate it, and it isn't helping me with my crocheting.
They wanted to send me to El Paso to get atmospheric dialogue on the
story I'm working on for Carole Lombard, Cary Grant and Richard Arlen,
an army cavalry post story, but thank God that's apparently too expensive
a trip or something, so instead I may go up to Frisco, especially at the expense of Paramount. So far I haven't done a picture, but they say they
like my work. What they really like is that a novelist is content to work for
what I'm getting."

As he sometimes did in letters to Tom, O'Hara now touched on matters
that were troubling him, and arranged his thoughts in the guise of advice:
"I don't suppose anything any Older Person ever said affected, to any important degree, the love life of any younger person. However, just a few
comments, if not advice: to begin with, I think you are fundamentally
decent. I think I was fundamentally decent, too, but on the other hand I
was — am — a weak character, and no one will ever know the number of
ladies I enjoyed life with — and suffered various kinds of remorse and fear
afterward . . . Don't ever fall for this line about Freedom. Freedom is a lot
of crap. Two people in love — that's all you can ask of life. Just about
everything in the world, with the possible exception of the South African
locust plague, was part of the great conspiracy to keep me away from
Margaretta Archbald. Don't let anything like that keep you away from
your girl, whoever it is. When you meet her you'll know it's the one. Marg
was the one for me; Pet I love actively and deeply, and she fills my waking
hours, but all those years with Marg, no matter how much I cheated on
her, haven't erased the handwriting on the wall of love, and you may have
ten such metaphors for a quarter by sending to Drawer B, Emporia Kansas.
It isn't that Pet is second best. It's just that she's second, that's all . . . Don't
be too cerebral with a girl. I'm sure now that an hour's conversation with
Marg would make me want to run screaming for an intellectual from
Union Square, but in three months I'd forget the intellectual and still be
pining for Marg. Not that I pine for Marg; Pet is the one I pine for, because she was my wife, and still is, really. I will add a few thoughts. The
most successful chaser in the world is far less happy than the man who
never knew anyone but his wife. The chaser, as a matter of fact, is only a
poor guy who is looking for just that one woman, and hasn't sense enough
to wait and see if this one or that one isn't The One. Also, your name is
O'Hara, and there is a congenital tendency in you to dominate your wife
or your girl. Here is the only piece of straight advice: never forget that
your girl or your wife is every damn bit as much a person as you are. She
regards you as another person, just as you regard her as another person; she
thinks the world revolves around her just as you do around yourself, just
as anyone does. She has a vote in life as well as in politics, she eats and

sleeps and suffers and loves and thinks (regardless of how badly you or I may think she thinks) like you and me. She was born, she lives, she's got to die; and for you to attempt to dominate her, to pinch her personality, is some kind of sin. And it won't make you any happier. I speak of conscious domination. Inevitably the man will dominate in the right ways. The woman will dominate by influence and suggestion; the man by being a man. I hope you are in love, but if you're not you will be. Be slightly critical, very discriminating, and extremely fastidious at the beginning of your friendship with every girl, even those you are strongly drawn to at first sight, and if you love her you'll most certainly know it and be unable to stop it no matter how carefully you check your brakes . . . You'll know the girl when she comes along, or if she has come along; and don't let any remarks of your betters or inferiors keep you away from that girl. If you want to get married, stall a while until you're fairly sure, and by that time maybe I'll be able to give you a start. Not a hell of a lot; but a couple of hundred bucks anyway. Maybe some movie company will buy the rights to my novel; never can tell . . ."

The favorable reviews that O'Hara hoped for appeared in large numbers all over the country and in New York, where they were especially important. Indeed, the press was more than "fairly uniformly good," and showed such enthusiasm for *Samarra* that its author was instantly and automatically raised above the rank of apprentice screenwriter, so that for the rest of his career he regarded moving-picture jobs as little more than paid vacations, never mastered the craft of writing screenplays, and gave up studio work altogether by the early 1940s. O'Hara's impact on the industry and his largest financial return from it was the result of selling screen rights to producers. Specialists wrote the scripts with varying degrees of success in capturing the mood of the big O'Hara novels. And all of this lay ahead as he opened the envelopes from his publishers and read clippings of the reviews.

Dorothy Parker wrote that *Samarra* was "a fine and serious American novel." She praised "this swift savage story, set down as sharp and deep as if the author had used steel for paper," and called it "of high importance both as a work of American letters and a document of American history." Scott Fitzgerald said, "John O'Hara's novel indicates the tremendous strides that American writers have taken since the war." John Chamberlain in the *Times* praised the author's "mimetic skill" and added, "For contemporary truth I have seen little writing as searching as Mr. O'Hara's." William Soskin of the *American*, who later became a publisher, wrote that "a quality which most novels of American life lack is very much present in *Appointment in Samarra*. Ever since I've finished it I've gone around knocking on wood and saying please make him write more novels. There are so few of his kind." Herschel Brickell of the *Evening*

Post gave judgment that *Samarra* was "a work of genuine talent, written vigorously in the American idiom, sophisticated, acute, and swift paced." Clifton Fadiman wrote in *The New Yorker* that O'Hara's book was "the most sheerly readable novel within miles. It is something we cannot lay down. You'll have to read it." These "selling" reviews were typical of almost all the rest; and the columnist Walter Winchell, who wielded nationwide influence through his hundreds of newspaper outlets, furnished valuable promotion for O'Hara's book when he called it a "grand novel" and worthy of "orchids," his expression of highest approval. Among influential weeklies, *Time, Newsweek,* and *The Nation* gave excellent notices, and the Communist *New Masses* said "O'Hara reports like Sinclair Lewis and has more guts than Hemingway."

When O'Hara returned to New York in October 1934, he appeared in his accustomed places, and walked the same streets in mid-Manhattan where the doormen had known him and the policemen on the corners said hello. He had earned a badge that he was to wear all the rest of his life, and although it was invisible, everyone in O'Hara's world knew it was there. He had taken on the role of successful author. Although it is akin to the public role of famous actor, this does not seem to be an easy part to play: Fitzgerald and Hemingway, for example, were uncomfortable as celebrities, and in comparison, O'Hara looks like a man with a rational approach to fame, riches, and the psychic problem of tearing the material for serious writing from personal emotion and experience. It was granting the adjective "serious" to O'Hara's work that marked his badge first class. To be popular and earn good money from a large audience with work of lasting value — how many writers succeeded in doing this? O'Hara was one of the few of whom it could be said that he had not only achieved success, but might be headed for greatness. Five printings of the first edition of *Samarra* showed the book's immediate wide acceptance. Within a year it had gone to a reprint house and was on its way to fifteen more separate editions in English, in forty-two printings, by various London and New York publishers and the Modern Library. Many foreign translations also appeared, and as the power of censorship waned in O'Hara's later years, moving-picture producers expressed willingness to put his first novel on the screen. By that time the author was able to tell his Hollywood literary agent H. N. Swanson that the price of *Samarra* would be one million dollars. O'Hara said, "It's like putting the Koh-i-noor diamond in Tiffany's window. They won't pay the price, but it brings them into the store."

O'Hara was particularly admired by readers who had perceived something more than magazine filler in his early *New Yorker* pieces. Some of these readers knew O'Hara, some did not, but they all felt the emotional stir inspired by recognizing a fresh, authentic talent. It was not easy to define the special quality of his appeal. Perhaps it was his ability to create a tension between characters that was likely to break out in an ugly quarrel, or the revelation of some old injury, or a visitation of malice by the strong on the weak. The late Frank Norris, a managing editor of *Time*, said "O'Hara writes of *treachery*. Chekhov says it is important that a human being never be humiliated — that is the main thing. O'Hara knows it happens just the same, and this is what makes his stories so true and good." While on his first trip to Hollywood, O'Hara had written a number of stories, aside from his "crocheting" for Paramount. This was his invariable custom whenever he was given access to a typewriter. He had an office on the fourth floor of the Writers' and Directors' Building, looking toward Melrose Avenue and the watertank tower on the neighboring RKO lot. Here he had written "The Deke Flag," a story that has not been published in book form, but can stand as an illustration of the way O'Hara created tension, and gave characters long memories. In the story one of O'Hara's typical complacent young men is talking to his friend Chuck about the difficulty of clearing out his bachelor apartment prior to moving into a honeymoon flat with his bride. After a passage indicating that the narrator has married a dreadful girl, the story closes with an echo when we hear:

> And I'll tell you something else. If you want it, I have a Deke flag I stole one time when you were a new boy. I did it in broad daylight. We were rushing a new boy, and it got around that he was thinking of going Deke, so just to show him what we thought of Deke, I went and stole their flag, right in broad daylight. You're not sore, are you? All that stuff — gosh, it seems so damn far away. All that collegiate stuff. You a Deke, and me a Delt. It doesn't mean a damn thing any more. And then when you stop and consider what it used to mean. You know, we weren't so damn collegiate when you stop to think, but I told Edith about stealing the Deke flag one time, and she thought it was the most childish thing she ever heard of. Well, maybe she's right. Of *course* she is. If it meant anything, would I be giving it back to you?

O'Hara wrote "It Must Have Been Spring" during that Hollywood stay, carrying his mind back to the pain of trying to get his father's approval. In this period he also wrote "Sportsmanship," about an ill-fated pool hustler, with details drawn from the Pottsville underworld, and "In the Morning Sun," which presents a young man to whom bad things have happened, including divorce, so that he is broken up inside, and sits in the sun, wearing his clean white shirt and white flannel trousers. His face is brown, but his ankles are "white and sick." His mother wants to help him, but knows that he is "through." "And his mother shivered, for there was nothing she could do."

Magazine stories of this quality, together with the enthusiasm for *Appointment in Samarra,* gave O'Hara something not far from the metropolitan rank he had predicted for himself a few years before. The editors of Henry Luce's *Fortune* would soon be publishing an article about status in Manhattan, recording their opinion that the owners of "21" would rather have John O'Hara as a patron than any number of rich Texans or other persons with nothing but money to recommend them. The managers of this place, like Sherman Billingsley of the Stork Club, sometimes found it advisable to seat O'Hara near the door, so that they could ease him out if the drink took a bad hold on him. When taken the wrong way, O'Hara would become argumentative, then belligerent, and apt to tell strangers he didn't like their looks. Thus he left an unfortunate impression on people who had seen him only when he was muttering objurgations at those who happened to catch his eye, and threatening to attack them. The owners of "21," who did indeed prefer O'Hara's trade to that of nobodies, as *Fortune* reported, had their bad times with him. They had to calm O'Hara, for example, when he tried to punch the world-famous neurologist Dr. Howard Fabing, also a select client of the restaurant. The Kriendler-Berns establishment was a legal resort after Prohibition ended (on December 5, 1933), and its atmosphere was quiet and dignified, so that O'Hara's outbreaks were more noticeable on Fifty-second Street than they would have been in Hoboken or on Tenth Avenue. Years after this period of the mid-1930s, a retired diplomat recalled, "I saw John O'Hara only once, but it was unforgettable. He was sprawled on a chair in the lobby on the right as you go into '21,' mumbling to himself. It was none of my business but I felt bad because he was such a fine writer." A woman in Baltimore had a distasteful recollection from these years: "I don't think I'll forgive O'Hara for the way he talked to me. It wasn't that he was drunk, he was nasty about it." On another occasion, O'Hara declared war on the actor Paul Douglas, followed him out of "21," and challenged him to fight. Douglas said, "Take it easy, John," and walked away. O'Hara trailed Douglas across Fifty-second Street and east to De Pinna's, where he aimed a blow at his head. Douglas sidestepped, pulled O'Hara's necktie so tight that his eyes almost popped out, and walked on down Fifth Avenue. Such scenes made little if any difference to those who respected O'Hara's talent, and believed he would accomplish even better things in the future. Dorothy Parker spoke for these friends when she said, "John was a writer who had more than any of them around. He was somebody who knew something and could do something. I would have staked my soul on it." A few years later, James Thurber summed up O'Hara's difficult side: "I guess a man cannot have an eye and ear and mind as sensitive as O'Hara's without also having feelings that are hypersensitive. He brings into a room, or a life, a unique presence that is John O'Hara. If he sometimes seems to exhibit the stormy emotions of a little boy, so do all great artists, for unless they can remember what it was like to be a little boy, they are only half complete as artist and as man. Who wants to go through life with only easy friends? Nothing would be duller."

Further support for O'Hara's literary reputation came from the collection of short pieces that he had mentioned to his brother, which appeared in February 1935 as *The Doctor's Son and Other Stories.* The title piece was O'Hara's working out of the material that came to him in the 1918 influenza epidemic, establishing James Malloy and his father in a semifactual relationship to John and Patrick H. O'Hara, with special reference to the emotional tension between them. The writing, which he had done in Bermuda while happy with Pet, came out plain and powerful. Stories in the book that showed O'Hara's abilities and aims were "On His Hands," "The Man Who Had to Talk to Somebody," "Lombard's Kick," "Early Afternoon," and others of merit such as "Pleasure," about a Negro woman who barely avoids starvation working as clean-up girl in a cafeteria, forces herself to save five dollars (out of sixteen) a week, and lights "a whole cigarette" because "a person has to have some pleasure." The collection also offered "Straight Pool," which is a development of the idea in "Fifty Cent Meal," and a monologue called "Except in My Memory," placed in a Kiplingesque frame, unusual for O'Hara, setting up the narrator's friend as audience for the tale of a young married woman who meets a former love on a cruise ship — and decides against reviving the affair. O'Hara closed the book with "Over the River and Through the Wood," introducing Mr. Winfield, a gentle and sensitive old man, his granddaughter, and her two vain and horrible school friends, who would be competent matches for Tod Sloane of "On His Hands." The climax puts Mr. Winfield in disgrace when he enters one girl's room by mistake, and finds her naked.

It was an axiom of the book trade that collections of short pieces did not sell, but *The Doctor's Son and Other Stories* went through two printings in 1935. Since then it has been internationally republished. Its appearance at a time when *Appointment in Samarra* had been out less than a year showed that O'Hara intended to keep on, and that he met the definition of a professional writer — a man or woman who brings out a book, and then brings out another one. Indeed, O'Hara did not count a collection of short stories as a new book, in spite of the fact that the title piece was published for the first time. O'Hara had another novel on his mind, and he began writing it in the early fall of 1934, working in comfortable quarters which he shared with John McClain in a brownstone house on East Fifty-fifth Street around the corner from Lexington Avenue.

John McClain was a young man of O'Hara's age, who had come to New

York from Marion, Ohio (President Harding's home town), by way of Kenyon College and Brown University. After a few months clerking in Wall Street, McClain landed the berth of ship news reporter on the *Evening Sun.* These were the closing years of the grand Atlantic passenger run, and each liner brought a cargo of celebrities to be interviewed by the New York press. The reporters came down the bay early in the morning on the pilot boats, boarded the liners, and then had a couple of hours to make notes, set off flashbulbs, and drink the coffee laced with brandy that the publicity people were happy to supply. Many of the more interesting and attractive of these passengers became intimates of McClain; while he had quite adequate talents as a journalist, he was almost a genius at making friends. John McClain was good-looking and solidly built, as befitted an ex-football star, and in manner so relaxed and pleasant that both men and women found it highly agreeable to spend time in his company. From ship news McClain went to Hollywood, then to an adventurous war. After the war he became drama critic and columnist for the *Journal American,* and died in 1967. This sort of man would have special interest for O'Hara, because McClain from his first day in New York behaved like an accepted insider, and in a short time that was what he became. No matter who you wanted to see, McClain could introduce you, and he would do so gladly, and without exacting any return. Part of McClain's charm lay in the broad tolerance of his views, and people felt comfortable around him because they knew he was not keeping score of their faults. His willingness to overlook shortcomings in others was so well known that the height of horror was expressed when some disgraceful affair took place and it was said that "even McClain was shocked." In a newspaper column of reminiscences, John McClain recalled the apartment shared with O'Hara as "the most amusing menage" he ever lived in. "O'Hara and I had the ground floor of an old brownstone. He had two rooms and a bath on one side of the hall and I had a similar arrangement on the other. *Appointment in Samarra* had come out and he was feeling the first twinges of the prosperity which was to follow. I had sold some stories to magazines and was convinced a fortune was dripping from the end of my pen, and so we hired a small butler named Burton to look out for us." Burton acted as chauffeur of O'Hara's Ford, and pleased his employers with expert valeting and bartending. But he left in six months, stating that "there was too much action around the premises."

That sounds as though a continuous party had gone on, but during those six months of October through March, 1934–1935, O'Hara wrote "Except in My Memory," "Over the River and Through the Wood," and the novel *BUtterfield 8.* The title suggested itself in the announcement of the New York Telephone Company that a distinguishing numeral was to be placed with the name of each central office; patrons were to dial the first two letters and the added number. BUtterfield 8 covered the middle upper East Side, where much of the action in O'Hara's story took place. The foundation of this novel lay in accounts of the mysterious death of a twenty-year-old girl who had the unforgettable name of Starr Faithfull. The morning papers of June 9, 1931, reported the finding of Starr Faithfull's body washed up on shore at Long Beach, Long Island. It was believed that she had attended a midnight sailing party on an outgoing liner, and failed to obey the warning for visitors to leave the ship. Investigation of Starr Faithfull's background soon raised the question of whether her fall from the ship had been accident, suicide, or murder. And it was never established as a certainty that Starr Faithfull had fallen from a ship; but in the weeks that her story occupied front pages, it began to appear strongly probable that more than one person might have been happy to see her go over the side. It became known that Starr Faithfull had been a recognized figure around the expensive speakeasies, where she often gave proof that her emotions were as unstable as her face and body were beautiful. Starr Faithfull had been a hard drinker, once under treatment for alcoholism at Bellevue; and she had spent some time in a psychiatric retreat. She lived in an apartment on St. Mark's Place a few doors from the sidewalk lamps that marked the residence of Mayor Jimmy Walker. Starr shared this home with her sister, who was also beautiful, her mother, and her stepfather, a retired chemical engineer. They were a family of the anonymous but presentable sort, just barely in the upper middle class, who used to inhabit Manhattan by the thousands. The disintegration of Starr Faithfull was fully revealed in the papers before the case was written off, perhaps under political pressure. She had been mistress to a rich man, and had kept a diary recording that friendship, also noting that she would sometimes wake up in bed with a stranger. The trouble with Starr Faithfull had begun in her childhood when a prominent man had sexually mistreated her: he paid twenty thousand dollars for professional care in an effort to mend the psychic damage. As Starr Faithfull's subsequent career was to show, the efforts were unsuccessful. In 1931, O'Hara stored this material in his mind, for it summed up much of the corrupt and destructive side of the speakeasy era following World War I. O'Hara used Starr Faithfull as the model for Gloria Wandrous, the heroine of BUtterfield 8, who like the original is corrupted by having been assaulted as a child. Gloria also is well known in the smarter speakeasies, and when the mood is on her, willing to go home with a casual acquaintance. This is the situation in the opening passage of BUtterfield 8, which lets us see Gloria waking up in the Park Avenue apartment where she has passed a wild night with the owner, Weston Liggett. He has gone to the country, but has left a note of apology for tearing Gloria's dress, and an envelope containing three twenty-dollar bills. The note closes, "'Will phone you

Tuesday or Wednesday. W.' 'You're telling me,' she said, aloud." Gloria inspects the empty apartment, puts on a mink coat belonging to Liggett's wife, and leaves. The chilling ugliness of this opening is maintained throughout the story, which ends with Gloria a suicide, torn to pieces by the side-wheel of an excursion steamer.

BUtterfield 8 resembled *Appointment in Samarra* in the presentation of a guilt-ridden alcoholic suicide as the main character. The secondary characters are an unhappy lot, with little kindness or grace to recommend them. Weston Liggett is Whit Hofman gone sour, his money and Yale education imparting a slight polish to a brutal selfish man. James Malloy is a young fellow in a difficult period, drawn by O'Hara from experiences of his first two years in New York. Critics asked with some asperity what Malloy had to do with Gloria Wandrous, whom he never sees in the story. It might be argued that Malloy represents a balancing theme, that of the young man who has a better chance of survival because he is a man, for life on the town is more destructive to a woman than a man. O'Hara establishes this point without dwelling on it, and makes the end of Gloria Wandrous the inevitable result of what he has revealed about her in the story. Along with his principal narrative, which accounts for the last few days in a neurotic's life, O'Hara brings on stage some forty or fifty other characters, mostly by means of one-line descriptions in crowd or party scenes, to create a panoramic background which he brings off with economy in 310 pages. Some of the bit-players seem to have come from O'Hara short stories. For example, there are Mr. and Mrs. Paul Farley, dinner guests at the Liggett apartment when Weston comes home beaten up after a speakeasy brawl. Emily Liggett has not met Farley, and isn't sure about him, although his wife is nice. But here is Farley "wearing a dinner jacket with shawl collar, a soft shirt, a cummerbund instead of a waistcoat, and pumps. The pumps were old and a little cracked, and in his hand he had a gray felt hat that certainly did not look new. Emily wondered where she had got the idea Farley would be dressed like something out of the theater programs . . ." The point is that this Farley, although Irish and Catholic, attended Lawrenceville and Princeton, has a fine war record, and is a fashionable architect, socially secure and inoffensively sure of himself. Farley is a gentleman, as he shows by the tactful way he meets the situation when the bloodied and dirty Weston Liggett staggers in. If Farley's presence in the story may be taken as thematic rather than plot material, he serves to balance the touchy and self-conscious Malloy, who is trying to convince himself *it is really all right* to be Irish and Catholic. The touch of the old cracked evening pumps is very good. Amid complaints about sordidness, there was agreement that O'Hara had written a powerful, convincing story. The novel was to outlive its author: it went to the reprint house in 1937, to the

Modern Library in 1952, to thirty-three other editions throughout the world, and is still in print in the early 1970s.

Those who took an interest in O'Hara considered him now launched on a serious career; he had three books to his credit and youthful energy that enabled him to work hard, live hard, and develop fresh material out of his intense curiosity about the people and things that came into his life. O'Hara had all sorts of friends, and he kept on searching, among those who were women, for the one woman who would fulfill his romantic ideal and be the love of his life. He had a serious affair with a married woman of family and position, which ended without scandal, and furnished some background for the final testament of James Malloy in *Sermons and Soda-Water,* written twenty-five years later when the emotions could be recollected in tranquillity. Among O'Hara's men friends was a lean and racy young sportsman named John Durant, who interested O'Hara because of his inherited position as a member of the inside world, and his remarkable career downtown and uptown. O'Hara had begun to realize that the origins of the higher internal crowd, for the most part, were in New England, and the Durant family had existed there for a long time with deep roots. John Durant was of the tenth generation in the Connecticut branch, his connections and forebears including Thomas Clark Durant of the Union Pacific Railroad, who drove the last spike in the transcontinental line with Leland Stanford, William C. Durant, founder of General Motors, and Henry Fowle Durant, founder of Wellesley College. John Durant's brother Tim was an associate of Charlie Chaplin in Hollywood, and he later rode three times in the Grand National, making his last appearance over that course in his seventieth year. Tim Durant is called "the galloping grandpa" in the British press, and now serves as a Presbyterian elder in Bodmin, Cornwall, where the family originated. The father was Harold Riggs Durant, heavyweight champion of Yale in the early 1890s. His sons also were Yale athletes, John a track star and Tim on the baseball nine. Mrs. Durant was a famous beauty, but her husband left her for another woman; as a result John Durant was estranged from his father for twenty-five years. On his deathbed Mr. Durant sent for his sons, and John later recalled, "He wanted to give me his split bamboo fishing rods (made by *his* father by hand) but I said No. We went to his funeral at Guilford and when they lowered him into the pit (in the rain) I could not cry . . ." John O'Hara found in Durant's career a fascinating example of what could be accomplished downtown. In the spring of 1928, Tim Durant had arranged a $50,000 loan so that his brother could buy a seat on the New York Curb Exchange. After a year, John Durant became a partner in W. E. Hutton & Co. and their broker "on the floor." This he accomplished by selling his Curb seat, now worth $100,000, and borrowing $344,000 from Hutton to make up the price of his membership on the New York Stock Exchange. Things looked different after the financial crash of October 1929, and John Durant found himself sharing in losses instead of profits, and working to pay off a debt of $500,000 while his Exchange membership shrank in value to $60,000, and later fell to $40,000. Durant then turned to his real vocation and became a writer, contributing to the *Saturday Evening Post* and other magazines, with encouragement from an expert journalist named Quentin Reynolds, and from Joseph Bryan III, a writer and *Post* editor who was a friend of Reynolds and O'Hara. John Durant solved the problem of paying off a half-million-dollar debt by absorbing his personal loss of $100,000 and turning over the Stock Exchange membership to W. E. Hutton & Co., who recovered their money when the value of seats passed $500,000 in the good times of the 1940s. The Wall Street part of Durant's life can be seen in some of Alfred Eaton's business dealings in *From the Terrace*, and Alfred Eaton also was estranged from his father. However, the surly and complaining Alfred bore no resemblance at all to John Durant, a cheerful, agreeable man, who was good company like his friend McClain. Durant liked packing into the deep north woods, and in the 1930s he leased some wild country in upper Quebec, and formed a small club, the Hook and Bullet. O'Hara accepted membership but never went there, although he listed the club in his *Who's Who* biography. He often played tennis with John Durant on indoor courts in Queens, formerly the Jay Gould family private courts. Durant's memory of those encounters was that "O'Hara for some reason I could never understand wanted to beat me badly and was always after me to play a match with him. He kept challenging me. I cannot recall an opponent that I ever faced with such confidence. O'Hara would call me up and we'd set the time. He would pack a suitcase in his apartment so he wouldn't have to go back there after the game and change for the evening. All I had to do was simply to get the ball back to him and he would eventually make the error. He was really a cinch. And every time I faced him he'd seriously tell me that this was going to be the day he'd get to me and from then on he'd always beat me. Once in a while he'd take a set, but he never left the court a winner for the day. This persistency seemed odd, but John could be delightful, and a good man to have around."

Good publicity and demonstrated talent were sufficient to place O'Hara in another Hollywood job immediately after he finished writing *BUtterfield 8*. It seemed that O'Hara was content to become known as a dialogue polish man, and this work of revising lines so that they would "play" — that is, come from actors' mouths in some semblance of natural speech — was relatively easy for a writer with O'Hara's ear. There is no evidence that O'Hara had any desire or plan to become a permanent member of the movie community. For a writer, that would require dedication to the screen as a medium of expression, along with expenditure of time and energy on studio politics, and a certain amount of luck in the assignment of stories, directors, and producers. Not all the people in control of the industry could be called civilized, and some of the producers and studio heads were fantastically unfitted for their jobs. One producer actually tried to teach George M. Cohan how to wave a flag, and another fought like a tiger, though fortunately without success, to persuade Harold Arlen that "Over the Rainbow" should be cut from *The Wizard of Oz*. Rather than risk too much of himself in battles with such people, O'Hara maintained the air of a spectator. In this he was not alone: To show how they felt about Hollywood, some members of Robert Benchley's circle, including O'Hara, had round celluloid buttons made, which they wore in their lapels, Around the edge of the button were the initials W.T.F.A.Y.D.O.H.A.C., and at the center in small type, NEW YORK 2500 MILES. The wearer's joy would be great and perhaps excessive when someone would ask what the letters meant, for he could reply, "What The Fuck Are You Doing Out Here Athletic Club." That was startling talk in 1935, even for Hollywood.

John O'Hara had periods of work at Twentieth Century-Fox, RKO-Radio, Metro-Goldwyn-Mayer, and in return engagements at his first studio, Paramount. He liked the Paramount lot, on Marathon Street behind Melrose Avenue in deep Hollywood, backed up against a cemetery that was landscaped with tall palm trees in whose tops there nested a tribe of large and intelligent rats. All around was good drinking and loafing territory where writers could play in life the screen role of the talented man who sees through it all. He sees through the false tinsel, as S. J. Perelman said, to the real tinsel underneath. There was a comfortable saloon across from the main entrance on Marathon Street, called Oblath's, which O'Hara recommended to any friend headed for Paramount. It was a haunt of film cutters and studio publicity people, in addition to the writers, who fielded an Oblath's softball team on which the producers forbade actors to play for fear they would get hurt while shooting was in progress. Nearby was a small bar catering to stunt men and back-lot laborers, sometimes tense with the hatreds of the industry's union wars. Either place was a fine drinking bar like the one O'Hara imagined in "Trouble in 1949" — with plenty of bottles on shelves, "labels to read." Across Melrose Avenue was a large restaurant called Lucy's, sufficiently expensive to attract agents at lunch. Lucy's had a small sunny courtyard with a fountain, pleasant for dreaming away an afternoon on Scotch and water, in those days before Los Angeles air was poisoned by smog into something not far different from the fatal draught inhaled by Julian English. And there was the Melrose Grotto, a vast, dim place with a bar so long that it required four bartenders. Studio electricians from Paramount and RKO came here, and various alcoholics in and out of the movie industry, who found the dimness soothing to their nerves. The Grotto operated twenty-four hours a day. There was much to be said for the Paramount lot and the area around it, for here were costume and property rental companies, worth a day's time whenever one cared to inspect acres of Civil War uniforms, cavalry sabers, Springfield rifles, stagecoaches, or enough tailcoats and hoopskirted gowns to dress five thousand extras for a Viennese ball. This was in addition to Paramount's property department, a subterranean robbers' cave with a ramp leading into it large enough for a locomotive. The theatrical part of moving pictures was here, and was not lost on O'Hara. He sometimes went to the sound stages and watched the actors, directors, and technicians at work. But moving pictures did not touch anything deep inside him. It is strange that of the many writers who worked for the industry, none came out with a great novel about movies. Scott Fitzgerald may have been on the track with *The Last Tycoon*, but he died before completing his story of a producer who had a creative feeling for the medium. It may be an illusion that the "big" film novel can be written. At any rate, O'Hara did not try for it. But during this time in Hollywood after *BUtterfield 8*, he assimilated material for a short novel called *Hope of Heaven*, which he finished in Philadelphia. He mentioned it in a letter to Joseph Bryan at the *Post*, which Mr. Bryan has kindly made available: "Here are two pieces which obviously were rejected by Collier's after being considered for a month. By the look of them they must have considered them by walking up and down on them, giving them an Underwriters' test to see if they were waterproof, and allowing Crowell's infant child to use them for paper dolls. However, occasionally typescript does come through, and perhaps there may be enough to please and purchase. I was in Philadelphia a couple of weeks ago, finishing my book. I locked myself in my room at the Ben Franklin, and then to show I was in earnest I immediately phoned you, but the office was closed on account of Lorimer* trouble, and also I saw that you were going to be in a (Oh, Bishop Kinsolving, your head is revolving) wedding. So then I called Jim Neville, who, according to the Princeton Club, is in California. Then I called Helen Hayes, but she wasn't in either. So I settled down and finished the book, an attractively bound volume bearing the mysterious title *Hope of Heaven*, to be published late in February, or 'Spring,' as the publishers call it. I hope they don't change to light underwear just because of that."

In this his third novel O'Hara presented James Malloy working in pictures after having achieved a New York reputation. Malloy is not happy and admits that he does not like himself very well. The opening scene

* O'Hara's reference was to the famous retired editor of the *Post*, George Horace Lorimer.

shows Malloy as narrator in his office, trying to get his "mind off the sound of the dynamo or the generator or whatever it was that made that sound. That sound never let up, and if you let yourself listen to it it had the effect of the dentist's drill, or the bastinado. That sound is in every studio I've ever worked in, and I never have been able to determine just what it is. Some say it's a dynamo; some say it's the ventilating system; others say it's just water in the pipe-lines. Whatever it is, it's always near the writers' offices." The story tells how Malloy becomes involved with a Lutheran minister's son from Gibbsville who has stolen five thousand dollars in travelers' checks and comes to Los Angeles under an assumed name. By coincidence the private detective on the case is the estranged father of Malloy's girl, an intellectual type who works in a Hollywood bookstore. The Southern California background is accurately rendered, and while *Hope of Heaven* is one of its author's lesser works, it is a controlled performance with a moment of honest emotion near the end. Malloy takes pleasure in his movie connection, is more than a name-dropper, a nickname-dropper — "Gretch" for Loretta Young — and like most creative workers at the studios, politically left-liberal. James Malloy is determined not to lose touch with New York, and makes a quick trip there and back between picture jobs. On his return to Los Angeles, he notes that all the way in from the airport the thing that keeps depressing him is that for three or four or five days he will not be able to see a New York paper that he has not already read in New York. *Hope of Heaven* met with a cool reception from many reviewers who said that O'Hara was not fulfilling the promise of *Appointment in Samarra*. Whether or not *Heaven* justified this ruling, there was vitality in the story, which went through two printings in 1938 and a British edition in 1939, then came to life again through paperback publication in 1946, 1947, and 1949, and started a run of fifteen international editions in 1956. In the time between *BUtterfield 8* and *Heaven*, O'Hara brought out eighteen short stories, including "Pretty Little Mrs. Harper," which appeared in *Scribner's* for August 1936 and has not yet been republished. This story showed O'Hara's recognition of the automobile as a common means of ending American lives. His own life almost ended in an accident to a car in which he and Madeleine Carroll were riding, with the director Lewis Milestone at the wheel. They went off the road but escaped with bruises and a few stitches. Charles Butterworth, one of the actors O'Hara liked, was to die on Sunset Boulevard when his imported racing car turned over near the Garden of Allah, headquarters of the New York crowd. Butterworth was on his way home from a party given by John McClain, now in California sharing a bungalow at the Garden with Robert Benchley. These cottages, grouped around a hotel that had once been the mansion of Alla Nazimova, were considered raffish by the moguls of the picture industry, but furnished ideal lodgings and gathering places for the irreverent, the unconventional, and the transient. It seemed a crowning irony that Robert Benchley should make his greatest impression on the movie business as an actor — indeed, as a star comedian who could inflict paralyzing laughter on an audience with his portrayal of a well-meaning man hopelessly beyond his depth. The hospitality of Benchley and McClain drew many guests who were in need of reassurance for one reason or another. The anxieties that beset actors and writers would vanish when these genial men welcomed their friends and pressed drinks upon them. McClain's recollection was that "because of Benchley's personal charm and the fact that our bar was always in good working order, the bungalow became a sort of salon. Any day, shortly after six in the afternoon, the living room would be cluttered with two or more members of the drop-in trade: John O'Hara, John Steinbeck, Dorothy Parker, Scott Fitzgerald, Roland Young, Donald Ogden Stewart, Mike Romanoff, Humphrey Bogart, Monty Woolley, Herbert Marshall, Irene Selznick, Charles Lederer, Charlie Brackett, Eddie Sutherland, Charlie Butterworth and scores of other amiable souls. The chatter and laughter could be heard a block or so . . ."

O'Hara also met Clifford Odets at this time, and Alfred M. Wright, Jr., a student at Yale on vacation. "Al" Wright, the son of a rich Pasadena lawyer, was to be an editor at Time, Inc., a hero of naval aviation, and one of the best-liked men in his generation. He was an easygoing man with a crooked smile of singular warmth — another of those natural insiders who fascinated O'Hara. During a stint at MGM, O'Hara met a man whose gift for friendship reminded him of John McClain. This was Carleton Alsop, a producer on the lot who did not take the movie business with overpowering seriousness. Sometimes in the early afternoon Alsop would look into O'Hara's office and say, "I think we've had about enough of this, don't you?" They would down tools and go out to play tennis. And it was at the Westside Tennis Club, in 1936, that John met Belle Wylie, one of the important people in his life and the mother of his only child.

When *Appointment in Samarra* appeared, Belle Wylie had been one of its readers, and said to her sister Lucilla, "I'd like to meet the man who wrote that book." At the time Belle was in her early twenties, a member of a family that was solidly established in Manhattan and Quogue, Long Island. Her father was Robert Hawthorne Wylie, a well-known physician, graduate of Yale, and descendant of an old Southern family. Belle had attended the Brearley School in preparation for St. Timothy's at Stevenson, Maryland, graduating in 1931. She was a dark-haired, slender girl, with keen intelligence and a gentle manner that could disarm the most difficult or self-centered person. Belle's sister Lucilla married Henry Codman Potter, a successful Broadway and Hollywood director who was a Yale graduate and the son, grandson, and grandnephew of Episcopal bishops. With her mother and her other sister Winnie (now Mrs. Henry Gardiner), Belle came to visit the Potters in California, played from time to time on the Westside courts, and there the meeting with John O'Hara came about through friends. O'Hara soon became seriously interested in Belle, and on returning to the East, he discovered that the Wylies' summer village of Quogue was much to his liking. Quogue is eighty miles from New York City, just over the line from Westhampton on Shinnecock Bay. It was and is a conservative, understated resort with neat hedges, shingled cottages, and some larger houses that call themselves cottages but are in fact mansions. Such was the Wylies' big house at the corner of Quogue Street and Shinnecock Avenue in the center of town. Along with the Gardiner family, the Wylies were the leading clan, and like the other summer people, they preferred Quogue exactly as it was — quiet, close-knit, and not interested in competition with the high-styled neighboring colony of Southampton. Some of the Southamptonites considered Quogue a dowdy sort of town where nothing happened, but O'Hara liked it on sight. Granted that the summer population was mostly Republican and Episcopalian, and that writers were unheard of, there was still much to be said for Quogue's restraint, good manners, and physical beauty. O'Hara's friend Charles Addams the cartoonist, who came to Westhampton in the summer, also approved of Quogue and liked to visit there. O'Hara rented a house on the Dune Road and passed an agreeable summer as an avowed admirer of Belle. Mrs. Wylie, a friendly and delightful woman, enjoyed talking with him. They shared a number of jokes, bits of nonsense they agreed were funny, and played some casual bridge, not expending too much mental effort on scientific evaluation of the hands. Mrs. Wylie was another Nelly Boone to O'Hara, who responded to her as he always did to sympathetic older women. The legend was that he had met her daughter in a speakeasy, and that Belle had remarked, "This used to be my house." There is a slight element of fact in this story, for while the doctor was living, the Wylies had a town house at 72 West Fifty-second Street, where the Onyx Club, formerly located across the way, established itself after Repeal. Here the horn men Ed Farley and Mike Riley informed audiences every night that the music went round and around (and it comes out here) in the room which had been the maids' dining hall.

In the summer of 1937 Belle went to Europe, and John reached a decision which resulted in his sending a cable asking her to come back and marry him. Belle returned, and O'Hara realized that he had almost no money on hand. Earning power he had, and royalties due every six months from what he had already published. But he had been spending at a fast rate in restaurants and nightclubs, and for transportation, clothes, and rent. Quogue encouraged simplicity, but it was the expensive kind. John now thought of an offer by his brother Tom, who had said he could lend up to one thousand dollars if need arose. In early September, John sounded the call for nine hundred dollars to get married on. Tom was working at the *Daily News* with Saturdays off; he took a train to Philadelphia and Pottsville on Friday night. In those days banks were open on Saturdays, and in the morning Tom walked down the hill from 606 Manhantongo Street, drew the money, and telegraphed it to John, who was then living in Tudor City at the eastern end of Forty-second Street in Manhattan. Tom went home and his mother asked him where he had been. He felt bad about it, but did not see how he could report what John had in mind, and so he answered, "I took a little walk downtown." Belle and John were married at Elkton, Maryland, after which they telephoned Winnie at the Wylie apartment in New York. Mrs. Gardiner has recalled that when she passed the news to her mother, Mrs. Wylie gave "a blood-curdling shriek, but she was all right about it and really quite pleased because of her liking and admiration for John."

Thus began a marriage during which, according to close friends, "John found himself." The process of self-identification did not take place overnight. In the moving-picture colony, O'Hara's usual role was that of observer: Sheilah Graham remembered him at the Garden of Allah, listening much and saying little. But O'Hara was unpredictable; his friends were not amused, for example, when he leaped on Benchley's back and almost sent him to the ground, while a cocktail party was strolling as a group down to the pool. The prank hints at the high spirits that could on occasion stimulate O'Hara and his associates in Southern California. Both in California and New York, Belle had her problems. Those who knew her were aware that there was more in Belle Wylie O'Hara than the gentle goodness she habitually displayed: underneath was a layer of steel for the protection of those she loved. O'Hara added to his private load of guilt at the times — in moods of spleen and irritability — he lashed out at Belle. When O'Hara lost emotional control, he became James Malloy at his least attractive, and he could arouse a sharp dislike if his rancor was public and its object Belle. A man who knew them in the early 1940s recorded: "I could have brained John in the Stork Club one night when he spoke sharply to Belle, who took it without flinching, then he began to needle her and kept it up, really bullying her and lousing up a nice dinner, until at last she burst into tears. It was a shameful performance and I never forgave him for it in my mind. Belle's offense, if there was one, was exceedingly trivial, but JOH took it big and never stopped. I left murmuring to myself, 'He may be a successful and talented writer but he is at heart a cheap bastard.'" The weight of O'Hara's talent made such severe judgments inevitable after displays of impatience or fretfulness that would be overlooked and forgotten in less interesting and important men. It was the same with Scott Fitzgerald, whose embarrassing and sometimes cruel misbehavior has been published in detail, though he has yet to attract the attention of an unfriendly biographer.

On May 22, 1971, five days before he died of a stroke at the age of fifty-five, Al Wright sat before his typewriter in Sagaponack, Long Island, bringing to mind for the author of this book some recollections of his friend: "Thoughts of John are always coming back to me in a thousand ways, perhaps because I am not yet used to the idea that he is dead. I frequently stay at the Yale Club when I'm in the city, and I get hung up for long periods in the hallways looking at all those photographs of the 1895 crew or the 1907 golf team or the Yale Battery of World War One. And immediately I think of John. That was the world he really loved — and lived in, or tried to. I don't think John gave a damn about anything that happened after World War Two. His era was that 85 years from the first shot at Sumter to the scene on the deck of the Missouri. You can leave out the rest of the history of the world. But if some guy with radar ears and eyes on the ends of three-foot antennae a couple of hundred years from now wants to know how people acted in that brief period — what they ate and said and thought — he had better read O'Hara.

"The time when I knew John best would be the period from 1937 through 1945. After that, I saw him only occasionally. Around 1955 I made his bad list over a silly incident involving someone else. I stayed on the list until I married Joan Fontaine, of whom John and Sister were fond, and then for several years I saw him quite frequently. But it was in that '36 to '45 period that I really knew him.

"John and I met, naturally, in a nightclub — the old Trocadero in Hollywood. It was just before my senior year at Yale, and John was sitting with a classmate of mine named Chad Ballard, a fellow from Indiana with a wooden leg whose father owned most of French Lick and the Sells-Floto Circus among other things. John had a snappy Ford V-8 phaeton and a Filipino boy who drove him in it and otherwise looked after him. John kept me drinking for several days after we met and then poured me on the Chief to return to New Haven. It must have been the Yale in me that attracted him, because I can't think of anything else I could have offered.

"He came up to New Haven a few times that year and drank himself into insensibility at the bar in the Fence Club. I would go to New York, and he would take me to Bleeck's and the Stork and '21' and introduce me to people like Bob and Adele Lovett and Heywood Broun and Dick Watts and Stanley Walker. Pretty heady stuff for a young college kid. John had a regular circuit around town, and he was as methodical about it as a night watchman. Bleeck's, '21,' the Stork, and finally Dave's Blue Room for a bowl of corn flakes. And always in a trench coat and big felt fedora. Also the white Brooks Bros. shirt.

"It was in the fall of that year, 1937, that John married Belle. I didn't see him again until he and Belle moved to Hollywood and lived in a small apartment in Westwood, actually several small apartments. John had his ulcer by then, and I think he was on the wagon for quite a stretch after he and Belle were married, but he went off rather strenuously after reaching Hollywood. I remember Belle phoning me in tears once and asking me please not to drink with John. Which was another way of saying, don't see him. If I didn't drink with him someone would, or he would drink alone.

"John didn't have a job most of the time in Hollywood, but he was writing short stories and living off them. He had a routine that would have killed the average man. On a good day, he would get up in time for lunch at the Beverly Derby around one. He had his regular table in the bar, which would grow through the afternoon with just about anyone — Scott Fitzgerald, Artie Shaw, Herman Mankiewicz, a few of the actors he liked. He would eat corned-beef hash with a poached egg on top (white of the egg always removed), wash it down with a glass of milk and then be ready for his Cutty Sark and water, or St. James and water. I think it was Cutty Sark at that time and St. James later, but it may have been vice versa. Belle would finally join him around dinner time, not at all happy with the way things were going, and they would then dine at Ciro's or Chasen's or some other expensive place. It always amazed me that John, who cared not a whit for food and rarely ate anything more esoteric than a lamp chop and creamed spinach, insisted on dining where the cuisine was so expensive and delicately prepared — '21,' Passy (one of his favorites in New York), Perino's in L.A., and so on. He had an elephantine memory for the names of waiters and captains and maîtres d'.

"To get back to John's Hollywood routine. After he and Belle had dined, they would proceed on to nightclubs, joining others or being joined until John could no longer function and had to be driven home by Belle, or the place closed at the merciful California hour of two A.M. If he was still upright when he reached the Westwood apartment, Belle would give him a bowl of cereal, and he would work until dawn. He would put his portable on a coffee table in front of a couch, get out that yellow copy paper he always used, and beat out a complete short story. Sometimes it did not go so well if he was too smashed to type decently, but I have seen one of his stories after a night of drinking without a single typographical error or any x-ing, and he would mail it off to the New Yorker without a correction.

"The next day after the drinking night, John was out of action. Belle would leave the curtains drawn in the apartment and tiptoe around while John slept until midafternoon. He would stay in his pajamas the rest of the day while Belle prepared his soft food, usually poached eggs on toast (with the whites of the eggs surgically removed), milk and whatever else was kind to his ulcer. Unless he had a really important engagement he would not leave the apartment. Minor appointments for dinner or whatever were cancelled. He would read and listen to the radio and write until after midnight, still in his pajamas, and then the whole cycle would begin again at the Brown Derby 48 hours after the previous one had started.

"John was rather sensitive about his social position in Hollywood. He was not on the list of the David Selznicks and the Sam Goldwyns and those places where the upper crust of Hollywood gathered, and he rather resented the fact that his old pal and roommate, John McClain, was. In fact, McClain and O'Hara were never close after that Hollywood period. I think the Hollywood guys would have liked to have O'Hara around, but I imagine they were a little frightened of him. Some of John's friends were through Belle, a couple of her pals from school who were married to guys working in Hollywood, and Belle's sister, Lucilla, who was married to H. C. (Hank) Potter, a successful director. John and Belle used to spend a lot of Sundays playing tennis and sunning by the pool at the Potters' big house in Brentwood. Their other friends were the New York émigrés — Dottie Parker and Alan Campbell, the Thurbers and others of the *New Yorker*, N.Y. newspaper set who happened to be in Hollywood. There was an occasional Friday-night poker game at the O'Haras' apartment with Fitzgerald and Sheilah Graham, sometimes Dottie and Alan and I forget who else. John's only club was the Westside Tennis Club out in that never-never land between 20th-Fox and MGM. John's tennis was not good, but he liked the conviviality of the bar with members like Gilbert Roland and George Murphy and other movie types.

"It will not surprise you that John enjoyed having a number of friends in Pasadena, which was out of bounds to Hollywood. John and Bob Benchley and Charlie Butterworth and McClain were about the only Hollywood people who had passes to Pasadena. You would usually see them at the sprightlier galas of the now-defunct Midwick Country Club, where the best polo in America was played, outside Meadowbrook, and John loved to go to the polo. He was not in the least interested in the Hollywood polo at Riviera and Uplifters, however, and made fun of it."

In 1939, Darryl Zanuck engaged O'Hara to work at Twentieth Century-Fox for $750.00 a week. Edmund Wilson, who never wrote for the screen, had compared the earnings of those who did to "fairy gold," that "melts at the frontier." The observation was accurate, for the luxury and fun of Southern California life came high, and little if any moving-picture money ever found its way to Eastern banks. Like most young people of the period who had high earning power, O'Hara did not bother with systematic saving or investment. Belle had property of her own, amounting to a modest competence. Her worries at this time were not financial, but had to do with trying to guide her temperamental husband, without his being aware of it, away from courses of action that could cause him to lose the strength of his vocation. In spite of Belle's underlying anxieties, their stays in Hollywood produced a great deal of laughter, for there were tempting targets on all sides for sophisticated wit. It is difficult if not impossible to convey a sense of amusement after the delightful moment is gone, and the question of taste so often arises, to congeal the printed word where the spoken word was airy and light; but it can be said that during his days and months of checking in and out at studios, O'Hara absorbed the material for a cluster of the best stories of his later years, and a novel about a movie star which he called *The Big Laugh*. Although this book did not appear until 1962, O'Hara was enjoying his personal big laugh from the time he first found his way to the Garden of Allah until the next turning point in his life, which came after World War II. During the year in which he had the contract with Zanuck, O'Hara published eleven *New Yorker* pieces, and five of them had to do with one of his most convincing characters — Joey Evans, the nightclub entertainer. Joey had first appeared on October 22, 1938, writing to his friend Ted, a bandleader. He had some resemblance to Lardner's Jack Keefe, who also told a story in letters. What Joey revealed in his first letter, written from the provincial hotel where he was appearing in the floor show, was his callousness toward the difficulties of a girl whom he had made pregnant. O'Hara called the story "Pal Joey," and followed it on November 26 with "Ex-Pal," which shows Joey in trouble because Ted has mentioned the contents of his first letter, and the word got back to Ohio:

> So you call yourself a pal . . . First of all the asst mgr of the hotel where I am singing he comes to me and says "Joey I just rec'd informaton that is not doing you any good around this town and I want you to level with me and tell me if it is true." What? I said. What informaton? "Well I do not exactly know how to put it man to man. We are both men of the world but this is what I have reference to, meaning that a certain mouse from this town had to leave on acc't of you and is now in N.Y. and instead of helping her you are writing letters to pals in N.Y. and shooting off your face about what a don Juan you are. That don't do you any good personally and I will state frankly that while we are highly pleased with your singing and drawing power as a personality here at the hotel however we have to look at it from all the angels and once it gets around that you are the kind of chap that writes letters to his pals in N.Y. mentoning his fatal attraction to the ladies why some nite some guy is just going to get his load on and you are singing and a guy will walk up and take a poke at you while you are singing. Think it over" he said.

The episodes appearing in 1939 were "How I Am Now in Chi," "Bow, Wow," "Avast and Belay," "Joey on Herta," and "Joey on the Cake Line." "How I Am Now in Chi" has Joey working in a South Side nightclub on Cottage Grove Avenue. The Ohio city has become too hot for him on account of his attentions to a banker's daughter. After having the girl examined by a physician, the banker sent a husky weighing over two hundred pounds to escort Joey to the Chicago train. At the end of 1939, Joey is still in Chicago, out of work but receiving a subsidy that keeps him on the cake line, which is considerably better than the bread line, and cheating a tailor over an evening coat.

In September of 1939, O'Hara published *Files on Parade,* a collection of stories that sold like a popular novel in three printings before the end of the year. The thirty-five gathered stories had such impact that critics began using the phrases "undoubted master of the form," "recognized as master," and the like. The collection included "Trouble in 1949," its background the quiet Pennsylvania roadhouse of the 1930s where future trouble might be brewing. This was a place whose quality you recognized when you saw the saintly white-haired Irish bartender. "Good-by, Herman" appeared along with "Are We Leaving Tomorrow?," the story of a wealthy young young couple always on the move, from one expensive resort to another, after the husband has done some unforgivable thing while drunk. "Their name was Campbell — Douglas Campbell, and Sheilah. They were the youngest people over fifteen in the hotel." The story leaves a feeling of lives being wasted, without hope — the mood of "Early Afternoon." Taken as a whole, the stories in *Files on Parade* showed O'Hara much concerned with people in pain. "The Cold House" lets us see Mrs. Carnavon preparing to turn out her dead son's room at their summer place. She realizes that she has harbored a "vague plan to lock this room and leave everything as she found it . . ." And she has been in danger of coming back to visit the locked shrine and "trying to squeeze out a tear . . . next August, next September, a year from next August and a year from next July . . ." O'Hara had observed some middle-aged ladies, as he showed in depicting Mrs. Carnavon breathing heavily from the exertion of descending from the car and walking up the three steps of the porte-cochere: "The thumb of her right hand was beating against the forefinger." Thus the pain of loss as O'Hara presented it in one story; he also made use of the pain that accompanies guilt in "A Day Like Today," which can be cited as an example of his economy in getting what he is after. In less than fifteen hundred words he gives us the meeting, in a shabby barroom, of a man in his forties and the girl, no more than twenty, whom he has seduced on the previous night. He says he wants to tell her he is sorry about last night, " 'sorry about the way it happened. I mean, I'm sorry about the *way* it happened. I'm not sorry it happened.' . . . She stood up. He took her hand. 'No, please don't go. Not unless you promise you'll see me tonight. Are you going to the Chase's party?' 'Yes, but I won't know you . . . We've got to be careful, Jim. *You* be careful, I don't know how . . .' " After the girl leaves, the man telephones his wife:

" 'Listen, what about not going to this thing of the Chase's tonight? I can't face another day like today.' "

O'Hara showed his knack for felicitous titles in *Files on Parade* for a collection of reprinted pieces. There was no need to explain that the phrase came from Kipling's private soldier in the ballad about the execution of Danny Deever, since this was probably the best-known set of verses in English. But some years later, Paul Palmer of the *Sunday World,* who had taken a high post at the *Reader's Digest,* was surprised to hear from O'Hara on the subject of this title. The *Digest* had headed a page of reprints "Files on Parade," and O'Hara accused the magazine of invading his rights. Palmer sent a soothing letter and a check for $100.00; he closed by saying, "We haven't heard from Kipling, yet." O'Hara replied with sincere thanks for the money, and added, "Speaking for myself and Corporal Kipling who just dropped in for a chota-peg, that would be the ideal way to settle all literary controversies."

Throughout 1940, *Files* continued to sell in an encouraging manner, and O'Hara had the pleasure and profit of seeing five books of his writing alive in the shops, and on the night tables and open shelves of people who read. During this year, O'Hara took on the "Entertainment Week" department in *Newsweek,* which he wrote from July 15, 1940, to February 16, 1942. The O'Haras rented a ground floor apartment in a remodeled town house at 27 East Seventy-ninth Street, near the New York Society Library. The house was deep, and the O'Hara flat seemed to go back indefinitely, giving a comfortable sense of shelter. Heavy walls and curtains made the place quiet for O'Hara's daytime slumbers, and absorbed the happy noise of friends who often gathered for parties. The O'Haras were good hosts: they did not object when guests had the inspiration, "Let's call Frank Sullivan," now returned to his native Saratoga. No matter how late the calls from Seventy-ninth Street went through, Sullivan was always cheerful, and never reproached anyone for waking him in the middle of the night. It was observed that O'Hara could survive long evenings at home without getting drunk. This was because Belle acted as his bartender, decreasing the amount of liquor in the highballs as the evening went on. But there was no stint for any guest, and the O'Haras tolerated some thirsty ones.

In contrast to the relaxed and agreeable atmosphere in O'Hara's home, the *Newsweek* columns almost always had an uncomfortable quality. The fact was that O'Hara should never have taken on any task of filling space on a regular schedule. James Malloy came to the fore — Malloy with power, settling grudges, airing prejudices, and writing all too often with an only partially concealed truculence. People who knew and liked O'Hara read his opening *Newsweek* columns, said to themselves, "John is better than that," and stopped reading. The first *Newsweek* piece took off from a memorial concert to George Gershwin at Lewisohn Stadium. Gershwin was three years dead, and O'Hara began handsomely with a salute to one who had achieved "enduring triumph after death." O'Hara mentioned his memories of parties at the Ira Gershwins' on East Seventy-second Street, with George "playing Gershwin endlessly — which was all right with me . . ." Then O'Hara wrote his memorable line, "George died on July 11, 1937, but I don't have to believe that if I don't want to." Heywood Broun could not have put it better; but O'Hara continued:

> I am a little sorry now that I did not like George, that I was not his friend. When I say that no layman knew and loved his work so well as I, I can almost prove it with an anecdote. One of those Saturday nights George was playing "Do Do Do," using an arrangement he had worked out for a phonograph record. When he came to the ending I said: "Why don't you play it the way you did on the record?" "I did," he said. "No, you didn't," I said. "Well now really, John, I wrote the piece. I ought to know." "Don't bet him!" said Ira to George. So I one-fingered the ending as it had been written in 1926, annoying George with a compliment, or what might have been regarded as a compliment but for my smugness and the fact that George rightfully enough considered himself the leading authority on his favorite subject, his music.

That was distinctly off-putting, but O'Hara would be capable of equal boastfulness on many an occasion yet to come. For all of that he was a competent columnist, and free of fancy-work in his writing. Still he would set one's teeth on edge by name-dropping ("both Benchley and I are stockholders in Romanoff's Restaurant . . . not only do I have as a fellow stockholder Mr. John Hay Whitney, but I am in the thing more than he is . . ."), by questionable judgments (placing George S. Kaufman above Bernard Shaw), and by a literary equivalent of the finger extended from the teacup ("Three times during the season I expect to step from my taxi into a shin-deep puddle of water, one of the occupational hazards of playgoing, and not very good for you when you wear pumps. I will turn up in tweeds for at least one white-tie opening, and on at least one other occasion, because I am going to a party later, I will be the only man in the theater in tails."). O'Hara gave us another peep into high life when he mentioned his appreciation for the society bandleader Emil Coleman. "There's a man who — well, he and his one-family band are so few and have given so much pleasure to so many. One night a few years ago I was at the Persian Room, had just danced with a pretty girl, and was dancing with her mother, and I looked down to see that the lady, my partner, was weeping. Had I said something wrong? No. But please let's dance over and say hello to Emil. 'He played for my wedding and my coming-out party, and he played for Dolly's party too. Let's dance over and say hello.' " We are not made uncomfortable because the lady was fortunate enough to be able to hire Coleman's band, but at O'Hara's gratification in being the lady's partner on the floor of the Persian Room. But again, one must beware of inflating foibles. In the piece that mentioned his partner at the Persian Room, O'Hara said he had danced to this music for about twenty years, which meant that he first heard Emil Coleman in the days of Shenandoah and the amusement parks around Pottsville. Since that time they had both come a long way.

By the middle of 1940, O'Hara saw that the Joey stories would add up to a short novel, and wrote two additional episodes, which did not have magazine publication, so that *Pal Joey* appeared as a book in fourteen chapters on October 23. A second printing was ordered in the following month, and Joey continued through eleven international editions. More than this came from the character when George Abbott, Richard Rodgers, and Lorenz Hart saw possibilities in Joey as the antihero of a musical play. In those days there had not been much experimenting with the idea of heel as hero, and the conception was daring and fresh. O'Hara turned out a highly professional libretto. He wrote tight scenes that "played," and his characterizations were funny and sharp, not only of Joey Evans, but of the older woman who falls in love with him, and of all the other people in the story. O'Hara had taken on the challenge of the Broadway musical theater at the height of its greatest period. It was a theater that tolerated no mistakes, but O'Hara's collaborators were veterans with many successes to their credit. The producer-director Abbott was perhaps the ablest in the business, while the music of Rodgers and the lyrics of Hart were standards of achievement in a period which also enjoyed the best work of Cole Porter, Vincent Youmans, Jerome Kern, Irving Berlin, and the Gershwin brothers. And so *Pal Joey*, a play with music, opened on December 11, 1940, at the Forrest Theatre in Philadelphia. Tom O'Hara was on the *Evening Ledger* at this time, and he interviewed his brother, noting that John did not seem to be the victim of anything resembling the nervous breakdowns that rehearsals sometimes caused in people trying to get a show together for New York. It turned out that O'Hara had superlative actors in addition to his eminent producer, composer, and lyricist. Gene Kelly was a Joey who managed to charm the audience at his most outrageous, and Vivienne Segal played the older woman with humor and style. Three weeks later *Pal Joey* was a success on Broadway — with some reservations by critics who thought the Joey-Vera situation improper, as indeed was intended. This aspect of the story troubled Brooks Atkinson of the *Times*, but *Time* magazine recognized the show's merits: "Since he came of age, John O'Hara has spent more time in nightclubs than many men have in bed. He has stayed till closing, seen all the sights, heard all the jargon . . . The play in O'Hara's slangy dialogue is gamy, funny, simple in outline: Joey is taken up by a Chicago society woman even harder than he is. She keeps him until she is tired of him, then gets the heel out of there. Meanwhile he has lost the affections of a nice young ingenue. Somehow the show performs the feat of making Joey an almost sympathetic character. As Joey, lean, dark Gene Kelly has a treacherous Irish charm, a sweet Irish tenor, a catlike dancing grace that makes vice almost as appealing as virtue." The success of *Pal Joey* made O'Hara the leading young all-purpose writer of the day: perhaps short of writing a long epic poem, he could do anything. Indeed, he had been heard to say that he had it in mind to attempt a narrative poem about a jazz musician. (The idea finally emerged as the story "I Spend My Days in Longing.") But so far as O'Hara and the stage were concerned, Dorothy Parker and others had little doubt that he would make a further contribution to the commercial theater. He seemed to have everything it required — wit, economy, the gift of putting life into characters. He was to write more plays, but they were never produced except by amateurs or in experimental one-night stands in summer theaters. There was one problem that would have made trouble had O'Hara continued to write for the Broadway stage: his apparent lack of understanding of the performer's contribution to a successful play. He had stated his dislike for most actors, and his portrayals of actresses in subsequent fiction were usually unflattering. Sidney Howard, who had won the Pulitzer Prize in 1924 with *They Knew What They Wanted,* had said that the only sound reason for writing a play was "a love of the brave, beautiful, ephemeral art of acting." The evidence is that O'Hara would not have agreed with this: he was always suspicious of Gene Kelly, for example, and apparently could not bring himself to see what Kelly had added to *Pal Joey.* O'Hara had told his collaborators that Kelly was perfect for the role; but he used the actor as the point of departure for a story in *Collier's* called "Conversation at Lunch," in which an ingrate fails to recognize benefits conferred on him. In the closing years of his life, O'Hara sometimes mused in conversation with his daughter Wylie about the satisfaction it gave him to think of "all the work he had provided" for actors, electricians, stage carpenters, and other people, in theaters and on the sound stages of Hollywood. He had overlooked the fact that no art or industry can be only one man deep, and that the technicians and actors would have been doing something else if not employed in an O'Hara story. It was obvious that O'Hara's temperament was not that of the theater, and he was not in fundamental accord with its people. But on one thing all hands could agree: Joey Evans was a triumphant creation, and one of the great parts on the modern American stage. Joey was absolutely convincing, and he lived without putting one in mind of an author at all, so candid and clear were his actions and speech. Additional evidence of Joey's vitality came when he got into the American language, by way of the *Daily News,* which began referring to Marshal Stalin as Pal Joey.

After his marriage, O'Hara started a lifelong custom of summering at Quogue. He and Belle occupied a cottage on the Wylie property until they were able to move into East House on the Dune Road, a place that looked over unlimited sea beyond its beach. Friends recall much laughter from the early summers at Quogue; although the village presented itself in a deliberately understated way, there were cocktail parties, dances, and an annual show called Quogue Quips, to which O'Hara contributed sketches. He enjoyed the social activities, tennis, and golf, and used his impressions for a number of stories about Long Island resort life, such as "The Next-to-Last Dance of the Season," and "The Last of Haley," which told how an Irishman ended his life by swimming straight out to sea on the night of a yacht club dance.

A close friend during this period was Frank Norris, a managing editor of *Time,* who admired O'Hara and his work. Norris was a red-haired half-Irish Tennesseean who had graduated from Princeton in 1929 after a lively career of writing for the college magazines when he was not in New York or traveling far and wide at no cost on the railroads of the United States, because his father was Ernest E. Norris, president and later board chairman of the Southern Railway. E. E. Norris was a craggy, sharp-eyed citizen with the early-American face of an Andrew Jackson, and he did not have the slightest idea who his son's friend was when introduced to John O'Hara. He also had only a dim notion of his son's employer, Henry Luce, connecting him in some way with the printing business. However, Mr. Norris was pleased to put private cars at Frank's disposal every spring for the Kentucky Derby, and so O'Hara had the gratifying experience of going to that race on the *Virginia* and the *Carolina.* Norris had married Lee Bacon, a red-headed beauty from Denver, and they made one of the handsomest couples in New York City and Dutchess County, where they occupied an estate called Willowbrook Farm. O'Hara renamed the main house "Birthplace of Millard Fillmore" because of its dignified Currier-and-Ives appearance. Norris recalled that when O'Hara visited them for a weekend, John liked to turn out in a Shetland country suit and cap, and enjoyed a walk over the fields, but he liked even more the long evenings in front of the Willowbrook fireplace. Next day, Norris remembered, O'Hara would wake up "nailed to the bed. His hangover was appalling. You felt for him because he obviously felt so bad. O'Hara would never be an alcoholic, that you could tell because he wouldn't take a drink in the morning. Instead, Belle nursed him like an invalid until the early evening when he began to feel better. Then he would again approach the jug, but with respect and caution."

Another valued friend was Joseph Bryan III, whom O'Hara had met in the early 1930s when Bryan was an editor at the *Saturday Evening Post*. For years, in letters and at luncheon meetings, they would discuss possible articles, stories, and serials. None of these ideas developed sufficiently to appear in the magazine, but the two men often exchanged bantering notes and telegrams, and got together on weekends. Bryan came from a long-established family in Richmond, Virginia; he was married to Katharine (Sister) Barnes of Long Island, and they lived at Jenkintown and later at Doylestown near Philadelphia before the war. Joe and Sister Bryan were among the most popular young couples of their time in Philadelphia, New York City, and Long Island. They liked to entertain, and their hospitality was much sought after, for it had an indescribable quality, to which they both contributed, of airy laughter and good cheer. The general opinion was that taken singly or together, the Bryans were just about the best company in the world. Joe Bryan had been chairman of the *Princeton Tiger* in 1927 when college humor magazines were in a good period. And it was a great satisfaction to O'Hara that Bryan conferred on him the little gold tiepin of the Right Wing Club, an organization of Princeton bloods, which had no political significance in spite of its name, but existed solely for the purpose of holding cocktail parties.

O'Hara liked to dance with Belle at Larue's, taking along another couple when it could be arranged. He also frequently visited the Stork Club on East Fifty-third Street between Fifth and Madison Avenues (now the site of a small park), a gathering place favored by such people as Quentin Reynolds, the sports writer Jimmy Cannon, the literary agent Mark Hanna, and the young ladies they escorted. Reynolds, Hanna, and Cannon had concocted a private language, based on double-talk, pig latin, and Broadway slang, which fascinated O'Hara. He made Jimmy Cannon into Jimmy Shott of "Portistan on the Portis," in which the reader hears that "The mains are coming to town. The semi-mains just took over Kansas City." From the same sources O'Hara developed the sinister man in "The Erloff" of the Joey cycle, who says, in regard to any situation, "It's the erloff, pal." The Stork Club had originated as a speakeasy. Its proprietor was a soft-spoken Oklahoman named Sherman Billingsley, who had perfected the use of publicity and kept a photographer on duty until four A.M.; a writer in *Cosmopolitan* magazine reported that when things got going, "the flashbulbs flickered like summer lightning around the floor." This was a good place to see Ernest Hemingway when he was in town. Hemingway was an agreeable companion on those New York visits, during which he did not attempt to work, other than to edit proofs in his hotel suite, and spent his nights looking for good conversation. There was no sign of the anxieties that beset him later, and the ultimate collapse. He resembled a genial champion boxer, and often spoke or wrote to writing friends as though they were all pugilists scuffling to get along. After the

appearance of *Files on Parade* Hemingway wrote to O'Hara that he liked
the stories, and admired the author's ear for dialogue, which he called a
perfect left, adding the suggestion that John cross with the right hand
once in a while. The analogy appealed to O'Hara, whose approach to
writing was completely professional at all times. One must not continually
exploit an advantage: dialogue called for the contrast of solid text.

When the United States entered World War II on December 7, 1941,
men of O'Hara's age saw an opportunity to imitate the college heroes of
the First World War. In that conflict the accepted thing had been to
enlist, or seek a commission, and it was the same in 1941 before and after
December 7. All that summer and fall the uniforms at Larue's had shown
the extent of reserve enrollments among young men of the upper middle
class. Throughout 1942, there was a brisk production of direct reserve
commissions for desk duty in the Army and Navy to mature men who
had college degrees, and to some who had not, while thousands of younger
men entered the officer candidate schools for ground combat or active
service in the Navy. It was the last innocent man's war for those who
believed in country right or wrong, when leftists and liberals also sought
service, because it was billed as an anti-Fascist fight. The broad front of
opinion, ideology, and emotion united this country as it has not been
drawn together since. O'Hara was sensitive to public and private emotions and to the general feelings of his time. He was thirty-seven years old
in 1942, and he intensely desired to serve in one of the uniformed forces.
He had the connections to get a hearing from any outfit he might care to
approach. For example, he could pick up a telephone and quickly reach
James Forrestal, Secretary of the Navy. Forrestal could give all that
might be needed in the way of recommendation for a Navy berth, but
meeting physical requirements was quite another thing. O'Hara's bad
teeth, poor eyesight, high blood pressure, and history of gastric ulcers
caused both Navy and Army doctors to turn him down. The rejections
strengthened O'Hara's conviction that he did not have long to live.

There was a feeling in the air that it was a privilege to go to war,
something like the privilege of going to Harvard or Yale. One afternoon
the O'Haras and the Philip Barrys saw a young man off for duty overseas,
and Barry expressed this feeling: "I won't wish you luck. You have the
luck." The luck held out for many of the internal crowd, and by mid-
1943 some of them — friends or acquaintances of O'Hara — were putting
on a good show. Al Wright was flying and fighting his way to a Navy
Cross; his Yale contemporary Henry Ringling (Buddy) North was preparing to take an Italian admiral from the Germans in a sortie arranged by
the Office of Strategic Services. Geoffrey M. T. Jones of Princeton College
joined a mountain guerrilla band by parachute; O'Hara's future brother-in-
law Charles Tracy Barnes was training in Scotland for an OSS drop into

occupied France, along with Stewart Alsop, with whom he had attended
Groton and Yale. A commendation and Silver Star were to be awarded
each of these young men for valor in the field. John McClain, whose
genius for being on the inside must have come to full flower in wartime,
had received a Navy commission — for he, too, was a close friend of
James Forrestal, and he could pass a physical — and then made connection with the OSS. Word came that someone had looked into a candle-lit
back room in Sicily, and there sat McClain over a bottle of brandy with
John Steinbeck and the movie actor Bruce Cabot. Two years later on
D-Day, David Niven of the Commandos dove for a Normandy ditch
when German shells began coming in, and when he peered out, he saw
McClain peering from the opposite ditch. Like one of those insouciant
British warriors in novels by Evelyn Waugh or Anthony Powell, McClain
seemed to turn up everywhere. He was waiting to greet Joe Bryan at
Fleet Headquarters in Honolulu when Bryan arrived as a lieutenant
senior grade to join Admiral Radford on *Ticonderoga*. Bryan was not surprised to see McClain, for members of their group were running into each
other on the Burma Road, flying the Hump, on back trails in the mountains of China, in Kandy or Trincomalee, or standing in line for coffee
on the ashpile called Ascension Island en route to the African shore. When
Bryan mentioned *Ticonderoga*, McClain said he had a reel of film relating to that ship which might be of interest. It showed two Japanese
planes plunging through the flight deck, and McClain remarked, "Those
crazy Japs can't fly for nuts. Notice how they get right over a ship, and
then just lose control of the plane, and fall right on top of you? Ever see
anything so ridiculous in your life? Hell, it's better than a Benchley short!
You'll be rolling on the deck all day long!" Previous to this Bryan had
received a letter in care of Fleet Post Office, San Francisco, which showed
O'Hara's frustration about military service. Writing from 27 East Seventy-
ninth Street, O'Hara said he had turned down $40,000 worth of Holly-
wood work while unsuccessfully seeking a commission and was now
considering a "pretty inviting" offer from Frank Norris at *Time*. He added,
"Norris said to tell you something but I forget what. Let him tell you
himself. Who does he think I am, a God damn messenger boy? [Noel]
Busch is back from some of the wars but I haven't seen him. Joel Sayre in
from Iran . . ." O'Hara laid bare his pain and disappointment when he
continued, "You see, old sport, I got the final No from the Army about
three weeks ago. Not only was I turned down; I was turned down for
waivers for limited service: When they gave me that one I was almost
afraid to test my strength in crushing a grape, but I finally took on a
brioche single-handed and tore it to pieces, so I don't feel so unmanly
now. Indeed, since I could not wheedle my way into the army, where as
a captain or major I might earn the Pour le Merite* or at least the Iron

* The highest German decoration.

Cross second class, I now feel I can do some mighty good work with John L. Lewis or at the very worst I can muscle in on the black market. And anyway a man of my brains ought not to concern himself with acts of violence. I shall devote myself to strikes, the nylon and roast beef enterprises, with now and then an occasional quart of deadly microbes in the ventilating system of the Interborough . . . [O'Hara's dots] If you think I'm kidding you're only about 98% right. I am so God damn mad I didn't get my commission that I never will forgive four guys. Two of them are obvious: Lovett and Forrestal; the others are Jack Ford and Bill Donovan. I have two more plans. One is the Red Cross, the other the Maritime Service. If Jack Miley can get a commission in the Maritime Service I should be a breeze, Breeze. As to the Red Cross, I saw Ward and Frankie Cheney the night Ward got back, and since Frankie's old man used to be chairman of the A.R.C. I figured she might still have an in there. Well, I figured good. She knows Norman Davis. So I am getting them to have Davis and me to dinner together, at which point I will outline to him what I think is a hell of a good idea. If he goes for it you can give that pape priest a hot scat to make room for me in your wardroom. Meanwhile I have been reasonably industrious for good old JO'H. I have made not only my regular bonus at The NYer, but also sold two short stories to Collier's (through high-priced Hanna,* who got me the most dough ever paid for that type of creation), and the big news is that I am to get a $2,000 bonus from The NYer because I have been so good about turning out the lights and flushing the can for 16 years. Just think! Four hash marks! Just think! Two g's."

The letter resembles those that John used to write to his brother Tom, or to Robert Simonds, in which he would reveal the hurt of a disappointment, and then recover his courage and spirits by reporting a success. In his letter to Bryan, O'Hara had reproached Forrestal and Colonel William (Bill) Donovan, but they had not let him down. Both were Americans of Irish background, like O'Hara, and both had achieved much: Forrestal as president of a big firm downtown, and Donovan as a lawyer and well-known citizen of New York. Now Forrestal headed the Navy, and Donovan had taken charge of the OSS, the department of unorthodox warfare. Donovan had distinguished himself on the battlefield in the First World War, and great things were expected from his agents in the war this country had now entered. This was of importance to O'Hara when, in spite of his physical disabilities, Donovan accepted him for OSS agent training, and he went through this regime at a secret base in Virginia. The students were instructed in the use of codes, hand-to-hand combat, techniques of espionage, and so on. Each man took a cover name for the duration of the course: John's pseudonym was "Doc." He also grew a beard, which made him look like a young General Grant. O'Hara's attend-

* Mark Hanna represented O'Hara during this period except in dealings with *The New Yorker*.

ance at this academy did not result in his joining the OSS; it did convince him that, as he later put it, he "lacked the physical resources to take responsibility for other people's lives." That was the vein of common sense in John O'Hara which often came to his aid when he was in danger of taking something too seriously. But he scrupulously preserved the security of the instructional school, and made no use of his experience there in fiction. It seems that this act of volunteering for hazardous duty, and attempting to qualify for it, relieved some of O'Hara's tension about getting into the war. He was able to write entertaining letters to Bryan in the Pacific with news about friends: "Went down to East Hampton last week for lunch and tennis with the Bill Lords. Others around were the Hugh Chisholms, the Phil Barrys, Buffy Harkness, the Johnny Haneses, Bob McCormick, Mrs. Mac Aldrich, and Mrs. John Cole. I guess they all hate you as your name never came up, and when I saw that I was afraid to bring it up myself as I didn't want to cause a scene. I remember they talked about Jo Forrestal, and plans for the dance Sat. night, and they said Di Gates and Dan Caulkins and Babs would be up this weekend, and Betsey Whitney and Mrs. Cushing were staying at Sea Spray. But they never once mentioned your name. This is interesting as Belle and I went down to my Mother's a couple of weeks ago. My aunt and my two sisters and two young people from Pottsville were there, and they didn't mention your name either. Looks to me like some sort of conspiracy of silence. Whatever it is they won't tell me anything about it and I'm dying to know. Today at the beach Penelope MacBride [from Richmond] did say she knew you, but she hasn't seen you for ages, she said, so I guess she ain't hep, or 'in on it,' whatever it is."

In April 1944 Bryan returned briefly to Washington; he was now a lieutenant commander, and when orders sent him back to sea, he informed O'Hara and other friends with hasty notes and took off in a hurry. O'Hara used V-mail for a plaintive message: "Belle just handed me your chit as I opened the soulful blues, and I give you my word what I said was 'That's not fair.' I mean it. I get not only a sense of loss, but a sense of theft. I thought you were going to be around for a while. Naturally there is a selfish reason: I was going to Washington this week to make you get the lead out of your keel and probe around for a spot for me, as you were supposed to do." O'Hara went on to tell how he had talked with Robert Montgomery, the cinema star now in the Navy, with Richard Barthelmess of the silent pictures who was an admiral's aide, and with the airline publicity man Rex Smith, now a lieutenant colonel — they had promised to do what they could, but O'Hara sensed that "nothing will come of any of this." He wrote that he would continue to be sitting at home "burning up all the available alcohol." O'Hara was sick of himself, and it was "a good thing I don't use a straight razor. Or live in a tall building." He was writing from the ground floor at 27 East Seventy-ninth Street, and he continued, "I am also sick of civilians, of all sexes. I just got turned down by Collier's on my feeler to go with the Navy . . . This is a cheery phillipic, what? I'll try to do better in my next. Anything you want me to do here, ask. Love from all here. — Landlocked."

O'Hara had observed Noel Busch coming and going from various zones of action as a correspondent for *Life,* and he knew that Joel Sayre was in Europe and the Persian Gulf for *The New Yorker.* Sayre had also been in the First World War — at the age of seventeen, in the Canadian Siberian Expeditionary Force as a member of an infantry squad whose corporal was Donald Meek, later much in demand as a character actor in Hollywood. Quentin Reynolds had become the equivalent of Richard Harding Davis for *Collier's,* and Jimmy Cannon was one of the sergeant-reporters for the Army publication *Stars and Stripes.* John Durant was a Naval officer somewhere in the Pacific. Ernest Hemingway was preparing to take the field as a fighting correspondent, festooned with weapons and a canteen of brandy, in a partisan campaign that produced no military results whatsoever. John Hay Whitney was a ground officer in the Air Force, and he escaped from Germans who captured him. John McClain had to lie low to avoid capture in a farmhouse surrounded by Germans. Some of these proceedings were not known at the time, but it *was* known that things of that sort were going on, and O'Hara had the sensitivity to understand that no matter what was being said, some of his friends were qualifying for creditable records in the war, or at least getting tickets to good seats from which to see it. His frustrations were partially relieved when he applied to *Liberty,* whose editors signed him as correspondent with the Navy in the Pacific. This meant a correspondent's uniform and privileges, which were those of a commissioned officer, and a chance for adventure and danger.

O'Hara took little pride in his connection with *Liberty,* a weekly magazine that ranked below *Collier's* and the *Post.* It was like working for Monogram or Republic after having been at Paramount and MGM. But it was better than nothing. O'Hara got to the Pacific in the summer of 1944, accredited to Task Force 38 of Admiral Bull Halsey's Third Fleet. He sent back only one piece for *Liberty,* an account of a Navy rest camp on the beach at Waikiki. O'Hara returned to the United States in early September 1944; he published a story called "War Aims" in *The New Yorker* on March 17, 1945. Here we have "Delaney, the middle-aged correspondent," talking to Forrest, a fighter pilot, who is "a friendly kid." Forrest confides his postwar plans in detail, about how he intends to get married, go to law school, and set up in practice; he has the furniture of his office precisely in mind. The squawk box summons all hands to battle stations, and Forrest says, " 'You come visit us, sir.' " But the reader feels that the young pilot's war aims are not going to be realized. And there was "The Skipper," which give us the commander of an oiler, a decent conscientious man who is interested in hearing about his idols Irene Dunne and Spencer Tracy. When a dangerous fire breaks out, this modest man behaves with natural courage. O'Hara also drew later on his Pacific experience for a descriptive passage in *From the Terrace*. But on the whole, he made little direct use of what he saw in TF 38. An opportunity for further dealings with the Navy came in early 1945; O'Hara later wrote to his brother Martin that Forrestal had offered him a captaincy. This was a rank seldom conferred by direct appointment, for a Navy captain equals a colonel in the Army. John told Martin O'Hara that he had to turn it down because Belle was pregnant. And on June 14, 1945, their daughter Wylie Delaney O'Hara was born.

The war in Europe ended on May 8, 1945, and the Japanese surrender followed on September 2. No one cared much about repeating the brass-band homecoming parades under triumphal arches of the First World War. The *Daily News* soon began warning readers against Pal Joey Stalin; but the nation was outwardly placid and calm under the rule of President Harry Truman, a man who looked like an out-of-town guest at a Times Square hotel. Those who had come through the war physically and mentally undamaged returned to their former modes of life. But things were not the same. Nobody ever gave it precise definition, yet all knew that something had gone wrong. It might be said that few American men and women of sensibility, whether or not they had direct contact with the war, finished their lives on the lines they thought they had been following before the war came along. Realization of this did not enter the mind immediately, and yet one knew by instinct that the silver decade of the 1930s represented something that would not come again. O'Hara observed the war veterans among his friends with care: he thought that certain ones, such as Al Wright, "had burned themselves out." In notes that he prepared a few years later for the unpublished and unproduced play *You Are My Sister* (from which he made the novel *Elizabeth Appleton*), he wrote of the hero: "What he did in the war is a-typical, as the War itself was anachronistic. The War was not real, and he was not himself. Call it a recess, that lasted too long." These notes are of additional interest as an example of O'Hara using Scott Fitzgerald's method of writing out preliminary discussions of what he planned to do. O'Hara usually carried that sort of material in his mind rather than in notebooks. He did make lists of characters and dates when he tackled his longer novels, all still to be written in 1945. But he seems to have depended on the momentum of a running start in preference to a detailed written plan, and among his papers are false starts on novels, which went to sixty or seventy pages before abandonment. He liked to save a character, or character's name, from aborted stories and plays. In *You Are My Sister* he brought on stage a Texan named Jack Tom Smith, a Rhodes scholar who was civilized and polite, in contrast to the brutal Texan of the same name in the novel *From the Terrace*. Another character in the play was Bruce Ditson, "Princeton, no club, no letter, Presbyterian clergyman's son." From this drab chrysalis comes the fashionable Porter Ditson of *Elizabeth Appleton,* who has money, mistresses, and New York connections. O'Hara finished his working notes for the play with four pages of handwriting on the question of why John and Elizabeth stay together after the final curtain. O'Hara had written years ago to Robert Simonds, before he achieved publication, that a story should always seem to promise a sequel.

Though he almost never used Fitzgerald's method of private writing to work up character and mood, O'Hara had been saddened when Scott died in 1940 at the age of forty-six. He said that "if ever a man was not meant to be fifty, he was Fitzgerald." But it was a depressing thing to O'Hara, to Dorothy Parker, and other writers, that Fitzgerald received perfunctory and inaccurate obituary notices, and that the papers tagged him as nothing more than the chronicler of some prehistoric period called the Jazz Age. But Frank Norris scheduled a respectful and sympathetic notice of Fitzgerald's death for *The March of Time*, read by one of its best actors, Richard Widmark.

The death of Robert Benchley in 1945 seemed at the time to have more significance than that of Fitzgerald, for Benchley, though by no means a happy man, had not gone out in apparent discouragement and failure, since he was a national celebrity whose face was known everywhere when he died at the age of fifty-six. O'Hara took Benchley's death as a placemark, and said that now the party was over. But the party did not shut down at once. John still liked convivial evenings with friends, who often enjoyed his hospitality at the apartment he and Belle had taken on an upper floor at 55 East Eighty-sixth Street. He frequently dined at "21" or at the Passy on East Sixty-third Street. One evening Joseph and Sister Bryan were in "21," entertaining John and Buddy North, at that time owners of the circus. The O'Haras came in and joined them, and O'Hara began to ridicule Sister's family. She said, "What did the Barneses ever do to you, O'Hara?" — and he desisted. Then after dinner they all went out to meet the circus train. All through the early postwar years the "inside" bantering continued. An example occurred when O'Hara published a story called "Like Old Times" in *The New Yorker,* with its narrator a Broadway character who goes to a nightclub and sees a grossly corpulent hoodlum who orders a steak sandwich and "eats it like a little hamburger. Picks it up, eats it like a hamburger, and boy you should have seen him devour it. He picks it up in his two hands and puts it in the one side of his mouth and he has these beady little eyes and by the expression of his face you'd of thought he was listening to himself eating it . . . I was fascinated, I never saw that before, a man taking a steak sandwich the size of that and picking it up in his fingers like a dainty little aw derve . . ." As soon as he read this story, Forrestal wrote to O'Hara, "Was it McClain or Reynolds?"

The collection of stories called *Pipe Night* appeared in 1945 and went through six printings with the original publisher in that year. It was to have ten more international editions and remain alive, like all O'Hara's writings, after its author's death. Stories showing sympathy with defeated people set the tone of this collection. There was, for example, "A Purchase of Some Golf Clubs," in which a frightened young woman comes into a saloon trying to sell a set of clubs and raise money for her husband, who is in jail for drunk driving. A young man gives her twenty-five dollars, although there is nothing in it for him. After she goes, he says to the bartender, who has been watching, "Anybody could tell it was worth twenty-five. The bag alone is worth forty, with leather going up these days.' 'Sure,' said the bartender." In "Too Young" a boy discovers that the older girl he worships is caught in a sordid affair with a bullying motorcycle cop. From *Collier's* O'Hara reprinted "Memo to a Kind Stranger," about the never-to-be-spoken love of a tired middle-aged man for a girl of seventeen. O'Hara showed the love and admiration between a Negro car-washer and his son in "Bread Alone," and he also included "The Erloff" in the thirty-one stories collected. The book opened and closed with studies in the futility of cramped lives: "Walter T. Carriman" and "Mrs. Whitman." A friend is writing an obituary article about Carriman, an obscure Philadelphian who is "able to trace his ancestry to one of the Hessian mercenaries who were defeated at the battle of Trenton." It appears that Carriman's life, going from one dull job to another, has added up to nothing. The same may be said of Mrs. Whitman in the closing story, which is a speech to be delivered on the occasion of Ella Miller Whitman's retirement after forty-five years as an office worker on the Gibbsville *Standard*. The title of *Pipe Night* came from O'Hara's membership in The Players, a mellow and distinguished club, similar to the Garrick in London, which actors shared with painters, writers, architects, and patrons of the arts. During the winter season the members gave monthly entertainments known as Pipe Nights. O'Hara resigned in 1947, as he would sometimes do after he had absorbed the flavor of a club. He also left the New York Athletic Club in its palatial home on Central Park South, and gave up the magnificence of the Metropolitan Club, designed by McKim, Mead, and White, at Sixtieth Street and Fifth Avenue. One afternoon while he held membership there, O'Hara invited

Richard Watts to come up and inspect Fifth Avenue through the tall plate-glass windows of the main lounge. Pointing to the crowds of people as they poured down the Sixtieth Street subway entrance, O'Hara said, "They envy us, Dick." Watts disagreed and said he believed the people only wanted to get home and couldn't care less who was peering down from club windows.

On occasion O'Hara would personally try out a background, as he seems to have done in playing this scene at the Metropolitan Club; he sometimes asked friends to go on trips, during which he proposed to look for story ideas and check his memories of former associations. For in spite of the amused attitude toward life that was still fashionable, John had begun to make it plain that he was giving serious thought to his vocation. The publishing of an omnibus volume called *Here's O'Hara*, in 1946, showed the weight of his work so far. For their money, purchasers got three novels, *Hope of Heaven*, *Pal Joey*, and *BUtterfield 8*, plus twenty stories, including "Are We Leaving Tomorrow?," "Trouble in 1949," and "Price's Always Open," in which a decent man pays a heavy penalty for a courageous act. Frank Norris featured the book in the daily network radio program called *Time Views the News*, in which the broadcasting editors asked the question, "How does O'Hara's writing stand up?" — and answered, "Like the Empire State Building." They commented on the variety of characters, selected "Price's Always Open" as an especially effective O'Hara story, and pronounced him "established and eminently worth while, in the American tradition of Edith Wharton and Henry James."

The next collection of O'Hara stories appeared in 1947 under the title of *Hellbox*, the composing room term for the container into which odd pieces of type were thrown to await melting down. The reviews used words like brilliant, powerful, sharp, savage, transfixing, and terrifying, and ceded to O'Hara a wide area that he could call his own from New York to Los Angeles, from rich to poor, and from high to low. The publishing history of *Hellbox* was like that of *Pipe Night*; by 1969 it had reached its tenth international edition (in the New English Library). Among other stories, the book gave readers "The Chink in the Armor," "War Aims," "Like Old Times," and "Common Sense Should Tell You," which takes place at an actual nightclub called Chez Paree in Chicago, and gives us all we need to know about Mr. Spring, the self-indulgent movie producer, on his way back to the Coast after consulting "the men at Johns Hopkins." Mr. Spring has eyes for a little girl in the chorus named Hilary Kingston. He had asked the Hopkins men about that sort of thing and they had said — the title of the story. With striking economy, O'Hara shows us the producer, the toadies in attendance, Hilary, and the owner of "The Chez." One could not forget "the feeling of a good swift kick all over the left side of your body" that lay in wait for Mr. Spring. There was a look at the underworld of Los Angeles and Florida in "Everything Satisfactory" and "The Moccasins," stories that had appeared in *The New Yorker*. And the book included another story of degradation, "A Phase of Life," that could not have been published in a general magazine at that time. Although the sexual activities took place offstage, the title and subject matter served notice of O'Hara's intention to write with unfettered realism: this phase of life was the evening of a pimp and a whore in a shabby apartment, entertaining a party of rich degenerates. The story was convincing with its businesslike air of services rendered and fees paid. After the customers leave, the two bawds settle down comfortably, one listening to the radio, the other reading a detective story. Aside from its impact as a collection, *Hellbox* had interest in its presentation of James Malloy in three stories: Malloy does lucrative work in Hollywood, and is able to buy a splendid foreign car at second hand. The last piece in the book is "Conversation in the Atomic Age," with Malloy listening to the chatter of Mrs. Schmidt, a Los Angeles society woman. The writing of this closing story was a virtuoso performance in the manner of the Delphian sketches of 1928, and emphasized O'Hara's continued mastery of the speaking voice.

In August 1948 Joseph Bryan contributed an essay on his home city to the *Saturday Evening Post*. O'Hara wrote to him at once: "I will never forgive myself for not helping you with the Richmond piece. In fact, ever since it came out I have gone around telling people that it is really my fault and not yours that you made such a botch of it. Of course the Post readers out in the provinces won't know that. All they'll think is that an ignorant man named Bryan, who probably never laid eyes on Richmond, was permitted to do the piece. I have therefore prepared a letter which the Post will print, and may take some of the heat off you. I first explain that Virginia is often called a boarder state. By a boarder state I mean just that; too poor to own property of its own, not related to the Family and never able to get the second piece of pie, the way a Star Boarder State like Maryland, or West Virginia does . . ." There was more in the same vein; the bantering showed that O'Hara was in a good mood, and he was feeling as cheerful a few months later when he wrote enclosing Bryan's old card of admission to the mess for officers in training at the Quonset Naval Station: "I find that I have got all the use I can out of the enclosed card. With that card I was able to establish credit here and there, and it was also useful when I picked up girls on trains and they wanted proof that Bryan was my real name. Naturally they didn't believe that a man of my commanding presence could be a mere lieutenant, and that made them suspect the rest of my story, until I produced the card. I must caution you not to use the name Bryan in Providence, New London, New Haven, Bridgeport,

Stamford, Newark, Trenton, New Brunswick, Wilmington, Baltimore or Catonsville, Md. Those were the towns where I had my greatest successes. I also lent the card to John McClain and Randy Burke.

"We are not planning to go to any more Princeton games, unless some real *gentleman,* like Jarvis Geer, provides lunch, tickets to the game, etc. However, there's nothing to stop you from coming to NY, as you must have saved up quite a bundle by this time, and we are always delighted to show out-of-town people around."

In spite of all the fun, the euphoria that followed the war was beginning to die down, to be replaced by a sense of desolation, and O'Hara's stories expressed this national mood even while the author sometimes indulged in chaffing with his friends. There was a story in *Hellbox* called "Doctor and Mrs. Parsons," which showed O'Hara's sympathy for an elderly doctor who has taken on grueling extra work in wartime, but finds himself unhappy in retirement. James Forrestal had stayed in Washington as the first Secretary of Defense. He now wrote to O'Hara that he could understand Dr. Parsons' fatigue. Forrestal was beginning to feel the acute anxiety that would drive him to suicide in 1949.

After the publication of *Hellbox,* O'Hara told an interviewer that he believed he had learned enough to attempt a long novel. In some ways his career up to this time had resembled those of Fitzgerald and Hemingway. Each man had written a short but significant and successful novel in his early maturity. O'Hara had fired off *Appointment in Samarra* like a cannon cracker, *The Great Gatsby* had been Fitzgerald's masterpiece, and Hemingway had put his expatriates into the American consciousness with *The Sun Also Rises.* And each man had written short stories that seemed to be permanent literature. Now here was O'Hara, as Hemingway said, with the old left in there pretty good — the dialogue, the ear. In addition, he had the strength and self-discipline to finish a big and solid book. He began it in New York in early 1948, continued that summer at Quogue, then settled to it at 55 East Eighty-sixth Street in the fall and winter. He wrote to Bryan on December 1, 1948, that he was about seven-eighths finished, and "available for lunch and/or dinner and/or both whenever a real sport comes to town loaded with flight pay. I know one whose initials are JB who was in town a fortnight ago but never called me . . . Some persons come to New York and spend their money for show, and then go home and pretend they were never in NY at all, and write letters asking if I am available for lunch/and/or/dinner, after they've spent all their money for show. I suppose the person I have in mind spent all his money trying to wangle an invitation to the Payson wedding and

* The politician Tom Dewey had recently received an autographed football from a college team.

then heard we were invited and now he wants to try to work it through us. Well, that person can go sign a Dewey football* is all I can say. If Charlie and Joan wanted him they'd have asked him is all I can say." Obviously the book was going well. The [Charles S.] Paysons referred to were John Hay Whitney's sister and brother-in-law. "Jock" Whitney was a man of charm and style who had played the role of sportsman with distinction in his younger days. He was now administering one of the country's largest fortunes, and he was later to be Ambassador to Great Britain, and final publisher of the *Herald Tribune*. Whitney was one of the last of the genuine sahibs to occupy a place of importance in American life, and he was also Katharine Bryan's cousin. So, of course, was his sister Joan, who had invited the Bryans to her daughter's wedding. O'Hara liked fashionable weddings, and his Wafer diary entries showed that he continued to attend them all his life. He drew from these gatherings what he called "special knowledge," and like anyone else he enjoyed the pleasure of being among those present.

During his year of work on the novel, O'Hara published three magazine pieces. One was a discussion of the Stutz Bearcat, a popular sporting car of the 1920s that had the same appeal as the Mercer Raceabout. This article appeared in *Holiday*, and there were two *New Yorker* stories. In "Nil Nisi" the question was, when Millicent Chapman drowned, was it an accident, or suicide? Either way, Ann Whittier had no reason to "give her a break," for Millicent had been Frank Whittier's lover. The voices of lower-middle-class Gibbsville are reproduced in "Requiescat," as a respectful crowd gathers at the gates of a mansion in which a leading citizen has shot himself. Aside from these magazine contributions, O'Hara put all his energy into the novel, which appeared in August 1949, entitled *A Rage to Live*. The book was almost 600 pages long, and its publishing record shows that there were eight printings in the remaining months of 1949, the reprint house took over in 1950, the public absorbed three large paperback printings from New York in 1951, and three British editions had come out by 1953. In 1957 a new American paperback edition took off, and had gone through twenty-eight printings by 1970, not to mention six more in Great Britain, and a number of translations. Indeed, *A Rage to Live* has been one of the outstanding best sellers of modern publishing; its acceptance shows that O'Hara had learned how to select and present a theme of universal interest. What he offered was the ruin of a woman's life because of physical passion for an unworthy man. He had found the title in two lines of Alexander Pope: "You purchase Pain with all that Joy can give, / And die of nothing but a Rage to live." For the central character, O'Hara went to the Pennsylvania of Walter T. Carriman and Mrs. Whitman, but on a higher economic level: Grace Caldwell Tate came from the big-rich, the old Protestant Scotch-Irish element that had dug so deeply into Pennsylvania in the late eighteenth and early nineteenth centuries. He also turned away from Pottsville and set the story in and around Harrisburg, which he called Fort Penn. The main action takes place up to and during this country's entrance into the First World War. Grace Caldwell of Fort Penn has married Sidney Tate of New York City, and they live on "The Tate Farm (old Caldwell place)," which is no farm at all but a handsome, well-staffed estate. Grace has been used to living in beautifully kept houses all her life. A telling detail indicated what Grace was accustomed to when O'Hara described a writing desk at the farm with a fountain pen ready in its holder: the pen was always full, and she had never filled it.

O'Hara at last came to grips with the Fourth of July in the long opening passage of *A Rage to Live*. The merchants of Fort Penn are holding a Red Cross Festival on Wednesday, July 4, 1917, using the grounds of the farm through the kindness of Mr. and Mrs. Tate. Distinguished guests are headed by His Excellency Governor Karl F. Dunkelberger, a low comedy Dutchman who is still believable, and his wife, who has the brains of the pair, and her own opinion of Grace Tate. The day is presented in fascinating detail until the lights go out on the lawn and the band plays "Home, Sweet Home." O'Hara then moves the reader along through many incidents affecting a large number of characters. The key episode is the physical surrender of Grace Tate to a cruel and reckless Irish contractor named Roger Bannon. Sidney Tate finds out, and so far as he is concerned, that ends the marriage. He is on his way to accept a Navy commission when he collapses, and dies of poliomyelitis. O'Hara's description of the funeral shows some of the atmosphere he got into the book:

To the dismay of the Fort Penn police it was a horse-drawn funeral. Fire-fighting apparatus, ambulances, and hearses were converted from the horse to the gasoline engine (often with only a change in the motive power while retaining the same bodies) without waiting for the invention of a reliable self-starter, and without much thought to local climatic conditions or to the hilly characteristics of most Eastern cities. . . . In the winter a horse-drawn funeral was enough to cause a Fort Penn traffic officer who knew about it in advance to report off sick, but in summer it was bad enough. . . . The waiting line of horse-drawn funeral coaches outside a church was not much more of a nuisance than a line of limousines, but in motion the carriages had nothing like the precise maneuverability of the automobiles, and what was more, the wheels of the carriages had grown dry and brittle and they sometimes ("always," the police said) split a spoke on the trolley tracks at busy intersections. As Connie had predicted, the funeral was large, one of the largest ever for a member of the upper crust who was not also identified with political life. [The undertaker's] promise that all the cops would be taken care of had kept the sick list down to a genuine minimum, but the prospect of a five-dollar tip was not enough to make the patrolmen happy. An out-of-town visitor commented that even the policemen looked sad . . .

Grace Tate bears up under the shock of her husband's death, but when her nine-year-old Billy shows symptoms of "infantile" and quickly dies of it, she is willing to believe it may be a judgment for her bad behavior. So ends Book Two and what would have been a satisfactory novel as it stood. But O'Hara had more to tell about Fort Penn, and he continued for another two hundred pages with a sociological survey of the city, centered around Grace Tate as the local great lady and owner of the principal newspaper. Her brother Brock Caldwell makes the town too hot for Bannon, who gets drunk and speeds to his death in an automobile. She becomes involved with a bright young newspaperman, his wife goes hysterical from hearing gossip about the friendship, and tries to kill Grace at a turkey-shoot where guns are lying around. Grace goes home and writes a letter to her older son Alfred, now at boarding school, using the silver-bound Conklin pen that she had never filled, to tell him that she plans to leave Fort Penn, travel, and then live mostly in New York. The novel ends with a short chapter called Postlude that shows Grace Caldwell Tate leading a meaningless New York life at the age of sixty-four, and in love with a man who is unhappily married.

Reviewers said good things about *A Rage to Live;* a writer in the *Atlantic Monthly*, for example, found the book "tumultuous, powerful, and moving." But there were others who disliked the candid treatment of sex, and a few who noticed that the story came to a halt with the deaths of Sidney Tate and Billy, then started again on the theme of a rich widow in a provincial city. There also was a tendency to rebuke O'Hara for writing a long book, and "trying to be a great author." It was asked if the characters O'Hara had drawn could be proper subjects for serious literature, and that question would be thrown at O'Hara many times, by amateur and professional critics. But the only review of *A Rage to Live* that gave him genuine distress appeared in *The New Yorker*, and caused O'Hara to sever his connection with the magazine for eleven years. The review was written by a staff writer and its tone was unfriendly, to say the least. The erotic aspect of *Rage* drew fire from the critic, who mentioned a compiler of sex statistics then in the news:

> The parallels between the Kinsey Report and the O'Hara report are unmistakable . . . Dr. O'Hara, our leading amateur, has had to go it alone, at his own expense . . . [with] recurrent passages of maudlin sexuality complete to even so worn a stencil as the prostitute with the loving heart and the high I.Q. . . . The author has intended to do more than out-

Kinsey Kinsey: he has intended to write nothing less than a great American novel . . . [and has produced] a sprawling book, discursive and
prolix . . . Dr. O'Hara's handy guide to healthy sex practices has been
tucked inside the disarming wrapper of the formula family novel, and the
one result . . . is the loss of the old sure-fire, ice-cold O'Hara dialogue . . .
It is hard to understand how one of our best writers could have written this
book, and it is because of O'Hara's distinction that his failure seems in the
nature of a catastrophe . . .

The damage to O'Hara's career that this review might cause lay in its
implication of a defeat that was not even honorable, for it accused the
author not only of failing to write a great novel, but also of using sex as
bait for readers. At the time the review appeared, O'Hara had contributed
215 pieces to *The New Yorker*, which made it all the more shocking that
hostile criticism should appear in its pages. James Thurber said as much
to Harold Ross, and the editor replied that he had not read the book,
but "couldn't see anything wrong with the review." Apparently it never
occurred to Ross that casting doubt on O'Hara's reputation cast doubt on
his own editorial judgment. Ross did not try to make amends, and indeed,
nothing could be done now that the review had appeared in print. There
were two O'Hara pieces already bought and on the shelf, and *The New
Yorker* published "Grief," which was another funeral piece, on October
22, and "The Kids," an underworld story, on November 26. Then followed the years without the O'Hara stories that had come to be as familiar
as the work of Arno, Addams, Sullivan, and Perelman. Whether Ross
cared to admit it or not, O'Hara's writings had been essential in the
magazine's early maturity. And Harold Ross had been nine years dead
before another story by O'Hara appeared in *The New Yorker;* on
September 17, 1960, the magazine carried the entire novella *Imagine
Kissing Pete.* The fee was $11,000, or 733 times the amount of his first
check cashed at the bar of Bleeck's saloon in 1928. After the appearance
of this novella, *The New Yorker* shared the best short fiction of O'Hara's
final period with *The Saturday Evening Post*, where his price was never
less than $3,500 a story.

At the same time that he severed connections with *The New Yorker,*
O'Hara got out of New York City. Belle had reached the conclusion that
he would accomplish more, with less wear on his nerves, in a quiet
suburban atmosphere, and Wylie's health furnished another argument
that it was time to go. Doctors said Wylie had developed an asthmatic
condition that would not improve in city air. The parents thought of
Saratoga, but Frank Sullivan's doctor said the winters of northern
New York State were not good for asthmatics. After making further
inquiries, the O'Haras decided on Princeton, far enough south for Wylie,
and convenient to New York and Philadelphia. They rented a house at

18 College Road West, near the McCarter Theater, and across the way from the grounds of the Princeton Theological Seminary; a little further west were the buildings of the Graduate College, and the Institute for Advanced Study. Professor Einstein lived nearby in Mercer Street. The O'Hara house was in one of the quietest parts of a quiet town, and it made an ideal residence for a writer. In a letter to Bryan on September 30, O'Hara said, "We are overboard on Princeton. Slowly and carefully we have been adding to our list of acquaintances and cautiously guarding our telephone number. I met Dean Gauss last night and he invited me for a drink, which I wouldn't miss, but we are not going to plunge into the local social life. I don't want people dropping in here just because I happened to be polite at a cocktail party. I am up for the Nassau Club, and Wylie started school today, so the more gregarious members of this family have that problem solved away from home. Free-loaders save your stamps. Students and Transients Beware of Dog. Right Wing '27 Welcome . . ."

There were all sorts of people in Princeton, some of them commuters to Philadelphia and New York. The area took its tone from the university, and the greatest literary celebrity in permanent residence, until his death in 1933, had been Dr. Henry van Dyke, the noted Presbyterian clergyman, professor, diplomat, and author. More recently Thomas Mann, T. S. Eliot, Thornton Wilder, and Ida A. R. Wylie had been among the writers working in Princeton. A large number of other people, all civilized and charming though with varying backgrounds and purposes in life, occupied houses in town or estates in the near countryside. Both town and gown played wealth and power in a low key, and the general atmosphere was relaxed and friendly.

After a year at 18 College Road West, the O'Haras rented the house next door, No. 20, which was a one-story structure of contemporary design. The lot sloped westward so that the large study window looked out over the Springdale golf course to Cleveland Tower of the Graduate College on the crest of the next hill. O'Hara could turn in his chair and enjoy the spectacular view whenever he wished to. However, his habit of working at night was established, and the view of Cleveland Tower usually served only as background for the conversation of friends who gathered in the study for coffee, tea, or cocktails in the afternoon. Friends also collected in the living room, where the atmosphere resembled that which the O'Haras had provided on Seventy-ninth Street and Eighty-sixth Street. When they first went into No. 18, John and Belle began a custom of giving a post-big-game party, that got off to a fine start with red-coated waiters from "21" serving food and drink to fifty people. In those days the Harvard or Yale game at Princeton was a sporting-social event: private cars and special trains stood on the Pennsylvania Railroad sidings south of Palmer Stadium, and the *Times* sent fashion reporters to answer the question of what the women were wearing. (The answer was tweeds.) After moving to No. 20, the O'Haras would entertain as many as one hundred invited guests at their annual party. It was an exceptionally pleasant occasion, with everyone in good humor, and much laughter to be heard. To see this cheerful group of people made one think that good things might be in store for everyone in the decade of the 1950s.

But when O'Hara settled to work in his study at No. 20, he had misgivings: too many people were getting into trouble, too many were dead. Philip Barry had died in 1949 at the age of fifty-three, and it was to him that O'Hara dedicated his next book. It was a short novel called *The Farmers Hotel*. O'Hara told the story mostly in dialogue, and divided it into three parts that suggested the acts of a play. And ten years later, he published *The Farmers Hotel* as a play, with little change except to recast the material between passages of dialogue into stage directions. The original hotel stood near Schuylkill Haven on the road to Oakland Farm, and can still be identified, a gaunt gray house with a long porch. In O'Hara's youth, there were Marmons, Stutzes, and Essex roadsters parked outside on winter nights. O'Hara made the place into a clean and cozy roadside inn, just opening for business under the management of Ira Studebaker, an elderly retired widower, who has taken over as an antidote for loneliness. He makes one think of Frank Craven in *Our Town*. His cook, Mrs. Fenstermacher, is locally famed for good food, and he has a resourceful bartender-handyman in Charles Moultrie Mannering, a tall, distinguished-looking Negro. The scene is the snug, newly renovated lobby, with its comfortable seats and small bar, where Charles and Mr. Studebaker are waiting for the first guests. Outside is O'Hara country, the village of Rockbottom, between Allentown and Bethlehem, Pennsylvania. A snowstorm is on its way, and O'Hara is obviously planning to use the magical focus of an inn and a group of benighted travelers, as had been done by Scott and Dickens, among others, to the great joy of readers. From the theatrical point of view there was much to be gained by the setting of a stormbound inn, although George M. Cohan had missed the mark in *The Tavern*, an attempt to burlesque romantic drama as played in the nineteenth century. There was no purpose of burlesque in O'Hara's mind, and he took this narrative so seriously, in fact, that he wrote in the preface to the published play that "*The Farmers Hotel*, novel and play, is an allegory, and very tightly written, and to tinker with the play would shatter the allegory." Be that as it may, the characterization was sharp, the story moved, and would undoubtedly work on the stage, though whether it would hold an audience for a Broadway run might be open to question. Charles would have been a fine part for Juano Hernandez, and there were many good touches, such as that of the two bedraggled show girls, only a little above the rank of whore, and their manager, who arrive out of the storm carrying "tired little satchels of striped canvas with stickers from a very minor airline." The kindly Frank Craven–Studebaker receives them with courtesy. Then there are two aristocrats, a man and woman caught by the blizzard while hunting the fox, who make their entrance in "riding boots and breeches under their polo coats." Lovers they are, and married, but not to each other. They are high-toned: while the man is telephoning, the woman says, " 'Any good brandy. A pony. Two. I think the gentleman will have one too.' " These lovers are destined for a horrible death when a villain wrecks their car after the storm subsides. O'Hara wrote that "There are those who like [The Farmers Hotel] better than anything I have ever written before or since." The play had a cast reading at the Actors Studio, and Cheryl Crawford of the Theater Guild produced it in a summer theater at Fishkill, New York. O'Hara wrote that "'The Fishkill opening night was sold out to the Rotary Club and my heart sank as I watched them enter the theater, in their white dinner jackets and summer frocks, and a few somewhat the worse for the Martini cocktail. They laughed, they cried, and there were some calls for the author. After the perform-ance, however, Miss Crawford had some suggestions that made me think she wanted to turn my play into Seven Keys to Baldpate . . ." O'Hara's feeling that The Farmers Hotel deserved a high place among his works was not unjustified; the dialogue was excellent and the characters dramatically right. The novel sold well, through five American and British editions in three years. Then in 1957, The Farmers Hotel exploded into the best-seller lists as a paperback with many printings.

On August 17, 1953, O'Hara was flying toward Martha's Vineyard as a passenger in a light airplane. Hitherto he had enjoyed flying, but now he suddenly felt apprehension and anxiety. He was shortly to discover that the evil sensation must have come from physical causes. Three days later, O'Hara came into New York from Quogue, planning to return that night. He went to "21" for lunch but could not eat, and decided he had best return to Quogue before he got worse. On the way to the Long Island side of the Pennsylvania Station in a cab, he began feeling so mis-erable he told the driver to take him to Mrs. Wylie's apartment at 116 East Sixty-third Street. He found nobody at home, and collapsed in a bathroom. By good luck Belle's sister Winnie came by and discovered him semiconscious on the tile floor, "white as a sheet." Doctors were mostly out of town in August, but Winnie finally reached one by telephone, who called an ambulance when he got to the apartment and found that O'Hara had vomited blood. On the way to Harkness Pavilion, she sat beside O'Hara, and he threw up more blood into basins she held for him as he gasped, "Winnie — I certainly am a busy body, aren't I?" Belle soon arrived at the hospital and the sisters passed an anxious night, for O'Hara's ulcer had penetrated so deeply that the blood loss was "massive," and his vital pressure fell dangerously low. He stayed in the hospital for a week, and spent the month of September recuperating at Quogue. O'Hara left Harkness determined to keep permanently away from alcohol, as he wrote to Pat Outerbridge. Later in the year he altered his decision to "May of 1954, at least." Before that date, however, he had reason to go back to his original resolve, which he kept for the rest of his life.

On October 16, 1953, word came that at the age of forty-six, Helen Petit O'Hara had closed her bright blue eyes forever. She had not remarried, and her life had been unhappy. Elizabeth Hart remembered, "John telephoned me from Princeton and asked if I thought he would be thrown out bodily by Mrs. Petit and Uncle Dee if he came to the funeral. I telephoned the latter and was told, 'He may appear but we will not speak to him nor shake his hand.' In a subsequent telephone conversation John and I agreed that Mrs. P. might not take such a purely negative attitude and he contented himself by sending flowers." Two years later, Uncle Dee gave the Wellesley College Library half a million dollars in memory of his niece.

On every hand O'Hara saw destruction at work in the lives of friends. Some were killing themselves with alcohol like the young man in the Owl during the late 1920s. Others were simply not living up to their potentialities. The tenets of John's early Catholic upbringing differed but little from the Protestant ethical system, grounded in the parable of the talents and the faithful servant, that urged all mankind to work, for the night was coming. He said to a friend who had survived a time of troubles, "Now you can peg your life to something real." The thing to do was work. Unexpected changes often came with news of rough places in friends' lives. Early in November 1953, for example, O'Hara got a note from Joseph Bryan, then living in Washington, saying that he planned to take a house in Princeton, for he and Katharine were separated. O'Hara answered at once, "Matter of fact we heard about the separation in a curious way. Mimi Linaweaver was here two weeks ago at Carolyn and Bob Wright's and said Katharine was in N.Y. and that you had gone back to Paris. So Belle called Katharine to invite her to our annual Princeton-Harvard or Yale party, and it was Katharine who told Belle you had separated, the word she used. She gave Belle no details, so we have an active, human curiosity about the bust-up after all these years (you know, of course, that Norris and Lee are getting a divorce), and needless to say we were saddened by it, whatever the reason. As a one-time loser myself I long ago learned that nobody, *nobody* outside the marriage ever really knows why a couple part company . . ."

During the last week in November of that same year, John picked up the *Times* and read of another in the toll of suicides among people he knew. Joe Brooks, ex-football star and Manhattan clubman, one of the best-liked men in his generation, had killed himself in his lonely Park Avenue apartment. It was said that Brooks had never recovered from the emotional turmoil of his divorce from Alicia Patterson, daughter of the eccentric publisher Joseph Medill Patterson, who founded the *Daily News*. O'Hara recorded that he would always remember Joe Brooks's remark, "You never know the tear in the lining of the other fellow's coat."

Not everyone knew it, but Belle O'Hara had a congenital heart weakness. She had begun to feel the need of extra rest, but used ingenuity in getting her naps and periods of relaxation when Wylie and John were occupied and did not need her attention. Belle was still capable of showing strength when she felt it necessary to protect their interests. Her good friend from St. Timothy's, Mrs. Gerald Bramwell, recalled an example of this protective energy: Kate Bramwell had carried on a lively discussion with O'Hara to a point where he seemed to find it unwelcome, and as they went to the dinner table, Belle said to her old friend, in a low voice between clenched teeth, "Kate — stop — baiting — John." And so it was understandable that her husband and daughter trusted and depended on Belle O'Hara to a marked degree. Wylie was eight years old, sensitive and shy. O'Hara had received some physical and emotional shocks in the past year. But the Christmas holidays passed pleasantly enough, until shortly after New Year's Day 1954, when Belle was stricken with pain, and went to the hospital. The truth was that her weakened aorta was about to give way. Wylie was told not to worry, but on the evening of the fourth day the child heard the telephone ring, and in a moment of clairvoyance, knew her mother was dead. Years later, as a grown woman with children of her own, she recalled the scene: O'Hara "mumbled something on the telephone" and then came into the living room to tell her what she already knew. They tried to comfort each other, but Wylie said, "I won't be able to go on living." O'Hara lifted her in his arms into his lap and said, "We'll have to go on."

FIVE

FROM THE TERRACE

FRIENDS AND MEMBERS of the family soon began arriving at 20 College Road West, where they found John outwardly calm, and "wonderful in his self-control," as Kate Bramwell among others saw it. Someone called a doctor who had treated O'Hara at various times, and he suggested whiskey as a nerve tranquilizer. That doctor is now dead, but with this suggestion he lost O'Hara's respect for the remainder of his life. Wylie's little dog had a cold, and O'Hara said to the doctor, "Before you go, you might look at the poodle." Shortly after that, O'Hara went into the kitchen with his brother-in-law Henry Gardiner and poured a quart of whiskey into the sink. He said, "That's one thing I don't need."

Four days later, the morning trains to Princeton Junction from Philadelphia and New York carried a noticeable number of neat, handsome women of the good-bone-structure type, and men who had in common a certain air of assurance. These people were using the trains because a snowstorm had caused poor driving conditions; they were gathering for Belle's funeral at Trinity Church, Episcopalian stronghold in a Presbyterian town. The mourners filled the nave of the imposing Victorian Gothic building on Stockton Street, and it could be seen that they were the same people who might have come there for a fashionable wedding; they were subdued because of grief for a kind and clever and good woman who had died before her time. Those who were near the front pews saw Wylie beside her father. Wylie had told him she did not think she could go to the service in the church; he had persuaded her that it would be a source of regret in the future if she did not go.

After the funeral and the burial at Quogue, which took place on the following day, O'Hara had moments of panic as the shock wore off and he faced life without Belle. He told Al Wright that he had considered suicide. Sometimes he would call Pat Outerbridge at eleven o'clock at night, Outerbridge would come over, and they would talk almost until dawn, when O'Hara became sufficiently tired to sleep. Other friends came for various periods of time to 20 College Road West, and all agreed that O'Hara was exhibiting the strength of character which they had believed him to possess, and that he was in no danger of killing himself. The danger of suicide lay behind the danger of alcohol: to wake up alone with the guilt of a "pretty good hangover" and then to realize why he was alone, might have started O'Hara toward the self-destruction he had flirted with in Pittsburgh. But waking with a hangover was one thing O'Hara now determined never to do, and he maintained this resolution as long as he lived.

Besides getting his emotions under control, O'Hara had to think of Wylie. There was some thought of entrusting the child to her uncle, Dr. Robert Wylie, and his wife; but O'Hara decided it would be best to keep her in Princeton. And he saw that his own health and sanity depended on the occupation and solace of writing. He labored at two journalistic jobs — a weekly column for the Trenton *Times-Advertiser*, and a page in *Collier's* which was called "Appointment with O'Hara." The magazine was publishing once a fortnight and headed for dissolution. But the editors paid O'Hara $1,000 per article, and beginning in February 1954 he made $68,000 at this job before the magazine's end on September 28, 1956. O'Hara had begun the Trenton column on January 3, 1954, and he continued it until August of that year, later collecting the material in a book called *Sweet and Sour*. The pieces were slight, and at their best mildly entertaining. In reviewing a book by the brilliant and discerning Louis Kronenberger, O'Hara got on to the John-callers — people who "call you John on the very first meeting. Kronenberger holds forth at some length on John-calling and he's right all the way . . . A little while ago . . . I made a few sarcastic remarks about people who write and address you as 'Dear John O'Hara,' not 'Dear Mr. O'Hara' or 'Dear John.' " Kronenberger had denounced this style of address as outrageous, and had written that he found it loathsome "because it even sounds ugly and unnatural." The pieces in *Collier's* resembled the *Newsweek* columns, and their competence and professionalism were unquestionable. Teachers of writing might well have used "Appointment with O'Hara" as a model for clarity of diction. But what he had to say usually amounted to little, and there was a tendency to drop names. The best of the *Collier's* articles went back to O'Hara's youth, as when he recalled Christmas holidays in Pottsville. In judging O'Hara as a journalist filling regular space, it should be noted that he lacked the temperament that makes a writer of light pieces the friend of his readers, though he did not slash at victims in the manner of Westbrook Pegler, nor explode firecrackers, like H. L. Mencken, under the seats of the mighty. Essentially his attitude toward column writing was: a day's work for a day's pay. And while *Collier's* lasted, and later for a year with *Newsday*, the pay was good.

When O'Hara had arrived at Trinity Church for the funeral, it happened that the first person he saw was Sister Bryan. In town from Quogue one afternoon that summer, O'Hara telephoned Sister at her mother's house on East Sixty-second Street and suggested dinner at the Passy. Sister said she had an engagement to go out with Mark Hanna, but was sure John would be welcome to join them. His answer was that he didn't wish to see Hanna, and so Sister asked Mark to excuse her, and went out with John. After that they saw more of each other; O'Hara proposed marriage, was accepted, and the wedding took place on January 31, 1955, which was John's fiftieth birthday, at Sister's East Seventy-fourth Street apartment. A woman judge performed the ceremony in the presence of Katharine's mother Mrs. Courtlandt Barnes (her father was dead), her sons Courtlandt and St. George Bryan, and John's mother and daughter. A few weeks before, O'Hara had written a note to Sister's divorced husband which might be included in a book of etiquette as a model for such letters. Bryan had been thinking of living in Princeton but had abandoned that idea at the time he wrote to express good wishes. O'Hara replied, "Dear Joe — Thank you for your note on Sister's and my coming marriage. Princeton, being the kind of heterogeneous community it is, is surely big enough for all of us; and the fact that Sister and I intend to spend most of our lives here should offer no problems to you. As to our own friendship, there naturally will be some early uneasiness, but time should smooth that out. We are not children. Again, thank you for your note. Sincerely, John O'Hara."

As things eventually turned out, Bryan married a delightful Frenchwoman, the Vicomtesse Jacqueline de la Grandière, and took up residence on a family estate near Richmond. And O'Hara entered into that remarkable third act in the drama of his life.

The early summer of 1955 found the O'Haras in a rented house at 143000 Sunset Boulevard in Pacific Palisades. A picture deal had been set up by H. N. Swanson, one of the few literary agents in whom O'Hara reposed confidence. Swanson had an editorial background, having published Scott Fitzgerald's famous essay on Princeton in his magazine *College Humor* before becoming a writers' representative on the coast. Now the Swanson office had negotiated a $25,000 contract for O'Hara to write an "original" about the songwriting team of Buddy de Sylva, Lew Brown, and Ray Henderson ("Button Up Your Overcoat," "You're the Cream in My Coffee"). John completed this task, but the shooting script or screenplay that went to the actors came from other hands. O'Hara was a transient professional, drawing high pay for piecework, while at the same time keeping up his signed page in *Collier's*, so that credit for the final script was not so important to him as it would have been to a permanent member of the cinema colony. In any event, O'Hara's credit on the picture about the songwriters was much more prominent than any to which a Hollywood writer could aspire: his contract called for name-above-title billing, like that of a star or an independent producer. Obviously the time had come for O'Hara to do a great deal of screen work — if he wanted to. His decision was to stay in California for the summer, but to use his energies in finishing a novel that he had planned and begun while getting married, dealing with agents and producers, and turning out his *Collier's* contributions. He wrote to Pat Outerbridge that he had refused a $75,000 screenplay assignment, because his novel came first. He added, "I am not so ivory-tower that I lost sight of the possibility that by finishing the novel I stood to make more in the long run than the fast 75. If I guessed wrong, you may taunt me on alternate Thursdays, when I can't afford the buffet at the Nassau Club. I have actually turned down 75 G's before, but that was an offer for Butterfield 8 when I was in the dreamland of $250,000, and also when Wylie was not yet in existence . . ." Meanwhile, Swanson had been working on a special arrangement for his client. As he put it in recalling the circumstances, "We showed John how he could make more money writing original screen stories at home than doing screenplay assignments at the studio." Under this agreement, Darryl Zanuck of 20th-Fox was to pay $75,000 each for three originals, a total of $225,000. Working under this arrangement in Princeton, O'Hara wrote two movie originals, of which *The Bravados* finally appeared on the screen, and the contract for the third story was cancelled at his request. During the rest of the stay in Pacific Palisades, O'Hara worked as fast and well as ever in his career, and the result was *Ten North Frederick*, the first Gibbsville novel since *Samarra*. This study of an unhappy man covered 410 pages, and the movie rights alone brought $175,000. The novel was critically acclaimed, and sales were prodigious both in hard-cover and paperback, making *Ten North* one of the largest-selling of all O'Hara novels with fifty-eight international printings by 1970.

They were burying Joe Chapin in the opening of *Ten North Frederick*, and memories of the service at Trinity Church in Princeton undoubtedly lay in O'Hara's mind as he wrote about the funeral in Gibbsville. This curtain-raising passage could be compared for its effectiveness with the Fourth of July festival that opened *A Rage to Live*, and served the same purpose of assembling characters and setting mood. And when the reader has finished the book, he knows that Joseph Chapin, member of the inner group of leading citizens, man of property, graduate of Yale, has been a failure and an emotional cripple who has scarcely passed one happy day. His law partner Arthur McHenry is the more able of the two, and his wife Edith the stronger partner in his marriage. There is a gallery of Gibbsville characters, including the politician Slattery and his lace-curtained, white-gloved wife and daughters, all conscious of Chapin as a fortunate man, none loving or respecting him as a good or valuable man. Julian English appears as an impertinent youth who can be agreeable when he wants to; but his father the doctor is neither kind nor capable. Chapin's well-intentioned mistakes cost him much pain; when his daughter elopes with a dance-band musician, he persuades her to divorce the young man and end her pregnancy by abortion. In this Joe Chapin resembles O'Hara's first mother-in-law, Mrs. Petit. A famous scene in the story has Chapin interviewing a national political committee on his prospects of nomination for the presidency of the United States. He would have made a superior Warren G. Harding, but the committeemen turn him down; nevertheless, the unfulfilled ambition costs Chapin $100,000 for the campaign chest. The life of Joe Chapin at last yields him a morsel of happiness through a brief love affair in New York with a girl, one of his daughter's friends, who says when they break off, "'. . . the middle-aged gentleman will be with her till the day she dies, in her heart.'" Dissolve to Gibbsville, 10 North Frederick Street. Chapin's life has come to nothing. Somehow his wife has found out about his one little period of happiness, but he tells her, "'There'll be no reprisals . . . good night, Edith.'"

At this point in the writing, O'Hara did a startling thing. Under the heading of Part Two, he ended the novel in fifteen pages, set in italics, that rapidly carried the reader to Joe Chapin's death, which could be called suicide by alcohol. Part Two opened with this paragraph:

The biographer has certain rights and duties and among them is the right, which is also a duty, to say that at such-and-such a point the biographee's life left one phase and entered another. It is not the same as saying that a change occurred overnight, for there are few occurrences — if there are any — that bring about radical and quick change in the lives of human beings. Change is almost always fluid; rapidly fluid, or slowly fluid; but even major events in a human life do not make the overnight personality changes that they are too often said to make. Marriage, parenthood, the successful culmination of an enterprise, a severe punishment, a dreadful accident resulting in blindness, a frightening escape from danger, an exhilarating emotional experience, the unexpected report of a five-inch gun, a sudden view of something loathsome, the realization of a great major chord, an abrupt alteration in a human relationship — they all take time, to be absorbed by the soul, no matter how infinitesimally brief a time they took in occurring or in being experienced. Only death itself causes that overnight change, but then of course there is no morning.

O'Hara left the middle passage of his life and entered its closing phase with his return to Princeton in the fall of 1955. There was no overnight change in his manner of working or reactions to the world. But he had "pegged his life," as he once advised a friend to do, and was now a completely serious man.

Back at 20 College Road West, O'Hara started on a short story, that ran to sufficient length for publication between covers as a novella, entitled *A Family Party*. Here he worked with memories of Lykens (Lyons in this and other stories), presented in a monologue, the method by which he had portrayed so many characters. We are present at a gathering of friends and neighbors who have assembled to honor Dr. Sam Merritt, a physician to whom the community is obligated not only for his help in illness, but also for his contribution toward founding a much-needed hospital. The speaker of the monologue talks in a manner that recalls the narration of "Walter T. Carriman" and "Mrs. Whitman." One can even hear echoes of Mr. Duffy of the Greens Committee. But the author's motivations are kindness and respect: Dr. Merritt deserves his testimonial dinner, and the revelation of tragedy — the insanity of his wife — comes without sentimentality, and touches the reader's heart. Unanimous critical praise greeted *A Family Party*, and the novella reached a sizable public through four hard-cover printings in the last five months of 1956 before it went out as a paperback in 1957. By that time O'Hara and his wife had left 20 College Road West and moved to Linebrook.

O'Hara had never been satisfied with 20 College Road West, in spite of its pleasing views. Accordingly, Sister began looking through the town and its environs for land that she could buy and build on. The university held property along the old Province Line Road, and was pleased to sell Mrs. O'Hara a little under three acres at the Pretty Brook intersection. The land lay in deep country, with large semiwild holdings along its borders so that the O'Hara house would have privacy and one could look from its windows down wooded lanes and across fields. O'Hara's workroom on College Road West had given a slight sense of crowding when he got his pictures and trophies into place. Acquiring further items of this kind would require more room, and it was already a problem to give proper housing to such things as Robert Benchley's banjo-mandolin, and a horn that had been blown on Mount Everest by a member of the Edmund Hillary expedition. The success of *Ten North Frederick* and O'Hara's triumphant dealings with Hollywood had made it possible for O'Hara to build a house if he wished to. But even more did he wish to build a substantial estate, for premonitions of imminent death were always with him. Sister decided that she herself would see to it that the O'Haras occupied a house that was suitable for an important writer who needed privacy and quiet; and it was her money that bought the land and built the house which made up the agreeable place they called Linebrook. Starting the project in early 1956, she was able to entertain the first guests at hospitable Linebrook a year later. However, although guests were welcome and by no means rare, these friends knew that O'Hara was spending most of his time on a big piece of work, by far the longest he had yet attempted. And in November of 1958 he presented to the world the gigantic novel *From the Terrace*.

The 898 printed pages of *From the Terrace* were set up from more than 2,000 typewritten pages, which O'Hara had composed as he settled at the new house. The book was to show in complete detail the life of a man named Alfred Eaton, from his birth in 1897 until shortly after World War II, when his failures have added up to a kind of death. An italicized introductory passage tells the reader that the novel is not to be *"a pretty story, but every life has some moments of beauty, and Alfred Eaton would be the first to point to such moments in his own life, even in his present anguish . . ."* The author also announces that he has a purpose in writing, additional to telling Eaton's story, which will be apparent *"when we come to the end of our work and can examine something that has been done."* When the readers reach this point, there is no question about Alfred Eaton's anguish, which is that of a formerly important and forceful man whose life has dwindled into futility. He had become one of those middle-aged men who can be found in clubs, always ready for a drink or a hand of bridge, who have given up making any effort to conceal the fact that they have nothing to do. To pass the time such men attend the funerals of obscure classmates, run trivial errands for friends who are busy, and read the ticker tape, if all else fails, every half hour. But his friends know that Alfred Eaton made a fortune as a partner in one of the big houses downtown, served as Assistant Secretary of the Navy during the war, and appeared to be established among the leaders of the country. What went wrong? There is much to consider as one looks back to the beginning of Alfred Eaton's story.

He was born at Port Johnson, a composite town made out of two or three small industrial centers in the Pottsville area. His father, who owned the Eaton Iron & Steel Company, was tight-fisted in business and grudging in the bestowal of affection on his family. Samuel Eaton cared only for Alfred's older brother William; when William died at the age of fourteen, the father did not conceal his wish that Alfred had died instead. O'Hara had drawn Samuel Eaton with deadly accuracy, a vain, dull, arrogant man with the kind of self-love that sees the favorite child as a second self. Samuel Eaton had wanted his first child born on the family farm, although the doctor had some practical objections.

Samuel Eaton said babies were born on farms every day of the week, and they were damned healthy, too. The doctor said, " I'm not interested in your pig-headed insistence on having the baby born on your property.'" Nevertheless, Samuel Eaton thought he was going to get his way. This brought on conflict with his wife's father, a member of the clan that had founded the town. Raymond Johnson thought that his house should be the birthplace, as it was readily accessible to the doctor.

"Well, now wait a minute, Mr. Johnson," Samuel Eaton said.

"I'm not going to wait a minute. I'm not going to wait anything. That farm of yours, how long's it been in your family? One generation, that's all. Well, I want you to stop thinking it's some royal palace, because it isn't. I want you to stop thinking of yourself as some duke or lord that has to have their child born in the — the — the palace. I want my daughter to have her baby in advantageous circumstances, with a doctor and a nurse and every medical precaution. And *that's* all I'm going to say about it."

Samuel Eaton's desire to found a dynasty introduced a theme that O'Hara developed in a later Pennsylvania novel, *The Lockwood Concern*. The immediate effect, on Alfred Eaton, was to give him a sense of not coming up to what was expected, which made him combative in life. When he was seventeen, he quarreled at a dance with his sweetheart Victoria Dockwiler and his friend Peter Van Peltz. Victoria and Peter drove off at dangerous speed in a borrowed, new red roadster. At five o'clock in the morning "a farmer discovered the Stutz and, a minute or so later, the bodies . . ." The episode of this dance, quarrel, and accident was prime O'Hara, and the scene in which the Van Peltzes paid a visit of condolence to the Dockwilers was shattering, because Victor Dockwiler was not able to "behave," as Mr. Van Peltz put it, adding that "'two young people are dead, Victor, not one.'" Alfred Eaton was not present, but he knew the feelings of all concerned, and his own sense of guilt grew heavier because his father withheld sympathy.

Alfred went to Princeton where he became the friend of Alexander Thornton (Lex) Porter, member of a rich New York family. After serving in the Navy in the First World War, Alfred went into the aviation business with Lex, who got the money from an uncle "who was never more than four blocks from one of his clubs." Alfred married Mary St. John; then the marriage went bad. By this time Alfred had broken off business relations with Lex Porter, and joined a Wall Street banking house, Mac-Hardie and Company. He found his true love in Natalie Benziger, a Pennsylvania girl whom he met on a tour of mining property. When the Second World War came along, Alfred got his big job in Washington, and traveled around the country on important errands, or errands that were thought to be important. Some suspected Alfred's biographer of indulging in satire with his detailed recordings of solemn, inside-stuff speeches by the Assistant Secretary to audiences of businessmen. In any event, Alfred had made a mistake in leaving Wall Street for Washington: during his absence, an enemy started undermining him at Mac-Hardie and Company. This enemy was a high-hat Irishman named Creighton Duffy, "whose father had owned the second Rolls-Royce on the north shore of Long Island." Duffy was MacHardie's son-in-law, and he owed Alfred nothing but kindness, for Alfred Eaton had met old James D. MacHardie on the winter afternoon when he rescued Duffy's little boy after the child fell through ice while skating. As he finished out the war in Washington, Alfred decided to divorce Mary in spite of whatever publicity might ensue. And he did so, with the help of a well-known attorney, Mr. Rex Easterday, who said to his client, on arranging an interview with Mary, " 'She'll be coming to my office at three o'clock. She had an affable sound to her voice and I only hope it lasts through lunch. I've seen too many ladies change from affable to hellcats after taking too many Martini cocktails.' " When the war ended, Alfred married Natalie and found that Duffy and other ill-wishers had so discredited him at the house of MacHardie that he had to resign. Lex Porter was killed when the Congressional Limited jumped the tracks; he had not yet found out that Alfred had slept with his wife. Next, Alfred considered going into a deal with the Texan, Jack Tom Smith. Then he almost died of a bleeding gastric ulcer. During his convalescence, Alfred talked with Natalie about failures and suicides, and she recalled the name of Julian English from Gibbsville. She said they should have known he was headed for self-destruction because of "little things" — his drinking, insulting important people, dangerous driving, and so on. Now Julian had been dead for fourteen years, she told Alfred, and you hardly heard his name mentioned any more. When he recovered his health, Alfred went to Los Angeles and worked on the deal with Jack Tom Smith, but they parted enemies when Alfred refused to allow Smith to bully him. The Eatons went back to New York and settled in a "small, easy-to-run apartment on East Seventy-eighth Street." Alfred began to loaf in clubs with older, retired men, or men who frankly wasted each day in its entirety as it came along. Natalie asked an old acquaintance to tell her the truth about Alfred. The man said word was out that Alfred was all washed up. Those who were inclined to be sympathetic held that Alfred " 'never got over the death of his son in the war, tried to forget it by working too hard, and finally wrecked his health so badly that it took him two years to be able to see people again.' " But why couldn't he make another connection like the one he had with MacHardie? The informant, an old and experienced man, gave his opinion: " 'I don't think he gave a damn for anyone else he saw, and I think that's the impression most men got . . . when your business is money, you stand to make an enemy every time you go into a deal . . . But Alfred didn't only make enemies. He failed to do the concomitant thing, which is to make a friend . . . people resented him all along the way. He's a very attractive man with an unattractive outlook on people." Not long afterward, this old acquaintance arranged for Alfred to be honorary chairman of a memorial committee, and Natalie found the pleasure it gave him both touching and alarming. At the end of Alfred Eaton's story, he was on his way to meet somebody's elderly infirm brother-in-law at Grand Central Station.

Thus O'Hara accomplished his primary stated purpose of describing the events of Alfred Eaton's life up to the time of anguish. O'Hara wrote in detail, presenting hundreds of scenes played by scores of characters. His method was not that of the author who works surrounded by notes, charts, and schedules, but he did call on Sister to keep a record of characters in a notebook, and he asked Pat Outerbridge to read along with him as he turned out the pages, on guard for anachronisms and conflicts of place or time.

The additional purpose announced by O'Hara at the start could be identified at the end: he was attempting to include in his novel a significant amount of the history of the first fifty years of the twentieth century in the northeastern part of the United States. So we were given material about the effects of two world wars, about school and college education, high finance, Washington bureaucracy, and morals, manners, and customs of both rich and poor in New York and Pennsylvania, with much besides, including some observations on Southern California. The host of minor characters came into sight on this flood of information, then disappeared from view, sometimes to return, sometimes not. The broad realistic treatment gave an impression of the uncontrollable occurrence of events, in too great profusion for any one person to understand them all, or force a symmetrical pattern over their insane diversity. This was life, to be sure, and a certain kind of social history. In offering all this, O'Hara made some demands on his readers, the greatest of which was endurance. You could not read *From the Terrace* at one sitting, and after Alfred's divorce, in the last part of the book, the going was rough. You continued reading, under the compulsion of the story, but the long, dense paragraphs in the pages that seemed to be made of solid type weighed heavily on the mind. This was according to O'Hara's theory and plan. Five years later he discussed his methods in a letter to William Maxwell at *The New Yorker*. O'Hara wrote that he used a technique of "mesmerizing the reader . . . I want to *control* the reader as much as I can, and I make the effort in all sorts of ways. (Punctuation is one of them) . . . What you tell me about Gibbs's theories did not all originate with Gibbs. Much of it came from me to Gibbs. Much as I loved Gibbs, he had a way of telling me something I had previously told him, and the attributional theories are in that category. It began with a discussion of modifiers ('No, thank you,' she said archly.), and went on to 'retorted' and 'chimed in,' etc. Most of the time the dialogue should stand on its own, but occasionally the non-modifier rule has to be broken . . . . There are times when I want to slow down the reader, almost imperceptibly, but slow him down . . . I can do it for a greater length of time with a big block of type, like the Caporetto retreat. I can make it easier for the reader by filling up that block of type with nouns — rifles, machine guns, tanks, motorcycles, ambulances, other non-think words — but the reader is still being slowed down. He picks up the pace, is forced to, when I go back to dialog. But since most of the stories I write for the New Yorker are in dialog, I have to use other tricks, and another trick I use is to dispense entirely with the attributive tag. The full name of a character will do that, if used sparingly . . . Finally I prefer 'said John Smith' to 'John Smith said,' for a number of reasons. It is easier on the eye to follow a comma and close-quotes with a small s than with a cap J. And 'John Smith said' is abrupt and full-stop where I don't want it to be. Now let us go out for a smoke."

When the solid pages gave way to dialogue, the only annoying technical fault in all of O'Hara's writing could be felt, if the scene consisted of many short speeches, and the reader lost track of who was talking. Granted that each character spoke with an individual voice, it was not the inner ear but the eye that lost the identities when the text went too long without "he said," "she said," or the characters' names. This is little enough to charge against a writer so free of mannerisms as O'Hara. It is hard to think of anything else that one might have wished to change: his occasional use of "oaken," "leathern," and "hempen" instead of the simple forms is perhaps the only literary affectation of which he can be convicted. And O'Hara would probably reply that those n suffixes added a quality that he wanted to get.

The difficulty about the dialogue in *From the Terrace* arose when there was too much of it. On these pages, O'Hara did not so much suggest con-versation as literally reproduce it, at tedious length, and he inflicted on the reader the weariness that comes from actual encounters with the long-winded. Nevertheless, readers stayed with Alfred Eaton till the end, and came to understand how Samuel Eaton's vanity, and obsessive preference for one son over another, had sent the surviving son through the world an empty man. At the close, near the place where Natalie recalled Julian English, O'Hara told briefly of another man, who lost the ability to main-tain his position in life, and solved the problem by stepping in front of a subway train. This brought to the minds of perceptive readers the chilling thought of a short sequel to Alfred's story. Perhaps somewhere beyond page 898, like Joe Brooks, Alfred would order his last drink at the club and go into endless night.

In spite of the death and disillusionment in *From the Terrace*, people read the book. Thirteen months after its first hard-cover printing, the novel went into paperback, and more than three million copies had been sold by 1970. There was encouraging critical response: John Hutchens praised O'Hara as an honest writer giving his vision of the world as he saw it. Others used such phrases as major work, great novel, gripping, smashing; the *Times* of New York hailed "this tremendous story" and the *Times* of Los Angeles recommended O'Hara for the Nobel Prize. But there were reviewers who said the book was too long, and others said O'Hara was too plain in his treatment of sex. In some cases it seemed that O'Hara had succeeded so well in making Alfred Eaton unattractive that reviewers felt resentment against the character, and by association his creator, as if they had run into Eaton in real life.

Whatever the critics might say for or against it, *From the Terrace* had showed O'Hara's vitality at the workbench, where he had to summon strength to complete his long projects. In February 1960, fourteen months after the publication of *Terrace*, he was able to go before the public with another novel, *Ourselves to Know*, a carefully planned work which displayed a sophisticated narrative construction. O'Hara took the title from a line in the *Essay on Man:* "And all our Knowledge is Ourselves to know." The new novel began and ended on O'Hara's Pennsylvania ground, allowing some European travels in the middle part. As the story flows, readers learn the truth about Robert Millhouser, who is first shown as an elderly man in Lyons (Lykens), Pennsylvania, through the eyes of a boy named Gerald Higgins. This youth expresses the non-Malloy side of O'Hara; he is a nice boy whose grandparents spoil him as he grows up with the privileges and advantages of an upper-middle-class child in a quiet community before the First World War. He differs from Malloy in not having a dominating father who causes resentments and a feeling of guilt. But at the end, Gerald is in more trouble than any that James Malloy ever blundered into. The story Higgins tells as narrator is a strange and engrossing one. He had learned that Mr. Millhouser, the sedate old man he saw walking the streets of Lyons, was a murderer: many years before, this man had deliberately killed his much younger wife. Robert Millhouser took a liking to Gerald as a bright, well-mannered boy who was interested in books, and by the time Gerald had gone on to graduate study in English, the old man was ready to entrust him with family papers and information necessary for a biography. O'Hara put Gerald Higgins into the Graduate College at Princeton, under the tower he used to see from his workroom at 20 College Road West. We learn what Millhouser's wife did to him, we are present when he kills her, we follow him through his three months' imprisonment and attend his trial, in which he is allowed to plead guilty and is released on probation, because the judge decides that the young wife's notorious promiscuity was a mitigating circumstance. This comes at the end, and we have now learned not only the story of Robert Millhouser, but also that of Gerald Higgins. In the last paragraph, Gerald records that Millhouser died, after many years of private penance, aged eighty-nine. Meanwhile Gerald has married, and joined the Navy in the Second World War, so that he is in the Pacific when Millhouser dies. And the last sentence of the book indicates a possible sequel, with Gerald committing the same crime that ruined the life of Robert Millhouser.

The critical response to this novel was mostly favorable, with some reservations by those who objected to unpleasantness in the main characters and the bluntness of O'Hara's treatment of sex. But on the whole, reviewers by now had begun to accept and praise O'Hara as a writer who derived power from presenting life as he saw it. Many of the English critics were friendly: the *Observer* said that O'Hara had created a world of his own in Pennsylvania like that of Faulkner in Mississippi; the *Sphere* said that *Ourselves* was O'Hara's most important book since *Appointment in Samarra*, with the conclusion that he was continuing to grow. In *Ourselves to Know*, O'Hara had shown that he could record a complicated series of fictional events from two points of view with conviction and economy. The book immediately appeared on the lists of best sellers, an imprecise ranking but an indication of popular demand. There were 100,000 copies rapidly sold in the hard-cover editions — although not O'Hara's greatest sale in this form — and *Ourselves* also received the unwelcome compliment of an offset edition by Chinese pirates. Seventeen paperback printings — over 1,500,000 books — had been issued by 1969 in England and the United States, a splendid commercial success for a book of serious intent.

The next O'Hara book followed in only eight months, to compete with *Ourselves to Know* in the stores, an unusual thing in itself and an indication of O'Hara's confidence in his work and his ability to produce it. What he now offered was three stories of about 35,000 words each, in separate slim volumes like those that Elbert Hubbard used to publish, boxed and sold together under the title *Sermons and Soda-Water*, a phrase from a line in *Don Juan* about repentance following dissipation. O'Hara called these novellas *The Girl on the Baggage Truck, Imagine Kissing Pete,* and *We're Friends Again*. The stories were memoirs of James Malloy, and at the end, the reader had a feeling that O'Hara had finally closed his relationship with this character. In the opening story, Malloy is working as a moving-picture press agent, sometimes insolvent but better organized, financially and socially, than the cub reporter of *BUtterfield 8*. He learns and tells the story of Charlotte Sears, a Hollywood star who has fought her way up from two-a-day vaudeville in the tank towns and whistle-stops. The point of the story is that a man from Gibbsville who claimed to be named Thomas Rodney Hunterden was born Thomas Robert Huntzinger, which is not much of a point. Huntzinger was another of the victims of automobiles who abound in O'Hara's fiction, and his death on the Long Island grade crossing saved him from prosecution for embezzlement. The central story, *Imagine Kissing Pete*, ends with Malloy showing a sympathetic side at the Princeton commencement exercises of the son of an old acquaintance: "I could not read the program because I was crying most of the time." The parents, Bobbie and Pete McRea, had gone down in the world through drink and promiscuity, losing their position in the Gibbsville social scheme. The low-life passages hold some of O'Hara's best writing, as Pete and Bobbie fight their way back to something that "wouldn't be a bad life for two ordinary people," although Lantenengo Street is gone. The bright son who wins scholarships brings hope — and the tears in Malloy's eyes — at the close. Third in the series of novellas came *We're Friends Again*, which shows how Malloy became intimate with carriage folk, and studied their ways. A New York society woman named Nancy Ellis has died of a stroke, and her husband Charley comes to Malloy for sympathy and help. Malloy has "been through it" and he tells Ellis what to expect from friends, takes him for a four-mile walk, and stays at his apartment overnight. The rest of the novella is Malloy's recollection of his friendship with Ellis, Nancy, a girl of fashion called Polly Williamson, and a man named Jack Preswell, who is another automobile victim (he walked in front of a taxicab while drunk) — all this summoned to mind by Malloy in his middle age as he looks back to 1937. James Malloy is now a successful writer, with the courage to recall the days of his early youth, the sort of memories that not everyone can face. But Malloy writes that "moments would come back to me, of love and excitement and music and laughter that filled my breast as they had thirty years earlier." The memory of music and laughter did not afflict him with homesickness, nor did he wish to live the excitements again. He experiences "a splendid contentment that once I had felt those things." Now secure in his vocation as a writer, Malloy understands why he had to mine his memory for those poignant recollections. "I had missed almost nothing, escaped very little, and at fifty I had begun to devote my energy and time to the last, simple but big task of putting it all down as well as I knew how." This in its way was a farewell both to Gerald Higgins and James Malloy. In his own character of John O'Hara, who was not entirely similar to either of the imagined men, O'Hara was organizing for a final assault on achievement and excellence. He stated this purpose in the author's preface to *Sermons:*

I want to get it all down on paper while I can. I am now fifty-five years old and I have lived with as well as in the Twentieth Century from its earliest days. The United States in this century is what I know, and it is my business to write about it to the best of my ability, with the sometimes special knowledge I have. The Twenties, the Thirties, and the Forties are already history, but I cannot be content to leave their story in the hands of the historians and the editors of picture books. I want to record the way people talked and thought and felt and to do it with complete honesty and variety. I have done that in these three novellas, within, of course, the limits of my own observations. I have written these novellas from memory, with a minimum of research, which is one reason why the novella is the right form. I am working on a big novel that will take two years' research — reading, correspondence, travel — but it is my practice to be writing while I am doing research, and by the time I am ready to start writing the longer book, I may well have written two shorter ones. It will take me two years to *write* the longer book, and at fifty-five I have no right to waste time. Two years' research could mean a lot of wasted time while I wait for answers to letters and go on trips and yield to reading distractions that have nothing to do with the material I need for my longer, longest novel. That one *will* pass the hefting test, if it comes to pass.

Why does this set one's teeth on edge? Unexceptionable it is, yet it strikes an ostentatious note that makes the reader uncomfortable. Perhaps one feels sorry for the historians and picture-book editors who receive gratuitous blows when minding their own business. But O'Hara was not addressing readers, though he seemed to be; he was encouraging himself to continue his labors, and warning himself against loafing and idle reading, two consumers of a writer's time. Under this rigorous self-discipline, he had some of his best writing ahead of him. He had signed this preface *Spring 1960 — Princeton, New Jersey*. O'Hara had ten years to go. But he had no way of knowing that, and sometimes said he thought there might be only five years left. Death the old enemy was circling closer, and did not appear to be the kindly fat man of Heywood Broun's fantasy. But O'Hara's anxieties came from the pressure of lessening time, and not from the fear of death, for which he was ready.

The "hefting" book that would take two years to write was *The Lockwood Concern*, which came out in 1965. Meanwhile, *Sermons* received a generally favorable press. Robert R. Kirsch of the Los Angeles *Times* had written that O'Hara deserved the Nobel Prize, and he now repeated that recommendation, adding that he considered O'Hara the "only American writer" who deserved it. Sales were good: the book had gone through nineteen international editions (in English, not counting translations) by 1967. All this entitled O'Hara to feel that a receptive public awaited anything he cared to bring out. Some might even suppose, from the tone of the preface to *Sermons*, that O'Hara had become a self-conscious professional great man along the lines of Frank Lloyd Wright. In fact, O'Hara's manner was quiet and at times diffident. He rarely harangued anyone, nor dominated the talk in gatherings of friends. He even occasionally took time off to construct a joke, in one case at least a quite elaborate joke: In the winter of 1961, when he may have recalled his efforts to organize a fraternity among the boys of Pottsville, he drew up the statement of purpose, rules, and by-laws of the Hessian Relief Society.*

In order to design regalia for the Society, O'Hara did some research on Hessian uniforms and equipment. He corresponded with military art galleries in Los Angeles, with the Stackpole Company of Harrisburg, who were publishers of books on guns and military subjects, and with the Company of Military Collectors and the German Information Center in New York. The correspondence revealed that almost nothing is known about the uniforms and gear that Hessian mercenaries carried into the Jerseys. Accordingly, the Founder decided to limit the insignia to a special tie, and he learned a great deal on this subject from Gieves, Ltd., of London, experienced makers of organization neckwear. The correspondence began in January 1962, and eventually O'Hara decided on an orange and blue stripe, of which he had Gieves make up three dozen. This was a more than adequate stock, for the Founder's list of men entitled to wear the tie of the Hessian Relief Society contained only twenty names, including Pat Outerbridge, J. H. Whitney, Courtlandt Barnes, Mike Romanoff, Nicholas Ludington, Hamilton Cottier and Rensselaer Lee of the Princeton faculty, and Richardson Dilworth and Edgar Scott of Philadelphia.

The organization of the Hessian Relief Society has significance because it shows that O'Hara had reached the place where he could make fun of "the badges" which he said had represented something important to him. He had received a badge of professional recognition as far back as 1955, in the National Book Award for *Ten North Frederick*. On acceptance, O'Hara remarked that more than twenty years had passed since the appearance of his first novel, and he was only just now receiving his first public award. The possibility exists that some honors were withheld from O'Hara because of his straightforward treatment of sex. In O'Hara's boyhood, there had existed a supposedly secret language spoken only by men, in saloons, barracks, and livery stables, which made use of half a dozen old blunt words, of singular power, having to do with physical functioning in animals and human beings. The words were universally held to be improper and unprintable. But authors felt need for the power in these

---

* The idea of self-conferred badges of distinction had amused John O'Hara for years. In 1940 he wrote to William Maxwell asking him to trace down an item in *The New Yorker* about a foreign legation that sold an Order, complete with medal and rosette, for thirty-five dollars: "Marc Connelly wears a ribbon which is a symbol of, I think, the American Academy of Arts and Sciences or something. It drives everybody crazy, and some night I would like to appear at a dinner with Marc, wearing the much more impressive and highly authentic decoration. Yes, it might even be worth $35. I've spent more for much less pleasure."

words, and after the First World War, began to use them in books. Along with this came a freedom of subject, and serious writers began to publish specific descriptions of sexual attraction and intercourse. As the years passed, many questions of taste became questions only of usage. It had been in 1876, after all, that Tolstoy took us to the very sofa on which Anna Karenina surrendered to Vronsky. But there was still a psychological difficulty in realistic writing about sex. The author took the chance of offending readers because of a set of taboos, not fully understood, which made the subject "dirty." And O'Hara often ran into charges that his treatment of sex was deliberately sensational. It was true that some of the scenes he depicted between men and women bore little resemblance to John Ridd plighting his troth to Lorna Doone. Or to put it another way, O'Hara was safe from any charge of prudery. But his evident purpose to present real life should have been enough to absolve him from accusations of catering to salacious tastes in readers. He had written on this matter in November 1958 to John Hutchens: "You raise the point that I seem to find a sexual motivation for 'virtually everything in life,' and it's okay to raise that point so long as you follow it up with the comment that 'they represent a dead honest writer's vision of the world as he sees it.' I do not think that the amount of sex in my novels is disproportionate to its effect not only on our motivations but even on our conversations. You do not think so; but in saying so you do not have recourse to cheap references to the Kinsey reports. This novel [*From the Terrace*] is almost 900 pages long and covers about fifty years (round numbers, old boy). Fifty years is, roundly, 17,250 days. Nine hundred mentions of sex, or a mention on every page, would be a remarkably small proportion of mentions in covering a period of 17,250 days, for sex certainly is a daily factor in all our lives, one way or another — and I don't even mention sex on *all* 900 pages. This is rather foolish talk by me, since all it can prove is that I don't think I mention sex disproportionately to its incidence in our life and in our lives. It could be argued that I don't mention money as much as I do sex, and we would then have to start building charts to show how much I mentioned money, food, water, air, and everything else that is basic in our daily lives . . ."

On occasion O'Hara could make himself laugh at charges that he dealt in gamy material. He touched on this while writing, in February 1960, to Courtie Bryan, who was serving his military obligation, after Yale, as a lieutenant in Korea. "I write you from a little corner of Korea that we have been getting ready for you. Perhaps I ought to explain. Due to some fault in the plumbing, every day at sundown for the past three weeks my study begins to smell as though six stallions had been having a pissing contest that ended in a tie. The pungency lasts until about 1 A.M., sometimes later, but between 5 P.M. and the early morning you might just as well be doing latrine duty. We have had experts in every day, but so far no one has been able to do anything about it. Your mother is thinking of suing Princeton University, which sold us the non-porous land, but . . . the retorts in my direction would not be good. There are plenty of people who say my books stink, and the fact that now my study does, etc., etc. . . ."

In this letter O'Hara went on to express anxiety about *Ourselves to Know,* which had just come out. It had appeared on the best-seller lists three weeks ahead of the official publication date; Random House had ordered 100,000 copies printed and bound. That was fine, but O'Hara thought that "because of the complex construction of this particular book I know damn well a lot of the critics, especially the out-of-town ones, will review it without reading it." He went on to sum up his position: "After 25 years, it is interesting to contemplate one's standing as a novelist. The professional Jews, the professional Catholics, the professional Marxists and the professional intellectuals want no part of me, whether they are laymen or in the book business as writers or critics. My strongest public is among educated, middle-and-upper-middle class, Protestant men and women, who do not inspect a book for its propaganda content. I couldn't be more pleased that this is the case, since I believe that among those people you will find most of the really decent, really tolerant, honest citizens of this country. They themselves are losing out to the others, since they are not an organized group or class and therefore cannot exert any pressure on government or in the large field of the arts. But they really made this country what it is at its best. With all their faults — and they were never vicious — they are the best Americans and when they cease to exist as a class, so will the United States as a nation. I will continue to write about them in critical but sympathetic terms, in the hope that a byproduct of my writing will be the continuation, even if only for a minute in time, of this class. The educated American Protestant made, I think, one mistake, that of postponing too long the assimilation of the educated American Irish-Catholic; but both sides were at fault there. The Protestants were pig-headed in their way, the Catholics soreheads in theirs, and both groups behaved as they did because they belonged to but did not practice religions . . ."

There seemed to be a faint echo of Mrs. Uhlein of the Afternoon Delphians in these remarks, even a suggestion of Harry Reilly. But O'Hara was offering conclusions based on life as he saw it. Many people thought his talent put him in a special class, in which there was no need to worry about whether or not a gang of canting Presbyterians and imitation-English Episcopalians preserved "the United States as a nation." That is the way one would expect an Irishman of spirit to see it: yet O'Hara was an Irishman of spirit, if ever there was one.

Prior to the publishing of *From the Terrace,* O'Hara expected to come under attack, and relieved his mind by writing to John Hutchens: "I like to think I am in a better defensive position than most authors. I have had to take the worst 'they' can dish out, and while I do not kid myself for a moment that I am invulnerable, I am toughened better than I would be if I'd always been handled gently, as [James G.] Cozzens was [before he wrote a book nearly all critics condemned]. As I've told you before, my chief concern with a new book is respectful consideration, which I get from you and Charlie [Poore of the *Times*] and which everyone else gets from you and Charlie. If I also get it from the people chosen to review the book for the Sunday sections, that's velvet . . . I am going to go right on while I have the strength; there are so many things I want to do, so very many, but I have to take a look at the calendar now and then. The calendar and the actuarial tables. This novel *From the Terrace* is enormous, but it could not be otherwise. I have a horror of sounding pretentious, but this is a private letter and I can level: if there has been one single controlling factor in my creation of this novel, it has been the Philadelphia Orchestra. Ever since I moved to Princeton I've been a regular at the Academy of Music. I used to go to the Philharmonic, too, as a season ticket holder, but I kept that quiet because too many of our mutual friends prefer to go on thinking of me as a drunken kid in a coonskin coat, and in a curious way they would have spoiled the Philharmonic for me if they'd known about it. I love music. But it is not as a sensual experience that symphonies have influenced me in this novel; it is hour after hour of sitting there and listening to Brahms while my intellect contemplates the simplicities and intricacies of symphonic construction. As far back as *A Rage to Live* I began to write novels that are not intended for one reading any more than a good symphony is for one hearing. I agree that most novels are so read until they get to be classics, but I can only say that the reader who does is not getting his $5 worth, give or take a buck. Although I am not a musician, I could have been a composer. All I lacked was the enormous but not impossible technical equipment. The distinction here is that I could have been a composer rather than, say, a great violinist or pianist. I taught myself to play the fiddle and years ago I used to play along with the Philharmonic on the radio on Sunday afternoons — the easy parts, of course, and substitute my voice in the hard parts. I was always closer to, let us say, Beethoven than I was to John Corigliano or Wallenstine. I like to believe that Rachmaninoff, who could combine the two accomplishments, would have liked my novels. God knows I admire him."

A little later, O'Hara wrote to Hutchens about something that failed to soothe him like a Brahms symphony — the presence of English literary ladies with positive manners: "I've never read anything by Miss Pamela Frankau, but your piece today made me recall the first time (of two) that I met her. My then wife and I were in Quogue — it was early in the war — and we drove over to East Hampton to have lunch at, I guess, the Phil

Barrys'. Because it *was* the war, Phil and I were the only registered males in a rather large company. Miss Frankau and, if I'm not mistaken, G. B. ('Petah') Stern were the guests of honor, and Miss Frankau, who had just arrived by train, was making fun of the names on the Long Island R.R. She took particular delight in Speonk. Speeeeee-yonk, she pronounced it. How could anyone think up a name like Speeeeee-yonk? And Center Moriches, of course she pronounced it Mo-reesh. What are they? Then she turned to me, old poker face, and said, 'Mr. O'Horra doesn't like what I'm saying. Have I offended you, Mr. O'Horra?' 'No,' I said. 'But I've lived in England and I don't see how an Englishman can kid American place names. How about Stewkey, pronounced Stiffkey?' 'Good boy!' said Barry. Several years later I met Miss Frankau again and she said, 'Oh, Mr. O'Horra doesn't like me.' 'Notta tall,' I said. 'Notta tall.' I left her to figure out how I meant it. A real phony dame, and an aggressive one."

In 1961, O'Hara issued his first volume of new short stories since 1947. Much of the book, called *Assembly,* had been composed during the previous summer at Quogue, in sessions of what O'Hara called "joyful writing." Ten of the stories had appeared in *The New Yorker* among his first contributions after his return to the magazine. These included "It's Mental Work," which John Gunther said was the best he'd read in twenty years by O'Hara or anyone else. The story told how a bartender and his girl cheated a crooked lawyer after threatening him with suffocation in an icebox. Among stories appearing for the first time was "Mrs. Stratton of Oak Knoll," which answered the question of what goes on in the houses of the formerly rich — houses that are too big to be properly kept up. (In this case, a brave old woman keeps living, to protect a moronic dependent son.) Another effective story for *Assembly* was "Mary and Norma," by contrast a study of domestic hatred in the lower middle class. Two young housewives are talking, and it develops that one of them is in danger of murder by her surly, jealous husband. One could feel a note of elegiac sadness in "The Pioneer Hep-Cat," which also was written directly for the book, and "You Can Always Tell Newark," in which a decent young man asks an older man for advice he hardly knows how to give.

The collected short stories that appeared in 1962, entitled *The Cape Cod Lighter,* earned a round of critical applause and again demonstrated the variety of things O'Hara could do when writing within these limits. Here were Gibbsville stories such as "Claude Emerson, Reporter," "Pat Collins," "Winter Dance," and "The Bucket of Blood," which inspired Quentin Reynolds to suggest a continuation: Jay the bootlegger organizes a chain of saloons, marries Jenny the whore, their son goes to Princeton, then to the moon as the first astronaut, marries Tallulah Bankhead, visits Russia, and defects to the Soviets. A man resembling Quentin Reynolds appears in "'The First Day," a story that suggests much that happened before its beginning and is likely to happen after its end. Ray Whitehill, a famous author and war correspondent, has come back to the small-city newspaper where he got his start. It is never stated in so many words, but we know he has been through bad times. Of course everything will be all right from now on, back with the *Ledger-Star*, and they are pleased and proud to have him — yet a tentative note gets in. We don't have to be told, we *know* that this isn't going to work out, the ruined celebrity will not make it, and will soon be on his way to something unthinkable. But everyone, including the publisher, is very nice on this first day. The same note of calm hopelessness could be found in "Things You Really Want," about an important man who has been advised to rest by a telephone conference of doctors. George Miles and his wife Elsie understand that what the doctors are really saying is, "Prepare to die."

The book of stories for 1963 was called *The Hat on the Bed*: again came flattering reviews of the old-master type. O'Hara offered a memorable picture of cruelty in "John Barton Rosedale, Actor's Actor," and a sad look at a young man headed for trouble in "The Ride from Mauch Chunk." It is remarkable how one's feelings are touched by the abrupt ending of this story. A young man of great facile charm flirts with a girl on a train, and she has an immediate tender feeling for him, though certain he is not a sound young man. Then the story jumps some years into the future: the girl reads in the paper that Jarvis Brittingham has received a harsh prison sentence for bribery. "The newspaper article reported that Mr. Brittingham heard the sentence with no show of emotion. 'I guess that was just the trouble,' said Maudie." O'Hara's understanding of old people was increasing as he himself grew older: here was a Los Angeles story called "The Friends of Miss Julia," which introduced an old lady transplanted from the Bronx to Beverly Hills by a successful son, and stricken with loneliness when her hairdresser dies. The same feeling appeared in "The Manager": Mr. Greene, who runs a summer resort, knows that old Mr. Wilbur is becoming a problem. And the manager also knows that "dignity of the right kind was the only protection the old people had."

A story of remarkable power in this collection was "Our Friend the Sea," in which a man named Donald Fisher falls in love with a perplexed girl in flight from trouble on an Atlantic liner heading for England. Donald stands between lifeboats and watches the sea flowing by: "He was there he knew not how long before he had a thought of himself, and when the thought came it was that he was alone and at peace, that there was nothing between him and the North Pole but all that restless water. Just below him the water streamed by, and lulled him to a wakeful sleep; and if he looked out beyond the racing stream, he saw the beginning of the vastness that lay between him and the top of the world. Behind him was the super-structure of the ship, and inside the ship were two thousand men and women; but he could not see them or hear them, and for as long as he gazed out on the sea, they did not exist. No one existed. He could not remember another time when he had had such a sense of being alone on the planet and feeling neither sorrow nor joy. Beyond the ship-made stream of the ocean the sea was quiet and not watery; more like a purple-black mass of sticky stuff for a Peter to walk on. And it was all there was between him and the top of the world — where there was no one either." Such descriptive passages are rare in O'Hara's work, and this one had a purpose, for it was into the ocean that Constance Shelber went when she decided things could never be straightened out. The steward handed Fisher her note: "The sea is a friend of mine, too." This story was one of twenty-six that O'Hara wrote for the *Post*, now his preferred market, where his last published work of short fiction, "Good Samaritan," appeared on November 11, 1969.

Sometimes a *Post* story and a *New Yorker* story would appear in alternate weeks; or there might be a run of stories in the *Post* like the five that appeared from February to March 1964, and also in that year's collection, *The Horse Knows the Way*. As the product of part-time work, O'Hara had now published 101 stories in four volumes, beginning with *Assembly*, after eleven years of no short stories. Like the other three recent collections, *The Horse Knows the Way* offered writing that entered the reader's mind and stayed there: "In the Mist," "I Spend My Days in Longing," and "The Gun," an example of O'Hara sleight-of-hand that seemed to reflect the existence of an entire novel about some Chekhovian characters in the Connecticut countryside, and an undefined danger which is due to something that happened long ago — or is it happening right now? O'Hara made "The Gun" a study in mood, while in the same collection he presented "School," a sharply defined character sketch of a boy at a fashionable boarding school, who hates and betrays his father. In another story O'Hara returned to Gibbsville and the brick and wooden houses climbing the hills near Dr. O'Hara's stable, houses which always seemed to ask, who lives here, and what do they do? Against this background, O'Hara made "Clayton Bunter" a glimpse of three frowzy lives, like dim lights behind curtains as one passes on a late winter afternoon. In his foreword to *The Horse Knows the Way*, O'Hara wrote:

> For a while, at least, this will be my last book of short stories. I know that Mme. Schumann-Heink, Sir Harry Lauder, and W. Somerset Maugham have made frequent farewell appearances that followed farewell appearances, and I have qualified my announcement by saying "for a while." I am also perhaps overconscious of the fact that at my age, fifty-nine, a man had better not be too sure that he is going to finish anything he starts . . . It is going to be difficult to resist the temptation to go on writing short stories — for me more difficult than it is to write them . . . I could live

nicely on my income from short stories and nothing else, even without movie options and television sales, and my taxes would not be so devastating. There is also a temptation to play it safe in my war with the academics and the critics, since they have a hard time rapping the stories and are driven to complaining against "the kind of people" I write about.

The period of O'Hara's refraining from issuing books of short stories proved to be only one year, for he came back in 1966 with *Waiting for Winter*, his fifth volume of stories since the eleven-year hiatus. In 1965 he had issued the long Pennsylvania novel on which he had been working for some time, *The Lockwood Concern*; and in 1966, he also released the fifty-two essays he had written for *Newsday* and its syndicate under the running title "My Turn." The book was not the success that O'Hara was accustomed to, although it did go into a paperback edition. The syndicated pieces had earned him $52,000, and the project had been close to his heart. O'Hara had given value, and supplied old Harry Guggenheim, the wealthy *Newsday* publisher, with some good copy, as when he remarked that certain snobbish political liberals like to feel that "Groton-and-Porcellian rubs off on them" when they associate with fashionable persons, a case of "gilt, as someone must have said, by association."

He began the "My Turn" series on October 3, 1964, with: "Let's get off to a really bad start." O'Hara announced that he was prepared to lose readers who would not agree with what he had to say: "I expect to lose some right now, before they have given themselves a chance to come under my spell . . . The whole thing may turn out to be a bomb, but if it does, what of it? When I was a young reporter I scarcely ever let a day go by without reading Heywood Broun and FPA, and I thought I would never get used to doing without them. But I have. One does. Therefore I have no illusion about my own indispensability. I have, of course, few doubts about my own wisdom. In this wondrous world you can say almost anything that comes into your mind, and sooner or later, you may turn out to have been right." The "My Turn" columns were O'Hara's most interesting writing as a regular contributor, superior to the *Newsweek* pieces in every way. Many readers wrote that they were "My Turn" fans. Perhaps these were "the Lawrence Welk people" for whom O'Hara said he proposed to say some good words. Be that as it may, editors began dropping the column, and, as O'Hara wrote, "it became an expensive feature for *Newsday*. Guggenheim then suggested a change in what he called the 'format.' He wanted me to stop commenting on current events and substitute a short story every week. That, of course, I would not do, and I am convinced that Guggenheim believed he was giving me an out. Even Guggenheim could not afford to pay me the kind of money I would demand for a weekly short story. So, in accordance with the terms of our contract, I duly notified him that after such-and-such a date, the column

'My Turn' would cease to exist. But I'll turn up on a newspaper some-where. I always do." Although *My Turn,* the collected pieces, had a limited sale and tepid critical response, the stories in *Waiting for Winter* were a success from all points of view. Here was "Afternoon Waltz," another feat of compression, the life story of a man on Lantenengo Street in twenty-seven pages. A Philadelphia specialist had to tell John Wesley Evans that he will soon be blind: " 'Have you got a friend, a very close friend?' 'One, yes,' said John. 'You're lucky,' said the doctor. 'Man, or woman?' 'A woman.' " It was Harriet Shields, who was waiting outside in a cab. " 'She wanted to come in with me, but I wouldn't let her. She's always right.' " When Harriet's elderly husband died, Gibbsville thought she would marry John Evans, the blind young neighbor to whom she was obviously devoted. They never got married, "but sometimes on a summer afternoon, or a favorable day in May, a warm day in September, there would be the sound of a waltz coming from Harriet Shields's talking-machine. It was not loud enough to disturb anyone."

Gibbsville also is the background for "Fatimas and Kisses," in which reporter James Malloy covers a murder, and discovers that the alcoholic homicidal maniac who committed the crime had gone crazy in a speakeasy while staring at "a pre-Prohibition framed brewery advertisement depict-ing a goat in Bavarian costume raising a beer stein." Just before he shot his wife and children, Lonnie Lintz thought he saw "a foreigner" who "had whiskers and wore those funny clothes. He had whiskers on his chin. All the girls were stuck on him." In the same collection was "Leonard," a story to be named among O'Hara's best, in which he used a Beverly Hills restaurant called the South Seas (the original stands on North Rodeo Drive), where

most of the patrons knew each other, if only by sight, and there was always a certain amount of table-hopping during the cocktail hours. The men patrons, who usually arrived a bit later than the girls, were likely to go to the bar first and have a drink before sitting with the girls. The men were also employed in the neighborhood shops and offices, the smooth-est and best-dressed being the salesmen and partners in the haberdasheries and tailoring establishments, and automobile salesmen. A few marriages had had their origin at the South Seas, but for the most part it was patron-ized by men and girls who were not bound by marriage or in any event were not too strict about the binding ties. Nobody had much money, nearly everybody could run up a tab, and a man who had the shorts did not hestitate to let a couple of girls buy his drinks. If he did it too often, he would be marked lousy and there would come the dread day when Teddy Hollander himself would say to him, "Don't come in no more, pal. You're in me for over a hundred dollars, and I don't like it when you free-load off these kids."

In the next paragraph, about four hundred words, O'Hara establishes the split-bamboo decoration, "Moon of Manakoora" played softly through the public address system, the doorman (a retired Negro prizefighter who wore a pith helmet, a khaki uniform, and a Sam Browne belt), the Filipino and Mexican waiters, the native American Chinese chef, Alma McHugh the hatcheck-cigarette girl, and her husband the bartender, who was a Jersey City Irishman who had served fifty-one months in the Marines. The McHughs were horse players, and deeply in debt to their employer. They often quarrelled but always went back together again. "Several of the older girls among the patrons, after a couple of McHugh's Guadalcanal Specials, would invite him to their apartment after work. The secret of the Guadalcanal Special was a big dash of Pernod; two dollars a drink and no more than two to a customer. They were popular with the girls who worked in offices, who dropped in on Friday afternoon and did not have to show up at the office on Saturday. Mac was a rye drinker himself." We are now prepared for the entrance into this little paradise of Leonard Dillman, the star customer. He is an older man, who looks like a banker. But there is something *wrong* about Leonard, though we never learn what it is. He spends money freely, but is most particular about his food, and can't eat his steak if it doesn't *look* just right — one sign of an alcoholic or drug user. What we see is Leonard's decline from the position of favored customer, until the proprietor notices that he interferes with the rhythm of the establishment through his attentions to the most popular of the "kids," Geraldine Williams. The other girls call her Jerry, or Character. "She could say anything to anybody and get away with it." Leonard takes Jerry out on a date after which she does not show up for three days, although Leonard is there at his usual table. Speculation about this begins to dampen the spirit of the cocktail hour, and hurt business. McHugh reports, "We're off about eighteen, twenty dollars." Teddy forces a dispute on Leonard Dillman, who tells him "subterfuge" is not necessary, and leaves the place. Jerry Williams also stops coming in and they never see her again, but Alma McHugh gets a postcard from Mexico City a year later, signed Jerry W. She is with Leonard. O'Hara's account of happenings at the South Seas ranks with two other saloon stories, "The Bucket of Blood" and "It's Mental Work," for the detailed background, complete even to the technical side of running the establishments, and the powerful suggestion that disaster lies ahead.

In the next three years, *Waiting for Winter* sold a million copies in paperback. O'Hara had explained, in a prefatory note,

I call this book *Waiting for Winter* because I wrote all the stories while doing just that. From the amount of work I do it might not seem that my industry is affected by the seasons, and it is true that I write all year long. But I prefer to work on novels in cold weather. I don't like warm weather much anyway; I feel better when the thermometer registers below 50° Fahrenheit, outside. When I can look out my window and see snow on the ground, I am impelled to go right to the typewriter; and a miserable, gloomy, raw rainy day has the same effect . . .

Long-writing weather is the late autumn and harsh winter and blustery spring. (In Pennsylvania we used to call it "eggy" weather. Probably comes from ague-y.) I put off getting back to an unfinished long novel [*The Instrument*], and while struggling against the vicissitudes of summer and a protracted Indian summer, I wrote most of these stories. Hence the title. Of course it has other implications as well.

The next collection, *And Other Stories,* appeared in 1968, and with it O'Hara added twelve more to those he had published since the hiatus, making a total of 139 stories in the six volumes that had appeared in seven years. He filled about a third of this book with a novella called *A Few Trips and Some Poetry,* which begins at the Farmers Hotel in Turnersville near Dr. Malloy's farm. The narrator is James Malloy, and the story appears to have some connection with the three novellas that O'Hara published as *Sermons and Soda-Water.* James summons up his memories of a girl friend, Isabel Barley. It seemed to him that Isabel was remote from the town and time, that "her life was being, and always would be lived elsewhere." When Malloy gets to New York he has a hard time at first and finds himself compelled to "eat and smoke" on a dollar a day when that much can be borrowed. His feeling about Isabel is a luxury, but when "you are reduced to the condition where you must measure the cost of a pack of cigarettes against a breakfast of coffee and toast, nearly everything is a luxury. And though you may not realize it at the time, the things that are happening to your pride and your self-respect have an effect that lasts long after the ordeal is over." Then Malloy's luck changes, he begins to sell his writing, and his life improves. He returns to Gibbsville for a visit; and here O'Hara presents one of his most incisive character drawings in the person of Horse McGrath, a jazz pianist and student of women who makes his living playing with pick-up dance bands and in cocktail bars from Philadelphia to Reading. When the Horse talks about women, one hears the voice of the essential pool-room loafer in concentrated form. Trouble ensues when Isabel and McGrath get together, and trouble follows her until the closing scene, thirty years on, when Malloy comes to see her at Turnersville, and finds her living with a young girl companion and dying of cancer. All that is left for James and Isabel is to say goodbye. Another memorable piece of work in *And Other Stories* was "The Private People," which gives us the privilege of meeting Jack Dorney, a retired picture star who saved his money and now leads a comfortable life playing golf and bridge, and catching up on his reading. His wife "is drunk at seven o'clock and he is alone with the TV and his reading until past midnight. He knows that when he has turned out his light she waits a little and then goes to the sitting-room and has some more to drink. Back in her bedroom she leaves the light on all night long. She cannot sleep unless the light is on. Oh, it is not a very bright light."

Jack Dorney had some resemblance to Hubert Ward, hero of *The Big Laugh*, the novel that O'Hara published in 1962. Although it seemed less important than *Ourselves to Know*, the novel was impressive in its picture of Hollywood as O'Hara had known it before the war. The story was his delayed goodbye to the laughter in the Garden of Allah — merriment that had often been derisive and scornful for all its spontaneity and wit. The book shows how Hubert Ward, an actor of moderate ability, is built into an international star because of an indefinable trait of personality that the camera catches, making him, as a producer says, "a clean-cut heavy." Hubert Ward's big laugh, which ends the story, is directed at everything and everybody — his fans, the other stars, the producers, his wife, and also at himself, for as we have found out, his career held many a disgraceful scene and shameful compromise.

The year 1962, in which *The Big Laugh* appeared, began half a decade of remarkable sustained production by John O'Hara. But if he had chosen to retire, and never publish another word, his accomplishment up to this point had been monumental. The trade magazine *Publishers Weekly* said that O'Hara's books had sold more than 20,000,000 copies. An additional million sales would soon be credited to *The Big Laugh*. And another O'Hara novel, which was to meet with similar success, came out in 1963. It was *Elizabeth Appleton*, the story of a rich woman who married a professor in a small Pennsylvania college. The question to be answered is, Will John Appleton succeed the retiring president of the college? The book is symmetrically controlled and organized: O'Hara presents three pairings of a man and woman, and the woman is the strongest member of each couple. (This is a theme that frequently appears in O'Hara's work, as in the marriage of Joe and Edith Chapin of *Ten North Frederick*.) Taken together, though they had no connecting characters, *The Big Laugh* and *Elizabeth Appleton* gave a panoramic view of the United States from the late 1930s until just after the war, presented in terms of the ambitions and rewards of two American pursuits, commercial entertainment and higher education. As soon as the typescript of *Elizabeth Appleton* was out of the house, O'Hara set to work on another long novel.

The new novel appeared on Thanksgiving Day 1965: O'Hara had now become committed in his own mind to issuing at least one book a year. When a collection of his stories appeared, he then would have two new titles before the public at once. Now here was another Pennsylvania novel to be considered, and this new book, *The Lockwood Concern*, proved worthy of standing as a companion piece with *Ourselves to Know*. Each of

these novels was controlled, organized, and effective in doing what it set
out to do. They made one think of mine buildings around Pottsville —
bleak and spare, communicating an emotion of total satisfaction to the
viewer as they mounted hills to the exact needed distance, then stopped.
Perhaps it is fanciful to say so, but O'Hara's sense of construction may
have come from these collieries, with their evident honesty of purpose, and
austere consummation of line. Construction is the theme in the opening
movement of *The Lockwood Concern:* George Bingham Lockwood has
ordered the building of a stone mansion on an old farm near Swedish
Haven (Schuylkill Haven), a small town tributary to Gibbsville. The time
is October 1926. George Lockwood is a member of a clan that O'Hara
created to indicate a subtle social shading: the Lockwood family is old,
but not good. It is the "bad stock" about which Dr. O'Hara grumbled.
The Lockwood concern, using the word in the sense of interest or purpose,
is to become a good family and produce a gentleman. They are not going
to do it with George, a cad of the first water who has nothing but money
to recommend him. The nearest he can get to honest emotion is mean
resentment or cold sensuality, and O'Hara shows Lockwood's quality in
the opening pages when an accident occurs at the building site. Lockwood has ordered the men to build a spiked fence around the property. A
boy who climbs a tree to see what is happening falls on a spike and is
killed. The minute this is reported to him, Lockwood leaves for New
York, with parting instructions to take the matter up with his Gibbsville
lawyers, Joe Chapin and Arthur McHenry. As the novel develops, it turns
out that George's son Bing also is a cad: he is expelled from Princeton,
goes west, and becomes a crook. So much for the Lockwood concern.
But George doesn't really care. At the end of the story, which comes five
years after the building of his house, Lockwood has found the ideal mistress in a skilled New York call girl he has met by chance while out drinking with an old college acquaintance. Back in Swedish Haven to think
things over (and driving a Buick trade-in borrowed from Julian English),
George is alone in his big house. He must go in to the Gibbsville Club
for dinner, Prohibition is still in effect, and he decides to bring up a bottle
of champagne from his cellar and take it along. George Lockwood had
ordered his contractor to put in a circular secret stairway from the library
to the cellar. This evening, George thinks he will go down for his wine by
way of this stairway. For various reasons — among them the aftereffects
of a heavy nap, and the emotional exhaustion from an ugly scene with a
gardener — his step is unsure, and he falls. O'Hara closes the book with
a remarkable passage:

> The stairway in the secret passageway wound around a central post and
> the steps were of uneven width, from zero to eight inches. He missed

the first step completely, and he fell to the cellar, buffeted from side to side all the way down. Before even coming to a jolting stop on the cellar floor he knew that his leg was broken. The pain seemed to prolong the fall, and when at last it ended and he lay still, he wondered why he had not landed sooner. In the blackness he was wholly blind and strangely deaf until a silence entered his ears and he realized that he had created the silence by pausing in the midst of his screaming. The lower half of his left leg had twisted itself crazily and did not belong to the rest of him except as the source of his agony. He reached down, impelled by irresistible curiosity, and forced his fingers along his trouser-leg until he could touch the broken skin. Beyond that his fingers would not go, and for the first time he fainted. But consciousness returned immediately; the pain was too lively for quick relief, and he was trying to shout again. Now a previously unnoticed pain competed with the shrill agony of his leg. He put his fingers to the right side of his skull and touched a sticky substance that he knew was blood. The scalp was cut. The roaring sound he was hearing could have been his own voice in a cave, and this passageway was a sort of cave. In the blindness of the dark he could not tell whether he had actually lost his sight, a symptom he vaguely remembered as having to do with a skull fracture. He held up his left wrist; he could not see the dial of his watch. He was blind.

He did not need his sight to observe the next development. It came out of his nostrils without extra pain but with an urgency that was like a bursting dam. It cascaded over his mouth and sickened him, and now he knew that he was going to die. He lost consciousness once more and this time when he awoke he found that his body — not he — was fighting for breath. A compartment of his intellect contained the information that he would not last the night, and that it would be morning before anyone could help him. Who would miss him? He had made no engagement for dinner. A woman in New York (he could not think of her name) was expecting him to telephone her, tomorrow. The man whom he had last seen, Kitzmiller, would not be there tomorrow. And who knew of the existence of the secret passageway? One man, Hibbard [who is in another town], and no one else but the vanished craftsmen who had built it. And so this was the way it all ended, to die hoping to die because there was no hope of living. He screamed again, but the cry was muffled by the stuff that was strangling him. Then soon — always soon, no matter when — came the moment that no one has ever told anyone about. And no one will ever tell anyone about, because it is a secret that belongs to Them.

During the time he was planning and writing *The Lockwood Concern,* O'Hara kept up correspondence with various people whom he liked. He did not write to those of whom he disapproved, and he disposed of letters from cranks and strangers by throwing them away. But when he thought a good man or woman was in trouble, he would try to say the right thing, knowing how important it was to feel that one is never quite alone, even if one is. Mrs. John Hutchens died in November 1963, and O'Hara wrote this message of condolence: "Dear John: As I said in my telegram, I was shocked and saddened to read about Katherine's death. Knowing nothing of the circumstances, I have assumed she died of a heart attack. Just ten years ago my wife died of an acute auricular fibrillation, and I know what you are going through now. Two things I can tell you: you must take on extra work. Whatever you are doing now, you must add to it. This is terribly important, and you should not delay it. You will have a hard time sleeping (and you will have dreams), but if you start right away to work on something new, besides what you normally do, you will go to bed at night exhausted and ready to sleep.

"The other thing: I was very lucky and fell in love a few months after Belle died, and a year later I remarried. This, too, is terribly important, and especially at our age. We know what we want and what we don't want in a woman. I have known my present wife for 35 years; and I had two marriages and she had one before we got together nine years ago, but we *are* together. I wish you the same good fortune. As always, John."

It was not true that O'Hara detested editors and refused to take their advice. Those editors for whom he had respect worked easily with O'Hara and he presented them with few problems. One editor he respected was William Maxwell at *The New Yorker*. When Wylie graduated from St. Timothy's School in June 1963, O'Hara found that the Maryland countryside brought back memories of Scott Fitzgerald, which he shared with Maxwell: "I was so sure I would weep at commencement that I practically didn't. I think I kept telling myself I was better off than Fitzgerald had been in the same area. We stayed in Towson, near the school, and it was one Sunday afternoon in Towson, in 1934, that I had Scott and Zelda in my car and I wanted to kill him. Kill. We were taking her back to her Institution, and he kept making passes at her that could not possibly be consummated. We stopped at a drug store to get him some gin. The druggist would not give it to him. I had to persuade the druggist to relent, and he got the gin. But I wanted to kill him for what he was doing to that crazy woman, who kept telling me she had to be locked up before the moon came up. That was the last time I saw her ..."

On January 31, 1966, Sister and John gave a lunch party at Linebrook to celebrate their eleventh wedding anniversary. The onset of a blizzard kept some of the invited guests in New York and Philadelphia, but those who got through found themselves present at a singularly agreeable gathering. The pale winter sunshine, reflected from snowdrifts, filled the living room with light like that in Edward Hopper's paintings. The highest ranking guest was Richard Hughes, Governor of New Jersey. His presence meant respectful state troopers in the hall and kitchen, like those who attended Governor Dinkelberger at Grace Tate's house in *A Rage to Live*.

Among the guests were George Frost Kennan, former Ambassador to Russia, and Mrs. Edgar (Zilph) Palmer, a sprightly and humorous old lady of the authentic dowager type, the reigning social figure of Princeton. Her late husband's name could be seen on a square, a laboratory, and a stadium. For years now the O'Haras had attended Mrs. Palmer's New Year reception: John and his hostess would talk for a few minutes in a side room, as he shrank from the noise of the general gathering. This was no affectation, but something any nondrinker can understand. O'Hara had paid Mrs. Palmer the compliment of using her name in a book — Zilph Millhouser was one of the sympathetic characters in *Ourselves to Know*. Today, the Edward Hopper light was steady all through lunch, with John at a large table, Sister at a smaller one with Kennan, Mrs. Palmer, and some old friends. There was one toast, proposed by O'Hara to Sister. Then, standing in front of the fireplace, Governor Hughes gave John something for his Rolls-Royce, the New Jersey motor license plate JOH-1. O'Hara was delighted. He had not only presided at a good party of people he wanted to see, but had finished a piece of work. In the study, he showed Mrs. Hughes the manila envelope containing the typescript of a new novel, *The Instrument*, which he would take to New York as soon as the roads were passable. He said the book had a New England background, and he had done special research to get New England speech right. The guests left soon after that, for the sky was beginning to darken, and the snow kept falling, heavily and silently.

The short novel in the typescript O'Hara had showed to Betty Hughes had to wait its turn on his publishing list. Ahead of it came the book of newspaper pieces, and *Waiting for Winter*, and so *The Instrument* did not reach the bookstores until Thanksgiving Day 1967. This novel records a few months in the life of a young playwright called Yank Lucas, who becomes a celebrity by writing a hit play. He goes to New England to write his second play, where he discovers that he is no genius, as he had thought, but an exploiter of other people's emotions. O'Hara seemed to be trying to see how repellent a figure he could make of his main character, and still not drive readers away. The cold and calculating Yank Lucas is conducted through the rituals of Manhattan success by the producer Ellis Walton, in pages of narrative that owe their authenticity to O'Hara's experiences when *Appointment in Samarra* first appeared. Critical response to *The Instrument* was good. The *Chicago Sun-Times* said O'Hara's name must now stand with those of Fitzgerald, Wolfe, Hemingway, and Faulkner; the *Atlantic* complimented O'Hara on his professionalism; and Charles Poore in the *Times* spoke of the author's "flawless ear" and recommended the book as something to be relished. All the best-seller lists included *The Instrument*, it went out as a Literary Guild selection, and the American market alone absorbed more than 1,000,000 of the paperbacks in the next three years. But for some reason, the Chinese pirates ignored *The Instrument*, which was quite all right with O'Hara and his American, British, French, and Spanish publishers, not to mention those who translated under his license into German and Dutch.

O'Hara used the prefaces to the collections of short stories as a means of telling readers how he felt about things in general, and also to give himself a fight-talk. In 1968, writing to introduce *And Other Stories*, he got back to a basic theme in his life and work when he mentioned Dr. O'Hara, "usually a good diagnostician," and his prediction that John would be lucky to reach thirty, and John's reply that he would be listed in *Who's Who* by that time, as he was. And now

> Big Seventy comes into plain sight . . . The thing I am going to miss most is the strength to work. At this moment I have a novel *[The Instrument]* in the upper half of the best-seller lists all over the country; I am writing a strange play, and I am well along with a long novel *[The Ewings]*. But the writing of short stories is becoming an expensive luxury at my age. No one writes them any better than I do, but in energy and time they have become costly because the energy and time come out of resources that I must budget for the long novel. It is not a good thing, especially at my age, to start forming bad habits, and the worst bad habit an author can form is that of leaving work unfinished . . . I believe, and I suppose I have always believed, that the writer who loafs after he has made a financial success is confessing that the money was all he was after in the first place. That was never my idea. Much as I like owning a Rolls-Royce, for instance, I could do without it. What I could not do without is a typewriter, a supply of yellow second sheets, and the time to put them to good use.

What O'Hara feared more than loss of strength was loss of memory. He was glad to seize an opportunity to show that his memory was still working well in April 1968, when Joseph Bryan sent him an old postcard depicting a scene in Pottsville. O'Hara replied, "Thanks for the view of — to give it its right name — the Soldiers and Sailors Monument in Garfield Square, Pottsville. As a small boy I spent many a happy hour climbing around the base and being chased off the cannon by the caretaker. The big house was owned by John Henry Swaving, M.D., my father's best friend. The churches are the Second Presbyterian, at left, and the English Lutheran, at right. The summer car is obviously making its way from Yorkville to Tumbling Run Park. I lived on Mahantongo Street, two blocks away from Garfield Square. I would guess from the shadows that the picture was taken at about 11 A.M., probably on a Tuesday in August, circa 1910. Other doctors on G. Square were Dr. Kramer, Dr. Herbein, Dr. Householder, Dr. Doyle, Dr. Veith, and the Rev. Drs. Lindemuth, Umbenhem, Walker, Nichols, and Talbott."

O'Hara's correspondence, on yellow second sheets like his novels and stories, had the same neat appearance of the typescripts he sent to editors, with almost no x-ing or correcting. His plain style was effective in showing his friends as much of his private self as he wished to reveal. Sometimes he revealed much, as when he wrote to John Hutchens in June 1962, at the height of his powers, yet in the mood of summoning courage to continue. One of the academics had written that O'Hara was a "sorehead" who was motivated by resentment at having come from "the wrong side of the tracks." John decided to correct this statement, and he wrote for Hutchens, at that time literary editor of the *Herald Tribune*, an article called "Don't Say It Never Happened," in which he presented convincing evidence that the O'Haras inhabited the *right* side of the tracks in Pottsville. There had been no dispute of this by anyone who knew O'Hara, but now for the benefit of future biographers he recorded his father's position in the town, the doctor's generous provision for the family, the club memberships, the farm, the automobiles, ponies, and horses. Hutchens sent the customary fee for the article, and O'Hara then wrote that he was glad to get the check: ". . . let me assure you that I am out for every buck I can get. I have reached the point of no return except income tax return, and I drive the hardest bargain I can. It is not mere greed. It is with an eye to the future, if any. Although I have made, and am making, an awful lot of dough, I have never been convinced that my drawing power is permanent. One of these days the people will get fed up and I will be back writing obits for Guild scale. That's why I keep my hand in at the Trib, and write long letters to the Princeton Packet. I told Barney Kilgore, who is a neighbor of mine and owns the Packet, that I want him to save a seat for me so that when D for Disaster Day comes, I will have a job. My wife and my daughter are fixed so that they don't really need me financially, but if I didn't have a desk to go to, I'd crumble and blow away. Of course I have a lot to do, stories and novels and plays to write, and there is in the works a TV deal that conceivably would more than double what I have been able to put away so far, but I don't really *believe* this money. When I used to work in Hollywood, I deposited my movie money in California banks, and my book and magazine money I sent back East. That was the hard money; the movie money was never real to me. One time, about to leave California, cleaning out my desk, I found about three months' royalty payments amounting to around $20,000 from *Pal Joey* that I had not yet deposited in the Eastern bank. I wouldn't even *squander* it in California. I have a small but well deserved reputation for being troublesome in contract negotiations, but when they're completed I want to forget them. My only extravagances — Peal shoes and a new Jag 3.8 and stuff like that — get paid for in my sterling account in London, and we live very simply. I can't drink, I can't eat fancy, I long ago stopped playing the races, and I don't like to travel except to Britain by ship, and that not too often to take the edge off it. I love to work. I have certain self-imposed family obligations, and that's it, as far as money's concerned. But I do drive a hard bargain, one of those new-fangled hard bargains with fourwheel brakes and balloon tires."

In September of the same year, O'Hara again wrote to Hutchens, telling of his dismay at the hostility of Them — not the dead whom George Lockwood joined, but an influential faction among academic and what might be called establishment critics toward his work: "At 57, and with all those years of honest and good work behind me, I sometimes wonder what the hell they are waiting for. I am quite sure that They will try to do, when I am safely dead, what they have done to Fitzgerald, which can be characterized as one of the most disgusting cases of necrophilia-cum-hindsight in all literature. They don't know what I have done; they have no idea what I've done; they don't recognize it even when I list my works in my books, where They can see the titles. Think of how many reputations have been built on a tenth of that list. They overpraise and have to make excuses for their favorites, and their favorites have to settle for that. I don't want people making excuses for me. And I'll tell you something else I most emphatically don't want: I don't want the overpraise They gave *Ship of Fools,* which They then follow up with a kind of squirming out from under. I haven't read the Porter book; I just watch and listen. I get sore, and when I get over being sore I go back to work. Perhaps that's one reason I don't get Their approval: I do go back to work, which is a sign that They have been unable to knock me out as They did Fitzgerald, with, of course, some help from Fitzgerald himself."

O'Hara sometimes wrote to share a passing thought. In July 1963, he informed William Maxwell that, "Ever since the invention of the helicopter I have had a strange desire to charter one and go to the Statue of Liberty and step out of the helicopter and down into the statue. This is strange for many reasons. I am and for ten years have been afraid of flying, although I have flown an airplane quite a few times and have had to use them to get places. I have never been in a helicopter and never expect to be in one. It would take me a week to climb up the statue. I get out of breath at the thought of it. My fear of flying, by the way, can be dated precisely: it came over me one day while flying in a small plane from Fishers Island to Martha's Vineyard. Three days later I was in the hospital with my big hemorrhage. The aerophobia could have been a warning that all was not well inside, because until then I loved to fly."

O'Hara's distaste for domineering literary women gave him something to tell Maxwell after attending a luncheon for writers in December 1964: "I was seated next to ———, who spit her food while talking, and when she is not spitting food, expectorates a stream of unpleasantness and untruth. She is my current candidate for the Academy of Horrible Women. On my right was a kooky woman who is related to friends of mine and whom I had never met before. She started our conversation by blaming all her troubles and her stepsister's troubles on the fact that they both attended convent schools in France where they learned to lie and to cheat, in an atmosphere of a barbaric religion. She then asked my advice on what to do if an intruder broke into her house. She has a shotgun, she said, but did I think she would be able to hold the intruder at bay while she telephoned the police? She has not been able to sleep well recently because she lies in her bed and tries to figure out how she would deal with the intruder situation. She apparently lives alone in a New Jersey farmhouse. She keeps the shotgun in her bedroom, but would she have time to get it? I had several suggestions of an unsuitably flippant nature, but quite obviously she has had the problem on her mind and has been unable to unburden herself to anyone else. So I had to be serious with her. Her eyes sparkled as she described her peril, and I think she was a little disappointed when I said that she would not actually have to shoot the burglar; that if she pointed the gun at him — a shotgun, mind you — he could be persuaded to get the hell out. Protect yourself, I said, and give him a chance to get away. I next suggested she buy some tear gas, but she didn't like that idea; you were just as likely to be blinded as the burglar, she argued. Then, I said, you ought to have some friend buy you a revolver, and we went into the matter of revolvers. She was much more interested in revolvers than in tear gas, and since I happen to know a lot about small arms, I was very entertaining. She found me so. I wanted very much to ask her if the French nuns had not included ballistics along with their training in lying and cheating, but she was having such a good time I did not have the heart. She said she had been everywhere in the world and had done everything, and I realized that at age 60 she is contemplating the joys of the ultimate experience, murder. At that, she was better balanced than the ———— woman, and now you see where I Get My Material."

Sometimes O'Hara discussed his books in letters, as he did when William Maxwell commented on the stairway that furnished George Lockwood's exit from life. Maxwell thought he recalled something about a secret stair in a detective story. He also spoke about the underlying intention of the novel. O'Hara answered: "what you remember is, I believe, an old thriller by Mary Roberts Rinehart called *The Circular Staircase*. She also wrote *The Bat*, hence the association.

"Second — and not as easy to answer. *The Lockwood Concern* is an old-fashioned morality novel, as are all my longer novels. I have a theological theory that God is, among other things, the Supreme Ironist; that no matter how long or short a time you spend in this life, it all evens up in the end. My mother, for instance, was a terribly *good* woman, guided by high principles all her life and extremely proud of her goodness. She took great pride in her ability to cope with adversity. She was not a stupid woman; she had brains and ability, she was well educated and she kept up with things. A musician of professional calibre, a woman who, for relaxation, used to get out my prep school trigonometry books and do trig problems. A great admirer of Eleanor Roosevelt, by the way, but at the same time a devout Catholic, an almost daily communicant. She never met my first wife, and refused to receive her and me until after we were divorced. She bore six sons and two daughters, and the only thing I ever heard her say about that was, 'Thank heavens all my children have well shaped heads.' Now the point about this strong character was that in the period between my father's death and my first success she had very rough going, but she enjoyed it. She baked cakes and sold them for $5, she gave French lessons and did crocheting, and she was also president of the Shakespeare Society, active in the D.A.R., gave recitals with The First Piano Octette of Pottsville, Pa., and not too humbly heard herself described as 'Katharine O'Hara is a remarkable woman.' She loved it. But when she was eighty-three she died of cancer, quite horribly, including what I now regard as unnecessary surgery. Life was fine, death was horrible, it all evened up in the end. The Supreme Ironist at work. . . .

"The same with George Lockwood. Completely self-centered, enormously selfish, enjoyed life, in his way, as my mother did hers in her way. It does not matter that he was evil and she was good. The Almighty system of checks and balances and compensations operated with both.

"I, of course, playing God, invented the secret staircase device to use as a symbol of Lockwood's secretiveness, withdrawal, superiority complex, to provide myself with the instrument of retribution. It is not supposed to be a bigger symbol than that, with more general applications, but if it works in the case of George Lockwood, it has served its purpose.

"But I must also tell you something else. The late Herbert Langfeld, a friend of mine who had been head of the psychology department at Princeton, told me one day that he had just gone through *all* of my writings, and that it might please me to know that from his point of view as a psychologist, everything I wrote was sound. I then told him that one reason for that was that I always used the psychological patterns, as I knew them, of real people. I have, of course, a psychological pattern of a real person for George Lockwood. He is still alive, but you don't know him. I shall be very curious to see how he turns out in real life and in death. The oddest thing, however, is that I have a neighbor [who] is a lot like Lockwood in many respects, and here is life mirroring art: at the very moment that I was struggling with the galley proofs of *The Lockwood Concern*, [this neighbor] was erecting a fence around his estate! It always amuses

me when some bush league critic says that the kind of people I write about
no longer exist.

"Emmy probably knows how the Supreme Ironist is at work on the lives
of —— and ——. It is brutal. But if I wrote it it would never get past
Shawn [editor-in-chief of *The New Yorker*]. It might not even get past
me, it is so brutal and incredible."

O'Hara liked to write letters to newspapers, and sometimes to magazines. In September 1964 he addressed the editor of *The New Yorker*, and
saw the letter published under the heading "Dept. of Correction and
Amplification," as follows:

The newspapers and magazines have been pack-jammed — or so it seems
to me — with half truths and misinformation concerning the name of that
good two-year-old [race horse] O'Hara. *The New Yorker*, for example,
says he was named after the "Boston miler." The human speed merchant,
Tom O'Hara, is, of course, from Loyola University, Chicago.

I can and must set the record straight. The horse is not named for me,
but I named him.

In August 1963 my wife and I were Saratoga house guests of Mrs. C. S.
Payson, who, as everyone knows, is co-owner with her brother, John Hay
Whitney, of the Greentree stables. Not everyone, but quite a few people
know that my wife is a cousin of Mrs. Payson's and Whitney's. After dinner one night a group of us were given paper and pencil and a list of about
a dozen unnamed Greentree colts and fillies, with the names of their sires
and dames. When I saw that one colt was by Ballymoss out of Track
Medal I thought immediately of Tom O'Hara, and suggested that name.
But my brother, Tom O'Hara, is a political writer on the *Herald Tribune*,
which is owned by Whitney. There were angry cries of "Nepotism!" and
"Double Nepotism!" So, as gracefully as I could, I backed down and
meekly suggested that the colt be named simply O'Hara. And so he was
registered with the Jockey Club. Since then several friends of mine have
said, "I see where Jock Whitney named a horse after you." Well, he didn't.

My interest in horses is lifelong and goes back at least two generations
before me. As a matter of plain fact, as a horseplayer I am slightly ahead,
largely through luck. For instance, once at Santa Anita I had a $5 bet
down on a horse whose name I unfortunately forget. I had him on the
nose and he ran third. But the win horse and the place horse were dis-
qualified, and my horse got the money. That oddity more than made up
for the time I bet on a horse called Dick O'Hara, which ran last in the
Kentucky Derby around 1928. I should have known better than to bet on
Dick O'Hara. Dick O'Hara was also the name of a heavyweight prizefighter whom Gene Tunney knocked out in two rounds.

The James O'Hara who was a founder of Bowie, and after whom half
of the Bryan-O'Hara race is named, was not a relation of mine, although
he was acquainted with an uncle of mine named James O'Hara. I believe

there was a horse named Jim O'Hara, but he sure as hell was not named after my uncle. The closest I ever came to having a horse named after me was a few years back when you could occasionally win a few bob on Joey's Pal. I made a few bob on Pal Joey, but that is another story. Or about thirty-five other stories.

To get you off the hook a little, there *was* a Boston foot racer named O'Hara years ago. But he was a marathoner, a twenty-five miler. A good distance runner.

Some of O'Hara's most revealing letters were written to his daughter Wylie during her years at St. Timothy's School. The first in the series was timed to reach her on the first day away from home: "My Dear: Welcome to St. Tim's! I am writing this on Tuesday afternoon. You are upstairs, I am in my study, unable to leave because I am expecting two telephone calls. Hot out, isn't it? By the time you read this you will have spent your first night in your new room, or so I imagine, and I am also imagining what your first day will be like. You will be doing and seeing so many new things and meeting so many new faces that you will wonder how so much could be crowded into one day, and you won't have a chance to think about it until you go to bed, the second night. That's the way it will be for a week — you must have had much the same experience at Interlaken and Ralston Creek. Then, almost without realizing it, you will find yourself a member of a new community.

"And that's something I would like to talk about. Just as I am going on a voyage, so are you embarking on a journey that is much more important than my quick trip. Mine will be over in a month, and the real purpose of my trip is to get away from my typewriter and my habits of work in order to get a new perspective and come back, I hope, the better for my holiday. But your journey is more important because you are entering into a new phase of your life. Beginning with the day you read this you cease to be a child. Your memories, naturally, will all be memories of childhood, the life you have led so far. But each day will be part of the future that you have been looking forward to all your childhood days. You will be assuming new responsibilities, but you will also find that responsibility does not necessarily mean something irksome. Responsibility, and responsibilities, can be a pleasure. The greatest pleasure I have in life is the responsibility of being your father. It is a greater pleasure than my work, which is saying a lot because I love my work. But a man is not born with a love of his work, and he *is* born with the nucleus of a love for his children, and his responsibility toward them, or toward her, in my case, is the only practical side of that love.

"In the Catholic Church you are taught to start each day by dedicating everything you do that day toward the greater honor and glory of God. Most Catholics forget that, and none of them remembers it every day, throughout the day. We are all human. But it is possible to copy something from the Catholics that is helpful: as I wrote you two years ago, 'to thine own self be true,' and if you do that every day you'll be all right. When I stopped drinking I did not say to myself 'Quit for a year.' I did it a day at a time; get through one day, then repeat it the next. Well, that's more than six years ago. And quite frankly, I still do it day by day. I take those damned exercises* every day, not with the thought that I will be taking them for the rest of my life, but with the thought that I will do them today — and let tomorrow's temptation to skip them take care of itself tomorrow.

"I hope you will write me while I am abroad. The address is at the bottom of the page so you can tear it off. After the 15th of October write me at home, as letters sent abroad will not reach me after that date.

"I wish you happiness in this new phase of your life. You have come through childhood as a fine person, with wonderful prospects for a wonderful future. You have made Sister love you as though you were her own. And I was born loving you."

In her first year, Wylie found herself at outs with one of the teachers. O'Hara gave the problem his attention as follows: "My dear: There will always be a villain. We always have villains, in school life, social life, business life. I have them; in my life the villains are the hostile critics, those who are against what I write even before I write it. There is nothing I can do about them. I can't shoot them. If I shoot one, there'll be another. The only thing I can do about them is to try to minimize their effect on me, which I do by thinking of the good critics who respect and admire my writing, and try to forget what the others say. I would have quit twenty-five years ago if I had believed some of the critics; but the amusing thing is that as the years go by, some of those same critics now like to think that they admired *Appointment in Samarra* when it came out. You have no idea what a beating I took from Atkinson of the Times when *Pal Joey* first appeared. But when it was revived 11 years later he voted for it for the Critics Circle Award as the best musical of the year. In other words, the villain changed; Pal Joey didn't; it was the same show.

"But the danger a villain can be, the harm he can do, is the harm that we do ourselves by brooding over his attacks. You get so that you blame the villains when your own work is at fault. In your case, you must concentrate on the people whom you like and who like you. Furthermore, you must remember that in your studies it is a matter of the subject and you. It is you and Math, it is you and History, it is you and Current Events. Forget the personality of the teacher, put the teacher out of your mind. I realize that that is asking the impossible, but I suggest you try it.

* For a chronic back ailment.

"I also urge you to work harder on the things that you like and the things you do well. I have never known it to fail that when you are excelling in one or two things, the hard things are made less difficult. Success begets success. I have a short story in this week's Saturday Evening Post. You may remember when I wrote it, last spring. I was then working on my new novel and it was going well. Because it was going well, I was able to write the short story in a few hours, although the novel and the short story were, you might say, two different subjects.

"You are in school to learn, this is the learning period of your life, and learning is never all easy. If it were, it would not really be learning, would it? But some things are easier to learn than others, and if you work harder on the easy things than you have to, I repeat, the difficult things will be less difficult.

"I saw The Doll's House too. (A Doll's House, actually.) Ibsen wrote that play in 1879, eighty years ago! And it's just as true to life now as it was when it first appeared. The woman who would not grow up, and who thereby got herself and others into trouble. That's why you found her unattractive when she was being coy with her husband. As you grow older, you will find that there are quite a few girls who resemble Nora, who won't grow up, who won't face facts, who try to get by on tricks. And she got a husband who was just as bad."

A typical letter from O'Hara to Wylie was written at Claridge's, London, in October 1960: "My dear: Our last full day in London. Tomorrow noon we take the flying machine for Paris, and a week from Thursday we head for home.

"We have had a fairly busy time of it, principally with theatergoing every night but one last week. Yesterday the Whitneys sent a beautiful Bentley to fetch us to their house in the country, about an hour's drive, and we had lunch with Jock [Ambassador Whitney]. Betsey was in bed with a cold, so it was just the three of us for lunch. Night before we had a drink with Commander and Mrs. Kenneth Cohen, he being my publisher's brother, and the night before that we went to the theater and supper with the Graham Watsons, he being my London literary agent. Night before that a dinner party at Dennis Cohen's, where I met a real fan. An old woman, fat and nearly toothless, named Baroness Woodburn,* who was once secretary to Gorki, the great Russian writer, and was also the mistress of H. G. Wells, who had quite a few mistresses in his day. She tawld me dat I had enreeched her life with my nowels and dat I was one of de truly great. When we were leaving she impulsively kissed Sister, whom she had never seen before that evening. At dinner I sat between a dame who went to college with my first wife and who also knew your mother — and who

---

* O'Hara had misheard the name of Baroness Budberg.

thought Sister had been the wife of John Hersey; and, on my right, a Lady Somebody whom I met a year ago, very attractive and nice, who proceeded to tell me her intimate family history. Daddy, what big ears you have!

"Paris will be quieter. Thursday night we are dining with Mrs. Gross, and that is the only engagement we have so far, but the baroness gave Sister the names of some plays we ought to see. One of them is in Sanskrit, and you know how good we are at Sanskrit.

"If I ever go abroad again it will not be in the fall. I love to be in Princeton in the fall, or Pennsylvania, or New England; and it is foolish to waste my favorite season in foreign lands. Right now I have no desire to go abroad again at all. You and Sister have been invited to visit a castle in Wales next summer. The people named Rogers whom we saw last week a couple of times. Sister will tell you about it when you begin to make your plans for 1961 vacation, which seems very far away but you should start planning during Christmas holidays as reservations even now are important. The London and Paris hotels are crowded as they used to be in the summer only.

"I am looking forward to your first weekend home, with whomever you want to bring. I like all your St. Tim's friends, those I've met anyway, although I guess Nancy is my favorite. By the way, no letter today, although we were expecting one. At least you are one up on Alex. Mrs. Gross said she has had no letter at all.

"A straight line is the shortest distance between two points. Q. E. D."

O'Hara wrote to his daughter as he would to an adult. In 1961, he sent encouragement after a report of grades that could have been higher: "My Dear: Far from being disturbed by your report (which just came), I think it is the most hopeful one we have had in two years. As Miss Watkins says on the bottom of the page: 'We feel that she is trying.' That, my girl, is the best news of all.

"Actually, when you get down to details, you have an Honor Grade in Latin, and that has not been the case for two years. You almost make it with a C Plus in French. We have yet to receive the detailed report from your various teachers, and that will be along before Christmas, but you have been given a 2 for Effort in all subjects.

"Miss Watkins also says: 'Now that Wylie understands what is required, I hope that she will improve her work by degrees.' I like that, because it implies an understanding of the difficulties that go with adjusting to a new environment. Notice she says 'by degrees.' In other words, she does not expect an overnight miracle.

"Once again I urge you to do that extra work on the subjects you do well in, so that you not only encourage yourself but also encourage your teachers. The most rewarding experience for a teacher is to see that *her* effort is bearing fruit. You will then discover, too, that success begets success. Thomas Jefferson when he founded the University of Virginia, established a policy that lasted for more than a century: if a man was doing well in one subject, he could stay in college, regardless of how badly he did in other subjects. Jefferson's theory was that if a man was doing well in one subject, he was *learning*, and the raison d'etre of every college was to learn. Jefferson himself was one of the most brilliant, versatile men who ever lived, and in a way he bears out my own theory. For instance, he was a good carpenter — and a good violinist. He was a great statesman — and a great farmer. Success begets success, Wylie. It does not all come at once, kerplunk. It comes by degrees.

"Every once in a while — not too often, but occasionally — you should stop and say to yourself: 'These are my years. These are the years in which I am making my future.' These years belong to you, the years before you fall in love, get married, have children and a home of your own. Time passes all too quickly, and when love and marriage and children come into your life, you will welcome them all. But these few years are your own. Treasure them.

"You are constantly in my thoughts, and the thoughts are pleasant. You are on your way, and you are proving it. I think you are even beginning to realize it a little yourself."

O'Hara's desire to reward Wylie for good work, and also to enjoy her company, was reflected by a note in December 1962: "My dear: I have written to Abe Burrows, author and director of *How to Succeed in Business Without Really Trying*, for seats for the matinee on December 20th, so don't make any engagements for that day. It is the biggest hit on Broadway in years. Music by Frank Loesser, and lyrics also by Burrows.

"Enclosed are instructions for ski exercise. The sooner you start, the better shape you will be in."

In the following year, O'Hara wrote to Wylie after a visit at home: "My dear: Sister and I enjoyed having you and your friends home with us. This does not directly concern me, but as a housewife Sister was terribly pleased by the consideration you all showed in tidying up, stripping the beds, etc. In these days when servants are few or non-existent it is especially important to do your share — but it was always important to have good manners, always will be. We also got nice notes from Lorraine and Louise, and these little things, which only take a minute or two, make life pleasanter.

"Well, you do things for old friends. Last night we went to NY to attend a dinner for my old friend Deems Taylor, who was getting a medal from NYU, his alma mater. I sat next to a woman called Ayn Rand, the author, whom I had often heard described as a terror, but we got along fine. She is an odd-ball, born in Russia, but what a talker! Fun, actually. She started right out by telling me that she was going to have to make a report on me to a Dr. Nathan Brandon, an associate of hers in the field of psychotherapy, because Brandon reads everything I write and has said that I never make a mistake about the psychological treatment of my characters. He is not the first to say that, by the way. She asked me what my philosophy was, and that, of course, got me going. Turned out that I am diametrically opposed to her philosophy, but I didn't know that till later, when Sister told me. I have never read Ayn Rand, and told her so.

"Saturday, Harvard game party. It's a damn good thing, by the way, that we told Mrs. Bundy we couldn't have her daughter. Sister won't get back till tomorrow night, and we would have had to disinvite her at the last minute. I had to give up going to Atlantic City for the NJ English Teachers awards — but that was no hardship.

"My friend Dick Dilworth took a pasting in Pennsylvania elections, so I wrote him a note inviting him to join the Losers Club. He lost the governorship, I lost the Nobel prize.

"A good review of *The Cape Cod Lighter* in the new Glamour, and quite by accident on the way to NY last night I read a rave review in the Philadelphia Bulletin. The book theoretically won't be out till Thanksgiving, but they don't wait any more. I turned down the NY Times for an interview, and a few minutes ago I said no to Newsweek, which wanted to take my picture. I suppose you saw this week's Life, with the picture they took last April and the snooty remarks about me and *The Big Laugh*.

"I meant to make this letter a thinking out loud about your future, but that will have to wait. I have some ideas that you might want to think about on the subject of post-school jobs, etc., which may influence you in your plans for the next year."

When writing letters to young people, O'Hara had the virtue of never talking down, and of always expressing himself with complete honesty. He told his daughter that "1962, in some ways, is Wylie O'Hara's Year of Decision. Some of the decisions you make this year will have an important bearing on decisions you may want to make several years hence.

"For example: suppose that when you are 20 or 21 you should discover that you want to participate in one of the many activities that will be open to young people in the federal or state government. The first thing they will want to know is what education and/or training you have had. Nowadays the minimum, absolute minimum requirement for hundreds of jobs is two years of college, either at a four-year college or at a junior college.

"For another example: you have said that you don't expect to marry before you are 23. Well, that is something you can't be sure of, but suppose you do wait till you're 23. Suppose your fiance-husband is a young man who is taking graduate work at some university — law, medicine, the sciences, government work, etc. — and you and he are living in the vicinity of his graduate school. You may want to do work on the college or the graduate school level yourself, but I assure you you will not be very enthusiastic about it if you have to start as a freshman of 23.

"Now I could go on at some length, but the point I am aiming at is this: I want you to think very, very seriously about what you are going to do after St. Tim's. You are not Miss Richbitch. You are not going to be Miss Churchmouse, either, but you must think in terms of being able to earn at least part of your own living. I don't think you are going to fall in love with a dumbhead. I think a dumbhead, rich or not, would bore the hell out of you. Therefore it is extremely likely that the kind of boy you will like and fall in love with is going to be one who uses his brains to earn his living. That almost automatically means that he will be taking either graduate work or special post-college training of some sort. And even if you have children right away, you will want to keep up with him intellectually.

"I can tell you from my own experience how important it is to have a wife with whom to discuss one's work. My first wife was a Wellesley B.A. and a Columbia M.A. and a diplomate, I think they are called at the Sorbonne. Your mother did not go to college, but she could have. Sister and your mother both graduated from good schools and took courses at Columbia and your mother even attended lectures at Oxford without having to enroll there. Both your mother and Sister loved to read and read a great deal, and Sister is multilingual. Both your mother and Sister disliked women's colleges, but they did not dislike higher learning. They found their dislike of college-girl types thirty years ago. The type has almost vanished, because the kind of girl your mother and Sister were then would be applying for college today. Everybody goes to college.

"Now this is what's on my mind: the tentative program you have outlined for yourself does not seem to me very 'realistic' in 1962 and 1963 and so on. I am hopeful that you will redirect yourself toward a good college so that you will get those two minimum-requirement years on your record and then be able, three years from now, to qualify for jobs or continue working for a degree. You will not regret having those two years on your record, whereas you might easily regret *not* having them. As your father I have a duty to point these things out to you. But once I have done that I have to leave the real decision up to you.

"I had a wonderful experience at Trenton. I waited on the platform, in case you did not take that train. Right in front of me there was a Pullman car, and I happened to notice that an austere woman was reading *Sermons and Soda-Water* (the three-volume edition). I knocked on the window, and she was understandably confused until I pantomimed 'book' with my hands and pointed to myself. She got it, got all excited, and spoke to her husband in the chair adjoining hers. He was delighted, recognizing me right away, and so did a woman who was in the other neighboring chair. Then the people in the other chairs, overhearing the excitement, all laughed and waved at me. So I clasped my hands like a prizefighter, and took off my hat and bowed. I'm sure I'll get a letter from my reader on the other side of the Pullman windows. It was fun."

Wylie had done well at school, but expressed anxiety to her father about not having made an even better record. He replied at once: "My dear: I want you to be head of school, captain of the Spiders [an official faction], tennis champion, and to get your classmates in a crap game in the Sixes Room and win $18,000 so that you could buy me a Rolls-Royce for Christmas.

"Seriously, if you think I am in any way disappointed in you, you are out of your little pink mind. I do not want you to be any of the things you are *not* at the sacrifice of the things that you *are:* a warm, human, honorable, decent, sensitive girl. Far from being the kind of person who makes a big splash in her, or his, teens, you are entering a future that is so exciting that I believe you sense it yourself, deep down. I believe you sense it because you are having a final struggle, wrenching yourself away from the past. It is almost like giving birth to yourself. Keep this letter and in ten years, or even five, see if the old man isn't right. I'll even put the date on this letter. And don't be *afraid* of the future. You'll get what you want, if it's what you want."

The Pulitzer Prize for 1963 went to William Faulkner for *The Reivers*. O'Hara by now was used to seeing that award go to other writers, and he wrote to Wylie about disappointment in general: "My dear: Sister is off to Quogue, so I am alone for the rest of the week, and I would have been even more miserable if you hadn't telephoned. But you did telephone, and that is over. I had a particularly rough time these past few weeks. A week ago yesterday I heard on the radio that Faulkner had been given the Pulitzer prize (instead of *The Cape Cod Lighter*, which rumor had it would or might get it); then an hour later my friend Edgar Scott telephoned to say I had been blackballed at The Brook Club. The reason? Certain members of the screening committee did not like what I have written about clubs and did not want it to appear that The Brook, by making me a member, appeared to approve of what I had written. Then I also bet on the Kentucky Derby, and my horse, No Robbery, ran out of the money and I had bet him across the board (win, place, and show) . . ."

When Wilder Hobson was dying in the spring of 1964, O'Hara wrote to Wylie: "My dear: I have been thinking about a lot of things, some but not all concerned with our conversation this evening. I did not, for instance, tell you that Mr. Hobson is in the hospital. He had a massive hemorrhage of the liver last night, and Mrs. Hobson phoned us at eight o'clock this morning, in tears. We went to the hospital this afternoon. We did not see him, of course. Archie had just come down from St. Mark's. Liza is at school in France and they have not yet told her. I'm afraid Mr. Hobson has had it. His hemorrhage is worse than mine of 10½ years ago, and the cause of it is, I think, probably worse than my ulcer. I know this much: a couple of years ago I asked your Uncle Bobby what would have happened to me if I had gone on drinking, and he told me I would have died. He said I would have died of what Mr. Hobson has now. Cirrhosis of the liver. . . .

"My affection for Hobson goes back 36 years, during which he often irritated me for one reason or another, principally in his selfishness. But he was fun to be with, intellectually stimulating, and we liked many of the same things. He was also rather pitiful, and one night he confessed that he had always been jealous of me. I had suspected that, but I was surprised that he knew it too. It is pretty hard for most writers not to be jealous of me, because I made it look easy and they know it is not. In Hobson's case it was sad, because he had ability and taste, and his confession was like a resignation from further effort. He had other problems as well.

"Why am I talking about him to you now? Because you are doing a lot of thinking about a friend of yours, whose faults you recognize and who is apparently unequal to her problems as Mr. Hobson has been to his. As I told you tonight, people do not change because of one dramatic episode, good or bad. It is the day-to-day meeting, facing up to, problems, or *not* facing up to them, that creates what is usually called character. You learn early, or you learn late, but if you learn too late you have lost. _____ is not hopeless; she has youth on her side. But she is going to have to begin a day-to-day struggle with procrastination and her own form of selfishness. Hobson did not work it out for himself, and I'm afraid he has had his last chance. It is a terrible thing to see a man telling himself that he is happy when he is, in everything he does, shouting that he is not."

The correspondence with Charles Poore was maintained for years; O'Hara wrote to him, for example, from 55 East Eighty-sixth Street, while working on *A Rage to Live,* to ask if he ever examined the citations of honorary degrees: "I always do. The Fordham ones indicate that the reverend Jesuit fathers have got the pipe that John J. McFetridge, Commissioner of Water Works in the city of Utica, N.Y., Papal Chamberlain, and member of the Class of '04, is right with God, having kept his hands out of the public till and off the departmental stenographers, and given six sons and two daughters to the service of God in the holy priesthood and the Sisters of St. Joseph. That's the Fordham-type citation.

"But the Yale-Harvard-Princeton type seem to have been written all by the same man, whose initials are H.S.C. [Henry S. Canby of the *Satur-day Review*]. The citations contain a nil-nisi-bonum theme, a cheerfully obscure presentation of the facts in the case, and a kind of antiseptic humor (often with a harmless pun) that make the gentleman who is being honored sound like someone slightly human but essentially too good for this world, which, as he is handed his diploma and moves his tassel, he ought to have the grace to leave within twenty-four hours.

"I have a strange relationship with Canby, whom I have never met. For years he put the knock on me in lectures at New Haven (I used to get letters from undergraduates). I in turn put the gentle knock on him when I spoke to the Elizabethan Club last year. But on the other hand I know from Phil Barry that Canby was in favor of my election to the Institute of Arts & Letters, and my candidacy at the Coffee House, where I was blackballed. I believe you said Cowley had written the comments you use today (I didn't save Thursday's paper), but Cowley, Canby, Schmowley, Schmanby . . .

"The pile of blank paper in this lonely room is getting smaller. I am now, at page 876, with about 200 more to go. I hope I know when to stop . . ."

During the same period, O'Hara wrote to Poore about an item in the Leonard Lyons column: "The other day he had a paragraph about Garson Kanin and Gertrude Stein. The anecdote matters so little that I promptly forgot it, but I have not been able to forget this one line: 'Garson Kanin, whose writing was influenced by Gertrude Stein . . .'

"There it was, just casually tossed away in a more or less routine paragraph; the answer to the question that has been bothering the literati since dear knows when: who influenced Garson Kanin? People have sat up half the night arguing the question. During the war, on troopships and foxholes, our GI's would while away the lonely hours with thoughts of the peanut butter the folks back home were enjoying, and with discussions of who influenced Garson Kanin. I wonder how many times a mischievous undergraduate has dropped in at the Lizzie Club and, over the tea and cookies, dropped that hot potato into the serenity of literary conversations about Walpole and Lefty Lewis. You could nearly always, by picking your man, relieve the tedium of a long train ride by saying, 'I beg your pardon, but I happened to notice that you're reading a book, and I wondered how you stood on the question of who influenced Garson Kanin.' Once in a while of course you would run into some stuffy fellow who would bristle and say, 'Nobody influenced Garson Kanin, sir. He is sui generis,' and hide himself behind the New Statesman. I understand that there was a dreadful scene at the Saturday Club between Archie MacLeish and M. A. DeW. Howe that all started over this controversial question. Some pundits have held out for Molière, some for Sheridan. Racine has been mentioned. Walter Pater, Corneille, of course. But nobody had thought of Gertrude Stein! Nobody, that is, except Leonard Lyons, who must have known it all along. Now at least I go to my grave with that problem solved."

One of O'Hara's letters to Poore, in 1955, gave an idea of what it means to bargain over literary properties of value, and the possibility of exploiting them without pay: "I am going to try to change your mind, or get you to change your mind on a matter that is not based on your literary judgment but on what might very easily be called the residual aspects of literary properties. It's this matter of parody.

"Several months ago my Hollywood agent was approached regarding a production of Pal Joey for TV. My price was high, and the deal fell through. Shortly thereafter the Frank Sinatra show (same network as the one that would not meet my price) announced that Sinatra was going to do a *parody* of Pal Joey. I quickly got my lawyers on their feet and notified Sinatra, the network, and the sponsor that if they did a parody of Pal Joey I would sue them but big. The parody was not done.

"You see? How could you parody Pal Joey on TV? It is so close to parody that you couldn't do it without using the original material, and of course the producers of the Sinatra show know that, but by announcing parody they think they have assumed the right to steal. There is no right to steal, but they'd have stolen if my lawyers hadn't gone to work. This is the perfect case, in that the network first wanted to *buy,* but being unable to buy, they were going to steal.

"Parodying properties has become in TV a handy device for stealing. This is particularly so where comedy is involved. A half-hour parody, a fifteen minute parody, is not parody. It is pure theft, in which the author of the original not only does not get paid, but he also suffers damage in that his original work is killed for subsequent presentation in its original form."

On a weekend at Quogue in 1957, O'Hara took time off to exercise his memory as he wrote to protest a statement in one of Poore's articles: "It isn't often I get a chance like this, and, knowing me, you will not be surprised to note how fast I get to the typewriter.

"Honestly, Charles, playwrights and novelists did not 'invent' the swaggering yellow-slickered reporter. The playwrights and novelists only reported him. In 1928, when I first went to New York as a breath of new life in metropolitan journalism, there was not a paper that didn't have from one (the Mirror) to 25 (the Times or the Trib) reporters of the type you mean. To begin with, we all carried canes. Ask any Silurian* of the present day, who was working in the late Twenties, not whether he carried

* Member of a veteran reporters' club.

a cane, but what kind of cane he carried. I must have had a dozen, not one of which I bought except for one I bought for a penny from Helen Hahn Haven Asbury. Let me rattle off a few names. Joel Sayre used to wear a blue blazer and a bowler hat. Gordon Kahn, a tiny little guy on the Mirror, actually wore a monocle. Red Dolan never wore a hat but he always, in those days, toted a malacca, which, by the way, was the most popular stick wood. Russ Porter was a cane man. I don't think Alva Johnson was, but he was unique in other ways: he was the best, for one thing and for another he was the only one who took his notes in short-hand and wrote them in flip-over notebooks, the kind stenographers use. But he had a slight eccentricity: he always wore the same suit, copied over and over again, and it made him look deceptively like a Methodist clergyman. (Light gray, single-breasted; plain necktie.)

"If you went to Bleeck's in non-overcoat weather you would see the canes hanging by their crooks from the old, backroom bar, and they would belong to Clare Briggs, Bill McGeehan, or the fresh kid from Pottsville, Pa. And, I believe, as a result of our taking up that fashion, it was also adopted by the town blades. I know that the Racquet Club types at Dan Moriarty's [speakeasy] took it up after we had established it.

"I dwell on canes? For one reason. We did not carry golden-knobbed canes like Mr. Morgan's. Mostly, as I said, malaccas. Mike Romanoff had one with a leather thong for his wrist. The thing about our canes was that they were part of the dash and the swagger. Ed Hill, it is true, rented a cutaway and diplomatted his way into an interview with, I think, Ramsay Macdonald, but that was part of the swagger. Red Dolan was not carrying a cane when he swam out to Lindbergh's yacht for a (refused) inter-view, and there were plenty of assignments where a cane got in the way. But we did have the swagger and the slicker. I even had a coonskin coat, in and out of hock, but I had it, and I am the guy who wore out one coonskin coat and got another.

"Now let me examine the Mercury legend. Did you ever see the maga-zine man, who peddled magazines in the editorial rooms of the Times and the Trib? I'm quite sure he sold more Mercurys than any other. At that time The New Yorker was not respected very much. It was kind of sissy, in the opinion of most working press, just as Time was kind of half-assed and laughed at as a journalistic hyena (which it was). But the Mercury printed Americana and the other short stuff as well as the longer stuff, and Mencken (but not Nathan) was considered to be a working newspaper man and closer to us, and his combination of erudition and beer and sar-casm had a great appeal below the managerial level. Ross, of course, was nearer to the newspaper man's idea of a newspaper man than Mencken was in actuality, but remember few people at that time had laid eyes on Ross or even knew much about him. In 1928 I arrived in NY and almost immediately made both Time and the NYer, and never did make the Mercury, but I'm giving you what the average NY newspaper man thought and not what I thought. The New Yorker was Peter Arno and Lois Long; the Mercury was Herbert Asbury and Mencken. You see the big difference from a working newspaper man's point of view? And the magazine did fit in the topcoat pocket. And it was more alive than the old Quality Group of the Atlantic, Harpers, and Scribner's, while still high-brow enough to suit the tastes of the men who voted for Norman Thomas because Al Smith was a Catholic (that's a big statement: most reporters came from good, solid Protestant families; they were intellectuals in college, etc., but they could not finally vote for a Catholic king).

"What I object to in your saying that novelists and playwrights invented the type is that it ignores the reality. When Winchell began to get power he pretended that the other type was rare, then he pretended that it did not exist, and finally he claimed to be (since he was not the other and never could be) the beau ideal of newspaperdom. The other type, in general, came of a good, middle-class family; Winchell was a Broadway sharpie. He began calling the real thing a scenario-writers' creation, and he was joined and assisted by Louella Parsons, so that when there was an occasional reporter who looked and acted like one, Louella and Winchell denied his authenticity.

"I am not claiming much for the type. He was often a sour, jealous, name-dropping frustrate, who got as far as he could with what he had and hated whoever and whatever was beyond his own achievement. And he *was* a type, but he was more interesting to read about or to see than his fraternity brother who became a customer's man, and he got written about and seen. But he had existed and been seen before he was written about by the novelists and playwrights. And may I remind you that he exists today in great profusion in Fleet Street? The English always copy the wrong things about us, and not very well. (Ever hear an Englishman try to speak Runyonese?)

"In about four or five months I will be coming to a point in my novel [*From the Terrace*] where I could legitimately develop some of these thoughts and maybe I will, if it flows right. Then a year or so later you will come upon some of this letter in quite another form, but remember, you saw it here first!

"Our best to Mary and to you. If what you really want to know is how my golf is, one day I played 9 holes, got three birdies, and still had a 45. I just can't win. I have been playing golf for 38 years and and I've never broken 80."

In the fall of 1958, O'Hara wrote to Poore with some thoughts on *From the Terrace* and other things: "I am very much interested in my own feelings about it. Have always worried about a new book, but if I am worried

about this one my worrying is secondary to a kind of fatalistic joy that I
was able to live long enough to finish it. Random are printing *and binding*
100,000 copies for a starter, and yet I feel that if only 100 copies existed,
my place in American literature would be established. I like to write, but
I have never known such pleasure as I have had with this novel; brutally
hard work, sure, but work with a pleasure and a purpose, the pleasure of
mastery of my characters and of technique. I swore after *Ten North
Frederick* that I would never work so hard again, but I did. The difference now is that if I were told that this had to be my last, I could say,
'Well, all right.' I told a literate friend of mine in the movie business that
for 24 years everything I did was, for comparison's sake, judged from *Appointment in Samarra* onward. Now, I think, they will go back from
From the Terrace.

"Poor Scott was, I sometimes believed, suspicious of me when I told him
how good *Tender Is the Night* was. As you know, I read proof for
him when he could no longer look at the words and lines and pages. I
believe he died without ever knowing how good it was. The atmosphere
was hostile when that book was published. It was the time for Odets and
Steinbeck and, to some extent, me, although I came in for some of the same
kind of hostility toward the kind of people Scott and Phil Barry were
writing about. The people who bought books and went to plays, and who
wrote about the books and plays, developed a mass bad conscience that was
a miniature social revolution but like many revolutions, came from unworthy origins for unpraiseworthy reasons. The handy victims were Vanity Fair, the Pierce-Arrow, the Hangar Club, and F. Scott Fitzgerald. Scott
should have been killed in a Bugatti in the south of France, and not to
have died of neglect in Hollywood, a prematurely old little man haunting
bookstores unrecognized (as he was the last-but-one time I saw him).
I am immodest enough to believe those who have told me that my preface
to the Viking Portable Fitzgerald started the revival that would have
started anyway, later or much later. I therefore feel involved in the revival
as I always felt involved with the living man, even before I ever laid eyes
on him. And feeling that way I sometimes go back to a thought that used
to bother me, oh, say, fifteen years ago. I would compare Scott's career
with mine: off to a good start with a first novel, then a pasting for the second novel. Then I would think about my next big one and worry about it
for fear it would have the same fate as *Tender Is the Night*. But my next
big one turned out to be *A Rage to Live* and I realized then that I had
been forcing the comparison, although the resemblance came to mind
again when I published *The Farmers Hotel*, with the rather major difference that *The Great Gatsby* was an instantaneous and enduring success,
while *The F H* had only a mild success and is only lately getting asked
about again. I supposed that I forced the comparisons between Scott's

career and mine because I was so full of admiration of his work that I tried to see resemblances in the two lives, resemblances that did not really exist. I go on at such length now because I can see my life and my career as mine and not for their similarities to anyone else's. From that you will infer that I have attained a retroactive self-confidence, and you will be right. And it is largely because of what I did and learned and learned about myself in this middle-aged novel.

"I suppose that I have had periods of unhappiness as painful as any man ever had, but I don't think they have been as damaging to me as they were to Scott and to Wolcott Gibbs (who actually were much more alike than Scott and I, or Gibbs and I). This leads me to wonder if my ability to bounce back hasn't something to do with the fact that in spite of the abuse I have given my body, I was always stronger than Scott and Gibbs. There was always something a little desperate about the humor of Scott and Gibbs; delicate, bitter, fragile, sharp are the words that come to mind. I could be subtle in ways that escaped them both, but here subtlety means restrained power, or strength, strength which I demonstrated to myself in my three big novels of the past ten years. Gibbs had all the equipment to become a first-rate novelist except strength, or endurance, if you prefer that word. A big book was beyond Gibbs (which is a real tragedy for Amer. Lit.), and a big book may have killed Scott.

"What am I saying? Well, among other things I am saying that your frequently repeated injunction to me — 'write more novels' — and McKelway's opening remarks in his review of *Ten North Frederick*, and the words of an anonymous reviewer on Time, of all places — 'you know that you are in the presence of a real writer' — have been decisively important to me . . ."

Although the Pulitzer committee had always overlooked O'Hara, he did not try to tell himself that the Pulitzer Prize was not worth having. In April 1959 he wrote to Poore: "When you talk to people about the Pulitzer Prize, meaning for the novel or the play, they say it is discredited. I go back to the storm of ennui created by the award to *Alison's House*, which was even before *Appointment in Samarra* was ignored. The novel and play category (I lump them for my present purpose) was given new standing with the award to *Of Thee I Sing*, but I beg leave to point out that that was about something and the only someone was Alexander Throttlebottom. The attempt to revive it a few years ago showed that it didn't have much but the Gershwin-Gershwin score. Kaufman and Ryskind really got a free ride on Ira Gershwin's satire. But let's concede that the committee deserve full marks for honoring an innovation; they crawled back into their shells until *Pal Joey* was safely past. The awards are generally gutless, and the criticism that they are discredited is all right, as far as it goes. But the term Pulitzer Prize has a prestige that the National Book Award has never had and never will (especially with a few more awards of the kind they've given as the N.B.A.). Pulitzer Prize, including the common mispronunciation of old Joe's name, is in the language, like Beech-Nut and Chevrolet and New York Yankees. It is a brand name, and the name of a brand, if you will. Consequently, it is an honor that you have and put away, as most men put away their Phi Bete keys. The man who averaged 84 instead of 85 can't knock the Phi Bete key, because to do so would be ungracious near-missing. The only people who can knock Phi Beta or the P.P. are those who got them or were never, never in the running. Meanwhile, to the ineligible public Phi Beta Kappa and Pulitzer each uniquely represents rewarded accomplishment.

"This, I feel sure, is my last chance to get it. The novel I am bringing out next year [*Ourselves to Know*] will not get it or anything else. It is transitional and will be baffling to most people and will make too many angry. It is not as good as *From the Terrace*, which is a hell of a thing to say to a man who will probably have to pass judgment on it, but as I say, it is transitional and evolutionary. Growing pains at 54! I shall go on trying to earn the Nobel, and maybe I'll be one of those horses that win the Derby and the Belmont, but lose the Preakness . . ."

O'Hara wrote Poore a long letter about his review of *Ourselves to Know,* but did not mail it. The unsent letter read as follows: "I have just read your review of *Ourselves to Know* and it started me trying to remember a drama critic — I seem to recall it was John Anderson, but I'm far from sure — who was annoyed at the Shuberts or somebody, and wanted to write a review of a play he liked without giving the Shuberts anything to quote. I must say you have made it tough for the advertising department of Random House, but then so do I, so I cannot chide you for that, when I didn't even have a new picture taken for this book.

"I am, of course, disappointed in your review, because there are things about *Ourselves to Know* that I expected as well as hoped yourself to know. You came close to discussing one of the things when you spoke of 'the novelist's right to omniscience.' It is a right, no doubt, but it is an option I don't pick up without justifying my action. The device I use in *OTK*, which bothers so many critics, is the best way I know to tell a lot of things that happened before my time. If you ever read this book again you will realize that I played entirely fair, that things that happened a hundred and more years ago could have been passed down in conversations between Moses and Robert and then to Gerald. In relating them I did not exercise my right to omniscience but only my ability to present them without merely stating them. I was acquainted with two men who served in the Mexican war; I go back that far in human contacts, even though I didn't talk with them about that war. I had a dear friend named Bill Irving, who lived in Lykens, Pa., my mother's home town, who was a

Civil War veteran. In spite of the great disparity in our ages whenever he came to Pottsville for the annual G.A.R. Encampment, he would call me up. And I spent many hours sitting on a bench with him — he smelled very strong of whiskey and cigars — watching the Lykens people go by and laughing and talking. I loved that old guy, and I loved that little old town, and as I got older it was not hard for me to unpeel the crusts of the decades going back to 1863. It is not the same thing as trying to reconstruct the Continentals in their ragged regimentals, although that would be one of the rights of the novelist. But the unorthodox construction I employ in *OTK* had not only to justify recollections of an ancient time, but also to justify the kind of probing into Millhouser's mind that was essential to the presentation of this character. Nothing annoys you more than passages in which thoughts and conversations are stated that the author could not possibly have known about, but in this case the narrator, Higgins, had every reason to know and was encouraged to inquire. I have noticed in the past year that you frequently object to the use of the flashback, but unless an author tells his story straightforwardly from very beginning to very ending, the flashback is unavoidable for exposition, among other things. And some stories should not be told as 'John was born . . . John died,' with a whole novel in between.

"As to detail, you qualify your beef by bringing up its effectiveness, which almost, but not quite makes it impossible for the author to rebut. You say, 'It wasn't effective,' and the author is supposed to shut up. Well, I won't. Detail and dialog furnish or should furnish the critic with the handiest clues as to the author's study and understanding of his characters. To me one of the most irritating elements in novels and plays is the sore-thumb anachronism, the Norfolk suit in 1928, the soldier-boy of 1918 saying 'You can say *that* again.' How many readers know that those things are wrong? Not many; but they make me distrust everything else about the play or the novel. You may say that I fail to answer the charge of excessiveness, but I will let you in on a novelist's secret: a big block of type which contains a lot of detail is restful. The reader who is not going to have to write about the thing he is reading sees a lot of nouns and relaxes, but he remembers. I have had two laymen's comments — a man and a woman — on the same detail, a crate of pigeons, and these readers said substantially the same thing, that the crate of pigeons gives you the whole picture. Well, it doesn't; but at the end of a block of detail it has that effect. A novelist who works as hard as I do to make the work look easy must play a lot of legitimate tricks on the unknown reader. One of the reasons I get such casual critical consideration is that I do make it look easy. Fadiman, for one, usually speaks of my 'readability' as if it were something I should unlearn. The curious thing so far (the book has really been out about a month; the booksellers jumped the deadline by that much) is that not one, not one layman has complained of the technique I used in *OTK*.

"By a coincidence, you and Johnny Chamberlain (tomorrow's Trib) are somehow reminded of Dostoevski, which is complimentary and intended to be. But this is not the first time, and I wonder what would happen to D. if he were to come out now as a brand-new novelist. I think I know my place in Am. Lit., as of five or ten years after I cool, but I would love to be able to enjoy some of it now, while I am alive. Now, especially, the author who writes for posterity is taking an awfully big chance. He always did.

"*From the Terrace* is a better novel than *Ourselves to Know*, but it is more obviously so and easier to say so. But *OTK* is a part of what *FTT* is a part of, that *Appointment in Samarra* was part of and all the rest of my Pennsylvania protectorate.

"Oh, what the hell? I wanted you to like this book more than you did, and in saying so I have given you a letter which you can enter in evidence on the charge of prolixity."

Both O'Hara and Poore objected to the use of jargon and imprecise terms in writing English. And they sometimes called each other's attention to words that had lost meaning through overuse, as when O'Hara wrote in May 1962 about a horrible example: "Like recording a bet at White's Club, I want to register with you my selection for the egg-head word that stands the best chance of equaling the popularity of valid-validity. My candidate is accommodate-accommodation.

"This word has already shown early foot, and so did valid. Denigrate and dichotomy were slow starters, did well in the back stretch, but had to drop out for lack of staying powers. Valid romped home to win the Triple Crown: first in the political world, the entertainment world, and with the public.

"Accommodate-accommodation may well be the Kennedy administration's answer to Truman's valid. Eisenhower's ghostwriters took up valid, and Kennedy went along with it, but now he has his own word. Of course it may also turn out to be as embarrassing to him as appeasement was to N. Chamberlain.

"To me, an old railroader, accommodation means a train that stops wherever the engineman sees two milk cans."

Because of the plainness of O'Hara's style, some readers were not conscious of his care to use precise meanings. He constantly looked up ordinary words in the dictionary to guard against inaccuracy and tautology and to achieve clarity of statement. O'Hara's desire for accurate expression was so keen that he invented a word, "dinch," meaning to grind the fire out of a cigarette against the surface of an ashtray. Characters dinched their cigarettes in "Alone," "In the Morning Sun," "You Don't Remember

Me," and "Sterling Silver." Although he permitted himself the coinage of a word, O'Hara went on strict rations in the matter of what is called "fine writing" or "the purple patch." He preferred a manner of communication which he called "fast writing." This did not refer to speed in composition, but to the ease with which the reader got the point and kept up with the narrative. More than once O'Hara stated his intention to keep his work entirely free from the use of metaphor. If this were made a general law, it would put Faulkner and Fitzgerald out of business, not to mention Kipling and Conrad. But in O'Hara's hands, the plain style could produce passages of remarkable power and realism, such as the accident which killed George Lockwood, the fight at the Gibbsville Club in *Samarra,* and the turkey-shoot in *A Rage to Live.* O'Hara gave some idea of his theoretical approach to the novel when he accepted an invitation to deliver two lectures at Rider College in Trenton, in the fall of 1959.

O'Hara had accepted the invitation to speak at Rider College because he felt the obligation of a neighbor. He had been a person of note in the Princeton-Lawrenceville-Trenton area from his first days of residence on College Road, when he took Mrs. Payson to tea with Professor Einstein. It is remarkable that no college ever conferred an honorary degree on John O'Hara, but such is the case. Year in and year out, the *Times* would publish the names of those who received the degrees, most of them highly forgettable nonentities, in many fields. Never O'Hara. His brother Tom recalled that in their youth, they went to Grandmother Delaney's house "by the Lehigh Valley Railroad from a station at a place just outside Pottsville with the beautiful name of Westwood Switch. Once when John was passed over for some public recognition I suggested he start a university and call it Westwood Switch University and maybe then his influence would win him some acclaim."

O'Hara helped in providing acclaim for Frank Sullivan, in December 1959, by traveling to Saratoga and appearing at a reception at the town library in honor of a new book by Sullivan called *The Moose in the Hoose.* Also making the trip was Russel Crouse, co-adaptor with Howard Lindsay of *Life with Father.* Sullivan wrote, "I'll never forget O'Hara for that kindness. Crouse either. One comical thing happened that night. I introduced the two boys to Mrs. Pirnie, an old friend of mine, and then left the three of them chatting. She told me later what happened. They asked her to have a drink. She doesn't drink but she thought, Well, here I am in the company of two distinguished guests and it would be rather churlish of me to refuse to drink with them so I'll break down and have a drink. So she ordered a Martini or something and then found she was drinking alone; both the boys were teetotallers."

The big moving-picture sales began in the early 1960s, and the rights for *A Rage to Live, BUtterfield 8, From the Terrace,* and *Ten North*

Frederick brought in $430,000 plus percentages on the rentals of each picture. And in the case of *BUtterfield 8*, this percentage amounted to an additional $400,000; at the risk of repetition, one must point out that income taxes took away eight-tenths of this money. When O'Hara set aside $19,000 to help educate his nieces and nephews, he remarked that he had to earn $100,000 to do it. His federal income tax for 1963 was $135,000; and he wrote to William Maxwell, "I wouldn't mind paying $135,000 income tax if I had made $270,000, but I didn't. That's why I'm a Republican, whatever that is, instead of a Democrat, whatever *that* is."

On June 3, 1963, *Newsweek* made O'Hara the subject of its cover story, "John O'Hara at 58: A Rage to Write." The carefully researched article mentoned *Elizabeth Appleton* as:

> his 22nd book and tenth novel since he shot to fame in 1934 with *Appointment in Samarra,* and his eleventh book and fifth major novel since his current outburst of activity began in 1955: This enormous productivity is unusual for any serious writer at any point in history, but it is particularly striking for a writer in this century. It used to be that an author approached his life's work with the unquestioning assumption that he would continue to create new works at more or less regular intervals until death or feebleness struck him down. With the turn of the century, though, something began to go wrong with the legs and wind of a great many of the world's most celebrated writers. Either they took increasingly long rests between outings or they went into full or partial retirement at comparatively youthful ages. Ernest Hemingway, for example, in the last twenty years of his life, published one novel and a novella; E. M. Forster, at 84, looks back no less than 39 years to the writing of his most recent novel.

At the time of the *Newsweek* piece, there seemed to be something indestructible in O'Hara. His general health was fairly good, although he had been suffering for years from a painful back. The doctors said he had a congenital spinal deficiency, for which he wore a brace, and performed the tiresome exercises he mentioned in his letter to Wylie. But O'Hara was producing at his best rate, and the results were some of his best work, in the spring of 1964, when word came that a substantial recognition of his achievement was at last to be accorded to him.

This recognition was the Award of Merit Medal for the novel, conferred by the American Academy of Arts and Letters and the National Institute of Arts and Letters, on the afternoon of May 24, 1964. O'Hara almost choked with emotion before he got through reading his short speech of acceptance. The previous winners of the Medal, which was awarded every five years, had been Theodore Dreiser, Thomas Mann, Ernest Hemingway, and Aldous Huxley. O'Hara said:

> I am honored indeed to make that quartet a quintette, to find myself in such company, and I trust that they are not made uncomfortable by my

company, even at this distance . . . This, then, is unquestionably the highest recognition, the top honor I have received in my professional career, which began forty years ago when I entered the newspaper business, and began again thirty years ago when I published my first novel.

Thirty years is the length of time that the anthropologists and the sociologists call a generation, and the coincidence that I am a whole generation removed from my first novel is a significant one. Today my first novel is studied in prep school English classes; when it came out, I was reviled and my book was banned. At least *some* of the liberties that the younger writers enjoy today were paid for by me, in vilification of my work and abuse of my personal character. That is one of the things I have in common with Dreiser and, to a lesser extent, with Hemingway. The public library that kept *Jennie Gerhardt* in the cellar — which is where I first read it — also kept *Appointment in Samarra* in the same cellar, in 1934. Go back, if you will, and read Sinclair Lewis on the subject of *Appointment in Samarra* and me, as of 1934, in what was then known as the Saturday Review of Literature. These obvious facts need re-stating today because in the context of present-day writing I am regarded as obsolescent, and rightly so. I continue to experiment in every story and every novel that I write, but the experimentation is in techniques rather than in point of view or in principles. There are things that I am for and things I am against, and they have not changed much in thirty years nor are they likely to. The fully rounded irony is that I can expect the same degree of abuse from the new critics for my 1964 conservatism that I got from my lack of restraint in 1934. But as long as I live, or at least as long as I am able to write, I will go to the typewriter with love of my work and at least a faint hope that once in a great while something like today will happen to me again. We all know how good we are, but it's nice to hear it from someone else. I thank you.

Another day of recognition for O'Hara came in 1966 when he joined other authors in accepting an invitation to the White House. The horrible taxation of O'Hara's earnings had not destroyed his feeling that the visit was an honor to him as an American artist, and perhaps he was right. He had another day of happiness in London on May 3, 1967, when he sat in the place of honor at the Foyles Literary Luncheon at the Dorchester Hotel in London. These luncheons, organized by the Foyles Bookshop, had been important literary gatherings from their beginning, when such writers as George Bernard Shaw, H. G. Wells, John Drinkwater, Dean Inge, Walter de la Mare, and Bertrand Russell were honored guests. American authors seldom appeared, which added to O'Hara's pleasure in accepting the Foyles invitation to mark the publication of *The Lockwood Concern* in the New English Library. John found it hard to finish his speech of appreciation, and part of the emotion came from his love of London. On this trip he dropped in as usual at the establishment of Swain, Adenay, & Brigg, which "made Mark Cross look like Bloomingdale's." O'Hara wrote to William Maxwell that he "very nearly bought a folding cane that is used for measuring things like the distance in feet between Buckingham Palace and St. Paul's or Westminster when they have a royal funeral march. No home should be without one, and if it's still there next time I go to London, I'll get it."

Before O'Hara's next trip to London, he walked up the church aisle in New York City in September 1967, with Wylie on his arm, to give her in marriage to Dennis J. D. Holahan. Wylie was a beautiful bride, and the ceremony and reception models of what a large formal wedding and its aftermath should be. Some who took their eyes from the bride, however, were startled and even shocked at O'Hara's appearance. In a short time he had aged. He looked heavy and tired. During that winter and in the following year, O'Hara's doctors, close friends, and family all worried about him. This was the time when Pat Outerbridge thought he noticed unsteadiness in John's walking — what little he did. Still O'Hara held himself to work and the production of a book a year. The novel that he wrote in 1968, for publication in the fall of 1969, was *Lovey Childs*, and some people called it a forced production, noticeably beneath the author's usual standard. Considered judgment, however, would give the book high marks for characterization, dialogue, and narrative, brought off with accustomed skill. But Lovey Childs, a Philadelphia girl, enacted a story that was scarcely edifying, and it may be that she was the most unattractive woman O'Hara ever created. So compellingly real was Lovey, that many reviewers and readers became indignant at the unpardonable things she did before settling down, with a conventional husband, "in Philadelphia, where they belonged." The Sunday *Times Book Review* had carried hostile writing on O'Hara's work, notably a malevolent blast at *From the Terrace*. And one would expect the Sunday *Times* to attack both Lovey Childs and her creator. On the contrary the reviewer, Richard Rhodes, wrote that O'Hara "is our data bank, our library, our ultimate resource." Mr. Rhodes's conclusion was that we should add the 249 pages of *Lovey Childs* to the thousands O'Hara had already written, to a huge body of work about the remembered past.

On September 20, 1969, O'Hara went to a hospital in New York for ten days. He was suffering from a sort of hernia in his swallowing apparatus, and spent an uncomfortable time forcing tubes down his throat. He was still having trouble with his back. But his weight was now under control, for he had taken off twenty-five pounds in the previous year by giving up most of his favorite foods, including pancakes. Three days before O'Hara's release, bad news arrived: Sister's older son St. George Bryan was lost at sea. The young man, who was living in Hawaii, had gone out in a boat with a friend, and they did not come back. Courtie Bryan and his sister Joan (Mrs. Peter Gates) immediately went to Hawaii, but no trace of "Saint" or his friend was ever found. Sister took the blow with courage and grace; and the autumn weather came to Princeton. It would be straining for effect to say that there was a note of autumnal sadness at Linebrook. The situation was that John had forted up for his last stand. He hoped to see another spring, and another fall, and more if the luck held out. But he had lived his life in readiness for the luck to go bad, and believed that the readiness was all. John began putting things in order. He made a will which superseded the handwritten note he had once given to Pat Outerbridge before flying to California, which said "Everything to Sister and Wylie." The more formal document also left his estate to those two, adding a few minor bequests, and a trust fund for his sister Mary. O'Hara had something to leave: he had become a genuine millionaire, as opposed to those who may or may not be able to put their hands on an actual million. John had a million dollars in his royalty account at Random House, which he could take out any time; and he had $220,000 in two Princeton banks. All this was aside from the value of his investments and copyrights. Unlike the Hofman Estate, the O'Hara Estate had received no benefits from depreciation allowances, and John had built it under the handicap of punitive income taxes.

The depression of spirit that O'Hara had felt because of poor health now left him. His color came back: he was able to work. He finished *The Ewings* in February 1970, and four days later began a book to be called *The Second Ewings*. It would be the first time he continued main characters from one book to another; but his Pennsylvania men and women had been visiting from book to book for years. We heard of Julian English, for example, in many places, such as the party in *Imagine Kissing Pete* where someone reported that there had been a silly scene at the country club, Julian English throwing a drink, nothing of any importance, the details confused. Two days later, they were shocked by news of the suicide. As recently as 1964, O'Hara had written a story called "The Pig," in which Lawrence Candler is dying of cancer at fifty-five, and says that if he decides on suicide, " 'I'll just make my plans and go ahead and do it. It'll be clean and orderly, unmistakably what it's intended to be. No shooting or anything like that. Ruth had a cousin, married to a guy I never met. They lived in Pennsylvania somewhere. But he had the right idea. You close the garage door and turn on the car engine.' " O'Hara qualified for the rating of genius by creating an imagined world; his stories and novels were reports from that world to the present world, written as he labored in the study at Linebrook. So many people were there in O'Hara's Pennsylvania, New York, and Los Angeles that he could never run out of material. Was he writing a real world? Not necessarily, but he was writing *O'Hara's world*. His artistic performance was so consistently good that another question came up, as it must when genius is under scrutiny — the question of the artist's fundamental view of life. O'Hara's conception of human existence was tragic and profound. In the short stories, he created more than a thousand characters, almost every one of whom is struggling with a burden too heavy to bear. In the novels, the main characters are destroyed by their own weaknesses and the malice of others, and go out heading nowhere. Julian English, Gloria Wandrous, Grace Tate, Robert Millhouser, Gerald Higgins, Alfred Eaton, George Lockwood, Yank Lucas, William Ewing, Joe Chapin, John Appleton, Hubert Ward, have failed to develop the best that is in them, which is the moral tragedy of O'Hara's novels. He also indicates that decent friendship is sometimes possible, and for those who are very lucky there may be love. The enemies of love, in O'Hara's vision, are egotism and selfish exploiting of the partner, the treating of sex as mechanics and nothing more. They accused Judge Williams in *Ten North Frederick* of having "a dirty mind," and he answered, " 'Well I don't give a damn what you think, or anybody else. Nothing personal. I just see what I see and I don't shut my eyes to it.' "

In the serene quiet of Linebrook, one would become aware of the ticking of several fine clocks, an indication of O'Hara's feeling for the value of time as measured in hours. The Wafer diaries recorded the days — in addition to work there were a few social engagements and swimming sessions at the university pool. John enjoyed this exercise and it seemed to do him such good that he gave the instructor a watch to show his appreciation. He contributed to the new building of the Young Men's Christian Association of Princeton, where a memorial reading room has since been dedicated in his name. He flew to London on February 22, 1970, bought a Lock hat, shopped at Asprey's, attended to business with agents, and flew back within two weeks. On this trip O'Hara saved his strength by using a wheelchair at the airports. But he felt well in Princeton on March 20, and went to the pool. The Wafer diaries show another swim on March 23. John was resigned to semi-invalidism, so long as brain and mind remained in working order and he could keep on writing. For all his devotion to work, he had never been a recluse. Yet some people said they found him hard to understand, which was not the way Sister saw him — she said, "John is just a very shy man." That was true. Sister also said, "And he is a methodical man   Tidy, tidy." O'Hara's friends who considered themselves judges of literature did not take the rough assaults on his writing too seriously, although they had to give up on the question of whether or not he should have published his lesser works, and his journalism. But one learned friend wrote to John, "I think your work is all of a piece, and the size of it is part of it." And on the shelf in the Eleventh *Britannica* stood the article by Edmund Gosse on R. L. Stevenson: "Very few authors of so high a class have been so consistent, or have made their conduct so close a reflection of their philosophy. This unity of the man in his work makes it difficult, for one who knew him, to be sure that one rightly gauges the purely literary significance of the latter."

The entries in the Wafer diaries carried John past April 11, the day he died. He was due for a swim on April 16 and 17, and he had noted an engagement for the eighteenth — to dine (black tie) with two special Princeton friends, Connie and Seymour Morris. The funeral took place in the University Chapel on April 16, a cool clear day. The sky, lawns, trees, and spring shrubbery in and around Princeton had the fresh look of a newly cleaned painting. The chapel is architecturally a cathedral, with nave, transept, lofty vaulting, and magnificent stained glass. A large crowd came that morning, photographers scouting in front for such celebrities as J. H. Whitney and Mrs. Payson. Old friends made the trip to Princeton, including Joel Sayre who could recall the days of the *Herald Tribune* and the coonskin coat. Also in the chapel were a number of young people from the university who were there because they felt that O'Hara had been important, and they wanted to show awareness and respect by coming to the funeral. Kate Bramwell had planned the service, which was conducted by Dean Ernest Gordon. Music of Bach and Brahms poured from the great organ, Dean Gordon read Scripture and said in his closing prayer, "We thank thee for the gift of life to thy servant, John, and for all the talents thou gavest him to be used during his earthly experience. We thank thee for the gift of his spirit, his personality, and his view of life. We thank thee for the Eternal Word which inspired men to express themselves in literature, thereby enabling people to see themselves in their humanity and need. We thank thee for the joy thou gavest thy servant in the use of words and in his understanding of others . . . We bless thee for giving him a goodly heritage, and a place to be in quiet and reflection . . ."

Some years before, O'Hara had suggested that Sister look for a burial plot, remarking, "Don't forget, I like to sleep on my right side." And when the time came they buried him in Princeton Cemetery, which has been in use since 1760. This is a peaceful place, and a walk under its old oak, pine, and poplar trees will always reveal something interesting or touching. Visitors to O'Hara's grave will find a headstone with the dates, and an inscription in his own words: *Better than anyone else, he told the truth about his time, the first half of the twentieth century. He was a professional. He wrote honestly and well.* You walk away wondering about the first four words of this inscription, until it occurs to you that O'Hara *did* tell the truth about his time, as he saw it, better than anyone else. His achievement was so great that it may take a while for us to realize its extent, as a mountain lifts above the shoreline in the eyes of travelers putting to sea.

CHRONOLOGY OF O'HARA'S LIFE AND WORKS

1905   John Henry O'Hara born January 31, first of eight children of Patrick Henry O'Hara, M.D., and Katharine Delaney O'Hara, at Pottsville, Schuylkill County, Pennsylvania.

1917   High point of an idyllic provincial childhood with ponies, dancing lessons, trips to Philadelphia; worships strong-minded father.

1919   Drives his father's car during the influenza epidemic, the remembered experiences of "The Doctor's Son."

1920   Leaves for first in series of boarding schools.

1924   Graduates from Niagara Preparatory School, but is excluded from commencement ceremonies for staying out previous night.

1925   Doctor O'Hara dies, leaving slender estate to family bereft of his earning power; John gets job as reporter on *Pottsville Journal*.

1927   Resolves to leave Pottsville; works way to Europe; tries Chicago but gets no encouragement.

1928   In New York City; works for brief period on *Herald Tribune*; sells first contribution to *The New Yorker*.

1929–   Works for *Time* magazine, promotion department of RKO-Radio
1931   Pictures, and at other jobs; meets Robert Benchley, Scott Fitzgerald, Heywood Broun, Dorothy Parker.

1931   Marries Helen R. Petit, a young Wellesley-educated actress.

1932   Has become a recognized *New Yorker* contributor and patron of speakeasies; Wolcott Gibbs, Dorothy Parker, James Thurber, and others say O'Hara has special talent.

1933   Helen Petit O'Hara goes to Reno for divorce; John works briefly as editor of magazine in Pittsburgh, and experiences near-suicidal despair; returns to New York and starts writing *Appointment in Samarra* in hotel bedroom.

1934   Instant success and high praise for *Samarra;* John goes to Hollywood for writing job at Paramount.

1935   Publishes *The Doctor's Son and Other Stories* and *BUtterfield 8*.

1936–   In Hollywood and New York: publishes eleven *New Yorker* stories
1937   and one in *Scribner's* magazine.

1938   Marries Belle Mulford Wylie of New York City and Quogue, Long
Island; begins his lifelong connection with Quogue as summer
resident.

1939   Publishes *Files on Parade*; is called master of the short story.

1940   The "Pal Joey" stories from *The New Yorker* appear in book form
and as a musical play with script by O'Hara, music by Richard
Rodgers, lyrics by Lorenz Hart; O'Hara becomes regular contributor to *Newsweek,* covering theater and movies; continues
column until 1942.

1943   Publishes "Walter T. Carriman" in *The New Yorker*: story shows
O'Hara's interest in Pennsylvania material from which novels of
later period will come.

1944   Goes to Pacific as war correspondent for *Liberty*; returns in
September.

1945   A daughter, Wylie Delaney O'Hara, is born to Belle and John; he
publishes a story collection called *Pipe Night*.

1946   Publishes *Here's O'Hara,* omnibus volume containing three novels
and twenty stories.

1947   Publishes a new collection of stories, *Hellbox,* including "A Phase
of Life," which is significant in showing O'Hara's unflinching approach to sexual side of humanity.

1949   Moves to Princeton, first at 18 College Road West, then next year
at No. 20; publishes *A Rage to Live,* his first Pennsylvania novel
since *Samarra*.

1951   Publishes *The Farmers Hotel* as novel (later a play); the scene is
near Lykens, where O'Hara's Grandfather Delaney lived.

1952   In the first of several revivals, *Pal Joey* returns to Broadway, and
receives the Drama Critics' Award; Joey Evans recognized as one
of the great parts of the modern American stage.

1953   Is near death for one night following hemorrhage of his gastric
ulcer; after a stay in Columbia Presbyterian Hospital he is placed
on strict diet with no alcohol which he observes for the rest of life.

1954   Belle Wylie O'Hara dies from congenital heart weakness on January 9; in August, a book of newspaper pieces, *Sweet and Sour,* is
published.

1955   Marries Katharine (Sister) Barnes Bryan, whose marriage to
Joseph Bryan III, has ended in divorce; *Ten North Frederick,* a
novel about Pottsville (the fictional Gibbsville) is published, and
receives the National Book Award.

1956 Publishes the Pennsylvania story *A Family Party*: the background is Lykens (the fictional Lyons); a collection, *The Great Short Stories of John O'Hara*, also appears.

1957 National Institute of Arts and Letters confers membership on O'Hara; Sister and John move to their new house, Linebrook, in the countryside near Princeton; his great closing period of production begins.

1958 Publishes *From the Terrace*: this longest of O'Hara's novels shows his intention of recording the history of his time and place, the first half of the twentieth century in North America.

1960 Publishes *Ourselves to Know* and *Sermons and Soda-Water*.

1961 Publishes the story collection *Assembly*, and *Five Plays*.

1962 Publishes *The Big Laugh* and *The Cape Cod Lighter* (stories); founds the Hessian Relief Society.

1963 Publishes *Elizabeth Appleton*, a Pennsylvania novel; *The Hat on the Bed* (stories); and *Forty-Nine Stories* in the Modern Library edition.

1964 Receives the Award of Merit in Fiction for the Novel from the American Academy of Arts and Letters, a recognition bestowed every five years; publishes collected stories, *The Horse Knows the Way*.

1965 Publishes another substantial Pennsylvania novel, *The Lockwood Concern*; on O'Hara's sixtieth birthday Thornton Wilder writes, "enjoy the decade."

1966 Publishes *My Turn*, fifty-two weekly columns written for *Newsday*; also publishes a collection of stories, *Waiting for Winter*.

1967 Publishes *The Instrument*, a novel about a playwright.

1968 Publishes *And Other Stories*; health begins to fail.

1969 Publishes *Lovey Childs, a Philadelphian's Story*; begins *The Ewings*.

1970 Finishes *The Ewings* in February; begins *The Second Ewings* four days later; health seems improved under treatment and work continues; dies on April 11, having completed seventy-four pages of the new novel.

INDEX